MANAGEMENT ACCOUNTING IN HEALTH CARE ORGANIZATIONS

MANAGEMENT ACCOUNTING IN HEALTH CARE ORGANIZATIONS

Third Edition

David W. Young

JB JOSSEY-BASS™

A Wiley Brand

Published by Jossey-Bass
A Wiley Brand
One Montgomery Street, Suite 1200, San Francisco, CA 94104-4594—www.josseybass.com

Jossey-Bass books and products are available through most bookstores. To contact Jossey-Bass directly call our Customer Care Department within the U.S. at 800-956-7739, outside the U.S. at 317-572-3986, or fax 317-572-4002.

Wiley publishes in a variety of print and electronic formats and by print-on-demand. Some material included with standard print versions of this book may not be included in e-books or in print-on-demand. If this book refers to media such as a CD or DVD that is not included in the version you purchased, you may download this material at http://booksupport.wiley.com. For more information about Wiley products, visit www.wiley.com.

Library of Congress Cataloging-in-Publication Data

Young, David W.
    Management accounting in health care organizations / David W. Young. – Third edition.
        pages cm – (Jossey-bass public health)
    Includes bibliographical references and index.
    ISBN 978-1-118-65362-3 (pbk.) – ISBN 978-1-118-65371-5 (pdf) – ISBN 978-1-118-65376-0 (epub)
    1. Managerial accounting.   2. Health services administration.   3. Medical care.   I. Title.
    RA971.3.Y68 2014
    362.1068–dc23

                                                                                          2013044625

Printed in the United States of America

THIRD EDITION

PB Printing   10 9 8 7 6 5 4 3 2 1

CONTENTS

LIST OF FIGURES, TABLES, AND EXHIBITS

Figures

Tables

This book is dedicated to the memory of Andy Pasternack,

a leader in the development of instructional materials for the

health care field, and a professional with quality standards that

the rest of us can only aspire to attain.

We all miss him.

This book provides introductory-level instruction for students of health care management who are studying management accounting for the first time, or for those who want a refresher as part of a course in advanced management accounting. It offers a user-oriented approach to management accounting concepts and techniques that will help prepare them for work in an environment where an understanding of management accounting is important to their success.

Management accounting is concerned primarily with the information needs of an organization's managers. In general, these needs arise in three areas: full-cost accounting, differential cost accounting, and responsibility accounting. The distinctions among these different types of accounting are discussed later in this preface.

To the Student

The working assumption of this book is that you have no prior knowledge of management accounting. My goal is that, on completing the book, you will be knowledgeable about both the uses and the limitations of management accounting information. To accomplish this, I place minimal emphasis on the technical aspects of preparing accounting information, covering only those technical matters that are essential to understanding the computations that the accounting staff typically makes. Most of the material focuses on the meaning and utility of accounting information for managers and other users.

In general, the learning process consists of developing new skills, which can be acquired only by practice. Learning management accounting is a bit like learning about a new city. If someone takes you on drives around the city, you will probably learn very little about how to get from one place to another. If you drive by yourself, however, you will learn a great deal about the city—acquiring far more knowledge on a single trip than you would in dozens of trips as a passenger.

In this book, you are the driver rather than the passenger. The idea is for you to practice (and learn) accounting while you read each chapter. You will have opportunities to prepare answers to problems that appear throughout the chapters and to analyze a practice case (sometimes two) at the end of the chapter. There are several features to keep in mind as you engage in this effort.

Minimal Memorization

Throughout each chapter, the important terms are defined in the margins. These terms also are contained in a glossary at the end of the book.

Having the definitions readily available means that you do not need to spend time memorizing them. Indeed, some management accounting terms are not used in a consistent way by everyone, so memorizing definitions may actually be counterproductive.

Rather than memorizing the terms, you should focus instead on mastering the concepts and analytical techniques discussed in each chapter. The book guides you as you work with these concepts and techniques so you can see how they are developed and applied. Please note that the discussion in each chapter assumes that you understand the material covered in the prior chapters, so it is important to work through the chapters in order.

Interactive Learning

A distinctive feature of this book is its interactive approach to the learning process. You are regularly asked to stop reading and work out the solution to a problem. The idea is to shorten the feedback loops in the learning process. Rather than answering questions or analyzing problems only at the end of each chapter, you can apply what you have learned about a topic immediately following the discussion about it. When the discussion of a topic is lengthy, problems may be presented throughout.

You may be tempted to shortcut this process, but please do not succumb to temptation. Shortcutting will compromise your mastery of the material. Indeed, the reasoning in the answer to a problem can be quite seductive: if you look at it before working out your own answer, you may find yourself in agreement with it, saying something like, "That's how I would have done it, if I had done it." But you may not have fully internalized the analytical techniques. Actually working through a problem, arriving at a solution, and then comparing it to the answer will give you an understanding of the logic behind the related accounting concept and allow you to apply it to real-life problems. To take full advantage of the interactive feature, you should answer each problem to the best of your ability before looking at the answer provided in the text.

In short, to learn management accounting, you must struggle through the process of arriving at solutions yourself, gaining understanding from both your successes and your mistakes. To prepare for this learning process, you should have a pencil, a calculator, and a supply of paper next to you while you are reading each chapter. A problem begins as follows:

PROBLEM

The problem statement is in a different typeface and is indicated with a question mark, as shown here.

ANSWER

The answer to the problem, also in a different typeface, immediately follows the problem, as shown here.

Use a blank sheet of paper to cover the answer as you work out the solution to each problem. Then compare your solution and associated reasoning with the answer provided. If your comparison shows that your solution is correct, continue reading. If you have an incorrect answer, spend as much time as you need to figure out where you went wrong. This may require rereading the section of the chapter immediately preceding the problem.

Short Chapters

Most of the chapters are relatively short. Reading a chapter and working your way through the problems can take several hours, however, so it's normal to feel that you are working slowly.

You should not try to cram the learning process into a short period of time, because you need to digest the material slowly as you go along. If you believe you already understand the material in a particular section and therefore do not need to read that section, you should prepare solutions to the problems in the section to confirm your understanding.

End-of-Chapter Tools

Each chapter contains, in addition to the problems for you to solve, three tools to help you verify your understanding of the concepts and techniques that were covered in the text.

To Bear in Mind

This section highlights two of the most significant issues in the chapter, with an emphasis on concepts that can be confusing or techniques that can cause difficulties when used in practice. These are just short "nudges" to make sure you understand.

Test Yourself

This section contains five questions (sometimes compound questions) that allow you to make sure you have grasped the chapter's major points. A short answer is usually all that is required for each question, although sometimes the answer can be longer. You should try to respond to each question as fully as you can before looking at the answer in appendix A.

Practice Cases

In addition to solving the problems in each chapter and answering the "Test Yourself" questions, you are asked to prepare an analysis of one or more practice cases at the end of each chapter. As with the problems contained in the chapter, you should attempt to analyze each practice case to the best of your ability before looking at the solution in appendix B. Each case covers some of the concepts discussed in the chapter and thus will give you an opportunity to test your knowledge of how the chapter's content would be applied in a practical setting.

The practice cases usually are rather short; some might even be thought of as extended problems. In some instances, however, the cases are longer and more detailed. Much depends on the chapter's content. The conventional distinction between an extended problem and a case is that a case usually presents a situation for which there is no single right answer. For many of the practice cases, there are right answers, although as you will see, there is sometimes more room for judgment than you might imagine initially.

Several practice cases are good candidates for relatively simple spreadsheet analysis, and you should use spreadsheet software in preparing your analyses of these cases. This approach not only will help you improve your spreadsheet skills but also will allow you to test alternative solutions more easily than if you had only written out the answer.

User Orientation

The book has a user orientation, focusing mainly on line managers and senior managers, and orienting the discussion to the decisions they make on a regular basis. Accounting details are discussed to the extent necessary for you to understand the concepts and techniques used in most organizations, but the text does not cover exceptions to the rules or some of the possible variations on each traditional theme.

Organizational Focus

Many texts use manufacturing examples to illustrate accounting concepts and principles. This book uses manufacturing examples, where appropriate, but these examples—as well as all the problems and practice cases—are set in the context of organizations that are in some way associated with the health care sector. Nevertheless, most of the examples, problems, and practice cases are about service organizations.

Although most management accounting concepts are universal, meaning that the type of organization used to illustrate a point is relatively unimportant, the learning process is much easier when the examples are related to your area of interest. The examples, problems, and practice cases have been chosen with the hope that they will resonate with you because they deal with organizations with which you may be somewhat familiar.

To the Instructor

This book has been written principally for use in a one-semester, user-oriented course in management accounting in health care. Each chapter is designed to be covered in a week, ideally over two classes of 1.5 to 2 hours each. Clearly a great deal depends on the depth you wish to pursue and how quickly or slowly you wish to move through the course. (The material in this book has also been used in a half-semester course on management accounting for MBA students. In this instance, each chapter was covered in a single 2-hour class meeting.)

Students' preparation for the first class session associated with a given chapter should include reading the chapter, engaging in the chapter's interactive activities, answering the "Test Yourself" questions, and analyzing the chapter's practice case or cases. Due to the interactivity, students will need considerably more time to read these chapters than they would if they were using a more traditional text. Moreover, they will need to spend time analyzing the practice cases.

It is sometimes useful to have an open class discussion after students have read a chapter and prepared the practice case or cases. This discussion can serve to clarify the chapter's concepts and address any difficulties the students are having in using them.

After this class session, each remaining class for a given chapter can focus on a case or cases that you select that will require students to use the chapter's concepts and techniques. This way, the concepts are first clarified and then applied in the analysis of case situations. At the end of each chapter is a list of suggested cases for that chapter.

If you would like assistance in selecting cases for your course, you may contact The Crimson Press Curriculum Center (www.thecrimson group.org) and review its online catalogue of materials. In addition, the Harvard Business School Press has a catalogue and a Web site (www.hbsp .harvard.edu) that can help you in selecting cases to supplement each chapter. An instructor who adopts the book for his or her course may obtain a course packet of cases from The Crimson Press Curriculum Center at no charge.

Case Method of Instruction

Educators increasingly are recognizing the power of the case method in teaching management accounting. The value of the case method lies in its ability to put students in the middle of the action, requiring them to be analytical—to apply principles rather than just memorize or reiterate them. In this way, it prepares students for work in an environment where analysis, judgment, and attention to nuance increasingly are required for success.

Changes for the Third Edition

This edition of the text contains several changes from the second edition:

- The chapter on absorption costing has been eliminated. Its important techniques and concepts have been included in the chapter on activity-based costing (chapter 5).

- A new chapter (chapter 1) has been prepared that sets the stage for the rest of the book. It discusses the many challenges health care organizations will face in the next five to ten years, such as the aging of the population and the presence of many more individuals with chronic conditions. Management accounting concepts and techniques have therefore become even more important than they were in the past.

- The cases without solutions have been eliminated. Only practice cases remain. As mentioned earlier, instructors who adopt the book for a course may select as many cases as they wish from The Crimson Press Curriculum Center without a need to pay the normal copyright clearance fees. This results in a shorter book as well as increased flexibility for professors to choose cases that meet their pedagogical needs.

- Five "Test Yourself" questions have been included at the end of each chapter. These questions help students to reflect on the concepts and techniques contained in the chapter.

- Several new appendices have been added that allow students to pursue material that was not discussed directly in the chapter, such as pricing in nonprofit organizations or undertaking benefit-cost analysis in public-sector capital budgeting.

Organization of the Book

Exhibit P.1 contains the book's learning objectives for each of its three major areas: full-cost accounting, differential cost accounting, and responsibility accounting. The book's chapters move from the design of good cost measurement systems to the design of good cost control systems. Cost measurement can take place without cost control, but controlling costs requires an ability to measure them. Therefore, the chapters need to be read in the sequence presented. The overall theme for each chapter is discussed briefly in this section.

Chapter 1: Management Accounting and Health Care's Impending Fiscal Crisis

Health care systems throughout the industrialized world are in trouble. As the population ages, and as people live longer, they will require increasing amounts of health care services, especially for the treatment of chronic conditions. In addition, individuals born shortly after the end of World War II (between 1945 and 1955) have now reached the age at which they will demand more services. Even nonelderly individuals who do not practice good health habits require greater care. This chapter discusses the details of this demographic and health behavior scenario. The inevitable conclusion is that if health care costs in industrialized countries are not better managed, there will be a fiscal crisis: either spending will skyrocket, or people will be denied needed care. Neither needs to happen if policymakers, managers, and physicians learn to understand their costs and manage them more appropriately. This chapter is, in effect, a call to action.

Chapter 2: Essentials of Full-Cost Accounting

"What did it cost?" is one of the trickiest accounting questions for all organizations, including those in health care. This chapter discusses the kinds of managerial decisions that are made in answering this question, as well

EXHIBIT P.1 Management Accounting Learning Objectives

Full-Cost Accounting

- The meaning of such terms as *cost object, cost center, direct costs, indirect costs, overhead, cost allocation methods,* and *cost systems*
- The way costs can be allocated to help determine the cost of a particular product or service
- The distinction between mission (or revenue) centers and support centers
- The nature of the managerial choices inherent in a full-cost accounting system
- The concept of an overhead rate, for attaching a mission center's costs to its cost objects
- The concepts of activity-based costing and cost drivers, including the use of multiple second-stage cost drivers

Differential Cost Accounting

- The rationale for the statement, "Different costs are used for different purposes"
- The distinction between full costs and differential costs, and when each should be used
- The nature of the factors that influence changes in cost, including the distinctions among fixed, variable, step-function, and semivariable costs
- The nature of alternative choice decision making, and the three major types of alternative choice decisions that most organizations make
- The concepts of unit contribution margin and total contribution, and their roles in alternative choice decision making
- The technique of cost-volume-profit analysis, how to prepare such an analysis, and its uses and limitations

Responsibility Accounting

- The definition of a responsibility center, the different responsibility center options, and the basis for choosing the most appropriate type of center
- The definition of a transfer price, and the role of transfer prices in a responsibility accounting system
- The phases of the management control process, and the characteristics of each phase
- The key elements in the budgeting phase of the management control process, and the relationship between budgeting and responsibility centers
- The meaning of the term *flexible budget,* and how it can be used in a responsibility accounting system
- The technique of variance analysis, and the different types of variances that can occur
- The uses and limitations of variance analysis, and the relationship between variance analysis and the reporting phase of the management control process
- Some of the difficulties involved in measuring nonfinancial (or programmatic) performance, and how to overcome them

as the utility of full-cost information for managers. Before managers can *control* their costs, they must know what they are. Unfortunately, many health care organizations do not have this rudimentary knowledge. Appendix 2A discusses the reciprocal method of cost allocation. Appendix 2B discusses the topic of pricing in nonprofit organizations.

Chapter 3: Cost Behavior

Chapter 2 classifies costs as either direct or indirect. This distinction is important for undertaking a successful full-cost computation, which is important for pricing and profitability analyses. For many managers, however, the distinction between direct and indirect costs is less important than the question of how costs actually behave. This chapter addresses cost behavior. It first distinguishes among fixed, variable, step-function, and semivariable costs. Next, it explains cost-volume-profit (CVP) analysis and the concept of contribution. It also discusses some tricky aspects of CVP analysis, including the approaches to take when step-function costs or multiple products are involved.

Chapter 4: Differential Cost Accounting

The notion that different costs are used for different purposes can be difficult to accept. This chapter explains why this notion is important, reinforcing the distinction between full costs and differential costs, and discussing when each should be used. The ideas contained in this chapter are important for managers when they are making what are called *alternative choice decisions*, such as outsourcing, keeping or eliminating a product that is unprofitable on a full-cost basis, or offering a special price.

Chapter 5: Activity-Based Costing

The discussion in chapter 2 focuses principally on what is known as stage 1 of a full-cost accounting system—the stage in which all costs end up in the organization's mission centers. This chapter looks at stage 2, which is the stage in which mission center costs are attached to the products that the center delivers. This *absorption costing* concept is applicable to service delivery units in almost all health care settings, ranging from a clinical department (such as surgery or medicine) to laboratories, radiology departments, and pharmacies, to name a few.

The major focus of the chapter is on the technique of activity-based costing (ABC), which is becoming increasingly prevalent in health care. Nevertheless, many users of ABC in health care organizations do not fully understand the kinds of problems it was designed to solve or the importance of what are called *multiple second-stage cost drivers.* The chapter shows how to make the computations, and it illustrates the importance of using ABC to determine the full cost of an organization's products.

Chapter 6: Responsibility Accounting: An Overview

There is an important distinction to be made between measuring costs and controlling them. This chapter makes that distinction, moving into the realm of responsibility accounting. To design a good responsibility accounting system, a manager must think about the system's structure and process. This chapter emphasizes structure, describing the different types of responsibility centers that can exist in an organization and the basis for choosing one type over another. The chapter concludes with a summary of the four phases of the management control process.

Chapter 7: Designing the Responsibility Accounting Structure

Chapter 6 raises but does not fully discuss several tricky issues involved in designing the responsibility accounting structure. This chapter takes the next step, discussing matters of fairness, goal congruence, the link between the responsibility center structure and an organization's motivation process, and the development of appropriate transfer prices for intraorganizational transactions.

Chapter 8: Programming

This chapter discusses some of the techniques for analyzing new programs or capital investments, emphasizing the concepts of net present value and internal rate of return. It also examines the issues involved in choosing a discount rate for assessing a capital project, and it assesses the impact of political and behavioral considerations on the choice of capital projects. Appendix 8A discusses the concept of present value, and Appendix 8B discusses some special programming issues in governmental organizations.

Chapter 9: Operational Budgeting

This chapter discusses the (usually) annual activity of forecasting operating revenues and expenses. Among the topics addressed are the key elements in the budgeting process, the relationship between budgeting and responsibility centers, the different contexts in which budgeting takes place, and the mechanical aspects of building a budget. Appendix 9A describes seven common budgeting "misfits," or areas where the operational budgeting phase does not align well with other activities in the organization.

Chapter 10: The Cash Budget

Moving from preparing the capital and operating budgets to preparing the cash budget requires an understanding of both financial accounting and financial management. This chapter is concerned with the choices managers make about (1) the use of debt or equity to finance assets, (2) the structure of debt, (3) the size of net income, and (4) the management of growth. It discusses the operating, financing, and revenue cycles, along with several key concepts that are important to understanding a cash budget: debt structure, leverage, and the role of profit (or surplus).

Chapter 11: Measuring and Reporting

Two important phases in the management control process are measuring performance and reporting the resulting information to managers. This chapter discusses these phases, beginning with flexible budgeting and variance analysis. It includes the uses and limitations of variance analysis and moves to the relationship between variance analysis and the reporting phase. It also provides some examples of reports that can communicate action-oriented information to managers. It concludes by addressing an emerging concern of many health care organizations—the measurement of nonfinancial performance.

Chapter 12: Implementing a New Responsibility Accounting System

The value of the concepts of structure and process that form the basis of responsibility accounting systems is in their application to real-world situations and problems. The ultimate goal is to develop a responsibility accounting system that facilitates improved operations, which requires assessing how such a system fits into a broader organizational context. This chapter first summarizes the key characteristics of a good responsibility accounting system. It then positions the responsibility accounting system in an organizational context made up of seven separate activities (or processes). It concludes with a discussion of some of the important issues that managers need to keep in mind when introducing a new or redesigned responsibility accounting system.

An instructor's supplement is available at www.josseybass.com/go/young3e. Additional materials, such as videos, podcasts, and readings, can be found at www.josseybasspublichealth.com. Comments about this book are invited and can be sent to publichealth@wiley.com.

ACKNOWLEDGMENTS

I thank reviewers Leslie K. Breitner, L. Kirk Harlow, Thomas E. McKee, Brandon Penick, Dennis Stillman, and Marci S. Thomas, who provided valuable feedback on the revision plan for this edition. John Raffoul and Simone Singh, along with Professors Harlow and McKee, provided thoughtful and constructive comments on the complete draft manuscript. I am grateful to them for their suggestions and guidance. Francie Jones did a masterful job of copyediting. Clearly, though, I am responsible for the final content of the book.

Davig W. Young is professor of management, emeritus, at Boston University (BU) School of Management, where he was nominated four times for BU's prestigious Metcalf Award for teaching excellence. During each of his last two years at BU, he was voted "best professor" by Cohort C of the school's MBA students. While at BU, he taught undergraduate, MBA, executive MBA, and executive nondegree courses on financial accounting, management accounting, and responsibility accounting systems. His courses were taught in for-profit, nonprofit, and health care contexts. During each of his last four years, he also taught the capstone course on competition, innovation, and strategy in the school's MBA program.

Professor Young has been a core faculty member for the past 37 years at Harvard University's School of Public Health, where he has taught in the Programs for Chiefs of Clinical Service and Leadership Development in Health Care. He has been the lead faculty member for the past 13 years in the Alliance for Academic Internal Medicines Executive Leadership Program for members of departments of internal medicine.

During the past several years, Professor Young has been a visiting professor in the international MBA and doctoral programs at the Universities of Ferrara, Messina, Bologna, and Pisa in Italy, and he has taught at the China Europe International Business School in Shanghai, the University of Reykjavik, ESADE and IESE business schools in Barcelona, and the Clinical Effectiveness Program in Buenos Aires. For the past three years, he has cotaught the managing public-private partnerships course at the Forlí campus of the University of Bologna. He also has lectured in Europe, Latin America, Asia, and the Middle East on a variety of topics.

In the late 1990s, Professor Young was appointed by the governor of the Commonwealth of Massachusetts to serve a three-year term as commissioner and chair of the state's Hospital Payment System Advisory Commission. This was a seven-member body charged with monitoring access, quality, and fair-market standards as the state shifted to a more market-oriented health care system. In 2006, he received the Special Recognition Award from the Association of Professors of Medicine, an award presented annually to a nonmember who has contributed the most to helping the association meet its mission of providing leadership and direction in the field of academic internal medicine.

In addition to his teaching and service awards, Professor Young has received several research awards, including "best article of the year" from both the American College of Healthcare Executives and (three times) the Healthcare Financial Management Association. In 2003, he published *A Manager's Guide to Creative Cost Cutting: 181 Ways to Build the Bottom Line, and Techniques of Management Accounting: An Essential Guide for Managers and Financial Professionals* (both have been translated into Mandarin).

This is the third edition of *Management Accounting in Health Care Organizations.* In 2012, Professor Young published the ninth edition of *Management Control in Nonprofit Organizations*; earlier editions of this text were translated into Italian and Japanese. Also in 2012, he published (with Emanuele Padovani of the University of Bologna) *Managing Local Governments: Designing Management Control Systems That Deliver Value.* His earlier book (coauthored with Richard B. Saltman), *The Hospital Power Equilibrium,* was a seminal study of the relationship between physicians and administrators in hospitals. Earlier in his career he served as a program economist with the US Agency for International Development in El Salvador, and as a consultant with the Social Administration Research Institute.

Professor Young earned a BA from Occidental College; an MA in economics from the University of California, Los Angeles; and a doctorate from Harvard Business School. He was selected to be a Milton Fund Fellow at Harvard Medical School, and he was elected to Beta Gamma Sigma (the national honor society for accredited business programs). For more information, visit his Web site, www.DavidYoung.org

MANAGEMENT ACCOUNTING IN HEALTH CARE ORGANIZATIONS

CHAPTER 1

MANAGEMENT ACCOUNTING AND HEALTH CARE'S IMPENDING FISCAL CRISIS

D uring the next five to ten years, hospitals and health systems will face a variety of financial challenges, including pressures related to the economy, health care reform, and increased demand for care. Addressing these challenges will require, at a minimum, an understanding of the costs associated with care delivery. It also will require these organizations to develop an ability to *manage*—rather than simply *measure*—their costs.

In a sense, then, this book represents a call to action. Cost-influencing decisions are being made in national, regional, state, and local health policy arenas, as well as in integrated delivery systems, academic medical centers, community hospitals, and even small home health agencies and nursing homes. These decisions require—but often lack—good analyses of the relevant cost implications. In addition, provider entities need to use much more sophisticated measurement and control systems than most now have. No one in health care is exempt from the challenges.

Organization of the Chapter

The chapter begins with a discussion of four forces that will affect costs in all health care systems in the industrialized world over the next five to ten years, putting most of the focus on the United States but also pointing out implications for other industrialized nations:

- The impact of demographic changes on the Medicare Trust Fund in the United States and on national health care budgets in other industrialized countries[1]

- The typical spending patterns for the elderly (sixty-five years old and older)

LEARNING OBJECTIVES

On completing this chapter, you should know about

- Four forces that are affecting health care costs: demographic changes, morbidity patterns, the special needs of the elderly, and the unusual structure of the health care market

- Five drivers of health care costs: case mix, volume, resources per case, cost per resource unit, and fixed costs

- Some alternative ways to address these cost drivers

- The nature of the health care "food chain" and its implications

- The impact of the Affordable Care Act on costs

morbidity
Refers to the state of disease within a population. It contrasts with *mortality*, which is the term used for the deaths in a population.

* The *morbidity* patterns in the nonelderly population

* The complex nature of the health care market

Collectively, the first three forces will create intense pressures on health care costs, and the fourth will limit the ability of market mechanisms to control cost increases. Combined, these forces represent a daunting challenge.

The chapter then addresses some potential responses to these forces. In particular, it focuses on ways that health care organizations can address their *cost drivers*. Finally, it discusses ways that management accounting systems can help organizations manage these cost drivers.

cost drivers
An activity that can be directly linked to an increase or decrease in costs. Cost drivers are frequently relatively easy to identify but sometimes difficult to measure. Thinking in terms of cost drivers allows managers to shift their focus away from the traditional departmental structure of an organization and toward the activities that cause the existence of costs and, perhaps most important, toward the managerial actions that can influence and control costs.

Four Forces Affecting Health Care Costs

Demographic Changes

Figure 1.1 shows how annual inpatient days per person change as people age. This is not surprising: as people grow older, they tend to use more inpatient care. The problem is that members of the baby boom generation—people born between 1945 and 1955—are now in their late fifties to late sixties. If the historical pattern continues, the baby boomers will demand

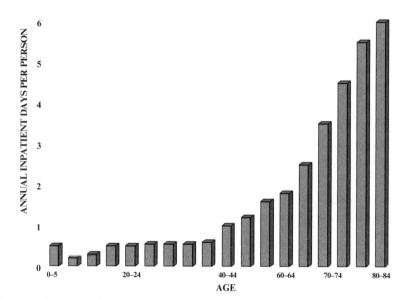

Figure 1.1 Demographic Trends
Source: The Crimson Group, Inc., adapted from presentation materials in company files.

geometrically increasing amounts of inpatient care. This idea is supported by an analysis from the Kaiser Family Foundation, which forecasted that Medicare spending would nearly double in an eight-year period, growing from just over $500 billion in 2010 to about $1 trillion in 2018.[2]

This problem is not confined to the United States. As figure 1.2 shows, several European countries will have an even more serious problem than the United States has in regard to the aging of their populations. In the Catalonia region of Spain, for example, costs in the first decade of the 2000s, shown in figure 1.3, increased by about 250 percent, from some €400 million to €1 billion; this represents a growth rate greater than that forecasted for the United States.

Spending Patterns for the Elderly

Medicare's spending (and, similarly, spending for the elderly in other countries) is not uniformly distributed among its beneficiaries. As figure 1.4 shows, approximately 20 percent of the program's beneficiaries consume well over 80 percent of its spending. Much of this spending is related to chronic conditions.

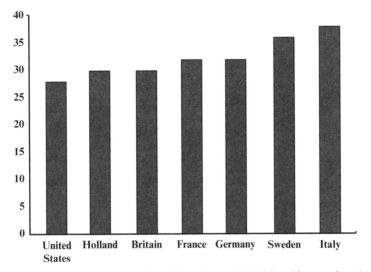

Figure 1.2 Percentage of the Population 60 Years Old and Over in 2015 in Selected European Countries and the United States
Source: Bernd Raffelhüschen and Jagadeesh Gokhale, "Population Aging and Fiscal Policy in Europe and the United States" (January 2000). CESifo Working Paper Series No. 237. Available at http://ssrn.com/abstract =263970.

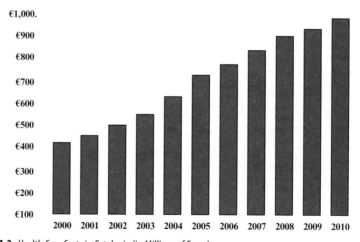

Figure 1.3 Health Care Costs in Catalonia (in Millions of Euros)
Source: La Vanguardia, November 28, 2010. *La Vanguardia* obtained the data from the Department de Salut, Barcelona, Spain.

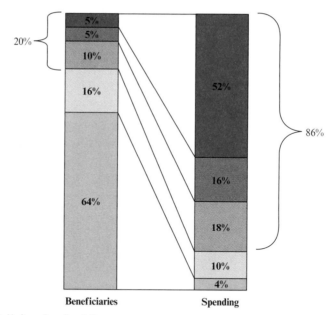

Figure 1.4 Medicare Spending Patterns
Source: The Crimson Group, Inc., adapted from presentation materials in company files. For more specific information, see Gerald F. Riley, "Long-Term Trends in the Concentration of Medicare Spending," *Health Affairs* 26 (May 2007): 808–816.

EXAMPLE

According to one analysis, approximately one-fourth of Medicare beneficiaries have five or more chronic conditions. These individuals account for approximately two-thirds of the program's costs.[3]

Morbidity in the Nonelderly Population

The elderly are only part of the story. As figure 1.5 shows, prior to becoming eligible for Medicare, many individuals experience high-cost medical conditions—mainly cancer and heart disease. In the United States, with some eighteen million individuals gaining insurance coverage in 2014 under the *Affordable Care Act,* the impact on insurers will be significant. Many countries with national health insurance—or that otherwise have insurance coverage for their entire population—are already facing this problem.

Affordable Care Act
A 2010 law in the United States that requires near universal coverage for health care and provides a variety of patient protection features. For details, see www.hhs. gov/healthcare/rights/law/index.html.

Complexity of the Health Care Market

The health care market is unlike any market described in an economics textbook. In no other market that we know of does Person A (a patient)

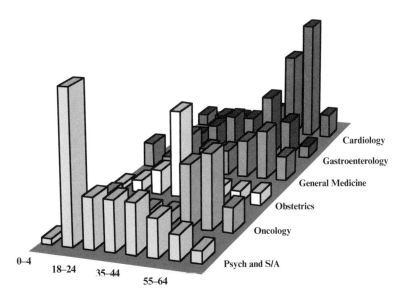

Figure 1.5 Morbidity among Those Not Yet Eligible for Medicare
Source: The Crimson Group, Inc., adapted from presentation materials in company files. Data are from a large California employer.

diagnosis-related groups (DRGs)

A DRG is a collection of several homogeneous diagnoses, and constitute a hospital's "products." A DRG is determined by "grouper" software, based on the International Classification of Diseases as well as the procedure performed, and the patient's age, sex, discharge status, including any complications or co-morbidities. A DRG determines how much Medicare pays a hospital for each of its products. For details, see http://medicaldictionary.thefreedictionary.com/DRG.

subcapitation

An arrangement when an organization that is paid under a capitated basis contracts with another organization also on a capitated basis. The first organization shares a portion of the original capitated premium with the second organization, but both are at risk for expenses that exceed the capitation payments.

receive services ordered by Person B (a physician), which are delivered by Person C (a hospital, clinic, or specialist), paid for by Person D (an insurer), whose revenue comes from Person E (the insured). Even when the setting is less complex, such as in a physician group practice, Person A has little say over the services ordered by Person B, which often are delivered by Person C (such as a lab or a radiology unit), and are paid for by Person D with revenue from Person E.

The result, shown in figure 1.6, is five separate markets:

1. A premium-sharing market (between an employer and its employees)

2. A per member, per month (PMPM) market (between an employer and an insurer, such as a managed care plan or a regional government)

3. A deductible market (between a patient and an insurer)

4. A copayment market (between a patient and a provider, usually a physician or a hospital unit, such as an emergency room)

5. A fee market (between a provider and an insurer)

The fifth market can be quite complex, including such payment approaches as fee-for-service (discounted or otherwise), *diagnosis-related groups (DRGs)*, bundled prices, and *subcapitation*. In the United States, under some of the provisions of the Affordable Care Act, bundled prices have been expanded from a single price that includes the hospital charge and the physician fee to a fixed amount for all aspects of an episode of care, including postdischarge services, such as home care.

Depending on how their health care systems are organized, some countries may not have all five market participants, but most have at least four. For example, instead of an employer, some countries may have a social

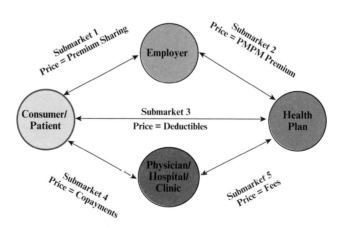

Figure 1.6 Five Separate Health Care Markets

security system; and some have tax payments (perhaps sequestered for health care) in place of premiums or premium sharing,. In all countries, however, there is a division among those who order the "product," those who provide it, and those who pay for it.

Responding to the Four Forces

On a conceptual level, it is relatively easy to describe how these four forces can be addressed. As figure 1.7 indicates, there are only five drivers of health care costs: case mix, volume, resources per case, cost per resource unit, and fixed costs. Each of these cost drivers relates to one or more of the four forces. Together they can help explain (1) why a country's (or state's, or hospital's) costs changed from one year to the next, (2) why one health system's or hospital's costs differed from another's, or (3) why actual financial results for a hospital or health system differed from budgeted ones.

Case Mix and Volume

Case mix and volume are related to morbidity patterns in the population, which result mainly from the environment, genetics, and health habits.[4] Although some improvements to the environment (such as cleaner air and water) may have an impact, nothing can be done about genetics (except asking people to choose their parents carefully!). According to the *Journal of the American Medical Association*, almost 35 percent of all deaths in the

Case mix and volume

Refers to the different types of diagnoses that can present themselves for treatment. Examples include diabetes, liver cancer, or psoriasis. Volume refers to the number of each type of case.

Cost Driver		Examples	Controlling Force(s)
Case Mix	Morbidity	Diabetes, cancer, heart disease . . .	Environment, genetics, health habits
Volume		10,000 cases diabetes, 15,000 cases cancer . . .	Environment, genetics, health habits
Resources per Case	Utilization and Efficiency	8 outpatient visits, 2 glucose tests, 2 complete blood counts (CBCs) . . .	Physicians, clinical protocols, available technology
Cost per Resource Unit		$40 per OPD visit, $25 per glucose test, $12 per CBC . . .	Service-providing units
Fixed Facility Costs	Technology	Plant and equipment depreciation, managerial and administrative staffing. . .	Senior management, physicians, health policy

Figure 1.7 Health Care Cost Drivers

United States are related to tobacco use, poor diet, and physical inactivity, which suggests that public health programs need to focus mainly on health habits. Public health officials must consider (1) prevention programs, such as laws that require the use of seat belts and motorcycle helmets; (2) early intervention programs, such as cancer screenings; and (3) wellness programs, such as childhood inoculations.

Computing the benefits of a prevention or wellness program is by no means easy, in part because it is not clear that people want to improve their health. Indeed, improving one's diet or increasing physical activity can be enormously difficult in a society where people do not adopt—or, apparently, *wish* to adopt—more healthy lifestyles.

EXAMPLE

A 2007 study by the Centers for Disease Control and Prevention (CDC) (www.cdc.gov/) found that 30 percent of the US population between fifty and seventy years of age had an average body mass index of 30 or above (30 is defined as "obese"). In an earlier study, the CDC found that the number of states with more than 20 percent of their population classified as thirty pounds or more overweight grew from zero states in 1991 to twenty states in 2000.

In addition to computing the financial benefits of each new programmatic endeavor in terms of, say, cost savings due to a reduction in morbidity, health policy analysts also must examine the relevant program costs; otherwise, a benefit-cost analysis will not be possible. But determining the program's costs can be difficult, in part because some of the program's "benefits" come in the form of cost reductions in the delivery system, such as from a decline in hospitalizations for conditions caused by obesity or smoking.

Program costs also must be analyzed in terms of both one-time investments (such as new facilities or equipment) and ongoing expenses (such as salaries and supplies). In many instances, a program's costs also will include a "fair share" of an organization's overhead. To assemble all the disparate pieces into one programmatic package is a daunting challenge, to say the least.

Resources per Case

The cost-related elements that are used in the treatment of a patient with a particular diagnosis. In a hospital, these resources include a day of care, a laboratory test, a radiological procedure, and a variety of non-clinical items, such as a meal or a pound of washed laundry.

Resources per Case

Addressing this cost driver means, in effect, lowering the bars in figure 1.1 (in addition to reducing the other resources used to treat a case, such as

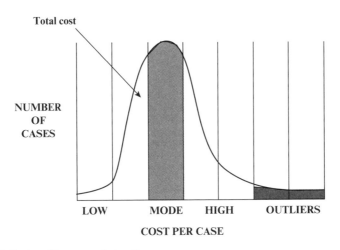

Figure 1.8 Number of Cases versus Cost per Case
Source: The Crimson Group, Inc., adapted from presentation materials in company files.

tests and procedures). Figure 1.8 demonstrates this idea conceptually. Because the vertical axis represents the number of cases and the horizontal axis represents cost per case, the area under the curve is the total cost. The obvious goal is to shift the modal (or average) cost per case to the left, which can be done by, say, using outpatient instead of inpatient care, engaging in preadmission activities or in-home care so as to shorten a patient's length of stay, or undertaking any of a variety of similar resource-reducing measures. (In this regard, note that a focus on outliers has very little cost-saving potential in most hospitals.)

EXAMPLE

The Dartmouth Atlas Working Group has studied how reductions in resources per case can be done without affecting the quality of care. The researchers examined the treatment for chronic conditions in the last two years of life in several organizations where the Centers for Medicare & Medicaid Services had rated the quality of care as similar.[5] They found variation between the "most aggressive" and the "most conservative" hospital of almost $61,000 per case ($105,067 versus $44,090, on average). Most of the variation was due to days in the ward (forty-two versus twelve), but there also were significant differences in regard to days in the intensive care unit (twelve versus four), specialist visits (ninety-seven versus eighteen), and primary care visits (thirty-four versus twenty-three).[6]

CURRENT PATTERN		OPTIONAL PATTERN	
Admit to Telemetry ALOS = 2.2 days	$2,800	Admit to Observation Unit ALOS = 23 hours	$1,000
Daily EKG × 3	$225	EKG × 2	$150
Enzymes and Full Bloods	$175	Enzymes and Limited Bloods	$75
Cardiology Consult	$150	Cardiology Consult	$150
Echo	$350	Echo	$350
Thallium Stress Test	$450	Non-Thallium Stress Test	$125
TOTAL COST	$4,150	TOTAL COST	$1,850

Figure 1.9 Alternative Treatment Patterns for a 48-Year-Old, Presenting in the Emergency Room with Atypical Chest Pain, Positive Smoking, and Family History, with a Normal Electrocardiogram (EKG)
Source: Robert Galvin, MD, personal communication, June 2005.

Resources per case also can be managed by physicians working collaboratively to determine the most appropriate resource mix for the average (or modal) patient with a given diagnosis or DRG. Figure 1.9 shows how this was done for the treatment of a patient with a certain presenting condition in a hospital emergency room.[7]

incidence rate

The frequency a particular event occurs. For example, if the incidence rate of a heart attack during a year is 1% and there are 1 million people, then 10,000 of them will have heart attacks.

PROBLEM

Assume there is an *incidence rate* of 5 persons per 1,000 insured (0.5 percent), which is fairly normal, and that there are about 1,000,000 insured people. Compute the annual savings to the insurer associated with the alternative care delivery pattern shown in figure 1.9.

It is extremely important that you write out your own answer before looking at the one given. Please do not shortcut this feature of the learning process. If you have not written out an answer yet, please do so before you continue reading.

ANSWER

The savings would be $11.5 million per year: 1,000,000 people × 0.5 incidence rate × $2,300 ($4,150 − $1,850) per person.

As this example and the Dartmouth Atlas research indicate, there are some important opportunities to address the growth in health care costs by focusing on resources per case. Happily, doing so need not be accompanied by a reduction in quality. In fact, by developing appropriate disease management protocols, quality actually may be improved.

One of the most dramatic efforts to address the issue of resources per case was made in Grand Junction, Colorado, a site often used as an example in health care reform discussions.[8] In Grand Junction, leadership by primary care providers (PCPs) resulted in a culture of incentives for cost control—a culture that was reinforced by the PCPs' deciding to *withhold* 15 percent of their fees to create a risk pool. The risk pool was managed by the Mesa County Physicians *Independent Practice Association.*

To better control resources per case, the Grand Junction PCPs, who on a per capita basis in Grand Junction were 185 percent of the national average of PCPs in a community, gathered data on the cost profiles of specialists and reduced their referrals to those who used above-average resources with no discernible quality differences. PCPs also led the way in the regionalization of services, resulting in one tertiary care hospital (many communities of a similar size have two or more *tertiary care hospitals*) that was fed by several secondary hospitals. Grand Junction's PCPs also supported end-of-life care that placed an emphasis on *hospice care* rather than on inpatient hospital care.

The results were impressive. Grand Junction saw

- A reduction in high-cost surgical interventions. Its *coronary artery bypass graft (CABG)* rate was 60 percent of the Medicare national average, and its inpatient coronary angiography rate was 55 percent of the national average.

- A decrease in inpatient days during the last two years of life to 61 percent of the national average, with hospice days rising to 174 percent of the national average. Deaths in hospitals declined to 50 percent of the national average.

In all of these instances, assessing the treatment options and making the needed trade-offs require an understanding of the relevant costs under alternative scenarios. Changing the way resources are used to treat a case without understanding the relevant cost implications is the health care equivalent of flying blind.[9]

Cost per Resource Unit

The distinction between resources per case and *cost per resource unit* is important. For example, the number of *complete blood counts (CBCs)* ordered for a patient during an inpatient stay is one measure of the resources used to treat a case. However, the cost of performing a blood analysis is a separate matter. Few hospitals have engaged in the activities needed to

withhold
An amount removed from a physician's (normally a primary care physician's) fee that is placed in a fund for later distribution if certain goals are met. If health care costs (and other goals) do not meet a certain defined target the withheld amount is not paid out.

Independent Practice Association
One form of a health maintenance organization (HMO). An HMO receives its revenue from monthly premium payments made by, or on behalf of, each insured person. Its revenue therefore is essentially fixed, and it must manage its expenses so that they do not exceed its revenue.

tertiary care hospitals
A hospital that deals with very sick patients. It contrasts with a community (secondary care) hospital that deals with moderately ill patients, and a quaternary care hospital, that deals with the sickest of patients. There are no primary care hospitals. Primary care is delivered by physicians in their offices.

hospice care
Focuses on palliative care for a terminally ill patient (one who is medically certified to have less than six months to live). For details, see http://hospicenet.org.

coronary artery bypass graft (CABG)
Pronounced "cabbage" is a surgical procedure performed to relieve angina (chest pain or discomfort) and reduce the risk of death from coronary artery disease. Arteries or veins from elsewhere in the patient's body are grafted to the coronary arteries to improve the blood supply to the heart.

cost per resource unit
The cost of each unit of service provided to treat a case, such as the cost of a complete blood count (CBC). It needs to be distinguished from the resource unit itself. For example, one cost driver is the number of CBS, but another is the cost of each CBC.

complete blood counts (CBCs)
A complete blood count. A fairly typical test for a patient in a hospital.

understand the cost of providing such physician-ordered resources as laboratory tests, radiology procedures, and other *intermediate products.*

Even without having good cost information, any hospital manager knows that cost reductions can take place with an increase in efficiency or a decrease in hourly wage rates or unit supply costs (for example, through a shift from name brand to generic drugs). However, computing the cost implications of these decisions can be tricky.

To make accurate unit cost computations, hospitals need to adopt the technique of activity-based costing (ABC). Although ABC is becoming increasingly prevalent in health care,[10] its use is not widespread. Moreover, many users of ABC in health care organizations do not fully understand the kinds of problems it was designed to solve, nor do they understand the importance of using what are called "multiple second-stage cost drivers." Yet to make informed decisions about ways to reduce the cost per resource unit, a hospital's physicians and managers must move down the ABC learning curve quickly. ABC is discussed in chapter 5.

Fixed Costs

Most health care organizations incur significant fixed costs. For example, plant and equipment depreciation expenses can represent a large percentage of a hospital's annual operating budget. Indeed, because the health care sector is characterized by a high rate of technological change, many hospitals (as well as other provider organizations) are likely to experience continuous growth in their annual depreciation expense. To avoid the resulting fiscal difficulties, senior management and physician leaders need to make judicious choices about the acquisition of new technology. However, few hospitals have shown a willingness to bite the technology-sharing bullet.

EXAMPLE

In Grand Junction, having one tertiary care hospital fed by several secondary hospitals helped curtail the growth of new technology while continuing to assure patients of access to needed resources. In effect, the Grand Junction PCPs helped ensure the sharing of technology.

Full-time employees, whose daily activities are largely unrelated to the volume of care provided, also constitute fixed costs. Unless there is a significant change in a hospital's average occupancy, the salaries of such people as admitting clerks, schedulers, housekeepers, dietitians, laundry staff members, and departmental administrators will remain largely unchanged over the course of a year. By the same token, if a hospital's average occupancy falls, it will need to make some difficult choices in regard to its staffing pattern. The nature of a hospital's costs (as well as cost behavior in general, and costs in other kinds of health care organizations) is discussed in chapter 3.

The Health Care Food Chain

Difficult cost-containment choices emerge, in part, because a reduction in one entity's costs in a health care system is accompanied by an equivalent reduction in another entity's revenues. As a result, implementing cost reduction efforts can become complicated.

intermediate products
Services that are provided to a patient during his or her stay in a hospital. The "final product" is a discharge from the hospital, but the intermediate products consist of all those services needed to provide the final product. They include lab tests, radiological procedures, meals, laundry, and others. They will be discussed later in the book.

EXAMPLE

Consider the scenario shown in the problem concerning alternative treatment patterns in an emergency room, and the ensuing consequences. The $11.5 million in cost reductions were for the payer, not for the hospital. That is, the payer (Medicare, a managed care organization, or some other insurer) would pay less to the hospital as a result of this change in resources per case, and the hospital would receive less revenue. If it did not find ways to decrease its costs, its operating margin would decline.

The nature of this *health care food chain* is shown in figure 1.10. As the figure indicates, at each step along the way, the expense for one entity represents revenue for another. Unless physicians and hospital managers have a good understanding of their costs—and unless they design good systems to control their costs—they will be at the mercy of entities higher up in the food chain. And, of course, the same principle applies to those entities, such as pharmaceutical and medical equipment firms, to which hospitals or physician group practices make payments.

In this respect, it is important to note, as shown in Figure 1.10, that many of the "suppliers" to which hospitals make payments are employees. Although perhaps this topic is not explicitly discussed in conversations about cost control, it should be noted that in a hospital or physician-hospital organization, where a significant portion of costs is in the form of salaries and wages, cost reductions no doubt will require a resizing of the workforce.

health care food chain
The idea that each entity's expenses in the health care system represent revenue for another entity.

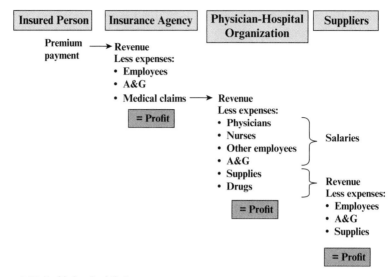

Figure 1.10 Health Care Food Chain

The Food Chain versus the Value Chain

The food chain need not have pejorative connotations. Considerable work has taken place on what now is known (perhaps euphemistically) as the "value chain." The idea, which was initially presented outside of the health care context by Michael Porter, Harvard University's strategy guru, is that each entity in an industry adds something to the final value of a product.[11] The value that it adds can be measured and accounted for financially in terms of such activities as inbound logistics, operations, outbound logistics, and the like.

value-based purchasing
The idea that cost is not the only consideration in a purchasing decision; benefits also matter. An example from the computer industry is a cheap (say, $300) computer. This computer will not have much RAM, hard-drive capacity, or processing speed. So, consumers will be willing to pay more if they perceive that their benefits (e.g. processing speed) increase in greater proportion to their costs.

In health care, the concept of the value chain was expanded some thirteen years ago to include the idea of *value-based purchasing*.[12] The basic argument was that costs do not constitute the only factor to be considered in decision making; rather, a purchaser must ask what benefits are being received for those costs. In the computer industry, for example, there are machines that sell for only a few hundred dollars, but they do not have the same features or benefits (processor speed, RAM, and so on) as computers that are more expensive. Thus, like computer purchasers, health care purchasers need to consider what they are receiving for their payments.

The Wharton School's health care group also addressed value. However, instead of incorporating the entities shown in figure 1.10, its value chain used a different mix of stakeholders: payers (government bodies, employers, individuals, employer coalitions); fiscal intermediaries (health maintenance organizations, pharmacy benefit managers); providers (hospitals, physicians, pharmacies); purchasers (wholesalers, mail-order distributors);

and producers (manufacturers of drugs, devices, supplies, and other similar items).[13]

Similarly, Michael Porter and Elizabeth Teisberg proposed that competition in health care should be value based and that entities should be rewarded based on their results.[14] In effect, this idea simply represented a return to the notion of value-based purchasing.[15]

Impact of the Affordable Care Act

There are some early indications of the ways that costs will be affected (or, as the current jargon goes, "how the cost curve will be bent") in the United States under the Affordable Care Act. The following efforts are expected to take place in an attempt to reduce resources per case:[16]

+ A focus on providing more coordinated care for patients with chronic conditions

+ An increase in the use of electronic medical records to help physicians choose the right tests and treatments

+ A reform of the health care system's infrastructure that will "enhance horizontal coordination among providers and provide more constant monitoring of patients"

+ An imposition of penalties for hospitals with high risk-adjusted readmission rates, to address the fact that 20 percent of Medicare patients are readmitted within thirty days after discharge

+ A provision of incentives for hospitals to adopt practices that reduce rates of hospital-acquired conditions, paid for via penalties for hospitals with high rates

+ The use of bundled payments to provide physicians and hospitals with incentives to coordinate care for patients with chronic illnesses

+ Evaluation and testing of new programs that enhance quality and reduce costs

All of the measures just listed, but especially the last two, will require an understanding of a hospital's costs and an ability to address the cost implications of alternative approaches to care delivery. These measures also will require an understanding of when to use full-cost accounting (discussed in chapters 2 and 5) and when to use differential cost accounting (discussed in chapters 3 and 4). And they will require hospitals and other provider entities to have much more sophisticated cost control systems than many now have. This last requirement occupies most of the latter half of the book, beginning with chapter 6.

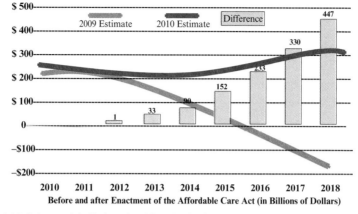

Figure 1.11 Estimates of the Medicare Part A Trust Fund Balance

Source: DGA Partners Analysis of Kaiser Family Foundation's Medicare Chartbook, 4th ed. (2010).

In summary, if the decline in Part A (hospital payments) of the Medicare Trust Fund balance is to be reversed in accordance with the estimates made after the passage of the Affordable Care Act (see figure 1.11)—that is, if the cost curve is going to bend—"something's gotta give"! To figure out what that something is and how much it must give, health policy analysts, hospital administrators, group practice managers, and physician leaders must have both a good understanding of their costs and an ability to control them.

The handwriting on the wall was revealed in a study of variations in 2009 Medicare spending among thirty-five hospitals for a ninety-day episode of congestive heart failure.[17] The results, contained in figure 1.12, showed a wide variation among the studied hospitals. If Medicare had drawn the payment line at some reasonable level (say, $15,000 in figure 1.12) and had bundled the price (as it probably will do) to include both hospital and physician payments, as well as both outpatient and inpatient care, some 77 percent of the hospitals and their attending physicians in the study would have had their payments reduced, with a corresponding need to reduce their costs.

Cost Control Is Everyone's Business

Controlling costs in hospitals, health care systems, physician group practices and clinics, home health agencies, nursing homes, and other similar entities requires the involvement of managers and clinical professionals at all levels in the organization. Accounting professionals can be helpful in making cost computations (discussed in chapters 2 through 5) and in

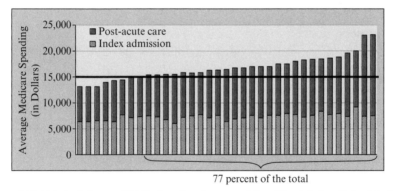

Figure 1.12 Variation in Average 2009 Medicare Spending among Selected Hospitals for a 90-Day Episode of Congestive Heart Failure
Source: Robert Mechanic and Christopher Tompkins, "Lessons Learned Preparing for Medicare Bundled Payments," *New England Journal of Medicine* 367 (November 2012): 1873–1875, doi:10.1056/NEJMp1210823.

establishing transfer prices (discussed in chapter 7). They also can help design a budget formulation process that relies on the five cost drivers shown in figure 1.7 (discussed in chapter 9). And they can prepare analyses of variances from the budget using these same cost drivers (discussed in chapter 11). However, both senior and middle managers throughout the organization must be solidly behind and deeply involved in the cost control efforts. Otherwise the resulting information may not meet their needs.

What is perhaps less obvious is that physician leaders also must be heavily engaged in cost control, for they alone can both establish clinical guidelines (resources per case) and monitor their colleagues' use of them. Indeed, without a collaborative effort among physician leaders, senior and middle managers, and the accounting staff, a provider entity may find itself being mercilessly devoured by entities higher up in its food chain.

Management Accounting Systems

As the preceding discussion has emphasized, an ability to understand and manage costs is essential for managers at both the health policy and provider levels who wish to address the four forces affecting future costs. Management accounting systems are needed in three broad areas: full-cost accounting, differential cost accounting, and responsibility accounting. The preface contains the book's learning objectives in each of these three areas, as well as a brief summary of the contents of each chapter.

Clearly, management accounting information is not the only information that managers need, nor is it the only element on the road to successful operations. But it is important, and the design of appropriate systems cannot be delegated completely to the accounting staff. Rather, system design efforts require the involvement of senior and middle managers as well as physician leaders. One of the goals of this book is to assist managers at all levels—clinical and nonclinical—in understanding their management accounting needs and communicating those needs to the accounting staff so that the appropriate information will be available for decision making.

KEY TERMS

Affordable Care Act	Independent Practice Association
Case mix and volume	(IPA)
Complete blood counts (CBCs)	Intermediate products
Coronary artery bypass graft (CABG)	Morbidity
Cost drivers	Resources per case
Cost per resource unit	Tertiary care hospitals
Health care food chain	Value-based purchasing
Hospice care	Withhold

To Bear in Mind

1. This chapter has distinguished between the external forces driving health care costs, such as demographic changes and morbidity patterns, and five cost drivers that can help managers address how these external forces will affect their organization's costs. Health care managers need to assess how the external forces in their communities will affect case mix and volume. They also need to address how they will manage the resources they use for each case type as well as the cost of each resource unit and their organization's fixed costs.

2. Conceptually, the food chain and the value chain are the same. They illustrate the zero-sum game that characterizes most health care systems, in which one entity's expenses are another entity's revenues. Value-based purchasing is somewhat different. It considers the bene fits as well as the costs of a particular product or service. Most of the remainder of this book focuses on the cost side of the equation, but managers should not ignore the benefit side.

Test Yourself

1. What are the four forces that will affect health care costs during the next five to ten years?

2. What are the five drivers of health care costs?

3. What is meant by the term *health care food chain*?

4. What does the term *value-based purchasing* mean?

5. How can physician leaders become involved in cost control? Why is it important for them to do so?

Suggested Cases

Boise Park Health Care Foundation (A)

Conglomerate, Inc. (A)

Conglomerate, Inc. (B)

Determination of Need Program

Heartbreak of DRGs

Hilda Cook

Wheeling Cardiology Associates

PRACTICE CASE

CENTRAL VALLEY PRIMARY CARE ASSOCIATES

I've got a week to finish this proposal. The information the hospital gave me on inpatient utilization was incomplete and so detailed that I had to have it summarized. Even so, I don't know if I'll be able to use it. How am I supposed to work with information like this to come up with a reasonable capitation rate for Continental?

The speaker was Maria Lopez, MD, board member of Central Valley Primary Care Associates (CVPCA) and chair of its subcommittee on finance, compensation, and risk. CVPCA was an independent practice association comprising 130 primary care pediatricians who worked in thirty-nine small group practices, located at fifty-seven sites. It worked closely with the Valley Children's Medical Center (VCMC) physician-hospital organization (PHO).

Background

VCMC was a teaching and research institution (with over 200 beds) that was considered to be one of the leading children's hospitals in the country. However, although it had a national reputation and was the only children's hospital in the three-state area surrounding the Central Valley region, it was not the only institution providing pediatric services. Several general hospitals were located nearby, each of which had a small (ten- to thirty-bed) pediatrics department. Moreover, whereas VCMC had both a residency program and an active research agenda, none of the other hospitals was engaged in either teaching or research. Patients in these other hospitals' had relatively uncomplicated diagnoses, requiring fairly standard treatment or procedures. Patients with complicated diagnoses or severe conditions generally were taken directly to VCMC or transported there shortly after admission to one of the other hospitals.

Central Valley Primary Care Associates

CVPCA had been formed several years ago. Its mission was to develop a comprehensive, integrated, primary health care delivery system to ensure quality and cost-effective care. Together with VCMC, it aimed to meet the total health care needs of children and adolescents in the tristate area. Dr. Lopez's subcommittee was one of six. Its charge was to "develop minimally acceptable capitation fees and fee-for-service compensation packages that directly correspond to the contractually covered services, and to outline acceptable risk components that may be included in the physician compensation program, such as withholds, risk pool sharing, and maximum stop-loss coverage."

Continental Health Care Request for Proposals

CVPCA originally had planned to contract with the PHO to provide community physicians for primary care. Recently, however, it had received a request for proposals from Continental Health Care, a large managed care plan, indicating that Continental intended to do business with primary care providers on a capitation basis rather than using the traditional fee-for-service approach. All primary care groups in the region had been asked to submit bids specifying the per member, per month amount they would charge Continental for a full-risk contract—that is, a contract that included the cost of all primary care, specialty care, and inpatient hospitalization care. Follow-up home health care and specialized services, such as occupational therapy, were excluded. The full range of inpatient services was to be included, however, including such traditionally expensive procedures as bone marrow transplants.

Continental had made it clear that it would not be awarding contracts to all groups in the area. Instead, it had said that it would focus its business on the groups that offered the best PMPM rates. Inasmuch as Continental currently had contracts that covered some 40 percent of the employees and their families in the region and was growing rapidly, failure to secure a contract would have serious financial implications for a physician group.

Analysis

In an effort to develop a budget and, ultimately, a PMPM rate, Dr. Lopez had asked her staff assistant, Tim Matthews, to gather all the relevant data that she would need to prepare a bid. She had decided to focus her efforts on a small subset of the total analysis, work out the methodology, and then instruct Mr. Matthews to use that methodology for the rest of the analysis. She commented on the rationale for her approach:

> I have to keep the job manageable. Any time I spend on this is time away from seeing patients. Also, I'm not an accountant, and have no desire to be one. However, Tim doesn't have the clinical knowledge he needs to figure out a methodology. So I decided to focus on children in the five- to eleven-year age group and to analyze the cost of their care for the three most frequent outpatient diagnoses and the three most frequent inpatient diagnoses. I figure that if I can develop a methodology for this set of children and activities, it'll be a relatively simple matter for Tim to extend the analysis to the whole practice.

Because physicians in the group frequently used VCMC's facilities and specialists for outpatient care, Dr. Lopez and Mr. Matthews had assumed that the hospital would be able to supply them with both outpatient and inpatient information. Indeed, Matt Barberi, the manager of marketing services for the hospital, had been extremely cooperative. He had supplied them with information on outpatient and inpatient diagnoses by age group; a fee schedule for the division of general pediatrics; and nursing wages and hospital charges and costs (contained in exhibits 1.1 through 1.4). He also gave them a list of the laboratory tests, radiology procedures, and pharmacy prescriptions that were associated with each inpatient diagnosis.

There were two complications with the data Mr. Barberi had submitted. First, the list of tests, procedures, and prescriptions totaled ten to fifteen pages per diagnosis. Dr. Lopez realized that working with such a long list for more than a few diagnoses would be extremely cumbersome. Under her guidance, Mr. Matthews had summarized the information according to the categories shown in exhibit 1.5.

The second complication was that Mr. Barberi had sent a letter along with the data that had not been especially encouraging. It read, in part:

> As you'll notice, there are some limitations to the data we have readily available. For example, on the outpatient side, we currently cannot tie diagnosis codes with resource utilization. Also, we cannot tie diagnosis with the kind and number of specialist referrals or consults.

It was this letter that prompted Dr. Lopez's comment at the beginning of the case, and that led her to conclude that whatever analysis she did would be based on a wide variety of assumptions. Nevertheless, she saw no alternative other than to push ahead.

Assignment

1. What are the salient strategic issues for Dr. Lopez to consider in her decision making?

2. How should Dr. Lopez approach the development of a budget for the expenses associated with CVPCA's five- to eleven-year-old patients?

   Note: You do not need to prepare a budget, but rather should outline an approach for Dr. Lopez to follow. To do so, you should structure the information available to Dr. Lopez in such a way that it is useful to her, identifying those places where she will need to obtain additional information.

3. What additional data are needed to complete the budget? How should Dr. Lopez obtain them? Where will she need to make assumptions?

4. How should Dr. Lopez translate her budget into a capitation rate that she can propose to Continental? What other issues should she consider in her proposal to Continental?

5. What issues should Dr. Lopez consider in working with the PHO, the hospital, and the specialists needed to care for pediatric patients so that she can increase the probability of meeting her budget?

EXHIBIT 1.1 Top 3 Outpatient Diagnoses for Ages 5 to 11 for the First 6 Months of the Current Fiscal Year*

Diagnosis	Cases	Percentage of Total
ROUTINE CHILD HEALTH EXAM	1,435	1.80%
CHR OTITIS MEDIA NOS/NEC	1,160	1.45%
ABN CLINICAL FINDING NEC	1,104	1.38%
TOTAL	3,699	4.63%

*Do not worry about the meaning of the diagnoses.

EXHIBIT 1.2 Top 10 Primary Inpatient Diagnoses for Ages 5 to 11 for the Last Fiscal Year*

	Diagnosis	Cases	Days	Charges
493.91	ASTHMA W STATUS ASTHMATIC	384	942	$1,509,616
486.00	PNEUMONIA, ORGANISM NOS	124	364	517,973
780.30	CONVULSIONS	97	239	393,685
540.90	ACUTE APPENDICITIS NOS	78	137	324,798
V58.10	MAINTENANCE CHEMOTHERAPY	74	246	670,878
519.10	TRACHEA/BRONCHUS DIS NE	61	150	243,505
313.81	OPPOSITIONAL DISORDER	52	570	319,344
540.00	AC APPEND W PERITONITIS	47	424	681,175
478.74	STENOSIS OF LARYNX	40	209	430,011
277.00	CYSTIC FIBROS W/O ILEUS	39	377	718,623
TOTAL		996	3,658	5,809,608
ALL OTHER DIAGNOSES		2,243	12,464	21,921,307
TOTAL REPORT		3,239	16,122	$27,730,915

*Do not worry about the meaning of the diagnoses.

EXHIBIT 1.3   Fee Schedule for the Division of General Pediatrics for the Current Fiscal Year (All Amounts in Dollars)

	Facility Fee	Professional Fee	Total
Well Child Care			
New visit	46.00	80.00	126.00
Subsequent visit	36.00	50.00	86.00
Anticipatory guidance (15 minutes)	0.00	30.00	30.00
Anticipatory guidance (30 minutes)	0.00	45.00	45.00
Anticipatory guidance (45 minutes)	0.00	60.00	60.00
Anticipatory guidance (60 minutes)	0.00	75.00	75.00
Sick Child Care			
New Visit			
Problem focused (10 minutes)	17.00	45.00	62.00
Expanded problem focused (20 minutes)	26.00	60.00	86.00
Detailed (30 minutes)	36.00	75.00	111.00
Comprehensive (45 minutes)	43.00	90.00	133.00
Expanded comprehensive (60 minutes)	50.00	125.00	175.00
Subsequent Visits			
Problem focused (10 minutes)	26.00	40.00	66.00
Expanded problem focused (15 minutes)	36.00	60.00	96.00
Detailed (25 minutes)	43.00	80.00	123.00
Comprehensive (40 minutes)	50.00	105.00	155.00

EXHIBIT 1.4   Wages and Prices for the Current Fiscal Year

	LPN	RN
Nursing Wages	$15 per hour	$25 per hour
	Charges	**Cost**
Day of Stay in Hospital	$1,800–$2,000	$1,000–$1,800

EXHIBIT 1.5 Tests and Procedures for the Top 3 Inpatient Diagnoses for Ages 5 to 11 for the Last Fiscal Year[*]

	Asthma		Pneumonia		Convulsions	
	Units	Charges (in Dollars)	Units	Charges (in Dollars)	Units	Charges (in Dollars)
Labs						
2669 TOTAL SPECIAL COAG	0	0	11	1,425		
92501 CBC	33	520	123	1,937	45	709
92503 DIFFERENTIAL	22	173	107	843	32	252
Several other items						
2702 TOTAL HEMATOLOGY	78	1,044	364	4,983	157	2,230
101503 POTASSIUM SERUM	34	536	0	0		
101508 GLUCOSE, BLOOD	126	1,985	21	331	34	536
102328 ARTERIAL BLOOD GAS	232	18,270	32	2,520	5	394
Several other items						
2703 TOTAL CHEMISTRY	1,607	41,992	713	11,001	960	17,094
2704 TOTAL MICROBIOLOGY	79	2,204	190	7,191	46	1,632
2705 TOTAL PATHOLOGY	5	243	17	997	6	497
2709 TOTAL LAB PROCESSING	0	5	307	8	458	
2710 TOTAL BLOOD BANK	0	112	4,033	0		
2717 TOTAL VIROLOGY	17	811	40	1,990	20	1,000
2801 TOTAL ENDOCRINOLOGY	1	42	0			
2805 TOTAL ENZYMOLOGY	0	0	9	908		
2806 TOTAL NEPHROLOGY	21	528	3	360	7	409
2812 TOTAL CRC LABS	1	30	3	113	0	
Radiology						
2697 TOTAL VASCULAR	0	4	257	10		1,369
160100 PORTABLES	67	1,829	39	1,065	8	218
170109 CHEST	238	13,745	159	9,180	16	924
Several other items						
2721 TOTAL RADIOLOGY	346	18,180	230	12,695	76	6,121
2722 TOTAL NUCLEAR MEDICINE	2	420	3	919	4	1,092
2806 TOTAL ULTRASOUND	2	331	6	789	1	164
2724 TOTAL CT SCANS	2	945	8	3,525	21	9,923
2725 TOTAL MRI	0	1	856	20	17,115	
Pharmacy (Several Pages of Items)						
2730 TOTAL PHARMACY	10,175	129,986	6,375	80,374	2,959	24,851

[*]Do not worry about the meaning of the various tests and procedures.

Notes

1. Medicare is a federal insurance program in the United States that pays for the health care costs of individuals sixty-five years old and older.

2. "DGA Analysis of the Kaiser Family Foundation's *Update on Medicare Spending and Financing Highlights from the 2009 Medicare Trustees' Report*, May 2009," *Healthcare Financial Management*, July 2009.

3. Robert Pear, "Consumer Risks Feared as Health Law Spurs Mergers," *New York Times*, November 20, 2010.

4. It is important to note that there are variations not only in the types of cases but also in severity (or acuity) within any given case type.

5. The Centers for Medicare & Medicaid Services, previously known as the Health Care Financing Administration, is a federal agency within the US Department of Health and Human Services that administers the Medicare program and works in partnership with state governments to administer Medicaid, the State Children's Health Insurance Program, and health insurance portability standards. For details, see www.cms.gov.

6. See "Tracking the Care of Patients with Severe Chronic Illness," *The Dartmouth Atlas of Health Care*, 2008, www.dartmouthatlas.org/downloads/atlases/2008_Chronic_Care_Atlas.pdf.

7. It is worth noting that only about one-third of all health care spending is for hospital care. The remainder is for other forms of care, including outpatient services, home health care, long-term care, rehabilitation care, and a variety of others.

8. Thomas Bodenheimer and David West, "Low-Cost Lessons from Grand Junction, Colorado," *New England Journal of Medicine* 363 (October 2010): 1391–1393.

9. Part of knowing the relevant cost implications is considering the clinical consequences before reducing resources per case. For a discussion of some of the related issues, see Peter J. Neumann and James D. Chambers, "Medicare's Enduring Struggle to Define 'Reasonable and Necessary' Care," *New England Journal of Medicine* 367 (November 2012): 1775–1777.

10. For a discussion of how ABC can be used in a health care setting, see Seema Pandey, "Applying the ABCs in Provider Organizations," *Healthcare Financial Management* 66 (November 2012): 112–116, 118, 120.

11. Michael E. Porter, *Competitive Advantage: Creating and Sustaining Superior Performance.* (New York: Simon and Schuster, 1985).

12. See, for example, David W. Young et al., "Toward a Value-Based Healthcare System," *American Journal of Medicine* 110 (February 2001): 158–163; David W. Young et al., "Value-Based Partnering in Health Care: A Framework for Analysis," *Journal of Healthcare Management* 46 (March–April 2001): 112–132; David W. Young et al., "Beyond Health Care Cost Containment: Creating Collaborative Arrangements among the Stakeholders," *International Journal of Health Planning and Management* 16 (July–September 2001): 207–228.

These publications extend the concept of value-based *purchasing* to value-based *partnering*. As they discuss, the distinction is important.

13. See Lawton R. Burns and Wharton School Colleagues, *The Health Care Value Chain: Producers, Purchasers, and Providers* (San Francisco: Jossey-Bass, 2002). See also http://pdfcast.org/pdf/the-wharton-school-study-of-the-health-care-value-chain

14. See Michael E. Porter and Elizabeth Olmsted Teisberg, *Redefining Health Care: Creating Value-Based Competition on Results* (Boston: Harvard Business School Press, 2006).

15. For additional thinking on the transition to value-based purchasing as well as some concerns about how the process may evolve, see Donald Berwick, "On Transitioning to Value-Based Health Care," *Healthcare Financial Management* 67 (May 2013): 56–59.

16. Peter R. Orszag and Ezekiel J. Emanuel, "Health Reform and Cost Control," New *England Journal of Medicine* 363 (August 2010): 601–603, doi:10.1056/NEJMp1006571.

17. Robert Mechanic and Christopher Tompkins, "Lessons Learned Preparing for Medicare Bundled Payments," *New England Journal of Medicine* 367 (November 2012): 1873–1875, doi:10.1056/NEJMp1210823.

CHAPTER 2

ESSENTIALS OF FULL-COST ACCOUNTING

In almost all organizations, managers need to answer the question, "What did it cost?" This question is especially important for those health care organizations whose prices are set by insurers or other third-party payers, or when senior management needs to assess the financial viability of different programs and services.

Answering the question is easy if we are discussing the purchase of inputs, such as supplies and labor, for the service delivery process. Even calculating the full cost of a unit produced—whether it is a surgical procedure or fifty minutes of psychotherapy—is relatively easy as long as the organization produces goods or services that are completely homogeneous. Complications arise when an organization provides multiple products that require different kinds and amounts of resource inputs.[1]

This chapter identifies some of the key decisions that are made in a full-cost accounting system, and it discusses how those decisions influence an answer to the question, "What did it cost?" As you read the chapter, you should be aware that there is considerable disagreement among managers and accountants about whether full cost is an appropriate calculation. Some accountants believe (for reasons that you will see in the chapter) that any such computation is inherently distorted and therefore of little value for managerial decision making. Nevertheless, we will assume for the moment that senior management wishes to know the full cost of a particular good or service, and we will examine the choices it must make to arrive at that figure.

Organization of the Chapter

This chapter begins with a discussion of the uses of full-cost information. It then turns to the issues that managers

LEARNING OBJECTIVES

On completing this chapter, you should know about

- The potential uses of full-cost information

- The relationship between full-cost accounting and the economist's three factors of production: land, labor, and capital

- Such concepts as cost object, cost center, direct and indirect costs, overhead, and cost allocation methods

- The distinction between mission centers and support centers

- Alternative ways to allocate support center costs into mission centers so as to determine each mission center's full cost

- The link between full-cost accounting information and pricing decisions

must consider in calculating full cost and links them to the economist's three factors of production: land, labor, and capital. Next, it outlines the decisions that must be made in calculating full costs, or the full-cost accounting methodology. The chapter concludes by looking at the effect of an organization's cost accounting methodology on the pricing of its products.

Uses of Full-Cost Information

Information about the full cost of carrying out a particular endeavor is used for essentially three purposes: pricing decisions, profitability assessments, and comparative analyses. Most managers use cost information for one or more of these purposes at different times and under varying decision-making scenarios.

Pricing Decisions

Cost information is not the only data that management uses in setting prices, but it is an important ingredient. (Some of the issues involved in setting prices in nonprofit organizations are discussed in appendix 2B.) In negotiating a contract with a managed care organization or a commercial payer, for example, a hospital or physician group practice is at a significant disadvantage if it does not know the full cost of the product under discussion. Even if its goal is to obtain a large volume of new patients by offering a price below the product's full cost, it needs to know the full cost.

Profitability Assessments

By contrast, many health care organizations are "price takers": they must accept the price that has been set by a third-party payer, such as Medicare or Medicaid. For these organizations, full-cost information allows senior management to assess whether a particular product is financially viable. Indeed, if a product is not covering its full cost, it is by definition a *loss leader*. Because an organization cannot survive if all its products are loss leaders, full-cost accounting serves to highlight where the cross-subsidization among them is taking place. This allows management to assess whether that cross-subsidization is consistent with the organization's overall strategy and, if it is not, to assess the financial implications of alternative courses of corrective action.

Comparative Analyses

Many organizations can benefit from comparing their costs with those of organizations delivering similar products. For example, an integrated delivery system (IDS) with a network of physician group practices, hospitals, and other service delivery units may make comparisons between similar entities within that system. Full-cost information can assist in this effort.

One difficulty with comparative analyses is that not all organizations of the same type (such as all hospitals or all home health agencies) measure their costs in the same way. This is not typically a concern for an IDS, however, because the cost accounting effort for, say, its physician group practices can be specified in detail. Otherwise, as we will see later, an organization attempting to compare its costs with those of similar entities may encounter a variety of methodological impediments.

PROBLEM

Concord Health Network, an integrated delivery system, is interested in comparing its cost per patient with the cost per patient in a similar IDS. What are some of the issues Concord must consider in making this comparison?

ANSWER

Concord must consider such comparability issues as the average occupancy rate of its hospitals versus that of the other IDS's hospitals; the existence of specialized programs—for example, in cardiology or oncology; and the provision of such services as social work and discharge planning. It also must consider whether it wishes to focus on an episode of illness, a hospitalization, or something else, and it must decide whether it wishes to include outpatient costs, home care costs, or both in the comparison.

As the answer to this problem suggests, the definition of what is to be included in a full-cost calculation is by no means clear-cut. Indeed, because such a wide range of choices is embedded in an organization's cost accounting system, managers frequently find it difficult to compare their organization's costs with those of other organizations, where different choices may have been made.

EXAMPLE

A study that compared the cost of an outpatient visit in a hospital with the cost of a similar visit in a physician's office identified two impediments to the comparison. One factor was noncomparable costs. For example, because of the way the hospital allocated its overhead costs, a fraction of the cost of the chaplain's office was included in the cost of each outpatient visit; there was nothing comparable to the chaplain's office in the physician's office. The other factor was scale-related costs. In the hospital, the cost of governance was high, entailing a great deal of time, effort, and expense to work with the hospital's board of trustees. Governance in the physician's office was much simpler.[2]

Because of these impediments to full-cost comparisons, many organizations simply compare their own costs over time rather than attempting to compare them with those of other organizations. They know that their full-cost accounting methodology has remained reasonably consistent from one year to the next, and therefore that there will not be problems with either noncomparable or scale-related costs.

Issues to Consider in Calculating Full Costs

If senior management does not wish to use full-cost information for pricing decisions, profitability assessments, or comparative analyses, it does not need to become involved in the effort to calculate full costs. Rather, it can delegate the task to the accounting staff. Although Medicare has paid hospitals on the basis of diagnosis-related groups (DRGs) for over thirty years, it continues to require hospitals to prepare a full-cost report. In general, however, such a report is of little interest to senior managers, and they can simply ask the accounting staff to prepare it as quickly and as easily as possible.

When a hospital or an academic medical center contracts with the federal government to do research, however, senior management no doubt will want to be more closely involved in the full-cost accounting effort. This is because the full-cost analysis must be prepared in accordance with the principles set forth in the Office of Management and Budget's Circular A-21, "Cost Principles for Educational Institutions." These principles provide for reimbursement of direct costs plus an "equitable share" of overhead costs.[3]

The overhead costs that Circular A-21 allows to be reimbursed include depreciation of buildings and equipment, plant operation and maintenance, general administration, departmental administration, student administration and services, and library services. Because these overhead costs can vary widely across organizations, senior management must be certain that the amount submitted to the government is legitimate and reasonable.

If senior management has decided to use full-cost information for pricing and other decision-making purposes, it must work with its accounting staff to select an appropriate methodology. The term *work with* is important. Because the issues are complex, the decisions cannot be completely delegated to the accountants. Full-cost information can be computed in a variety of ways, most of which can be defended as valid, but each of which can produce a different result. Moreover, full-cost accounting efforts in health care organizations are complicated by a variety of factors, such as patient or service mix, standby capacity, and alternative treatment modalities. Thus, senior management must set the ground rules and guide the accounting staff's work. Otherwise, the resulting information may be of little managerial use.

Because there are no full-cost accounting rules similar to Generally Accepted Accounting Principles (GAAP) in financial accounting, we first need to discuss the conceptual structure that underlies full-cost accounting. We then can turn to the various cost accounting decisions that will affect the way the accounting staff gathers and presents the information.

Resource Use: A Conceptual Framework

The fundamental issue that cost accounting addresses is the use of resources. At a conceptual level, these resources are the classic ones of the economist: *land, labor,* and *capital.*

Land

Land is the simplest of the three. It can be somewhat complicated for agricultural firms or companies in the extraction industries (oil, coal, and so on), but in general—and certainly in health care—it is the site where the organization is located.

If an organization has multiple sites, as many large academic medical centers and integrated delivery systems do, the land resource might be divided between *mission* and *support* facilities. Mission facilities are those where patients and other clients receive services; support facilities are used not for patient or other mission purposes (such as research), but instead for administrative purposes.

Labor

Labor in health care and other service organizations also can be classified as being either mission (sometimes called professional) or support (sometimes called administrative). Mission labor consists of the individuals who actually deliver the organization's services and thus are directly associated with the organization's main mission. Support labor consists of everyone else in the organization.

Support labor can be divided into *direct* and *general.* Direct support activities include scheduling patients or providing secretarial assistance for a research project. General support may be related to mission services, or it may be part of general administration. If the former, it includes centralized functions that assist the organization's mission departments but are organized separately from them, such as maintenance or cleaning.

General administration is the organization's central office staff—the people who engage in activities that typically are not related to specific professional departments. These people are engaged in such activities as computer operations, payroll processing, purchasing, legal work, and billing.

Capital

Capital also can be looked at as either mission or support. The former includes all capital resources needed to provide direct support to the organization's service delivery activities. Mission capital can be divided between *short-lived* (used up in one year or less) and *long-lived* (used up over several years).

Short-lived mission capital is sometimes called direct materials. In health care, it includes items related to patient care, such as syringes in a physician's office, food in an inpatient ward, blood products in an operating room, floss in a dentist's office, and pharmaceuticals. Long-lived mission capital comprises the equipment used in service-related activities.

Support capital can also be either short- or long-lived and includes items that provide general support rather than items that are directly associated with service delivery. Supplies used in the CEO's or controller's office of a hospital are short-lived support capital, for example. Such equipment as centralized photocopying machines, fax machines, and computers in a computing center are considered long-lived support capital.

Units of Measure

Land is rather easily measured in terms of rent (for example, for a square foot for a month). Labor is measured by wages, either per unit of time (such as an hour) or per unit of activity (such as a visit). Short-lived capital—either mission or support—usually is measured in terms of the factor price per unit, that is, what the organization paid to obtain the item. Long-lived capital typically is measured in terms of depreciation per unit of time.

Limitations

The principal objective of a full-cost accounting effort is to measure as accurately as possible the consumption of resources associated with producing a particular good or delivering a particular service. In some instances, the measurement process is quite easy. An organization that produces a single product would have little difficulty calculating the full cost of each unit. All costs associated with the organization, and hence with the product, could be added together and divided by the number of units produced during a particular accounting period to arrive at a cost per unit. For example, a freestanding laboratory that processed only complete blood counts (CBCs) would have a relatively easy time calculating the full cost of each CBC.

But few health care organizations produce a single product. Most provide multiple products (usually in the form of services) and therefore have a more difficult time measuring resource consumption for each. To do so, they must identify the factors that influence the use of resources—and therefore costs. Thus, identifying these factors is an important activity.

Cost Drivers

Cost drivers are organizational activities that can be linked directly to costs. Chapter 1 discussed the five cost drivers that exist in most health care organizations. Table 2.1 describes them, and divides the cost per resource unit (shown in figure 1.7 in chapter 1) into two parts: efficiency and factor prices. It also gives some examples for a hospital. Note that this classification scheme does not revolve around the traditional departmental structure found in most organizations. Instead, it lists and classifies the activities that cause costs to exist. We will return to this idea in chapter 9 when we look at how an organization can use cost drivers to build a budget.

The Full-Cost Accounting Methodology

We turn now to some concrete aspects of the cost accounting methodology. As indicated earlier, an organization that produces a single good or service usually has little difficulty in calculating the cost of each unit. In

Table 2.1 Examples of Cost Drivers in a Hospital

Cost Driver	Examples
Case type: The type of diagnosis a patient has; sometimes called case mix	Myocardial infarction; pneumonia; appendicitis
Volume: The number of cases of each type	10 cases of myocardial infarction; 50 cases of pneumonia; 30 cases of appendicitis
Patient needs: The resources typically used by a patient with a particular case type	For myocardial infarction: 2 days in a coronary care unit; 4 days of care in a ward; 3 days of level III nursing care; 2 days of level II nursing care; 12 laboratory tests; 7 X-rays
Efficiency: The number of resource "inputs" needed for each unit of output	Nursing hours per patient at each level of nursing care; time and supplies per radiological procedure; time and supplies per lab test
Factor prices: The cost per unit of each resource input	Hourly nursing wage; hourly technician wage; price per unit of laboratory reagents
Fixed costs: The costs incurred to allow the organization to be ready to serve patients	Costs for rent, professional staff, and administrative personnel needed to run, say, an open-heart surgery, renal transplant, or alcohol detoxification program

contrast, organizations that produce a variety of goods, services, or both, each requiring different amounts of land, labor, and capital, have a more difficult time determining the cost of each unit sold.

To address this more complex process, an organization must make six full-cost accounting decisions: (1) defining the final *cost objects*, (2) determining mission and support *cost centers*, (3) distinguishing between *direct costs* and *indirect costs*, (4) choosing *allocation bases* for support center costs, (5) selecting an *allocation method*, and (6) attaching a mission center's costs to its cost objects. Together these six decisions constitute the full-cost accounting methodology.

cost objects
The purposes for which costs are gathered. A cost object is aligned with a price. Examples include DRG100 or an ambulatory care visit.

Decision 1: Defining the Final Cost Objects

The final cost object is the unit for which we wish to know the cost. In general, the more specific the cost object, the more complex the accounting methodology. At one time, for example, some acute care hospitals defined their cost object as an all-inclusive day of care—a cost object that included surgical procedures, laboratory tests, radiology exams, pharmaceutical usage, and so on. For these hospitals, calculating their cost per day—their cost object—was simple: total costs divided by total days.

Most hospitals now use more specific cost objects. A "day of care" might comprise "routine" factors only (such as room and board and nursing care), with separate cost objects for other activities, such as laboratory tests. Some hospitals use a discharge or an episode of illness, rather than a day of care, as the cost object. If a discharge is the cost object, the hospital needs to include all costs associated with the patient's inpatient stay (that is, for all days of care rather than just an average single day). If an episode of illness is the cost object, the hospital includes costs for all admissions associated with a particular illness for a given patient, in addition to outpatient and home care costs. In 1983, with the introduction of DRG reimbursement, Medicare effectively specified that a hospital's final cost object was a discharge of a patient (classified by DRG). Because there are hundreds of DRGs, hospitals now have several hundred different final cost objects.

To compute the full cost of each cost object, many hospitals have identified what they call intermediate cost objects: the various services that a patient receives while in the hospital (referred to as "patient needs" in table 2.1).[4] Thus, the full cost of caring for a patient with a particular DRG would be the sum of the costs of all of the resources (intermediate cost objects) that he or she used during the hospital stay—laboratory tests, radiology procedures, and laundry services, for example.

Decision 2: Determining Mission and Support Cost Centers

Cost centers can be thought of as categories (or buckets) used to collect cost information. To understand how they work, consider again an organization that delivers a single product. The organization could treat itself as a single cost center, thereby creating a relatively simple cost accounting system. In this case, the category used to collect cost information would be the organization itself.

Alternatively, the organization could subdivide itself into several cost centers—such as direct care delivery, administration, housekeeping, and so forth—for the purposes of its cost accounting effort. When this is done, the cost of a particular final cost object will be the sum of the costs attributed to it in each of the cost centers.

From a managerial perspective, having several cost centers provides better information for decision making. For example, a multiple-cost-center structure can be used for pricing or submitting reimbursement claims to third parties. If each program (or service) is represented by a mission center, the costs of that center can be used as the basis for setting the appropriate prices.

cost centers
Categories used to collect costs. They are divided into two categories: support centers (such as housekeeping, laundry, and plant maintenance) and mission centers (such as medicine, surgery, and pediatrics).

PROBLEM

Homecare, a small home care agency, is considering the use of four cost centers: housekeeping, administration, patient services, and patient education. Cost data are available for housekeeping salaries ($30,000) and supplies ($4,000); administration salaries ($100,000) and supplies ($36,000); patient services salaries ($175,000) and supplies ($125,000); and patient education salaries ($105,000) and supplies ($25,000). The agency provided 8,000 hours of service last year. What are the costs in each cost center? What is Homecare's cost per hour? You should make the computation before reading the answer.

ANSWER

Using these four cost centers, our analysis would be as follows:

	Cost Centers				
Cost Items	Housekeeping	Administration	Patient Services	Patient Education	Total
Salaries	$30,000	$100,000	$175,000	$105,000	$410,000
Supplies	4,000	36,000	125,000	25,000	190,000
TOTAL	$34,000	$136,000	$300,000	$130,000	$600,000
COST PER HOUR	$4.25	$17.00	$37.50	$16.25	$75.00

PROBLEM

What concerns would you have about the breakdown of Homecare's costs in the answer to the previous problem?

ANSWER

Patients receive services only in the patient services and patient education cost centers. Therefore, the cost per hour in the housekeeping and administration cost centers is not an especially useful number. Moreover, the cost per hour in the patient services and patient education cost centers will depend on how the 8,000 hours of service are divided between them, but we do not have this information. (We'll get it in decision 3.)

In a multiple-cost-center structure, an organization's cost centers generally are divided into two broad categories: mission centers and support centers (which sometimes are called service centers). Mission centers are associated with the organization's main focus (or mission); normally they charge for (or are reimbursed for) their activities. In fact, some hospitals call them revenue centers (because they earn revenue by charging for their activities).

Support centers accumulate the costs of the activities the organization carries out to assist its mission centers. In the Homecare problem, housekeeping and administration would be support centers, and patient services and patient education would be mission centers. In a hospital, institution-wide depreciation, human resources, plant maintenance, laundry, housekeeping, and the like generally are support centers, whereas programs and patient service departments are mission centers.

With these distinctions, the amount of a final cost object now depends on (1) the mission center or centers where a patient received services, (2) the number of units of service that he or she received in each, and (3) the cost for each unit of service. The cost per unit of service in each mission center depends, in part, on that center's fair share of the organization's support center costs.

Decision 3: Distinguishing between Direct Costs and Indirect Costs

A third decision in designing a cost accounting system begins with distinguishing between direct and indirect costs. Direct costs are unambiguously associated with, or physically traceable to, a specific cost center. Indirect costs apply to more than one cost center and thus must be *distributed* among them.

Again, under the simplest of circumstances, whereby an organization produces one product in one cost center, there are no indirect costs, because it is not possible to have costs that apply to more than one cost center. The creation of multiple cost centers means that some costs become indirect, thereby necessitating their distribution (sometimes called their assignment).

direct costs
A cost that can be attributed unambiguously to either a product or an organizational unit. If the former, it is classified as either direct material or direct labor. If the latter, it can be somewhat complicated. For example, depreciation of machines in a plant is a direct cost of the plant; however, it is generally considered an indirect cost of the products produced in the plant.

indirect costs
A cost that cannot be attributed unambiguously to either a product or an organizational unit. It must be divided among the units to which it applies.

PROBLEM

The staff members in the patient education cost center at Homecare are supervised by someone whose salary is contained in the patient services cost center. What kind of a cost is the supervisor's salary? Why? What should be done with the salary? Write a general answer to each question.

ANSWER

The salary is an indirect cost because it applies to activities in both the patient services and patient education cost centers. This means that it must be distributed between them.

   To distribute the salary to the two cost centers, we might ask the supervisor to maintain careful time records. If we do this, we effectively convert the indirect cost into a direct cost, because we will have created a situation in which the cost (time) is physically traceable to each cost center. Alternatively, we might create a formula that uses, say, salary dollars or number of personnel in each cost center as the distribution mechanism.

PROBLEM

Assume that Homecare decides to use hours of service as the mechanism to distribute the supervisor's salary among the relevant cost centers. Also assume that 6,000 service hours were provided by the staff in patient services, and 2,000 hours were provided by the staff in patient education. The supervisor's salary is $60,000. How would the salary be distributed?

ANSWER

Homecare can perform the following calculations:

Cost Centers	Hours of Service	Percentage of Total Hours	Assigned Supervisor's Salary
Patient services	6,000	75.0	$45,000
Patient education	2,000	25.0	15,000
TOTAL	8,000	100.0	$60,000

The cost centers would then have the following total costs:

Cost Centers	Cost
Housekeeping	$34,000
Administration	136,000
Patient services	285,000 (that is, $300,000 − $15,000 for supervisor)
Patient education	145,000 (that is, $130,000 + $15,000 for supervisor)
TOTAL	$600,000

> Note that this approach has divided the supervisor's salary between the two relevant cost centers based on a distribution formula. Of the $60,000 salary, $45,000 remains in the patient services cost center, and $15,000 has been transferred to the patient education cost center.

Decision 4: Choosing Allocation Bases for Support Center Costs

In the Homecare problems, the hourly cost of patient services and the hourly cost of patient education include more than the direct costs and distributed indirect costs of those activities. Their costs also include each mission center's fair share of the organization's support center costs. (As you might imagine, the notion of "fair" can be highly debatable in cost accounting, just as it is in other aspects of life.)

Because of the need to allocate support center costs, the fourth decision in the cost accounting methodology is the selection of *allocation bases.* That is, we must choose a metric for each support center that measures its use by the remaining cost centers (frequently including other support centers as well as mission centers) as accurately as possible. To accomplish this, we are seeking the *activity* that *causes* the existence of a support center's costs.

allocation bases
The metrics used to distribute a support center's costs to other support centers and mission centers.

Let's begin with housekeeping. Our goal is to find an allocation basis that measures as accurately as possible the use of the housekeeping resource by the other cost centers. Although several allocation bases may be available, one that seems to be quite appropriate is square feet (or square meters) of floor space. That is, the more floor space a cost center uses, the greater will be its share of the housekeeping expense.

PROBLEM

Assume that the following information on square feet is available for Homecare:

Cost Center	Square Feet
Administration	1,000
Patient services	3,000
Patient education	1,000
TOTAL	5,000

How much of the cost of the housekeeping cost center will be allocated per square foot for each of the other cost centers? Make your computations before continuing reading the answer.

ANSWER

The rate is $6.80 per square foot: $34,000 of housekeeping ÷ 5,000 square feet of floor space.

With this information, we are now prepared to allocate housekeeping costs to the three remaining cost centers. All we need to do now is multiply the rate by the number of square feet in each.

PROBLEM

How much of the housekeeping cost should be allocated to each cost center at Homecare? Write out your computations and allocation amounts, using the following headings:

Cost Center	Computation	Allocation
Administration		
Patient services		
Patient education		
TOTAL		

ANSWER

The amount of housekeeping allocated to each cost center would be calculated as follows:

Cost Center	Square Feet × Rate	=	Allocation
Administration	1,000 × $6.80	=	$6,800
Patient services	3,000 × 6.80	=	20,400
Patient education	1,000 × 6.80	=	6,800
TOTAL	5,000		$34,000

Note that housekeeping has been allocated to the administration cost center as well as to the patient services and patient education cost centers—that is, in this approach, a support center's costs have been allocated to another support center as well as to mission centers. We examine alternative approaches later in the chapter.

Given this approach, Homecare now must allocate the costs of the administration cost center to the remaining cost centers. To do so, it must choose an appropriate allocation basis. There are several bases we might use, such as number of personnel, salary dollars, or number of visits. Assume that salary dollars are used as the allocation basis and that the following information is available:

Cost Center	Salary Costs	
	Initial	With Supervisor Salary Assignment
Administration	$100,000	$100,000
Patient services	175,000	160,000 ($15,000 removed for supervisor)
Patient education	105,000	120,000 ($15,000 added for supervisor)
TOTAL	$380,000	$380,000

Computing the allocation rate per salary dollar for administration is somewhat more complicated than it was for housekeeping, because total costs in the administration cost center have been increased by the housekeeping allocation. When we include this allocation, the total costs in the administration cost center are $142,800, calculated as follows:

Direct (and distributed) costs	$136,000
Housekeeping allocation	6,800
TOTAL COSTS TO BE ALLOCATED	$142,800

Because the administration costs are to be allocated to the remaining cost centers (patient services and patient education), and because the basis of allocation is salary dollars, we need to determine the allocation rate—that is, administration costs per salary dollar.

PROBLEM

Given the figures supplied, how much of Homecare's administration costs should be allocated for each salary dollar? Please make your computations before looking at the answer.

ANSWER

The administration costs per salary dollar would be calculated as follows:

Total costs to be allocated	$142,800
Divided by salary dollars in cost centers receiving administration's services	$280,000
Equals rate of administration costs per salary dollar	$0.51

Note that we have used only the salary dollars in the two *receiving* cost centers, that is, the cost centers to which the administration costs are being allocated. If we were to use all salary dollars—those in housekeeping, administration, patient services, and patient education—we would end up with a rate that does not fully allocate the $142,800. (This idea is a little tricky. If you are having trouble with it, try doing the allocation using a rate that includes salary dollars in all cost centers.)

Determining the Allocation Rate

We can use the previous two problems to derive a general principle for determining the allocation rate:

$$\frac{\textbf{Total costs in the support center to be allocated}}{\textbf{Total allocation-basis units in the receiving cost centers}}$$

An important point to note here is that the denominator of the formula does not include the allocation-basis units in the cost center from which the allocation is being made. Nor does it include any units from cost centers that have already been allocated. It includes only the units in the *receiving* cost centers.

PROBLEM

Given the previous calculations, how much of Homecare's administration costs should be allocated to each cost center? Write out your computations and allocation amounts using the following headings:

Cost Center	Computation	Allocation
Patient services		
Patient education		
TOTAL		

ANSWER

The amount of administration costs allocated to each cost center would be calculated as follows:

Cost Center	Salary Dollars × Rate	=	Allocation
Patient services	$160,000 × $0.51	=	$81,600
Patient education	$120,000 × $0.51	=	61,200
TOTAL	$280,000		$142,800

With this information, we now can determine the full cost of each mission center:

Cost Center	Direct Plus (Minus) Distributed Costs	Housekeeping Allocation	Administration Allocation	Total Costs
Patient services	$285,000	$20,400	$81,600	$387,000
Patient education	145,000	6,800	61,200	213,000
TOTAL COSTS				$600,000

Note that the total costs of $600,000 remain the same as they were prior to the allocation of support center costs, but they now reside only in mission centers. We have fully allocated the housekeeping and administration costs, first by allocating the housekeeping support center's costs to the administration support center as well as to the two mission centers, and then by allocating the administration support center's costs (with its housekeeping allocation included) to the two mission centers.

In summary, the total costs in a given mission cost center are the sum of (1) the center's direct costs, (2) the indirect costs distributed to (or removed from) it, and (3) the support center costs allocated to it. In the Homecare problems, our bases of allocation were square feet and salary dollars, but an allocation basis can be almost anything that (1) can be measured and (2) has a reasonable cause-and-effect relationship with the use of a support center's resources.

In the context of deciding on allocation bases, it should be noted that increased precision generally requires greater measurement efforts and hence higher accounting costs. Thus, the decision to use a more accurate basis depends largely on senior management's planned use of the information. In some instances the information can improve pricing decisions, and in others it will have an effect on reimbursement from third-party payers. These and similar considerations will determine whether a more accurate allocation basis should be used.

Let's look at this precision issue in the housekeeping support center. A common basis of allocation for housekeeping is square feet of floor space. Computation of square footage for all cost centers is a one-time activity. After it has been completed, housekeeping costs can be allocated quite easily.

However, not all square feet are equally easy to clean. Therefore, although the use of square feet for the allocation is relatively easy, it is not completely accurate. By contrast, using hours of housekeeping service as the allocation basis, which is more accurate, requires ongoing measurement (or at least a one-time measurement and ongoing verification) of housekeeping hours (the number of units of the allocation basis). Obviously, the use of square feet can lead to over- or underrepresentation of the actual use of housekeeping services by a given cost center, whereas using hours of service as the allocation basis presumably would not result in this problem.

In general, the more precise the allocation basis, the more accurately one captures true consumption of a support center's resources. Measurement of the more precise basis can be a time-consuming and complicated process, however. Occasionally a less accurate basis is adopted in response to time, staffing, and technical constraints.

EXAMPLE

In one study of the precision of allocation bases, the researchers found that the use of a more precise basis in only three service centers changed the cost in several mission centers by about 15 to 20 percent.[5]

Distribution versus Allocation

In choosing allocation bases, it is important to keep in mind that *distribution,* discussed in decision 3, precedes allocation and serves to place costs into both support and mission centers. Costs that are direct for a given cost center need not be distributed, whereas indirect costs (those that apply to more than one cost center) must be distributed into the relevant centers. In contrast, allocation is the process of transferring support center costs into mission centers to determine the full cost of each mission center.

This terminology can be confusing, because the terms *distribution, allocation,* and (sometimes) *apportionment* can be used interchangeably. In addition, *support centers* are sometimes called *service centers,* and their costs are sometimes called *indirect costs* or *overhead costs.* As a result, attempting to memorize precise meanings for the various terms is not especially useful. Rather, by understanding the process that is at work, you generally will find that the context clarifies the meanings of the terms.

Decision 5: Selecting an Allocation Method

Three methods can be used to allocate support center costs to mission centers: (1) direct (or one-stage), (2) stepdown (or two-stage), and (3) reciprocal.

Direct Method

Using the direct method, support center costs are allocated to mission centers only and not to other support centers. This is the simplest method of the three and is used by many organizations. It is the least precise of the three, however, in that it does not include the cost effects associated with one support center's use of another support center.

Stepdown Method

We used the *stepdown method* for Homecare. It sequentially "trickles down" support center costs into other support centers and mission centers. This process of "stepping down" begins with the first support center in the sequence and spreads its costs over the remaining support centers as well as the mission centers. The distribution is based on each cost center's use of the support center's resources as determined by the chosen allocation basis. This process is followed for all remaining support centers.

stepdown method
One of three methods for allocating support center costs to mission centers. Sometimes called the "Two Stage" method. It allocates costs to both support centers and mission center, but all costs eventually end up in mission centers.

Because it allocates each support center's costs to other support centers as well as to mission centers, the stepdown method is more complicated than the direct method, but it is also more precise in that it includes the cost effects associated with one support center's use of another. Once a support center's costs have been allocated, however, it cannot receive an allocation, which means that the stepdown method does not account for the cost effects of a given support center's use of another support center that comes later in the sequence.

Reciprocal Method

The reciprocal method is the most complex technique. With it, support centers make allocations to and receive allocations from each other, as well as make allocations to all the mission centers. The allocation amounts are determined by a set of simultaneous equations. Because all support centers can both make and receive allocations, the reciprocal method is the most accurate of the three.

An example of the reciprocal method is contained in appendix 2A at the end of this chapter. As it demonstrates, even when only two support centers are used, the simultaneous equations make the method quite complicated. When the number of support centers (and hence simultaneous equations) exceeds three, a human has considerable difficulty using the reciprocal method. It is relatively easy for a computer to solve the equations, however, and software packages are available to do this.

Because of its precision, the reciprocal method is preferred by the Cost Accounting Standards Board (CASB).[6] Despite the CASB's preference, many health care organizations find that the stepdown method strikes about the right balance between accuracy and ease of use. It is the method preferred by the American Hospital Association for use in hospitals, and Medicare requires hospitals to use it to receive reimbursement.

Choosing a Support Center Sequence

When the stepdown method is used, the sequence followed in allocating the support centers can affect the costs in each mission center. The sequence will not affect total costs, however, which will remain the same under all sequences (for example, $600,000 for Homecare). On occasion, the effect of the sequence decision on a particular mission center may be significant, and this decision should therefore be considered carefully.

In general, the approach to choosing a sequence is to allocate support centers in order of their use by other support centers. That is, the support center that uses other support centers the *least* is allocated *first*, and the support center that uses other support centers the *most* is allocated *last*. Clearly, considerable judgment is required to determine this sequence.

PROBLEM

What judgment has management at Homecare made in deciding to allocate the housekeeping cost center before the administration cost center? Is a similar judgment involved in choosing the sequence of mission centers? Why or why not?.

ANSWER

Management's judgment apparently is that the housekeeping department uses the administration department less than the administration department uses the housekeeping department. (That is, less effort is spent administering the housekeeping department than is spent cleaning the administration department!) With regard to mission centers, their sequence is unimportant because there is no allocation *out of* mission centers.

An Illustration

Figure 2.1 shows the same support and mission centers that have been discussed up to this point in the chapter. As before, the allocation process begins with the housekeeping support center and uses square feet as the basis for allocation (as shown by including the term *square feet* in

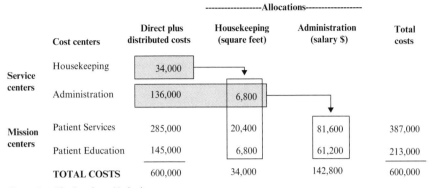

		------------------Allocations------------------		
Cost centers	Direct plus distributed costs	Housekeeping (square feet)	Administration (salary $)	Total costs
Service centers Housekeeping	34,000			
Administration	136,000	6,800		
Mission centers Patient Services	285,000	20,400	81,600	387,000
Patient Education	145,000	6,800	61,200	213,000
TOTAL COSTS	600,000	34,000	142,800	600,000

Figure 2.1 The Stepdown Method

parentheses in the column headed "Housekeeping"). As this column shows, the $34,000 in the housekeeping support center has been allocated across the remaining cost centers.

Looked at a bit differently, the total direct costs (plus distributed costs if there had been any) in housekeeping are $34,000, which is shown in the *row* labeled "Housekeeping." The total *allocated* costs of $34,000 are shown in the *column* labeled "Housekeeping." The row amount is shaded; the allocations are shown in the outlined box, with a total at the bottom.

With the allocation of the housekeeping costs, the administration support center now has a total of $142,800 ($136,000 + $6,800) to be allocated—that is, its $136,000 of direct costs (plus any distributed costs), plus the $6,800 of housekeeping allocated to it. These two amounts are shown in the shaded box in the "Administration" row.

Administration costs are allocated using salary dollars, and the outlined box shows how those costs were allocated to the remaining cost centers—the two mission centers in this case. The total amount allocated ($142,800) is shown at the bottom of the column.

The total costs in the mission centers are determined by combining their direct and distributed costs and adding the costs allocated to them from the support centers. This process was discussed in the section on allocation bases. The stepdown method is the formal approach to the same process.

Key Aspects of the Stepdown Method

There are several important points to keep in mind when allocating costs using the stepdown method:

- Only support center costs are allocated. Mission center costs are not. Mission centers receive costs from support centers, but once a cost has been allocated to a mission center, it stays there.

- To carry out the stepdown process, a basis of allocation must be chosen for each support center. The basis is used to measure the use of that cost center by the other cost centers—both support centers and mission centers. For example, in organizations that have laundry services (such as hospitals), the number of pounds of laundry frequently is used as the basis for allocating the costs of the laundry support center. Each cost center thus receives a portion of laundry costs in accordance with its proportion of the total pounds of laundry processed. If a particular cost center did not require any pounds of laundry to be washed, it would not receive any allocation from the laundry cost center.

- The amount of a given support center's costs allocated to a particular mission center will depend in part on whether that support center's costs are allocated early or late in the sequence. If they are allocated late in the sequence, they will contain some costs from support centers allocated earlier in the sequence. If they are allocated early, they will not.

- Total costs do not change. All that changes with different allocation bases and stepdown sequences is the distribution of costs among the various cost centers and, ultimately, among the mission centers.

Decision 6: Attaching a Mission Center's Costs to Its Cost Objects

A final decision to be made in a full-cost accounting system concerns the way mission center costs are "attached" to its cost objects. A *process system* typically is used when all units of output are roughly identical, as on a production line. All production-related costs for a given accounting period are calculated and then divided by the total number of units produced to give an average cost per unit. When hospitals used an all-inclusive per diem, they were using a process system.

A *job order system* is used when the units of output are different. An automobile repair garage is illustrative. Adding all costs for a given accounting period, such as a day, and dividing the total by the number of cars repaired to determine an average cost per repaired vehicle would provide misleading information to management (as well as unfair prices to customers). Instead, a job order system uses job tickets. On each ticket the time and parts associated with that repair effort are recorded separately, and the costs are computed by means of hourly wage rates, unit prices, and so on. We will examine these choices and their impact on the cost of a cost object in chapter 5.

Managerial Judgment

Of the six cost accounting decisions we have discussed, the two that typically require the most managerial judgment are defining the cost object and the determining mission and support cost centers. The distinction between direct and indirect costs is largely a matter for the accounting staff to address. The choice of allocation bases and the selection of an allocation method require some involvement by senior management, but largely in regard to establishing the balance between the precision that a particular basis or method provides and the cost of using it.

Defining an organization's cost objects requires senior management's judgment about how well a given set of cost objects fits with management's pricing policies. In Homecare's case, the final cost object probably would be a visit to a patient, because this is how most patients think about Homecare's work. However, senior management also would be interested in the cost per hour—which would be its intermediate cost object, and which would be likely to differ across mission centers.

Determining the Impact on Customer Prices

Information structured into multiple cost centers can be extremely useful for pricing purposes. If we assume for the moment that Homecare's management wants a 10 percent markup over costs when pricing the agency's services, the multiple-cost-center approach will give a pricing structure very different from that of the single-cost-center approach.

PROBLEM

A potential client has asked Homecare for a bid on a weekly home visit, which the manager estimates will require three hours. Another potential client has asked for a bid on educating an elderly relative, which the manager estimates will require one hour a week. Homecare uses a 10 percent markup in setting its prices. How would the prices Homecare proposes to these potential patients and clients differ depending on whether Homecare is using a single cost center or multiple cost centers?

ANSWER

The price per hour for either patient services or patient education would be the cost plus 10 percent, computed as follows:

Cost per Hour

One cost center	$600,000 ÷ 8,000 hours = $75.00
Multiple cost centers	
Patient services	$387,000 ÷ 6,000 hours = $64.50
Patient education	$213,000 ÷ 2,000 hours = $106.50
Price per Hour	
One cost center	$75.00 + $7.50 = $82.50
Multiple cost centers	
Patient services	$64.50 + $6.45 = $70.95
Patient education	$106.50 + $10.65 = $117.15

The weekly cost-based prices for the two jobs would therefore be as follows:

One Cost Center	
Patient services	3 hours @ $82.50 = $247.50
Patient education	1 hour @ $82.50 = $82.50
Multiple Cost Centers	
Patient services	3 hours @ $70.95 = $212.85
Patient education	1 hour @ $117.15 = $117.15

Note that with the multiple-cost-center approach, the price per hour for patient services decreased by about 13 percent, and the price for patient education increased by about 43 percent. If we assume that the multiple-cost-center approach gives us a more homogeneous collection of activities in each cost center, then the cost on which the price is based comes closer to the true consumption of resources needed for each hour of service.

Some Pricing Complications

As discussed in chapter 1, the fee market between a provider and an insurer can be quite complex, including such payment approaches as fee-for-service (discounted or otherwise), DRGs, bundled prices, and subcapitation. In many instances a health care provider is a price taker and does not have the opportunity to propose a price and perhaps negotiate a mutually agreed-on amount with an insurer. Hospitals, for example, have little or no influence over the DRG payments it receives from Medicare. Similarly, physicians can bill whatever fee they wish, but that fee generally is adjusted by the insurer to an amount often called "usual, reasonable, and customary."

There are some instances in which a hospital or its physicians have an ability to negotiate fees with a managed care plan. These negotiations can become complicated, depending on such factors as the number of "lives" under discussion (and therefore the impact of the additional volume on costs) and the nature or complexity of the service being provided, which also can affect the cost.

In both cases, however, a hospital must know its full costs. Whether it is negotiating a bundled fee with a managed care plan in conjunction with its physicians or whether it is a price taker, it cannot make strategic decisions about loss leaders (or gain trailers) or about how much to propose in a contract unless it has a good full-cost analysis as its starting point and has done a good job of attaching a mission center's costs to its cost objects.

As we will see in chapter 5, many hospitals are deficient in regard to attaching mission center costs to cost objects. Most have done a good job of allocating support center costs to mission centers, but they have done a poor job with decision 6: attaching a mission center's costs to its cost objects. One can only imagine how much more difficult profitability analyses will become for hospitals when the pricing bundle is expanded to include care provided outside the walls of the hospital, such as in home health agencies or nursing homes.

Summary of Cost Accounting Choices

The choices in developing a full-cost accounting system can be tricky and usually require some managerial judgment. Moreover, they are highly interdependent. The choice of cost centers will influence the distinction between direct and indirect costs. The choice of a particular final cost object frequently will require the use of certain intermediate cost objects or call for certain kinds of cost centers. Allocation of support center costs will be determined in part by the choice of the support centers themselves, in part by the distribution process for indirect costs, in part by the chosen allocation bases, and in part by the allocation sequence.

In this context, it is important to emphasize that any change to the full cost of one mission center always will be accompanied by changes in another direction to the full cost of one or more other mission centers. That is, once costs have been incurred, they do not change. Total costs will therefore always be the same on any set of cost reports prepared for the same organization for the same time period. As a result, the effect of any change in methodology is solely one of making shifts among mission centers. Sometimes these shifts can be quite significant, however.

You are now ready to work on the practice case for this chapter, Mossy Bog Laboratories, which will give you practice in using the stepdown method. Work through the case to the best of your ability before looking at the solution in appendix B at the end of the book.

KEY TERMS

Allocation bases	Direct costs
Cost centers	Indirect costs
Cost objects	Stepdown method

To Bear in Mind

1. This chapter has focused on mission and support centers and the allocation of support center costs to mission centers. This way of viewing costs has some limitations. Specifically, the allocation methodology says little about a cost's actual behavior as the volume of activity in a cost center increases or decreases. For this reason, full-cost information is not especially useful for a category of decisions known as alternative choice decisions. The kinds of costs appropriate for these decisions are discussed in chapters 3 and 4.

2. In this chapter you have learned about stage 1 of the cost accounting effort. At the end of this stage, all costs reside in mission centers. In stage 2, mission center costs are attached to the cost objects passing through those centers. We discussed this activity briefly in terms of the choice between a process system and a job order system, but it is trickier than it might seem. Stage 2 is discussed in detail in chapter 5.

Test Yourself

1. What are the three purposes for which full-cost accounting is most often used?

2. What are two factors that can complicate a comparison between the costs in a hospital outpatient department and those in a physician's office?

3. What is the breakdown of costs (from a managerial perspective) that corresponds to the economist's three factors of production (land, labor, and capital)?

4. What are the six decisions that constitute the cost accounting methodology?

5. Of these six cost accounting decisions, which two typically require the most managerial judgment?

Suggested Cases

Harbor City Community Center

Carroll Hospital

Croswell Hospital

Jebah Hospital

Riverview Community Health Clinic

University of Miami Department of Medicine

PRACTICE CASE

MOSSY BOG LABORATORIES

Mossy Bog Laboratories, an organization that contracts with hospitals to perform various kinds of laboratory tests for outpatients—has two support centers (maintenance and administration) and two mission centers (sophisticated tests and simple tests). The sophisticated test department is highly equipment intensive, whereas the simple test department is highly labor intensive. Management has decided to allocate maintenance costs on the basis of depreciation dollars in each department, and administration costs on the basis of labor hours worked by the employees in each department.

The following data (dollar amounts in thousands) appear in the organization's records for the current period:

| | Support Centers | | Mission Centers | | |
	Maintenance	Administration	Sophisticated Tests	Simple Tests	Total Costs
Direct plus (minus) distributed costs	$1,160	$2,400	$8,000	$4,000	$15,560
Depreciation dollars*	$200	$2,000	$3,000	$800	$6,000
Labor hours	20,000	10,000	10,000	40,000	

*Depreciation dollars are included in direct cost figures. For example, the $1,160,000 of costs in the maintenance department includes $200,000 of depreciation.

Assignment

1. Allocate the support center costs to mission centers using the step-down method, and determine the relevant total costs. Begin with the maintenance department.

2. To what use might a manager put this information? Please be specific about the next steps that should be taken based on this information.

Appendix 2A: The Reciprocal Method of Cost Allocation

To see how the reciprocal method of cost allocation works, let's use the example of an express mail delivery company with two support centers, housekeeping and administration. We wish to allocate the support center costs to the two mission centers: next-day delivery and two-day delivery. Management has decided to allocate housekeeping costs on the basis of the square footage in each department, and administration costs on the basis of the number of hours worked by the employees in each department. Table 2A.1 (dollar amounts in thousands) shows how the initial data for the company might look.

Note that there are no square feet shown for housekeeping and no labor hours shown for administration. Because we are using square feet as the basis of allocation for housekeeping and labor hours as the basis of allocation for administration, we exclude these measures from the two departments. In other words, we do not calculate the cost of cleaning the housekeeping department or the cost of administering the administration department. We will, however, calculate the cost of administering the housekeeping department and the cost of cleaning the administration department.

To perform the reciprocal allocation, we must set up two equations with two unknowns; the unknowns are the amount of administration costs to be allocated (designated as A) and the amount of housekeeping costs to be allocated (designated as H). Because housekeeping costs are allocated on the basis of square footage, and because administration occupies one-fifth $(1,000 \div 5,000)$ of the total square footage,

$$A = \$1,200 + (1/5)H$$

Table 2A.1 Basic Information for a Reciprocal Cost Allocation

	Administration	Housekeeping	Two-Day Delivery	Next-Day Delivery	Total
Area occupied (in square feet)	1,000		1,000	3,000	5,000
Labor hours		100	100	400	600
Mission center costs			$1,500	$4,000	$5,500
Support center costs	$1,200	$2,400			$3,600
TOTAL COSTS					$9,100

Therefore, the amount of administration costs to be allocated to the other cost centers is the sum of the administration department's direct costs plus its share of housekeeping costs.

Because administration costs are allocated on the basis of hours worked, and because housekeeping uses one-sixth ($100 \div 600$) of the hours,

$$H = \$2,400 + 1/6(A)$$

That is, the amount of housekeeping costs to be allocated to the other cost centers is the sum of the housekeeping department's direct costs plus its share of administration costs.

We now can substitute terms as follows:

$$A = \$1,200 + (1/5)(\$2,400 + [1/6]A), \text{ or}$$

$$A = \$1,200 + \$480 + (1/30)A. \text{ Therefore,}$$

$$A = \$1,738.$$

And because the value of H is $\$2,400 + (1/6)A$,

$$H = \$2,690$$

To complete the reciprocal allocation, we remove $1,738 from administration and allocate it to the remaining three cost centers on the basis of labor hours, and we remove $2,690 from housekeeping and allocate it to the three other cost centers on the basis of square footage. The result is that the costs of each support center are fully allocated to the other support centers and to the mission centers. After all this is done, total costs reside only in the mission centers. These allocations are shown in table 2A.2.

As pointed out in the chapter text, once the number of support centers exceeds three, solving the set of simultaneous equations becomes too complex for a human, although it can be done easily by a computer.

Table 2A.2 Allocation of Support Center Costs to Mission Centers (in Thousands of Dollars)

	Administration	Housekeeping	Two-Day Delivery	Next-Day Delivery	Total
Initial costs	$1,200	$2,400	$1,500	$4,000	$9,100
Housekeeping allocation[a]	538	(2,690)	538	1,614	
Administration allocation[b]	(1,738)	290	290	1,158	
TOTAL COSTS			$2,328	$6,772	$9,100

[a] $2,690 from formula. Allocated 1/5 to administration, 1/5 to two-day delivery, and 3/5 to next-day delivery.
[b] $1,738 from formula. Allocated 1/6 to housekeeping, 1/6 to two-day delivery, and 4/6 to next-day delivery.

Appendix 2B: Pricing in Nonprofit Organizations

Setting prices in many nonprofit organizations is a tricky proposition. Full costs, differential costs, and a variety of other configurations can be used to determine prices. The choice depends in large measure on the scenario under consideration. Unfortunately, many nonprofit managers give little thought to pricing policies. In fact, many tend to regard all marketing activity as something to be ignored. Such an attitude can result in their giving insufficient attention to client needs. It also can result in the organization's pricing its services in a way that is unfair to some of its clients or developing pricing policies that inhibit the achievement of strategic goals. This appendix addresses these issues and discusses several matters that affect pricing decisions in nonprofit organizations.

Importance of Appropriate Pricing

Pricing policies are important in most nonprofit organizations because prices (1) influence the behavior of clients, (2) provide a measure of output, and (3) influence the behavior of managers. The issues to consider differ somewhat in each of these areas.

Client Behavior

The amount that a client (or third party on behalf of a client) pays for a service indicates that the service is worth at least that much to the client. Indeed, the better a set of prices fits with client decision-making options, the more powerful its impact on client behavior. For example, residents of a city or town can be charged for water use in at least three ways: (1) everyone can be charged the same amount; (2) everyone can be charged a monthly or quarterly flat rate based on the number of bathrooms and kitchens in their respective residences; or (3) everyone can be charged individually for the water they actually consume, as measured by a meter. In the first case, residents are not motivated to conserve water, and consumers who use little water subsidize those who use more. In the second case, the charge is somewhat more equitable because water use tends to vary with the number of outlets. However, such a system does not motivate consumers to conserve water (although it may influence their decisions in regard to adding or deleting bathrooms). If meters are installed, however, consumers are more likely to conserve water. Indeed, some years ago, the installation of meters in New York City led to a drop in consumption of nearly 50 percent.

Prices that affect clients directly tend to have the greatest influence on consumption. Normally, as the price for a unit of service increases, clients consume fewer units. In some situations, however, price is a mere book-keeping charge with no direct effect on client behavior. Some universities, for example, allocate computer resources by providing students and faculty with monetary allowances that entitle them to a certain amount of computer time. These allowances may be set so high or may be so easily supplemented that they do not motivate at all, doing little more than helping track computer usage. The motivating force of such systems would be much stronger if students were allowed to trade "dollars" of computer time for other resources, or if they were to receive a refund for time not used.

Measure of Output

Measuring output in nonmonetary terms, such as the number of visitors to a community health center or the number of courses faculty members teach, is likely to be cruder than using monetary measurements. If, for example, each service furnished by an organization is priced on the basis of full costs, the organization's total revenue for a period will provide a good approximation of the total amount of services it provided during that period.

Even if reported prices do not measure the real value of an organization's services to individual clients or society, the revenue-based approximation may provide managers with useful information. For example, if revenue in one year is lower than that of the previous year (after adjustments for inflation), managers have a good indication that the organization's real output has decreased.

If the quantity of services provided varies across an organization's clients, a single price will not accurately measure the variations. At one time, for example, hospital patients were charged a flat rate per day, even though the services they received varied greatly based on their illnesses. Today hospital charges vary more directly with the quantity of services provided. Moreover, if the unit price of a service reflects the relative magnitude of that service, then total revenue is in effect a weighted measure of output—that is, it incorporates differences in the services rendered.

Behavior of Managers

If services are sold, the organizational unit that sells them frequently becomes a "profit center."[7] In general, profit center managers are motivated to think of ways to (1) render additional services so as to increase revenue, (2) reduce costs, or (3) change prices. Under these circumstances, the manager of a profit center in a nonprofit organization behaves much like a manager in a for-profit company. For example, in an organization with a computer center, if computer services are furnished without charge, assignment of computer time is the responsibility of the manager of the center, and time assignments are made according to his or her perception of users' needs (or sometimes friendship with users). In any case, the manager has little financial incentive to provide quality computer services in a cost-effective manner. In contrast, if the computer center were set up as a profit center and dissatisfied users were free to go elsewhere, the manager would be motivated to offer quality services at competitive prices—or risk underused facilities, unmet revenue goals, and poor per-formance. In addition, when internal clients must pay for their use of computer resources (which reduces the profit in their respective profit centers), they tend to think much more carefully about their use of those resources.

In this and other pricing situations, if customers do not buy a product in the quantity that managers think is reasonable, it is an indication that something is wrong. Perhaps not enough of the customers believe the product is worth the stated price. Perhaps they can obtain a similar or better product at a lower price elsewhere. Whatever the reason, manage-ment will want to reexamine the product and its price.

In general, prices should be set prior to the delivery of services. When this happens, managers have an incentive to keep costs within prescribed amounts. No such incentive exists for managers who know that costs will be recouped no matter how high they are. Of course, this principle works well only when the cost of a service can be estimated with reasonable accuracy. With many research and development projects, there is no reli-able basis for estimating how much money should be spent to achieve the desired result.

Normal Pricing

In general, the price of a good or service provided by a nonprofit organiza-tion should be its full cost plus an appropriate margin. This is the same approach that is used in normal pricing in the for-profit sector, except that in for-profit companies the margin ordinarily is higher due to the need to provide a return to shareholders.

Rationale for Normal Pricing

Although the basic goal of a nonprofit organization is to provide services, it nevertheless must generate revenues that at least equal its expenses, or it will go bankrupt. Beyond this, a nonprofit organization also must earn an excess of revenue over expenses if it is to generate some of the funds needed to grow, acquire new assets, and replace existing assets as they wear out. In this respect, there is no difference between for-profit and nonprofit organizations. Like their for-profit counterparts, nonprofit organizations need an excess of revenue over expenses to finance working capital (such as for inventories and accounts receivable) and fixed assets (such as new or replacement buildings and equipment).

Like their for-profit counterparts, nonprofit organizations can finance some of their working capital and fixed asset needs by borrowing. However, there is a limit to the amount that any organization can borrow. Consequently, nonprofits need equity capital for basically the same reason that for-profit companies do—because lenders are unwilling to provide an organization's total capital needs. Moreover, many nonprofits believe that financing entirely with borrowed funds is too risky, especially if their revenues are uncertain from one year to the next.

Assuming a nonprofit organization can finance some portion of its capital needs through borrowing, it must then finance the balance of its needs from equity funds: either contributions or surpluses from operations. In the absence of a constant and predictable source of capital contributions from donors or other sources, the organization will need to generate equity capital in the form of a surplus. Furthermore, a nonprofit organization needs a reserve against "rainy days," or periods when revenues do not equal expenses. Earning a profit during good times will assist the organization in weathering bad times.

In summary, the purpose of having an excess of revenue over expenses is to increase the retained earnings portion of the nonprofit's equity. The need for equity capital is smaller in nonprofit organizations than it is in their for-profit counterparts because they do not have stockholders who expect cash dividends or stock price appreciation. In other respects, however, the need to generate equity capital from operations—as a source of financing and as protection against bad times—is the same in both types of organizations. These matters are discussed more fully in chapter 10.

Approach to Normal Pricing

In setting a normal price, a nonprofit faces three tricky issues. First, the relevant costs are not historical costs, but rather estimates of future costs. Making these estimates can be difficult, especially when the nonprofit's environment has a great deal of uncertainty.

The second issue is whether the cost analysis should include depreciation on buildings and equipment that were financed with contributions. Some people argue that such buildings and equipment were acquired at zero cost and therefore there is nothing to depreciate. Others maintain that depreciation is necessary to help provide for replacement of these assets.

Also, some people argue that the services a nonprofit organization provides are just as valuable as the services provided by a for-profit company, and that clients should pay a comparable amount for them. Thus, by including depreciation as an element of cost, nonprofits are behaving in accordance with the pricing practices of for-profit companies. Indeed, many clients of nonprofit organizations, including government agencies, are willing to have depreciation on contributed assets included as an element of cost.[8]

The third issue concerns revenue offsets. Some services are partially financed by revenue from endowment or other contributed sources, and opinions differ as to whether these revenue offsets should be deducted from costs to arrive at the price a client should pay. For example, in a university, endowment spending that is specifically designated for financial aid to students clearly should be taken into account in arriving at annual tuition. When this approach is taken, however, it may be desirable to report this amount as a component of the program's or service's revenue on the operating statement rather than as an offset to costs. Then the operating statement will show the total resources earned by the program or service.

Estimating the Margin

The best way for managers to estimate their required margin is to calculate the cost of using the equity capital that the organization needs, and to include this cost in the total cost of a service. Most managers do not make such calculations, however, and rely on rules of thumb instead. For example, there is a widespread belief among managers of hospitals that their organization's margin should be 3 or 4 percent of revenue. There is little empirical justification for this figure, however. Moreover, because each hospital has a different strategy and different needs, its margin quite probably will need to differ from the rule of thumb.

Some organizations base their prices on a conservative estimate of volume, planning for no surplus. When actual volume exceeds the estimate, the incremental contribution (that is, revenues minus differential expenses) provides the necessary margin. For example, a college may base its tuition on an enrollment that is 5 percent lower than what it actually expects. If its actual enrollment reaches the expected level, the difference in contribution is its surplus for the year. Similarly, an organization may make a conservative estimate of its revenue from annual giving, with the expectation that the anticipated excess will be its surplus.

This approach works well when the estimate of volume is truly conservative. When volume falls below the anticipated level, however, an organization's revenues do not cover its expenses. In such circumstances, continued existence is precarious and often rests on the hope that, in times of crisis, special appeals to donors will bail the organization out. For example, it is said that for many years, the Metropolitan Museum of Art presented its annual deficit to its board of trustees, and the trustees then wrote personal checks that totaled the needed amount. Today, few nonprofit organizations (including the Met) are able to do this.

The Role of Outside Forces

Some prices are set by outside agencies. Examples are the DRG prices that Medicare uses to reimburse hospitals as well as the price ceilings sometimes specified by government agencies as a condition for providing a grant. In these instances, managers still need to make cost calculations even though their selling price is given. Some hospitals, on discovering that the full cost of treating a patient with a particular diagnosis is greater than the associated DRG price, may attempt to avoid treating these patients. This approach gives rise to the phenomenon of "DRG orphans." If the approach extends to too many hospitals, it is a fairly clear signal to the payer (Medicare in this case) that its price is too low.

Price may also be influenced indirectly by outside forces. For example, no college could charge much more than its competitors, because to do so would indicate that it was inefficient. Nor would most colleges charge less than their competitors, because they could make good use of any additional amount to strengthen their curricula. Furthermore, most colleges are convinced that small differences in tuition do not influence a student's decision as to which college to attend. In 1990 the Department of Justice considered investigating the possible incidence of illegal price fixing by a group of colleges whose tuition charges were within 5 percent of one another. Its decision not to pursue this matter was probably influenced by the recognition that such behavior is likely among competing organizations.

The Pricing Unit

In general, the smaller and more specific the pricing unit, the better. Such a unit improves senior management's knowledge of and decisions about cross-product subsidization, and also is a more accurate measure of output. By contrast, a price that includes several discrete services with different costs is not a good measure of output because it masks the actual mix of services rendered. The practice of isolating progressively smaller units of service for pricing purposes is called unbundling.

Managers who unbundle services should be mindful of two qualifications. The first such qualification, and an obvious problem beyond a certain point, is that the paperwork and other costs associated with pricing tiny units of service outweigh the benefits. Some hospitals charge for individual aspirin tablets, for example, a practice that is difficult to defend.

The second qualification is that the consequences of such pricing should be consistent with the organization's overall policies and goals. This qualification extends beyond the size of the unit to matters that are much more strategic in nature. For example, undergraduate English instruction costs less than undergraduate physics instruction, and these differences could be reflected by charging different prices for these courses. However, a separate price for each course might cause students to select courses in a way that university management considers to be educationally unsound.

In contrast, in most universities there are significant differences in the overall costs of graduate and undergraduate programs, such that there may be good reasons for charging different tuition rates for graduate and undergraduate students. University administrators who unbundle in this way do not feel that the differences motivate students to make unwise choices.

Hospital Pricing as an Example of Unbundling

Exhibit 2B.1 shows several approaches to pricing the services provided by a hospital. Moving from column A to column D, one can see pricing practices that involve (1) an increase in record keeping, (2) a corresponding increase in the amount of output information available for senior management, and (3) a basis for charging patients that more accurately reflects the services they received. At one extreme, for example, the hospital could charge an all-inclusive rate—say, $820 per day. This practice (shown in column A) is advocated by some on the grounds that patients can know in advance what their bills will be (assuming their lengths of stay can be estimated), and because record keeping, at least for billing purposes, is simplified.

A common variation on the all-inclusive price is shown in column B. Here the hospital charges separately for the cost of each easily identifiable special service and makes a blanket daily charge for everything else. In fact, rather than there being a price per film (as shown here), radiology prices could be calculated according to a rather detailed point system that takes into account the complexity of the procedure, with each point worth a few cents. (Of course, there is some incongruity in calculating prices for certain services in terms of points worth a few cents each, while at the same time lumping other service costs into a large overall rate.)

EXHIBIT 2B.1 Pricing Alternatives in a Hospital

A	B		C		D	
All-Inclusive Rate	Daily Rate plus Special Services		Daily Charge per Type of Service		Detailed	
$820 per day	Patient care, per day	$500	Medical/ surgical:		Admittance	$500
	Operating room, per hour	$300	1st day	$550	Workup, per hour	$50
	Pharmacy, per dosage	$7	Other days	$475	Medical/ surgical bed, per day	$400
	Radiology, per film	$35	Maternity:		Maternity bed, per day	$150
	Special nurses, per day	$75	1st day	$350	Bassinet, per day	$125
	Etc.		Other days	$300	Nursery care, per hour	$30
			(Plus special services as in B)		Meals, per day	$40
					Discharge (Plus special services as in B)	$50

Column C unbundles the daily charge. Different charges are made for each department, and more is charged for the first day than for subsequent days. This pricing policy accounts for the admitting and workup costs associated only with the first day of a patient's stay.

Column D is the job-cost approach that managers in many for-profit companies use. Managers of automobile repair shops, for example, price each repair job separately. Each repair includes charges for the services of mechanics according to the number of hours they work on the job, as well as for each part and significant item of supply required for the job's completion. The sum of these separate charges is the basis for the price the customer pays. Customers of a repair garage would not tolerate any other approach. They would not, for example, agree to pay a flat daily rate for repairs, regardless of the service provided.

Variations from Normal Prices

There are many situations in nonprofit organizations in which circumstances call for variations from the normal approach to setting prices. In some instances, these situations arise because of the presence of third-party payers. In others, they arise because the organization wishes to distinguish between services provided as part of its main mission and those that are more peripheral. As a result, there are several areas where the organization may wish to use some approach other than normal pricing.

Cost-Plus Pricing

With cost-plus pricing, the purchaser of an organization's goods or services agrees to pay the full cost plus an agreed-on increment, usually a percentage. Many government contracts are written this way, especially in the defense industry, in which the argument is made that the activities needed to design and manufacture the product are so uncertain that it would be impossible to determine the cost in advance, and therefore also difficult to set a reasonable price.

Although the intent of cost-plus pricing usually is for the purchaser to pay the full cost of the service, the definition of the term *full cost* can vary among purchasers. In particular, some purchasers define certain costs as "unallowable." These are costs that, although incurred by the organization, may not be included in the cost pool used to arrive at the payment rate. Purchasers also may specify ceilings for certain items, such as the compensation of executives or the daily amount that can be spent for travel.

Market-Based Pricing

Nonprofit managers may use normal pricing for services that are directly (or closely) related to their organization's principal objectives but use market-based pricing for peripheral services. For example, many universities use normal pricing for room and board charges because students live in dormitories and eat in dining rooms as a necessary part of the educational experience. By contrast, these universities often use market prices for space rentals to outside groups, because these outside groups' activities are not closely related to the university's main objectives. Similarly, many universities use normal pricing for tuition for graduate and undergraduate programs but market rates for executive education programs.

In making pricing decisions, managers often have difficulty drawing the line between programs that are closely related to the organization's objectives and those that are more peripheral. For example, market rates seem appropriate for executive education programs, but whether they should be used for university extension courses or community education programs is much less clear.

Subsidized Pricing

A subsidy exists when price is set below full cost. Most subsidies are intended to encourage clients to use a service. For example, many public bathing beaches and other recreation facilities charge a lower price on weekdays to encourage off-peak use. In general, nonprofit organizations use three types of subsidies: (1) subsidies for certain services, (2) subsidies for certain clients, and (3) subsidies for all clients.

Subsidizing Certain Services

A nonprofit organization may decide to price a certain service at less than the normal price to encourage use by clients who are unable or unwilling to pay the normal price. Or, as a matter of policy, the organization may want clients to select services on some basis other than their ability to pay. Examples come from public education and low-cost housing. In most circumstances, providing a service at a subsidized price is preferable to providing it for free, because a price, even if low, motivates clients to give thought to the service's value. However, an organization should be careful to determine whether the price deters clients from using needed services. For example, some years ago, when Medicaid patients in California were charged $1 per visit for primary care, there was a sharp decline in the number of primary care visits. Some months later, however, there was an increase in these patients' rates of hospitalization—hospitalizations that could have been avoided had the individuals received timely primary care. Overall, the cost to Medicaid was higher as a result of this pricing policy.[9]

An organization may decide to use the same price for all services even though some cost more than others. In this case, the higher-cost services are subsidized by the lower-cost ones. Although cross-subsidization is frowned on in some settings, there may be sound reasons for using it. For example, Latin and Greek courses in a college typically have small enrollments, resulting in a faculty cost per student that is considerably higher than that for courses that are more popular. Because the college does not want to discourage enrollment in these courses, however, it charges the same tuition to all students. Thus, low-enrollment courses are subsidized by high-enrollment courses.

Even if managers do not use cost as the basis for pricing, they may find it helpful to calculate the costs of subsidized services. Knowing the difference between price and full cost can help flag areas for managerial decision making. For example, if a service does not cover its full costs, managers have several possible courses of action:

- Accept the loss, recognizing that the service is either a loss leader or sufficiently important to the organization's strategy to warrant subsidization

- Reduce the variable costs or fixed costs directly associated with the service

- Increase volume (if the service makes a contribution, there is some breakeven volume at which full costs will be covered)

- Raise the price of the service

- Phase out the service

Subsidizing Certain Clients

A client who is not charged the same amount as other clients who receive the same or comparable services is being subsidized. The reason for this subsidy is that the organization's objective is to provide the services to all qualified clients, some of whom are unable to pay the normal price. For example, colleges and universities provide subsidies to certain students in the form of scholarships and other financial aid. Similarly, nonprofit hospitals, as charitable (and therefore tax-exempt) organizations, are obligated to provide certain levels of care to indigent patients.[10]

In some instances, a class of clients is subsidized even though some members of the class have ample resources. Examples are subsidies given to the elderly and to people with disabilities for transportation, movies, restaurants, drugs, and a variety of other services. In theory, the subsidy should be limited to those in need, but finding a practical way to apply this concept is difficult. A "means test" usually is not feasible because it is expensive and time consuming, and, more important, because many people resent being classified as needy. Moreover, such a subsidy tends to be politically popular, and any attempt to eliminate or modify it would encounter considerable resistance from lobbying groups.

Subsidizing All Clients

Some organizations receive contributions or appropriations intended to subsidize their services for all clients. When this happens, no client pays the normal price for services. Museums, symphony orchestras, and state universities are examples.

Free Services

Some services are provided free to clients. This sometimes happens when public policy officials determine that it would be discriminatory to charge for a particular service, or when managers determine that attempting to collect for a service would be impossible, unfeasible, or politically untenable. Services in the former category include welfare investigations and legal aid services. Examples of services in the latter category are public tours of the White House and Capitol.

The most important class of free services comprises those that are provided for the benefit of the public in general rather than for specific users. They are well described in the following passage:

> These are goods and services that simply cannot be provided through the market. They have two related qualities. First, they inevitably have to be supplied to a group of people rather than on an individual basis. Second, they cannot be withheld from individuals who refuse to pay for them.

> Take national defense, for example. The national security provided by our military forces is extended to all persons in the country. They all receive the same protection, whether they are willing to pay for it or not. There is no way of withholding the service, or creating a market which separates those who pay from the freeloaders. In fact, in this type of situation, rational consumers who are interested only in economics will never pay since they will get the benefit in any event.[11]

Quasi-Public Goods

Many services that seem to meet the definition of public goods turn out, upon analysis, to be services for which prices could be charged. For example, a somewhat classic public good is a lighthouse. It is said that one ship's "consumption" of the warning light does not leave less warning light for other ships to "consume," and there is no practical way that the lighthouse keeper could prohibit ships from consuming it. At the same time, a ship cannot refuse to consume the light. It can be argued, however, that ship owners, as a class, should pay for lighthouses. Then, if lighthouse costs become too high, the objections of ship owners may help bring them back in line.[12]

The lighthouse example is similar to the practice of charging users of highways for their cost via tolls or fuel-related taxes, or of charging airlines and owners of private aircraft for the cost of operating the air traffic control system. In many countries, the airwaves are considered a quasi-public good, and users are charged for them through a tax on television sets; in the United States, the airwaves are regarded as a public good.

Peripheral Services

Even when the principal service of an organization is a public good, managers may be able to charge for certain peripheral services. For example, the US Congress charges a fee for copying certain documents in its files, federal agencies charge fees for copying documents made available under the Freedom of Information Act, municipal governments charge for dog licenses, and some public school systems charge for after-school athletics.

Other Free Services

In addition to the general class of public goods, there are other situations, such as the following, in which prices should not normally be charged for services:

* Services are provided according to public policy, but clients cannot afford to pay for them. Examples include welfare investigations and legal aid services.

* It is public policy not to ration the services on the basis of ability to pay. Examples include the services provided by legislators, who do not charge fees for assisting constituents, even though a legislator's time is a valuable resource.

* A charge is politically untenable. Examples include public tours of the White House and Capitol. The public clamor over such charges could be harmful to overall organizational objectives, even though a charge might be equitable.

* Client motivation is unimportant. A nominal charge to a public park or bathing beach will not measure actual output, nor will it influence a client's decision to use the facilities. A charge equal to full cost, by motivating less wealthy individuals to avoid using these facilities, may be inconsistent with public policy.

Summary

The prices that a nonprofit organization charges (or decides not to charge) for its services influence the behavior of clients, provide a measure of output, and influence the behavior of managers. The price that is usually charged is the normal price—the full cost of a service plus a modest margin.

Prices charged for subsidized services are lower than normal prices. Subsidized prices may be charged only for certain services, only to certain clients, or to all clients. In some instances, for sound public policy purposes, a service may be provided free of charge.

Pricing decisions exist not only between an organization and its clients but also between two units in a single organization. The price established in this instance is called a *transfer price*. Transfer prices are discussed in chapter 7.

Notes

1. Technically, a *product* is either a good or a service. The term could refer to a lab test, an X-ray, an operative procedure, or a discharged patient. Using the term in this way is not intended to suggest that a patient is a product or an output unit, but rather to clarify a shorthand that will make it easier to discuss the concepts without a great deal of excessive verbiage.

2. David W. Young, "Cost Accounting and Cost Comparisons: Methodological Issues and Their Policy and Management Implications." *Accounting Horizons,* March 1988, 67–76.

3. For details, see www.whitehouse.gov/omb/circulars_a021_2004/

4. Hospitals that use bundled pricing, one of the fee options discussed in chapter 1, need to increase the number of intermediate cost objects. In addition to products provided in the hospital's various departments (such as the laboratory), the intermediate cost objects now must include physician visits and individual services provided to a patient after discharge (such as home care).

5. David W. Young, Elinor Socholitzky, and Edward W. Locke, "Ambulatory Care Costs and the Medicare Cost Report: Managerial and Public Policy Implications," *Journal of Ambulatory Care Management* 5 (February 1982): 13–30.

6. The CASB is part of the Office of Federal Procurement Policy. Its main concern is to ensure that costs are accounted for properly under cost-based contracts that are issued by the federal government, mainly the Department of Defense. For details on its regulations (which are massive), see www.whitehouse.gov/omb/procurement_casb

7. A profit center is an organizational unit in which both outputs and inputs are measured in monetary terms (that is, using revenues and expenses). The manager of a profit center is responsible for operating the unit in such a way that it achieves the budgeted difference between revenues and expenses. Profit centers are discussed in detail in chapter 6.

8. The government does not permit inclusion of depreciation on equipment that it has contributed (or otherwise paid for already), however, because to do so would be double counting.

9. Milton I. Roemer et al., "Copayments for Ambulatory Care: Penny-Wise and Pound-Foolish," *Medical Care* 13 (June 1975): 457–466.

10. Until recently, hospitals deducted revenue lost from charitable care from the gross revenue that measured charges for all services rendered. A 1990 pronouncement by the American Institute of Certified Public Accountants (AICPA) changed this practice for external reporting purposes. Managers of hospitals that follow the AICPA's recommendation will not have as sound a measure of actual output as they had under the previous practice. See American Institute of Certified Public Accountants, *Audits of Providers of Health Care Services* (New York: Author, 1990), para. 7.2.

11. Otto Eckstein, *Public Finance*, 2nd edition (Englewood Cliffs, NJ: Prentice Hall, 1967), 8.

12. In a fascinating article, Ronald Coase describes the history of British lighthouses, showing that they in fact successfully charged fees from the seventeenth century until the present. Ronald H. Coase, "The Lighthouse in Economics," *Journal of Law and Economics* 17 (October 1974): 357–376.

CHAPTER 3

COST BEHAVIOR

A basic tenet of cost accounting is that different costs are used for different purposes. The full-cost accounting principles discussed in chapter 2, although useful for pricing, profitability analysis, and cost comparisons, have some important limitations. Specifically, they do not address how costs vary with changes in volume (or other factors, such as time). Yet information on cost behavior is important for several types of decisions that managers make on a fairly regular basis. As this chapter and the next discuss, using full-cost information as a basis for deciding which costs will change, or how costs will change under different decision-making scenarios, may lead managers to make decisions that are financially detrimental to their organization.

Organization of the Chapter

The chapter first addresses the nature of costs. Once terms and concepts have been defined, we take up the subject of cost-volume-profit analysis. We look at CVP analysis (sometimes called breakeven analysis) in its most basic form and then examine a variety of special considerations that can complicate it.

The Nature of Costs

Fundamental to any discussion of management accounting is the question of cost behavior. Chapter 2 identified the distinction between mission and support center costs. This chapter takes a different view of costs, classifying them as either fixed or variable. In general, the fixed-versus-variable distinction lets us see more clearly how a change in the volume of activity will affect an organization's costs. We also need to include the refinements of

LEARNING OBJECTIVES

On completing this chapter, you should know about

- The definitions of fixed, variable, step-function, and semivariable costs

- The technique of cost-volume-profit (CVP) analysis, how to prepare such an analysis, and its uses and limitations

- Some of the special considerations involved in preparing a CVP analysis

- The concepts of unit contribution margin and total contribution

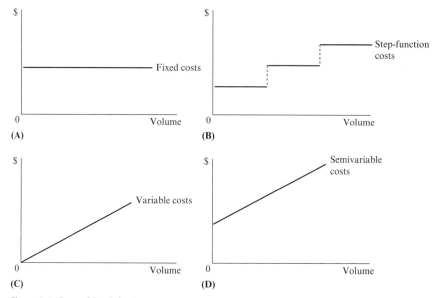

Figure 3.1 Types of Cost Behavior

Fixed costs

A cost that remains unchanged over a wide range of volume. The classic example is rent. Fixed costs ordinarily have a relevant range, that is, a certain number of units or volume of activity over which they remain fixed. Rent, for example, would increase if an organization's volume of activity increased to such an extent that it needed to move into larger and more expensive facilities.

semivariable and step-function costs. These four types of costs are shown in figure 3.1.

Fixed Costs

Fixed costs are independent of the number of units produced or hours of service provided. Although no costs are fixed when viewed over a long enough period, the *relevant range* for fixed costs (that is, the span of units over which they remain unchanged, or the period within which they are considered) generally allows them to be viewed graphically as shown in quadrant A of figure 3.1.

A good example of a fixed cost in most organizations is rent. Regardless of the number of units of service provided or other volume of activity, the amount of rent the organization pays will remain the same.

Step-function costs

A cost that is essentially fixed but for which the relevant range is relatively small. A good example of a step-function cost is supervision. When the number of employees increases to a certain level, a new supervisor must be hired. Supervision salaries thus increase or decrease in a step-like fashion rather than smoothly.

Step-Function Costs

Step-function costs are similar to fixed costs, except that they have a narrower relevant range, so they increase in a stair-like fashion. They take the form shown in quadrant B of figure 3.1, where the dotted lines represent discontinuous jumps.

An example of a step-function cost is supervision. As the number of employees increases, supervisory personnel must be added. Because it is usually difficult to add part-time supervisory personnel, supervision costs increase in a stair-like fashion. Similarly, if the number of employees decreases, supervision costs would be expected to decline in steps.

Variable Costs

Variable costs have a linear relationship to changes in volume. That is, as volume increases, they increase by a constant proportion. The result is a straight line, the slope of which is determined by the amount of variable costs associated with each unit of output, as shown in quadrant C of figure 3.1.

An example of a variable cost is medical supplies in an outpatient clinic. The cost of these supplies will increase in almost direct proportion to increases in the number of patient visits. Some organizations have relatively high variable costs per unit of output, resulting in a line that slopes upward steeply; others have relatively low variable costs for each unit of output and a variable cost line that is less steep. In a hospital, for example, the pharmacy's cost line will have a steep slope, whereas the social service department will have almost no variable costs per service unit.

Variable costs
A cost that increases in an almost linear fashion with volume. For example, as the number of visits in an outpatient department increases, the cost of medical supplies increases at about the same rate. See fixed cost and step-function cost.

Semivariable Costs

Semivariable costs (sometimes called *mixed* or *semifixed costs*) share features of both fixed and variable costs. A portion is fixed, but the cost line then rises with increases in volume. The result is a line that begins at some level above zero and then slopes upward in a linear fashion, as shown in quadrant D of figure 3.1.

A good example of a semivariable cost is electricity. An organization typically incurs some base cost each month for electricity service, even if it uses no electricity. Costs then increase linearly, in accordance with the number of kilowatt-hours used. Similar cost patterns exist for other utilities as well, such as telephone, gas, and water.

Semivariable costs
Sometimes called mixed or semi-fixed costs. A cost that shares features of both fixed and variable costs. A portion is fixed, but the cost line then rises. The result is a line that begins at some level above zero and then slopes upward in a linear fashion.

Separating the Fixed from the Variable

To separate the fixed and variable components of a semivariable cost, we need at least two historical or projected data points. We can then use algebra to make the computations.

EXAMPLE

Assume that an organization used 10,000 kilowatt-hours of electricity in June and 12,000 kilowatt-hours in July. The June electric bill was $1,500; the July electric bill was $1,700. To compute the fixed and variable components of the cost line, take the following steps:

1. Compute the difference in total costs: $1,700 − $1,500 = $200.
2. Compute the difference in volume: 12,000 kWh − 10,000 kWh = 2,000 kWh.
3. Compute the variable cost per unit by dividing the two: $200 ÷ 2,000 kWh = $0.10 per kWh.
4. Compute total variable costs for one data point: June = $0.10 per kWh ×10,000 kWh = $1,000.
5. Compute fixed costs for the same data point: $1,500 − $1,000 = $500 fixed costs.
6. Describe the line: Total cost = $500 + ($0.10 × kWh).
7. Test the line with the second data point: $500 + ($0.10 × 12,000 kWh) = $1,700.

If we have several data points, we can plot them on a graph, manually fit a straight line to them, and extend it to intersect the vertical axis of the graph, which is the fixed cost component. We then can compute the line's slope to determine the variable rate. This is called the *scatter diagram method.*

Alternatively, we could use a statistical technique, such as *linear regression* (or *least squares*), to fit the points to a line. When using this method, we must eliminate outliers so that the fit will reflect the general experience. This of course raises the question of what constitutes an outlier. Because of this complexity, many analysts prefer the scatter diagram method. Indeed, because we usually are using the information to project future costs, and because the future is unknown, we must be careful not to be seduced by the alleged precision of the linear regression method.[1]

Relationship between Cost Behavior and Full-Cost Accounting

The analysis of differential costs would be simplified if all support center costs were fixed and all mission center costs were variable (as occasionally is assumed to be the case). Unfortunately this is almost never true. Figure 3.2 presents four cost types and their distinctions among fixed, variable,

	Fixed Costs	Variable Costs
Mission Center Costs	Supervisor's salary in patient services	Medical supplies in patient services
Support Center Costs	Portion of the executive director's salary (which is a cost of administration) that is allocated to patient services	Cleaning supplies (which are cost of housekeeping) that are allocated to patient services

Figure 3.2 Fixed and Variable Costs versus Mission and Support Center Costs

mission center, and support center costs. This example refers to the costs of Homecare, the organization discussed in chapter 2. In reviewing figure 3.2, keep in mind that terms can vary. Sometimes, as discussed in chapter 2, support center costs are called *indirect costs,* and sometimes they are called *overhead costs.* In general the context will make the meaning clear.

Cost Behavior in Organizations

To assess an organization's costs, we must divide them into the categories of fixed, step function, variable, and semivariable. Doing so requires analyzing the actual or expected behavior of each cost item to determine how it can be expected to change with changes in the volume of activity.

PROBLEM

The Hawthorne Dental Clinic currently provides 1,200 patient visits each month. At this level of activity, it incurs the monthly costs shown here. Classify each cost into one of the four categories: fixed, step function, variable, and semivariable.

Hygienists	$25,000
Cleaning supplies (for example, floss, gloves, disposables)	6,000
Other supplies (for example, uniforms)	2,000
Utilities	1,000
Rent	6,000
TOTAL	$40,000

ANSWER

Hygienists are probably step-function costs: they will remain fixed until the number of visits increases by some fairly sizable number. Cleaning supplies, in contrast, most likely are variable costs: they change in direct proportion to a change in the number of visits. Other supplies are a little tricky. If we assume that they vary with the number of personnel, they can be treated as step-function costs. Utilities most likely are semivariable costs: the clinic probably pays a fixed amount each month with a variable component based on usage, which probably is proportional to the number of hours the clinic is open, which is related, in turn, to the number of visits. Rent probably is fixed, although with some ceiling on the number of visits: once visits reach a certain number, the clinic will need to rent a larger facility.

Classifying costs is only the first step. The next step is to estimate how they will change with changes in volume and to develop formulas that indicate the cost-volume relationships.

PROBLEM

Senior management of the Hawthorne Dental Clinic plans to increase the clinic's volume to 1,800 visits a month. It has determined that (1) each hygienist can provide 12 visits a day, or 240 visits a month (the clinic hires only full-time hygienists, and each works a twenty-day month); (2) cleaning supplies are variable costs; (3) other supplies will increase to $2,500 when the number of visits reaches 1,800; (4) utilities are semivariable costs and are $400 a month regardless of the number of visits; and (5) rent remains at $6,000 as long as the number of visits does not exceed 2,000.
    What will the clinic's costs be for these five items at 1,800 visits?

ANSWER

Let's look at each cost item separately:

1. *Hygienists.* The clinic currently has 5 hygienists (1,200 visits ÷ 240 visits per month per hygienist), who have a total monthly cost of $25,000. Therefore, the cost per hygienist must be $5,000 per month ($25,000 ÷ 5 hygienists). At 1,800 visits per month, Hawthorne will need 7.5 hygienists (1,800 ÷ 240), but because it hires only full-time hygienists, it must have 8 hygienists for 1,800 visits, at a cost of $40,000 (8 × $5,000). Alternatively, you may have decided to "stretch" 7 hygienists (asking them to work faster or to work additional hours with no

additional compensation) and not hire the eighth person until total visits reach 1,920 (8 × 240). That is a possible (although tricky) approach. If you do that, the hygienist cost for 1,800 visits will be $35,000 (7 × $5,000).

2. *Cleaning supplies.* Because Hawthorne's costs were $6,000 with 1,200 visits, and because the costs are variable, the variable cost per visit must be $5 ($6,000 ÷ 1,200 visits). This means that at 1,800 visits, the total cost will be $9,000 (1,800 × $5).

3. *Other supplies.* These were given as $2,500.

4. *Utilities.* Because utility costs are semivariable, they have both a fixed and a variable component. We were told that the fixed component is $400. Because they totaled $1,000 at 1,200 visits, the variable component must be $600 ($1,000 − $400). Therefore, these costs must increase at a rate of $0.50 per visit ($600 ÷ 1,200 visits). Thus, the utility costs at 1,800 visits will be $1,300 ($400 + [1,800 × $0.50]).

5. *Rent.* This was given as $6,000 as long as visits don't exceed 2,000.

To summarize, the cost figures are as follows:

	1,200 Visits (5 Hygienists)	1,800 Visits (8 Hygienists)	1,800 Visits (7 Hygienists)
Hygienists	$25,000	$40,000	$35,000
Cleaning supplies	6,000	9,000	9,000
Other supplies	2,000	2,500	2,500
Utilities	1,000	1,300	1,300
Rent	6,000	6,000	6,000
TOTAL	$40,000	$58,800	$53,800
AVERAGE COST PER VISIT	$33.33	$32.67	$29.89

The fact that the per-visit cost declines as the number of visits increases indicates that not all costs increase in proportion to volume. As we have seen, several costs either are fixed, have fixed components, or are step function in nature.

Cost-Volume-Profit Analysis

An important technique used in a variety of managerial situations is cost-volume-profit analysis. The purpose of a CVP analysis is to determine (1) the volume of activity needed for an organization to achieve its profit (or surplus) goal, (2) the price that it needs to charge to achieve its profit goal, or (3) costs (fixed, variable, or both) that it needs to adhere to if it is to achieve its profit goal.

CVP analyses usually are done for a particular organizational activity, such as establishing a new product line or program. A CVP analysis thus begins with this fundamental equation:

Profit = Total revenue (*TR*) − Total costs (*TC*)

Total revenue for many activities is easy to calculate. If we assume that the activity's price is represented by the letter p, and its volume by the letter x, then total revenue is price times volume, or

$$TR = px$$

Total costs are somewhat more complicated. CVP analysis requires recognition of the different types of cost behavior discussed in the previous section. Let's begin with the simplest of cases—one in which there are no step-function or semivariable costs. In this instance, the formula is quite simple:

$$TC = \textbf{Fixed costs} + \textbf{Variable costs}$$

Algebraically, fixed costs are represented by the letter a, and variable costs per unit by the letter b. Thus total variable costs can be represented by the term bx, where, as before, x represents volume. The resulting cost equation is

$$TC = a + bx$$

This means that the fundamental profit equation can be shown as

$$\textbf{Profit} = px - (a + bx)$$

Figure 3.3 represents the formula graphically.

Point x_1, where $px = a + bx$, is the *breakeven volume*—the volume at which total revenue, px, equals total costs, $a + bx$. At a volume above x_1, the activity earns a profit; below x_1, it incurs a loss.

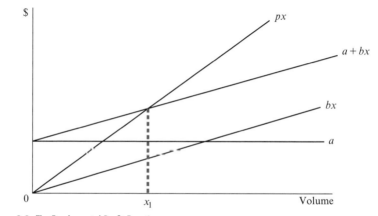

Figure 3.3 The Fundamental Profit Equation

To illustrate how this formula can be used, let's assume that an organization wishes to determine its breakeven volume, which is the volume at which profit is zero. If we know price, fixed costs, and variable costs per unit, and if we set profit at zero, then we can solve the formula algebraically for x, which would be the breakeven volume.

PROBLEM

Littleton Home Health Agency publishes a monthly health and nutrition newsletter for the elderly and homebound. For this activity, the agency incurs fixed costs of $100,000 a month and variable costs of $0.80 per newsletter. It charges $1.80 per newsletter. What is its breakeven volume (number of newsletters per month)?

ANSWER

We can begin with the CVP formula and substitute the known elements. We can then solve for the unknown, which in this case is volume, or x:

$$Profit = px - (a + bx)$$

At breakeven volume, there is no profit; therefore, as discussed earlier,

$$px = a + bx$$

$$\$1.80x = \$100,000 + \$0.80x$$

$$\$1.00x = \$100,000$$

$$x = 100,000$$

Breakeven is thus 100,000 newsletters. To confirm:

Revenue: $1.80 × 100,000	=		$180,000
Less:			
Variable costs: $0.80 × 100,000	=	$80,000	
Fixed costs		100,000	180,000
PROFIT			$0

Unit Contribution Margin

An important aspect of CVP analysis is the concept of *unit contribution margin*. This is the contribution to fixed costs that comes about as a result of each unit that is sold. In effect, the unit contribution margin is the difference between price and unit variable cost, or $p - b$. By rearranging the

unit contribution margin
The amount that each unit of product sold contributes to the recovery of fixed costs. Normally, it is calculated as price minus variable costs per unit.

terms of the CVP formula, we can see that breakeven volume is simply fixed costs divided by unit contribution margin, as follows:

$$px = a + bx$$

$$px - bx = a$$

$$x \times (p - b) = a$$

$$x = a \div (p - b)$$

In effect, price minus unit variable cost tells us how much each unit sold contributes to the recovery of fixed costs. When we divide this amount into fixed costs, we arrive at the volume (number of units of activity) needed to recover all fixed costs. This is the breakeven volume.

To illustrate, the Littleton Home Health Agency's newsletter has a unit contribution margin of $1.00 ($1.80 – $0.80). When we divide this amount into the newsletter's fixed costs of $100,000, we arrive at the breakeven volume of 100,000 newsletters.

Incorporating Other Variables into CVP Analysis

Thus far we have been using CVP analysis to solve only for the breakeven volume. Clearly, if we know how many units of a product an organization expects to sell, the product's fixed costs, and its unit variable costs, we can determine the price it needs to charge to break even. Similarly, if we are in an environment where price is market driven, if we know about how many units we can sell at that price, and if we know our fixed costs, we can set up unit variable costs as the unknown and solve for it.

Profit or Surplus Considerations

We also can incorporate a need for profit (or surplus) into CVP analysis. The easiest way to do this is to add the amount of desired profit to the fixed costs and then to calculate a breakeven point using that new level of "fixed costs." Similarly, if the organization needed a margin of safety, we could incorporate that amount also, arriving at a new level of fixed costs.

Special Considerations in CVP Analysis

A number of special considerations can complicate a CVP analysis: semi-variable costs, step-function costs, and multiple products or services. Let's look at each of these.

CVP Analysis with Semivariable Costs

Incorporating semivariable costs into a CVP analysis is relatively easy. Because these costs have a fixed component and a variable component, we simply add the fixed component to the fixed cost total and add the unit variable component to the existing unit variable cost figure.

PROBLEM

In addition to its other costs, Littleton Home Health Agency has electricity costs for its newsletter operation that are $2,000 a month regardless of usage, plus an additional amount per kilowatt-hour of use. Electricity usage is tied directly to the number of newsletters produced. The agency's accountants have determined that the rate is about $0.04 per newsletter. Given this semivariable cost, what is the agency's new monthly breakeven volume (number of newsletters)?

ANSWER

Again, we can begin with the basic formula, insert the known elements, and solve for the unknown:

$$px = a - bx$$

$$\$1.80x = (\$100,000 + \$2,000) + (\$0.80x + \$0.04x)$$

$$\$0.96x = \$102,000$$

$$x = 106,250$$

Breakeven is 106,250 newsletters

CVP Analysis with Step-Function Costs

Introducing step-function costs into a CVP analysis is somewhat more difficult than you might at first imagine. Ideally we would like to be able to assume that for any given relevant range, we could simply add together the step-function costs and the fixed costs to give us the total applicable fixed costs. We then could use the basic formula. Unfortunately, the process is not quite that simple, as the following problem illustrates.

PROBLEM

Return to the first problem featuring Littleton Home Health Agency (that is, ignore the electricity costs). In addition to the $100,000 in fixed costs stipulated in the first problem, Littleton also has supervision costs that behave as follows:

Volume (Number of Newsletters)	Supervision Costs
0–50,000	$10,000
50,001–100,000	$20,000
100,001–150,000	$30,000
150,001–200,000	$40,000

What is Littleton's breakeven volume now? Careful—this is a little tricky.

ANSWER

If we attempt to solve the breakeven formula at the first level of fixed costs, we get the following:

$$\$1.80x = (\$100,000 + \$10,000) + \$0.80x$$

$$\$1.00x = \$110,000$$

$$x = 110,000$$

The problem with this solution is that the breakeven volume is 110,000 newsletters, but the relevant range for this level of step-function costs ($10,000) is 0 to 50,000 newsletters. Thus, a breakeven of greater than 50,000 newsletters is invalid, and we must move to the next level of step-function costs ($20,000), which gives us the following:

$$\$1.80x = (\$100,000 + \$20,000) + \$0.80x$$

$$\$1.00x = \$120,000$$

$$x = 120,000$$

This solution is also invalid because the relevant range maximum is 100,000 newsletters. Only when we get to the third level ($30,000) do we encounter a valid solution:

$$\$1.80x = (\$100,000 + \$30,000) + \$0.80x$$

$$\$1.00x = \$130,000$$

$$x = 130,000$$

The conclusion we can draw is that the incorporation of step-function costs into a CVP analysis requires a trial-and-error process to reach a valid breakeven volume.

CVP Analysis with Multiple Products or Services

Thus far we have made all of our CVP calculations for situations involving only one product. When there are two or more products, the analysis becomes more complicated. Consider the following problem.

PROBLEM

Quicky Surgicenter, an ambulatory surgery center, has three surgical case types: regular, hard, and extra hard. Annual fixed costs are $2,565,000. Other information is as follows:

	Regular	Hard	Extra Hard
Fee per case	$3,000	$4,000	$5,000
Less: Variable costs per case	1,800	2,200	2,500
Equals: Unit contribution margin	$1,200	$1,800	$2,500
Cases per year	1,000	400	600

What is the breakeven point for the center?

ANSWER

To determine the breakeven point under these circumstances, we must calculate a weighted average unit contribution margin and then divide it into fixed costs. The easiest way to calculate a weighted average unit contribution margin is to begin by calculating total contribution margin for all case types, as follows:

	Regular	Hard	Extra Hard	Total
Unit contribution margin	$1,200	$1,800	$2,500	
Cases per month	1,000	400	600	2,000
Total contribution	$1,200,000	$720,000	$1,500,000	$3,420,000

The weighted average unit contribution margin then can be calculated by dividing total contribution by total cases:

$$\$3,420,000 \div 2,000 = \$1,710$$

We now can calculate the breakeven point by dividing fixed costs by the weighted average unit contribution margin, or

$$\$2,565,000 \div \$1,710 = 1,500 \text{ cases}$$

Thus the organization must have 1,500 cases a year to break even.

The Impact of Product Mix

One problem with the weighted average approach is that changing the mix of products (case types in the Quicky Surgicenter problem) will change the breakeven point. In the problem, changing the mix of cases (but keeping the total number of cases at 2,000) will change total contribution. This in turn will change the weighted average unit contribution margin. The result is that fixed costs will be divided by a different number from that used before, resulting in a different breakeven figure.

To see this point more clearly, answer the following problem.

PROBLEM

Assume that Quicky Surgicenter's 2,000 cases are distributed as follows: 800 regular, 300 hard, and 900 extra hard. Also assume that all other cost and fee figures given in the previous problem remain the same.

What is the breakeven point with the new mix? Why, if the cost and price figures have remained the same, has the breakeven point changed?

ANSWER

The computations are as follows:

	Regular	Hard	Extra Hard	Total
Contribution margin	$1,200	$1,800	$2,500	
Cases per month	800	300	900	2,000
Total contribution	$960,000	$540,000	$2,250,000	$3,750,000

The weighted average unit contribution margin now is $1,875, calculated as follows:

$$\$3,750,000 \div 2,000 = \$1,875$$

Breakeven now is

$$\$2,565,000 \div \$1,875 = 1,368 \text{ cases}$$

The breakeven number of cases has changed because the mix of cases has changed. This will happen any time an organization's various products have different individual unit contribution margins. In this situation, the new mix has more cases with a higher unit contribution margin. Other things being equal, a higher unit contribution margin means a lower breakeven point. That is why the breakeven point fell (from 1,500 cases to 1,368 cases) with the change in mix.

An important conclusion to be drawn here is that a breakeven figure with multiple products can be very unstable—as mix changes, so will the breakeven figure. It is important to bear in mind, however, that an unstable breakeven figure comes about only when the individual unit contribution margins are quite different. When they are roughly the same, changes in mix, even if they are large, will have relatively little impact on breakeven.

In this regard, it should be noted that individual unit contribution margins can differ for a single product when there are multiple payers for that product, each paying a different rate. This is a particularly problematic issue for hospitals, as they usually are paid by a variety of third parties (such as Medicare, Medicaid, and Blue Cross). In short, having only one product in a breakeven analysis does not solve the "mix" problem, as there can be a mix issue in terms of payment rates as well. In effect, different payment rates create different unit contribution margins, thereby creating a similar problem to a difference in product mix.

CVP Analysis for a New Product

Because of this potential instability, CVP analysis tends to be used relatively rarely in organizations with multiple products. However, it frequently is used in conjunction with an analysis of the possible introduction of a new product. Indeed, it is an essential aspect of a good marketing analysis for a new product.

To understand the process for a new product, let's look at a hypothetical company, Clearwater Ambulance Service. Clearwater operates just one ambulance and charges $2.00 per mile for each emergency mile driven. Last year, the ambulance drove 60,000 emergency miles. The variable cost per mile (mainly gasoline) was $0.40. The driver was paid a salary of $40,000 per year. Rent and administration were fixed costs totaling $60,000. As the following analysis shows, Clearwater lost money:

Item	Amount		
Revenue	$2.00 × 60,000 =		$120,000
Expenses:			
Variable costs	$0.40 × 60,000 =	$24,000	
Driver		40,000	
Overhead costs (rent and administration)		60,000	124,000
PROFIT (LOSS)			$(4,000)

In thinking about how to address this problem, management has decided that one possibility is to add a second ambulance.

PROBLEM

Assume that ambulance 2 will charge the same amount per mile as ambulance 1, have the same variable cost per mile, and require a driver at the same salary as the driver for ambulance 1, but it will require no additional overhead costs. How many miles must it drive to eliminate the loss that Clearwater currently incurs?

ANSWER

Let's follow the format suggested earlier, whereby we compute a unit contribution margin and divide it into the sum of the fixed costs and the desired profit. Unit contribution margin is price minus unit variable cost, or $1.60 ($2.00 − $0.40). Fixed costs are $40,000 (the driver), and we need $4,000 in profit to cover the loss from ambulance 1. Therefore, we divide $1.60 into $44,000, and conclude that ambulance 2 must drive 27,500 emergency miles to cover its costs and earn a $4,000 profit.

Now assume that management believes ambulance 2 will actually drive 30,000 miles during the upcoming year, and that overhead costs will remain at $60,000. It has asked the accountants to prepare an analysis of the profitability of ambulance 2. The accountants allocate overhead on the basis of number of miles driven, and ambulance 2 is expected to drive one-third of the miles (30,000 of a total of 90,000 miles).

PROBLEM

What would the accountant's profitability analysis for ambulance 2 look like?

ANSWER

The accountant's profitability analysis might look as follows:

Revenue ($2.00 × 30,000)		$60,000
Expenses:		
Variable costs ($0.40 × 30,000)	$12,000	
Driver	40,000	
Overhead costs (1/3 of $60,000)	20,000	72,000
PROFIT (LOSS)		$(12,000)

This analysis raises a perplexing problem for management. When overhead costs are included, ambulance 2, which was projected to drive more miles than needed to earn a $4,000 profit (30,000 miles versus 27,500 miles), is being presented as a money-losing proposition.

Contribution

The problem, of course, lies in the allocation of overhead. Because of situations such as this, many managers prefer to think in terms of the contribution of each product to the organization's overhead costs. *Contribution* refers to the amount of money that remains after a product's direct costs have been deducted from its revenue. These include variable, semivariable, fixed, and step-function costs. The amount left after deducting these costs *contributes* to the recovery of overhead costs.

More generally, a product (an ambulance in this case) provides some revenue and incurs some direct costs. The difference between revenue and direct costs (both fixed and variable) is the contribution of that product to the organization's overhead costs.

A contribution income statement has a different format from a more traditional income statement and can be used to analyze situations such as the one at Clearwater. A typical construction is as follows:

Contribution
Usually the difference between revenue and variable costs but sometimes the difference between revenue and the sum of variable costs and direct fixed costs of, say, a department or a program. An example of the former is the contribution of a dialysis procedure to the dialysis unit's fixed costs. An example of the latter is the contribution of the dialysis unit to the organization's overhead costs.

Total revenue
    Less: Total variable costs

Equals: Margin (for fixed and overhead costs)
    Less: Product's fixed costs

Equals: Product's contribution to overhead costs
    Less: Allocated overhead costs

Equals: Profit (loss) on a full-cost basis

PROBLEM

Prepare a contribution income statement for Clearwater, assuming that ambulance 2 drives 30,000 emergency miles. To do so, fill in the following table:

Item	Ambulance 1	Ambulance 2	Total
Total revenue			
Less: Total variable costs			
Margin (for fixed and overhead costs)			
Less: Product's fixed costs (drivers)			
Contribution (to overhead costs)			
Less: Overhead costs			
PROFIT (LOSS) ON A FULL-COST BASIS			

ANSWER

The contribution income statement would look as follows:

Item	Ambulance 1	Ambulance 2	Total
Total revenue	$120,000	$60,000	$180,000
Less: Total variable costs	24,000	12,000	36,000
Margin (for fixed and overhead costs)	$96,000	$48,000	$144,000
Less: Product's fixed costs (drivers)	40,000	40,000	80,000
Contribution (to overhead costs)	$56,000	$8,000	$64,000
Less: Overhead costs			60,000
PROFIT (LOSS) ON A FULL-COST BASIS			$4,000

The key figures here are the contribution amounts, which show that each ambulance is making a positive contribution to overhead—meaning that eliminating either one (or not initiating ambulance 2) would leave the organization worse off. In fact, it is ambulance 2's $8,000 contribution that led to the change from a $4,000 loss to a $4,000 profit.

Now test yourself with the following two problems.

PROBLEM

Quicky Surgicenter's surgeons work in three departments. Each department is responsible for one of the case types: easy, hard, or extra hard. Each department also has some direct fixed costs. The organization's total fixed costs are shown in the following table, along with some other basic information:

	Fixed Costs	Fee per Case	Variable Cost per Case
Regular department	$500,000	$3,000	$1,800
Hard department	700,000	4,000	2,200
Extra-hard department	1,000,000	5,000	2,500
Overhead (centerwide)	365,000		
TOTAL FIXED COSTS	$2,565,000		

Using the mix of cases shown earlier (1,000 regular, 400 hard, 600 extra hard), structure Quicky's revenues and costs into a contribution income statement format. Try to do so without looking back at the earlier examples.

ANSWER

Using these data, Quicky's contribution income statement would look as follows:

	Regular	Hard	Extra Hard	Total
Revenue	$3,000,000	$1,600,000	$3,000,000	
Less: Variable costs	1,800,000	880,000	1,500,000	
Margin	$1,200,000	$720,000	$1,500,000	$3,420,000
Less: Fixed costs	500,000	700,000	1,000,000	2,200,000
Contribution	$700,000	$20,000	$500,000	$1,220,000
Less: Overhead costs				365,000
SURPLUS				$855,000

PROBLEM

How would Quicky's contribution income statement look with the second mix of cases discussed earlier (800 regular, 300 hard, 900 extra hard)? Try to prepare a new contribution income statement without looking back. As a member of the senior management team at Quicky, how might you respond to this change in the mix of cases?

ANSWER

Using the second set of data, a revised contribution income statement would look as follows:

	Regular	Hard	Extra Hard	Total
Revenue	$2,400,000	$1,200,000	$4,500,000	
Less: Variable costs	1,440,000	660,000	2,250,000	
Margin	$960,000	$540,000	$2,250,000	$3,750,000
Less: Fixed costs	500,000	700,000	1,000,000	2,200,000
Contribution	$460,000	$(160,000)	$1,250,000	$1,550,000
Less: Overhead costs				365,000
SURPLUS				$1,185,000

The organization's senior management presumably would be pleased with the change in the mix of cases because it has increased the surplus from $855,000 to $1,185,000. Management might wish to look at the hard cases to see whether eliminating this category of cases would result in a reduction in the number of the other two types of cases. If not, the surplus could be improved by $160,000 by eliminating this category of cases. Moreover, if some of the overhead costs could be reduced with the elimination of the hard category, the surplus could be improved even further. A key issue, of course, is that the surgicenter no longer would be able to offer a full line of surgical services, and this might lead to a decline in cases of the other two types. We will look at situations such as this in greater depth in chapter 4.

You are now ready to work through the two practice cases for this chapter. Huntington Hospital allows you to analyze cost behavior. Jiao Tong Hospital allows you to work through the issues involved in a CVP analysis when there are multiple products. The solutions are in appendix B at the end of the book.

KEY TERMS

Contribution	Step-function costs
Fixed costs	Unit contribution margin
Semivariable costs	Variable costs

To Bear in Mind

1. Some beginning students confuse fixed and variable costs by reasoning that if the rate stays the same, the cost must be "fixed." This is incorrect. The easiest way to dispel this notion is to think about the cost of gasoline for an automobile. Assume that gasoline sells for $3.00 a gallon and that your car gets thirty miles to the gallon. This means that your gasoline cost is $0.10 a mile. As long as the price of gasoline remains at $3.00 and you continue to get thirty miles per gallon, your gasoline cost *per mile* is fixed. This does not mean that gasoline is a fixed cost, however. Rather, it is a variable cost that increases in a linear fashion with mileage at a rate of $0.10 per mile. Your total variable cost for gasoline will be the total miles driven times $0.10. If you do not drive for a day, you will not incur any gasoline costs.

2. A CVP analysis in a situation with multiple products is unstable only if the unit contribution margins are significantly different. When there are significantly different unit contribution margins, a change in mix (of either products or payers) will change the breakeven volume. Under

these circumstances, a contribution income statement generally is more useful.

Test Yourself

1. What are the four different kinds of costs that an organization can incur?

2. What is the formula for a CVP analysis? Be specific about its elements.

3. What is the formula for calculating unit contribution margin? What does it measure?

4. When would a breakeven analysis with multiple products or multiple payers be unstable? When would it be relatively stable?

5. What is the format of a contribution income statement?

Suggested Cases

Abbington Health Center

Carlsbad Home Care

Harlan Foundation

Springfield Visiting Nurse Association

PRACTICE CASE A

HUNTINGTON HOSPITAL

The dietary department at Huntington Hospital uses a "transfer price" to "sell" meals to the clinical departments (such as surgery) for their patients. The hospital's goal is to break even. Information for the past three months of operations is contained in exhibit 3A.1.

Assignment

1. Develop a cost equation for the dietary department that can be used to predict total monthly costs.

2. During February, how much would the price per meal need to be for the department to break even?

3. If the department's price is $12.00 per meal, how many meals must it sell to break even?

EXHIBIT 3A.1   Dietary Department Information for 3 Months

	December	January	February
Number of meals served*	3,000	5,000	8,000
Costs:			
Food sold	$18,000	$30,000	$48,000
Staff salaries and fringe benefits	14,500	16,500	19,500
Rent and depreciation	4,000	4,000	4,000
Utilities and other	2,100	3,300	5,100
TOTAL	$38,600	$53,800	$76,600

*The department expects to serve 10,000 meals in March.

PRACTICE CASE B

JIAO TONG HOSPITAL

Xiong Yin, a recently-graduated MBA, had been hired three months ago as assistant director of Jiao Tong Hospital. Prior to earning his MBA he had worked in several manufacturing firms, but he had never worked in a hospital. He knew little about Jiao Tong's programs or the health care matters that concerned the professional staff, but he had decided to take the job because he had been impressed with the hospital's attempts to provide high-quality health care for the residents of his community.

Despite his lack of experience in hospitals, Mr. Xiong had brought some much-needed management skills to the hospital's operations. In his short tenure with the hospital, he not only had introduced some new management techniques but also had regularly made attempts to educate the professional staff in the use of those techniques.

This afternoon's staff meeting was no exception. In attendance would be the hospital's director, Furong Huang, and the physician coordinators of the hospital's three outpatient programs: Cheng Liew (obstetrics and gynecology), Min Li (pediatrics), and Chao Yang (internal medicine).

Mr. Xiong planned to instruct the attendees on the concept of CVP analysis. To do so, he had gathered some data on the revenues and costs of the hospital's three outpatient programs (see exhibit 3B.1). Using this information, he had determined that each outpatient visit contributed ¥40.73 to fixed costs after covering its variable costs. Given fixed costs of ¥2,185,000 (¥1,385,000 in the programs and ¥800,000 allocated to the outpatient department overall), he had calculated that 53,645 visits were needed to break even.

He had prepared a breakeven chart that he planned to distribute to everyone at the meeting prior to giving a short lecture on the concept of CVP analysis. His intent was to make clear to everyone that outpatient visits were almost exactly at breakeven, which did not allow any margin of safety, and to encourage the program managers to increase the activity in their respective programs by a few patient visits each so as to provide a more comfortable margin of safety and, if all went well, a surplus for the department.

The Meeting

At the meeting, several issues arose that Mr. Xiong had not anticipated, and a rather hostile atmosphere developed. Dr. Cheng pointed out that 13,800 visits was the maximum her program could accommodate, given current space, and she wondered exactly how Mr. Xiong expected her to increase her program's visits. Dr. Min said she would be happy to expand her program by another 4,000 visits, but to do so, she would need to hire another nurse practitioner (NP) at a cost of ¥62,000. She wondered how Mr. Xiong might include this fact in his analysis, and whether the NP should be considered a fixed or a variable cost. Dr. Chao said that he had been planning all along to add another 4,000 visits to his program, and he asked why Mr. Xiong had not checked with him about this prior to preparing his analysis. He too would need to hire another NP, however, at a cost of ¥65,000, and also wondered whether this was a fixed or variable cost.

Ms. Furong seemed quite perplexed by the discussion, and she began her comments by asking Mr. Xiong why he was using averages when the outpatient department had three separate programs. She also indicated that ¥21,800 was far too low a surplus, because she was hoping to have some extra money available during the year for painting and some minor renovations, which would cost about ¥300,000. She asked Mr. Xiong how he might incorporate this need into his analysis. She also expressed some concern about Mr. Xiong's per-visit fees, stating that in conversations with people in other hospitals, she had learned that Jiao Tong's per-visit fees were about 10 percent below what other hospitals were charging. She thought an across-the-board price increase to make up the difference was called for.

Finally, all three of the program coordinators questioned Mr. Xiong about his figures for variable cost per visit. They asked him how he had derived these figures and whether they included some recent price increases of about 5 percent in the hospital's supplies. Mr. Xiong stated that his figures accounted for these supplies, but he confessed that he had not included any price increases in his calculations.

Next Steps

The meeting ended on a less-than-happy note. Mr. Xiong had not had an opportunity to give his lecture, the program managers felt frustrated that their concerns and plans had not been included in his analysis, and Ms. Furong was quite upset because it appeared as though the hospital would not have the funds necessary to pay for the much-needed painting and renovations.

Mr. Xiong returned to his office and wondered whether his decision to work at the hospital had been a wise one. Perhaps, he thought, life would be simpler in a manufacturing firm.

EXHIBIT 3B.1   Program Cost Analysis, Normal Year

	Obstetrics and Gynecology	Pediatrics	Internal Medicine	Average/ Aggregate
Patient visits at full capacity				63,000
Actual number of patient visits	13,800	17,280	23,100	54,180
Fee per visit (after discounts and bad debts)	¥80.00	¥65.00	¥75.00	¥73.08
Variable cost per visit	¥30.00	¥20.00	¥43.00	¥32.35
Net revenue	¥1,104,000	¥1,123,200	¥1,732,500	¥3,959,700
Total variable cost	414,000	345,600	993,300	1,752,900
Contribution to program fixed costs	¥690,000	¥777,600	¥739,200	¥2,206,800
Less: Program fixed costs	350,000	470,000	565,000	1,385,000
Contribution to allocated costs	¥340,000	¥307,600	¥174,200	¥821,800
Less: Allocated fixed costs*	215,000	285,000	300,000	800,000
SURPLUS (DEFICIT)	¥125,000	¥22,600	¥(125,800)	¥21,800

*Fixed costs are allocated on the basis of square meters.

Assignment

1. What assumptions are implicit in Mr. Xiong's determination of a breakeven point? Be sure you understand how he arrived at the figure of 53,645 visits. What is your assessment of the utility of this figure?

2. On the basis of the suggestions and comments made at the meeting, and making assumptions where necessary, prepare revisions to exhibit 3B.1. What is the new breakeven volume for the outpatient department? What is it for each of the three programs? Which is the more useful figure?

3. Based on the information in exhibit 3B.1, Ms. Furong has decided that it would make good financial sense to eliminate the internal medicine program so as to improve the hospital's surplus. What advice would you give her?

Notes

1. A variety of other statistical methods also can be used, such as multiple regression. Some are available on spreadsheet software. In all instances, the calculations are based on past experience, and these methods therefore must be used with caution when forecasting the future.

CHAPTER 4

DIFFERENTIAL COST ACCOUNTING

An important tenet of cost accounting is that different costs are used for different purposes. The Clearwater Ambulance Service problems in chapter 3 illustrated how full costs can be used inappropriately and why managers need to understand cost behavior. In this chapter, we go one step further, showing how full costs are inappropriate for several types of decisions that managers frequently make, called *alternative choice decisions*. The three primary types of these decisions are (1) keeping versus discontinuing a product line or service that is unprofitable on a full-cost basis; (2) making versus buying (for example, performing an activity internally versus outsourcing it); and (3) accepting versus rejecting a special request (for example, selling a product below full cost so as to use some otherwise unused capacity). To make such alternative choice decisions, the appropriate accounting information is *differential costs*.

In effect, differential costs are those costs (and sometimes revenues) that will change under the optional arrangements in an alternative choice decision. If a product line or service is discontinued, for example, some costs will be eliminated, but so will some revenues. In an outsourcing decision, certain costs will be eliminated, but other costs will be incurred. In the special request situation, certain revenues will be received, but costs will not change in accordance with the indications of a full-cost analysis.

As this chapter discusses, using full-cost information as a basis for deciding how costs will change under these sorts of alternative arrangements can lead managers to make decisions that are financially detrimental to their organizations. A different analytical approach is needed.

LEARNING OBJECTIVES

On completing this chapter, you should know about

- The rationale for the statement, "Different costs are used for different purposes"

- The distinction between full costs and differential costs and when each should be used

- Sunk costs and their role in alternative choice decision making

- The role of allocated overhead costs in alternative choice decision making

alternative choice decisions
A decision with one or more options. The three primary types of these decisions are (1) keeping versus discontinuing a product line or service that is unprofitable on a full-cost basis; (2) making versus buying (for example, performing an activity internally versus outsourcing it); and (3) accepting versus rejecting a special request.

differential costs
Costs that will change depending on a choice made by management. Differential costs are calculated for make-or-buy, keep-or-discontinue, special-price, and obsolete asset alternative choice decision making. They include the variable costs of any products involved and may include both step-function and fixed costs, depending on the circumstances. If a cost will be the same regardless of the alternative chosen (as depreciation will be, for example), it is not a differential cost.

Organization of the Chapter

The chapter builds on the concept of *contribution* discussed in chapter 3, going deeper with the analysis. It begins with the differential cost concept, discussing some of its key principles. It then addresses the tricky issues of sunk costs, nonquantitative considerations, and the role of allocated overhead. As the chapter discusses, allocated overhead cannot always be ignored, and a portion of it may be relevant to the decision under consideration, especially when a strategic perspective is employed.

The Differential Cost Concept

Differential cost analysis seeks to identify the behavior of an organization's costs under one or more scenarios that relate to a decision under consideration. With an understanding of fixed, variable, step-function, and semivariable costs, all discussed in chapter 3, we are in a position to undertake such an analysis. Let's begin with the Clearwater Ambulance Service situation that was discussed in chapter 3, but put it into a slightly different decision-making context. Recall that the full-cost analysis looked like this:

Item	Ambulance 1	Ambulance 2	Total
Revenue	$2.00 × 60,000 = $120,000	$2.00 × 30,000 = $60,000	$180,000
Expenses:			
Variable costs	$0.40 × 60,000 = $24,000	$0.40 × 30,000 = $12,000	$36,000
Drivers	40,000	40,000	80,000
Overhead costs	40,000	20,000	60,000
(rent and			
administration)			
TOTAL EXPENSES	$104,000	$72,000	$176,000
PROFIT (LOSS)	$16,000	$(12,000)	$4,000

PROBLEM

Would Clearwater Ambulance Service's financial performance have been improved had ambulance 2, which lost money, been discontinued at the beginning of the year? By how much would the company's financial performance have changed? Before reading further, make your computations and identify any assumptions you used. If you have difficulty with this problem, return to the discussion about Clearwater in chapter 3.

ANSWER

An answer to this question must be structured in terms of differential costs. The question is not whether ambulance 2 lost money on a full-cost basis (as it did), but rather the nature of its differential costs and revenues. Specifically, how would Clearwater's revenues and costs have changed if ambulance 2 had been discontinued?

Although some assumptions are needed, the data appear to indicate that discontinuing ambulance 2 would have eliminated its revenue and its variable costs, as well as the fixed cost of the driver. From all indications, however, the overhead costs (rent and administration) would have continued (that is, they were not differential). The result would have been a shift from a profit of $4,000 to a loss of $4,000, as the following analysis indicates:

Item	Ambulance 1
Revenue	$2.00 × 60,000 = $120,000
Expenses:	
Variable costs	$0.40 × 60,000 = $24,000
Driver	40,000
Overhead costs (rent and administration)	60,000
TOTAL EXPENSES	$124,000
PROFIT (LOSS)	$(4,000)

This situation illustrates several important principles.

Principle 1: Full-Cost Information Can Be Misleading

The information available from most full-cost accounting systems can produce misleading implications when used for alternative choice decisions—in this instance a "keep or discontinue" decision. The full-cost data suggested that Clearwater could increase profits by dropping ambulance 2, but this clearly was not the case.

Principle 2: Differential Costs Can Include Both Fixed and Variable Costs

Although this principle may seem counterintuitive, differential costs can include both fixed and variable costs. In the Clearwater case, for example, the driver was a fixed cost of ambulance 2, and yet the elimination of ambulance 2 eliminated this fixed cost. The key point is that as long as Clearwater operates ambulance 2, it has the fixed cost of the driver's salary, which does not fluctuate in accordance with the number of miles driven (within the relevant range). But when Clearwater eliminates ambulance 2, it also eliminates this cost in its entirety; the cost is therefore differential in terms of the alternative choice decision under consideration.[1]

Principle 3: Assumptions Are Needed

Differential cost analysis invariably requires assumptions. Although the Clearwater analysis focused on what would have happened in the year prior, the real intent of such an analysis is to assist management in making a decision concerning the future. One assumption that underlay our analysis was that next year's prices, costs, volume, and so forth would be the same as last year's.

Of course, it is not true that next year will be just like last year. Inflation will affect costs, and the organization may be able to raise prices. The general state of the economy, along with a wide variety of other factors, will affect next year's volume, such that it is quite likely to be different from last year's. These matters raise some important concerns about the reliability of the analysis.

Despite these concerns, and because we do not have perfect knowledge of the future, we must speculate about how costs will behave. In Clearwater's case, we made two important assumptions about the future: (1) the number of miles driven by ambulance 1 would not increase with the elimination of ambulance 2, and (2) Clearwater would not be able to reduce its rent or administrative costs with the elimination of ambulance 2. Changes in either of these assumptions would have an impact on the new profit (or loss) figure and might in fact make it financially beneficial to eliminate ambulance 2.

Principle 4: Causality Is Needed

For an item to be included in a differential analysis, it must be *caused* by the alternative under consideration. For example, if we assume that there will be an increase in the miles driven by ambulance 1, that increase would need to be caused by the elimination of ambulance 2. If ambulance 1 would have driven more miles anyway, then the increased mileage is irrelevant for the differential analysis. If, however, we assume that the elimination of ambulance 2 means that some people who would have used it will now use ambulance 1 instead, then the increased mileage is relevant for the differential analysis. We would then need to include that additional mileage in computing ambulance 1's revenue and variable expenses under the one-ambulance scenario.

The same issue must be considered for such cost items as rent and administration. If Clearwater planned to reduce its administrative costs with or without ambulance 2, then that change is irrelevant for the differential analysis. If, however, the elimination of ambulance 2 would allow Clearwater to reduce its administrative costs (for example, by eliminating a portion of the dispatcher wage expense), then we would need to include this reduction in the differential analysis.

Principle 5: Sensitivity Analysis Can Be Helpful

Because assumptions play such a crucial role in a differential analysis, it is important to identify and document them as completely as possible and to explore how changes in them would affect the conclusions of the analysis. This latter activity is called *sensitivity analysis*.

If we were doing a sensitivity analysis for Clearwater, we might try to determine how many more miles ambulance 1 would need to drive to maintain the $4,000 profit. Or if we thought Clearwater might be able to reduce its rent and administrative costs with the elimination of ambulance 2, we might ask by how much these costs would need to fall to maintain the $4,000 profit. We would follow this sensitivity analysis with an assessment of whether management could take action that would allow the assumptions to become reality.

PROBLEM

Assuming ambulance 2 is eliminated and there is no increase in the number of miles driven by ambulance 1, by how much would rent and administrative costs need to fall to maintain the $4,000 profit? How would you incorporate this information into a sensitivity analysis?

ANSWER

Because profit fell by $8,000 (from a positive $4,000 to a negative $4,000) when ambulance 2 was eliminated, Clearwater would need to reduce rent and administrative costs by $8,000 to maintain the $4,000 profit.

With this information in hand, we can now ask whether the elimination of ambulance 2 will allow Clearwater to reduce its administrative costs by more than $8,000. This reduction would be a differential item that is directly associated with the elimination of ambulance 2, and thus should be included in a sensitivity analysis.

Principle 6: A Contribution Income Statement Can Be Useful

The Clearwater situation illustrates the value of a contribution income statement, which was discussed in chapter 3. However, even a contribution income statement does not deal with the underlying assumptions. Specifically, in the Clearwater case, a key assumption was that overhead costs (rent and administration) would not be reduced by eliminating ambulance 2. As indicated earlier, and as will be discussed in greater detail later in this chapter, an assumption of this sort is not necessarily valid. Nevertheless, in most instances, an analysis of differential costs is most easily performed by preparing a contribution income statement. If you have forgotten what a contribution income statement looks like, you should return to the section of chapter 3 where it is discussed.

sunk cost

A cost that is associated with a past decision. It either has been committed (like the rent payments on a lease, for example) or has actually been spent (like the depreciation on a machine, for example). Sunk costs are not relevant for alternative choice decision making as they will remain the same regardless of the option that is selected.

Sunk Costs

One of the most difficult aspects of differential cost analysis concerns the role of what are called sunk costs. Because alternative choice decisions always look toward the future, full-cost analyses—which typically rely on historical data—have some serious limitations. Nevertheless, even when we focus our analytical efforts on the future, we frequently are plagued by history, particularly when it presents itself in the form of sunk costs.

A *sunk cost* is an expenditure that was made in the past and that results in an expense on a full-cost report. But because this expenditure has already been incurred and the decision cannot be reversed, the expense is inappropriate for future considerations. Consequently it should be excluded from a differential cost analysis.

Sunk Costs and Intuition

For most people, the notion of sunk costs is very difficult to accept intuitively. Because sunk costs are present in many alternative choice decisions, however, you should be comfortable with them. The next problem illustrates their counterintuitive nature.

? PROBLEM

Two years ago, you purchased 200 shares of stock in ABC, a company traded on a major stock exchange. You paid $60 per share, for a total of $12,000. Today, the stock is selling for $45 a share. A trusted financial adviser has suggested that you purchase

100 shares of stock in XYZ, whose share price is $90. He tells you that he believes the future prospects of XYZ are far superior to those of ABC, and after some investigation, you decide that you agree with him. However, you have no additional cash to invest. Assuming that there are no transaction costs, should you sell your 200 shares of ABC for $9,000, thereby incurring a loss of $3,000, and use the funds to purchase 100 shares of XYZ?

ANSWER

If your decision was influenced by the $3,000 loss on the sale of ABC shares ($9,000 sales price minus $12,000 purchase price), you, like most people, have difficulty accepting the idea of sunk costs. The $3,000 is gone, and there is nothing you can do about it. Your choice now is between investing the available $9,000 you have in XYZ, or leaving it in ABC. If you believe that the future prospects of XYZ are superior to those of ABC, you should sell your ABC stock and purchase 100 shares of XYZ.

Sunk Costs in Organizational Settings

The classic example of a sunk cost in an organizational setting is depreciation, the technique used to spread the cost of an asset over its economic life. Although depreciation will appear on a full-cost report, accountants traditionally consider it inappropriate for differential cost analysis because it will not change regardless of the alternative chosen. That is, like the $12,000 you invested in ABC, it is a sunk cost.

Despite being a sunk cost, depreciation can play a role in a differential cost decision if we shift our perspective from the short term to the medium or long term—or what might be called the *strategic perspective*. To examine this idea, let's look first at the accounting view of sunk costs, and then examine them in a more strategic context.

Accounting View of Sunk Costs

Accountants typically consider sunk costs from a relatively nonstrategic perspective, meaning that they look at the remaining economic life of the assets that are involved in an alternative choice decision but exclude consideration of a decision to replace those assets. To illustrate the distinction, consider the following outsourcing decision.

PROBLEM

Newton General Hospital (NGH) has a machine with a book value (purchase price minus accumulated depreciation) of $40,000 that is depreciating at a rate of $10,000 per year. The machine is a highly specialized one, used only for a specific, esoteric type of test. Because of technological changes, the machine has a market value of $0. (A scrap dealer has offered to remove it at no charge, however.)

A private physician group practice has offered to perform the same tests (on NGH's site) for $15,000 a year. Is the book value of the machine a relevant cost to consider in deciding whether to accept the offer? Be as specific as you can in your reasoning.

ANSWER

The answer is no, because the $40,000 book value is the same whether or not NGH outsources the work. Leave aside for the moment the cost of the contract with the group practice. If NGH scraps the machine (that is, receives nothing for it), it would no longer have any depreciation on it, and its income statements for the next four years would look something like the following (assuming a financial surplus before depreciation of $100,000):

	Year 1	Year 2	Year 3	Year 4	Total
Surplus before depreciation	$100,000	$100,000	$100,000	$100,000	$400,000
Less: Depreciation	0	0	0	0	0
Surplus before disposal of assets	$100,000	$100,000	$100,000	$100,000	$400,000
Less: Loss on disposal of machine	40,000	0	0	0	40,000
NET SURPLUS	$60,000	$100,000	$100,000	$100,000	$360,000

If NGH continues with the existing situation (that is, if it does not outsource the work), it would have entries such as the following for each of the four years of the remaining life of the machine:

	Year 1	Year 2	Year 3	Year 4	Total
Surplus before depreciation	$100,000	$100,000	$100,000	$100,000	$400,000
Less: Depreciation	10,000	10,000	10,000	10,000	40,000
Surplus before disposal of assets	$90,000	$90,000	$90,000	$90,000	$360,000
Less: Loss on disposal of machine	0	0	0	0	0
NET SURPLUS	$90,000	$90,000	$90,000	$90,000	$360,000

In either case, net surplus for the four-year period is $360,000, and the machine expense is $40,000. The only difference is that in the first alternative, NGH incurs the expense in a single year, whereas in the second alternative, the expense is spread out over four years.

If NGH were a for-profit entity, and if we were being completely accurate, we would consider, as a differential item, the time value of the cash generated from an earlier reduction in income taxes in the first alternative. For purposes of simplicity—and because most hospitals are nonprofit—this calculation has been excluded. Similarly, if NGH can sell the machine today for, say, $12,000, then the $12,000 salvage value is a differential item: it is cash NGH will receive if it outsources that it would not have received otherwise. The operating statements then would look as follows:

	Year 1	Year 2	Year 3	Year 4	Total
Surplus before depreciation	$100,000	$100,000	$100,000	$100,000	$400,000
Less: Depreciation	0	0	0	0	0
Surplus before disposal of assets	$100,000	$100,000	$100,000	$100,000	$400,000
Proceeds from sale of machine	12,000	0	0	0	12,000
Less: Book value of machine	(40,000)	0	0	0	(40,000)
NET SURPLUS	$72,000	$100,000	$100,000	$100,000	$372,000

The fact that NGH sold the machine changes the impact of the transaction on its surplus, but it does not change the fact that the book value of the machine was reduced by $40,000. The $40,000 is the sunk cost.

Because the $40,000 book value of the machine is a sunk cost, accountants do not include it in a differential cost analysis that focuses on the short term. Rather, they look only at the out-of-pocket expenses that would be eliminated as a result of outsourcing and compare them to the cost of the subcontract. These items would affect the "surplus before depreciation" figure shown earlier. In this case, if NGH could reduce its annual out-of-pocket (that is, nondepreciation) expenses associated with the tests by more than $15,000 (the price of the contract), then, other things being equal, outsourcing would be financially beneficial.

Implications for Differential Cost Analysis

The example just given has some important implications for the accounting approach to a differential cost analysis. Specifically, from a pure accounting perspective, an alternative choice decision (whether or not to outsource, in the NGH case) excludes consideration of the book value of any equipment that is involved (here, $40,000). The book value is not relevant because it would be the same whatever the organization does. The amount the organization could receive from selling the equipment (here, $12,000) is a relevant item, however, because it is differential, and because it occurs only if the organization accepts the subcontractor's offer. (If the organization were going to dispose of the machine anyway, then the $12,000 would be nondifferential with respect to the decision under consideration.)

Conceptually, then, in assessing an outsourcing decision, an organization looks at both the costs that would be eliminated and those that would be added if it were to outsource the work, as well as any revenue that would be received as a result of an action, such as selling the machine in the NGH case. In the category of eliminated costs, NGH would use all existing variable costs, including such items as variable labor and supplies associated with the tests. It also would include in the computation any fixed costs that would be eliminated if it outsourced the work (such as the salary of a machine operator). But from an accounting perspective, the book value of the machine that would be eliminated is not differential. This same principle can be applied to any other asset an organization would dispose of if it accepted a subcontractor's offer, such as an inventory that would become obsolete if the organization began to outsource some work that it historically had done itself.

And, of course, the revenue from the disposal of an asset is a one-time cash inflow, in contrast to most other items in a differential analysis, which are ongoing. We thus must be careful to include this revenue only in year 1.

The Strategic Perspective

Although depreciation is a sunk cost and therefore a nondifferential item in any alternative choice decision, we treat it differently when the decision-making perspective is more strategic—that is, when the time period under consideration extends beyond the remaining years of a machine's economic life. From the strategic perspective, the question is, "What will the organization's costs and revenues be over an indefinite (or at least long) time period?" In answering this question, the amount of depreciation can assist in the analysis.

The strategic perspective may be appropriate in decisions about both outsourcing and eliminating a product or product line. Let's look first at another outsourcing situation, and then at the decision to keep or drop an unprofitable product line.

The Outsourcing Situation

Senior management, in making a decision to outsource an activity, typically is unconcerned with revenue. Instead, senior management compares costs under two scenarios: performing the activity itself, or contracting with another organization to perform it.

PROBLEM

The Magnetic Resonance Company (MRC) manufactures a line of body scanners with automatic shutoff switches that are activated when the patient is wearing a metal object. The shutoff switches are made in a special department that uses some highly specialized equipment. The annual full costs of the auto switch department are as follows:

Direct labor	$150,000
Materials	70,000
Department manager	50,000
Depreciation	30,000
Allocated overhead	20,000
TOTAL	$320,000

MRC has received an offer from a local firm that specializes in automatic switch devices to manufacture the same annual volume of shutoff switches at an annual cost of $280,000. The contract is for five years. If MRC accepts this offer, it will be able to totally eliminate the auto switch department. In assessing this offer, management has determined the following:

- Although the machines used in the department have five years of depreciation remaining, they are technologically obsolete and have no market value (they can be removed at no charge, but that is all). They can, however, be used for another five years before they need to be replaced.
- No inflation or salary increases are expected.
- The department manager is willing to accept early retirement (at no additional cost to the company) if the department closes. That is, her salary will be eliminated, and she will draw her retirement income from the company's pension fund, which is a separate entity.
- None of the allocated overhead is differential; that is, it will be reallocated to other departments if the auto switch department is eliminated.
- The expected number of automatic switches needed for each of the five years of the contract is well known and will be the same as it was during the year when the figures given earlier were computed.
- The local firm making the offer has an excellent reputation for quality and delivery.

Identify the relevant costs to consider in the analysis of this outsourcing decision, along with your reasoning.

ANSWER

If MRC were to adopt the traditional approach to this analysis, it would use the following costs:

Savings from Outsourcing

Direct labor	$150,000
Materials	70,000
Department manager	50,000
Depreciation (sunk)	0
Allocated overhead (nondifferential)	0
TOTAL	$270,000
Less: Cost of contract	280,000
NET FINANCIAL BENEFIT (LOSS)	$(10,000)

If MRC adopts a more strategic perspective and includes depreciation in the analysis (even though it is a sunk cost), it would use the following costs:

Savings from Outsourcing

Direct labor	$150,000
Materials	70,000
Department manager	50,000
Depreciation	30,000
Allocated overhead (nondifferential)	0
TOTAL	$300,000
Less: Cost of contract	280,000
NET FINANCIAL BENEFIT (LOSS)	$20,000

PROBLEM

In the previous problem, all else being equal, under the first cost analysis the organization would reject the offer, whereas under the second analysis it would accept it. What should management do?

ANSWER

A short-term, cash-maximizing perspective would lead management to reject the offer. The organization would save only $270,000 in expenses and spend $280,000 for the contract. The traditional approach, which excludes sunk costs, most certainly would lead to this conclusion.

From a longer-term, strategic perspective, the focus shifts to what might be called steady-state operations. This focus recognizes that at some point the organization will need to replace the equipment, and thus the analysis includes depreciation as a surrogate for the cost of the replacement equipment (in fact, some analysts would use the *estimated* depreciation on the replacement equipment). Under these circumstances, management would accept the offer because it would improve financial performance over the long term.

Ideally, of course, management would wait five years to accept the contract. Much could change in the interim, however, that would affect the decision. More important, this option most likely is not available.

Keeping or Dropping a Product Line

In deciding to keep or drop a product line, senior management must carefully assess the behavior of both revenue and costs under the scenario that involves dropping the product line and must compare these results with the revenue and costs involved in keeping it. Again, sunk costs present some analytical difficulties.

PROBLEM

Sunshine Laboratories conducts a variety of blood tests. The annual revenue and full costs of the department that does complete blood counts (CBCs) look as follows:

Sales revenue (net)		$600,000
Less:		
Direct labor	$200,000	
Supplies	260,000	
Department administration	120,000	
Depreciation	80,000	
Allocated overhead	110,000	770,000
PROFIT (LOSS)		$(170,000)

The accountants have recommended that the CBC department be discontinued because it is losing money. The manager of the department has asked his staff assistant to prepare a contribution income statement. How would you construct this statement using the data just given? Assume that direct labor is a fixed cost.

ANSWER

A contribution income statement for the CBC department would look as follows:

Sales revenue (net)	$600,000	
Less: Variable costs (supplies)	260,000	
Margin (for fixed and overhead costs)		$340,000
Less department fixed costs:		
Direct labor	200,000	
Department administration	120,000	
Depreciation	80,000	400,000
Contribution to overhead costs		$(60,000)
Less: Allocated overhead costs		110,000
PROFIT (LOSS)		$(170,000)

PROBLEM

Assume now that you are the department manager. How would you react to this contribution income statement? Can you prepare an argument that the department is indeed financially beneficial to the company despite its negative contribution?

ANSWER

If you argue that the depreciation expense is a sunk cost and choose a short-term perspective for the analysis (that is, one short enough that the machines do not need to be replaced), the contribution income statement would look as follows:

Sales revenue (net)	$600,000	
Less: Variable costs (materials)	260,000	
Margin (for fixed and overhead costs)		$340,000
Less department fixed costs:		
Direct labor	200,000	
Department administration	120,000	320,000
Contribution to overhead costs		$20,000
Less: Allocated overhead costs		110,000
PROFIT (LOSS)		$(90,000)

As the department manager, you could argue that the CBC department is making a contribution to the recovery of overhead costs, at least in the short run, and that it therefore makes sense to keep it.

PROBLEM

As senior management, how would you react to this argument?

ANSWER

Senior management would probably focus on the following issues:

1. In the very short run (the next six months or so), it makes sense to keep the department because it is contributing $20,000 in cash to help cover the laboratory's overhead costs.

2. In the medium run (the next year or so), we need to answer two questions:
   - By discontinuing the department, could we eliminate more than $20,000 of the allocated overhead costs? Suppose, for example, that there is someone in the administrative service center who works full-time on matters related to the employees of the CBC department, and that this person's salary plus fringe benefits totals $30,000. It might be possible to eliminate this position and save the $30,000. This savings would more than offset the $20,000 contribution, making it financially beneficial to discontinue the department.
   - If we are capacity constrained (that is, if we cannot add a new product without discontinuing an existing one), can we find some other product line to pursue that would generate more than $20,000 in contribution? The difference between the contribution from this new product line and the $20,000 becomes the *opportunity cost* of keeping the CBC department.

3. In the long run, can we find another product line to pursue that would cover all of its costs, including depreciation and allocated overhead? If so, and if none of our other departments is affected, then we should pursue that new product line. Again, the difference between the contribution from the new product line and that of the existing one represents an opportunity cost—what we are giving up to have the existing product line.

opportunity cost
The cost of an option not chosen. If we could earn $20,000 in contribution from selling product A and $30,000 in contribution from selling product B, and we choose to sell product A, the difference ($10,000) is the opportunity cost of selling product A.

More generally, the issue of opportunity cost is an important ingredient in a differential cost analysis. We always must keep in mind the fact that whatever we are doing—whatever programs we are offering—represents choices not to offer other programs. Thus, we always must ask the question, "If not this, then what else might we do with the space and other resources?"

Sporadic Use of the Strategic Perspective

Traditionally the strategic perspective has been used only when an organization is deciding whether to purchase replacement equipment. At that time, management looks at the annual cash flows associated with the proposed investment in new assets and compares them with the amount of the proposed investment. (Chapter 8 discusses techniques for performing an analysis of this sort.) The problem with this approach is that it occurs only when an equipment replacement decision is under consideration, but not when an outsourcing offer or another alternative choice decision presents itself. As a result, the equipment replacement decision is made in relative isolation.

The traditional approach to the strategic perspective also is incomplete if multiple fixed assets are involved. If a particular product line uses several assets, for example, it is unlikely that all of these assets will require replacement simultaneously. Applying a strategic perspective to the replacement of a single asset when a product line uses several assets will result in a partial analysis only. To analyze the situation fully, senior management must consider either the current or the forecasted depreciation amounts for all assets associated with the product line.

To correct for these shortcomings, senior management must consider the strategic perspective whenever an opportunity to outsource presents itself, or when it is considering the replacement of one piece of equipment in a department with multiple fixed assets. Many managers will include depreciation in the analysis so as to approximate a "typical year's" costs. Because the continuation of the product line or activity requires eventual replacement of all machines or other assets, including depreciation helps management assess the situation more holistically.

Precision of Depreciation

Clearly, depreciation is not a precise measure. Because inflation and new technology will change the cost of a replacement asset, depreciation provides only a rough approximation of steady-state operations. Nevertheless, having a rough approximation is better than completely excluding the cost of the associated assets.

Growing Importance of the Strategic Perspective

As organizations develop strategic alliances with their suppliers, as some health care organizations are doing, and as their daily operations become more and more automated (that is, as the number of fixed assets increases), the strategic perspective takes on greater significance in alternative choice decisions. As a result, it is becoming increasingly important to move away from the more traditional approach that excludes depreciation (as a sunk cost) and to focus on the longer-term implications for the organization's strategy.

Nonquantitative Considerations

Any alternative choice decision involves factors that cannot be quantified easily, if at all, but that can tip the balance in one direction or another, frequently overriding the financial analysis. This is especially true when the financial analysis indicates that the approaches under consideration have roughly similar cost or revenue implications.

In the decision to keep or drop a product (or product line), nonquantitative considerations usually include product interdependencies—that is, the extent to which revenues from some of the organization's other products are dependent on the product being considered for elimination. In some hospitals, for example, the pediatrics department loses money, but most hospitals would find it unwise to eliminate pediatrics as a product line. Many other more profitable product lines serve adults who have become familiar with the hospital because of taking their children to the pediatrics department.

In an outsourcing decision, nonquantitative considerations typically include such factors as quality, service, delivery, and vendor reputation. They may also include market issues, such as the difficulty and cost of switching from one vendor to another if the initial relationship does not work out. A health care provider that outsources snowplowing services for its parking lot, for example, typically has an easy time switching from one vendor to another. There are many individuals with pickup trucks and snowplowing blades who can provide this service. Conversely, a hospital that outsources some highly specialized laboratory testing and then is dissatisfied with the vendor's performance may have difficulty finding a replacement vendor.

Another nonquantitative consideration in outsourcing is the cost of switching back to internal service provision. Once an organization outsources an activity, it may eliminate the associated facilities, equipment, and trained personnel. If it later wishes to resume internal service provision, it may find that purchasing (or leasing) new facilities and equipment as well as training new personnel are quite costly. The more costly these items are, the more important the nature of the market for vendors becomes. In a highly competitive market, an organization that is dissatisfied with one vendor can simply hire another. In a more oligopolistic market, however, it may be difficult to hire a new vendor. Under these circumstances, an organization that has eliminated its capacity for internal manufacture may find itself at the mercy of its vendor. Rarely is this desirable.

These issues are summarized in figure 4.1. As the figure suggests, as one moves northeast and toward the rear of the cube, the *outsourcing risk* increases. The impact of poor vendor performance on patients or clients is greater, the market is more oligopolistic, and the switching costs are higher. This does not suggest that outsourcing a high-risk activity should be avoided, only that the vendor selection process needs to be more rigorous, and the vendor management process more thorough.

outsourcing risk
The chance that an outsourcing activity will have problems. It is a combination of patient (or client) sensitivity to the service's quality, the competitive nature of the market for the outsourced activity, and the cost of switching back to internal production or engaging the services of another vendor.

Allocated Overhead

Additional complexities are introduced into the differential cost analysis when overhead costs are associated with the particular effort being analyzed. There are two such complexities, each of which relates to one of the full-cost accounting issues discussed in chapter 2: allocation bases and the stepdown sequence.

Misleading Allocation Bases

Although many health care organizations, especially hospitals, attempt to measure the use of support center resources as accurately as possible, situations still occur in which a given support center's basis of allocation does

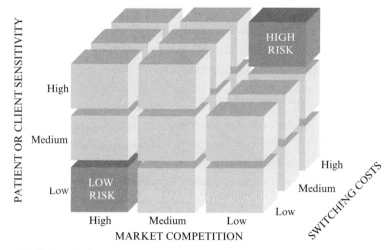

Figure 4.1 Outsourcing Risk

not accurately reflect the actual use of its resources by receiving cost centers. This becomes an important consideration in alternative choice decisions.

PROBLEM

Homecare (the organization from chapter 2) is considering the possibility of dropping its patient education product line. If it does so, it will be able to eliminate all the direct costs of the patient education mission center. Because the center uses 1,000 square feet of space, it is allocated $6,800 of housekeeping costs. What do you think will happen to these costs if the patient education product line is eliminated? How does the allocation basis for housekeeping help management understand the behavior of housekeeping's costs?

ANSWER

It is likely that some of the costs in the housekeeping support center are differential with respect to the number of square feet. It is highly unlikely, however, that the entire $6,800 will be eliminated if Homecare eliminates the patient education product line. The allocation basis for the costs of the housekeeping support center therefore does not give an accurate picture of the behavior of that support center's costs.

To analyze the behavior of the housekeeping support center's costs, we must determine the nature of each cost: variable, semivariable, step function, or fixed. With this information, we can assess with reasonable accuracy what will happen to costs in the housekeeping department if we eliminate the patient education product line.

In short, if an organization outsources some services, or if it discontinues a particular product line, it probably will find that some of the support center costs allocated to the mission center in question will decrease. But in most instances, few of those support center costs will actually be eliminated. Only the variable, the semivariable, and perhaps some of the step-function costs allocated to the mission center from the support center will be eliminated. The remaining costs will be reallocated to other cost centers.

EXAMPLE

Consider the expenses of an administration support center whose allocation basis is salary dollars. A reduction of staff in a given mission center will lead to a reduction in total salaries in that mission center. Because administration costs are allocated on the basis of salary dollars, the amount of administration costs allocated to the mission center will be reduced. It is highly unlikely, however, that there will be a comparable reduction in the costs associated with the administration support center. Thus, rather than being reduced, most administration costs will be reallocated to other cost centers.

Effects of the Stepdown Sequence

As discussed in chapter 2, in preparing a stepdown analysis, the costs in each support center are allocated to all remaining support and mission centers. The total costs allocated from each support center include both the center's direct and assigned indirect costs plus the costs that were allocated to it from previous support centers in the stepdown sequence. As a result, the total costs of the support centers that come late in the sequence will include costs from support centers above them.

EXAMPLE

If the social service department is far down in the stepdown sequence, the total social service costs allocated to a particular mission center will have a significant allocated component (for administration, housekeeping, laundry and linen, and so on). It may be possible to reduce the use of social workers in a mission center by reducing the number of patients treated or changing the treatment plans. However, the impact of the cost reductions in social services will be overstated if the organization uses the fully allocated social service totals (including previously allocated support center costs). This occurs because the costs being allocated from the social services cost center contain costs from a variety of other support centers that may not be affected at all by the reduction in the mission center's volume of activity or its use of social workers.

Now, test your understanding of the material just discussed by analyzing the following problem.

PROBLEM

Concord Rehabilitation Hospital treats patients with a variety of chronic conditions. Treatment in its physical rehabilitation department involves several exercise machines. The unit currently performs 10,000 rehabilitation sessions a year, for which it charges $140 each. The department's exercise unit has twelve stations, each of which contains highly sophisticated equipment. Total depreciation on the equipment is $120,000 per year, and other fixed costs are $500,000 per year. Variable costs (such as disposable supplies and electricity usage) are $80 per training session. Service center costs allocated to the unit total $330,000 a year. The hospital's accountants have suggested that the unit should be discontinued and the patients referred elsewhere for treatment because the unit is losing $350,000 a year, calculated as follows:

Revenue (10,000 × $140)		$1,400,000
Less: Variable costs (10,000 × $80)	$800,000	
Depreciation	120,000	
Other fixed costs	500,000	1,420,000
Contribution		$(20,000)
Less: Allocated service center costs		330,000
PROFIT (LOSS)		$(350,000)

Do you agree with the accountants' suggestion and calculations? If so, why? If not, prepare your own analysis using the data provided.

ANSWER

If the time perspective is a relatively long one, and if the "other fixed costs" are all associated with the exercise unit, the accountants are correct that the unit is losing money. Unless strategic reasons dictate its continuation (perhaps because senior management believes it is important for the hospital to treat a patient's entire set of needs), it should at least be evaluated against other activities that might be more financially beneficial.

If, however, the time perspective is a short one—in this case, one in which the machines can continue to be used rather than being replaced—then the unit is making a positive contribution to the hospital, as follows:

Revenue	$1,400,000
Less: Variable costs	800,000
Margin	$600,000
Less: Fixed costs (other than depreciation)	500,000
CONTRIBUTION TO HOSPITAL OVERHEAD	$100,000

This situation arises because, as discussed earlier, depreciation is a sunk cost and thus is irrelevant to the decision to discontinue the unit in the short run. Unless a substitute activity with a higher contribution can be found, the hospital is financially better off with the unit than without it.

Before reaching a final conclusion, however, management needs to examine the allocation of support center costs. If the hospital could eliminate more than $100,000 of these costs by eliminating the exercise unit, it is financially better off without the unit. Assume, for example, that by discontinuing the unit, the hospital could save $120,000 of the $330,000 of allocated support center costs. In that case, by discontinuing the unit, the hospital loses $100,000 in contribution but is able to eliminate $120,000 in support center costs. It is thus $20,000 better off financially by eliminating the unit.

The Analytical Effort

Recognizing these complexities and incorporating them into the analytical effort is one of the most challenging aspects of differential cost accounting. Determining which costs are indeed differential and how they behave can be very tricky, particularly when a stepdown cost report is the principal source of information. There are no easy answers to this dilemma, just a lot of hard work and careful analytical thinking.

You are now ready to work through the practice case for this chapter. The Narcolarm case allows you to analyze differential costs. The solution is in appendix B at the end of the book.

KEY TERMS

Alternative choice decisions	Opportunity cost
Differential costs	Outsourcing risk
	Sunk cost

To Bear in Mind

1. An important nonquantitative factor in outsourcing is the risk an organization runs if the vendor does not perform according to expectations. Outsourcing risk can be assessed along the three dimensions of market competition, patient (or client) sensitivity, and switching costs.

An activity that is outsourced in a high-risk environment (where there is high patient [or client] sensitivity, limited competition, and high switching costs) must be managed much more carefully than one in a low-risk environment.

2. When making an alternative choice decision, you might try, as a first step in your analysis, to structure the financial information in terms of a contribution income statement, as follows:

Total revenue	$XXX
Less: Variable costs	XXX
Equals: Margin (for fixed and overhead costs)	$XXX
Less: Department fixed costs	XXX
Equals: Contribution to overhead costs	$XXX
Less: Allocated overhead costs	XXX
Equals: PROFIT (LOSS)	$XXX

You will frequently find that this sort of analysis sheds some interesting and useful light on the financial aspects of the decision.

Test Yourself

1. "If a cost is fixed, it is nondifferential." Comment and explain your thinking.

2. You have spent $15,000 so far on tuition in a two-year graduate program, and have finished the first year. Because of a tuition increase, the second year will cost you $16,000. You have just received a very attractive job offer—one that you were hoping to get after graduation, and one that, if you don't take now, will not be available when you graduate. If you accept the offer, you will need to drop out of the program. A friend has told you that you are crazy to drop out of the program because you have already paid $15,000 in tuition. What role, if any, should this $15,000 play in your decision to accept or reject the offer?

3. What is the difference between the traditional accounting perspective associated with an alternative choice decision and a more strategic perspective?

4. What are the three categories of nonquantitative factors that should be considered in an outsourcing decision?

5. Besides outsourcing, what are the other two major types of alternative choice decisions?

PRACTICE CASE

NARCOLARM

Not long after completing her fellowship in neurology, Mary Lou Black, MD, became quite disenchanted with the practice of medicine. Shortly after she began her private practice, she was beset with more administrative and regulatory reporting requirements than she had ever thought possible. Moreover, the hospital at which she had admitting privileges began to insist that all its physicians participate in determining clinical treatment pathways for patients with the most common diagnoses, a practice that Dr. Black found completely distasteful.

During her residency and for the years that followed, she had specialized in the treatment of narcolepsy, a neurological disorder resulting in individuals' falling asleep during periods of high emotional activity or stress and occasionally during periods of relative inactivity. Although drug treatments had been found that would allow narcoleptics to lead relatively normal lives, the one area where they frequently encountered difficulty was in driving. For obvious reasons, if a narcoleptic's drugs failed to work while the individual was driving, the results could be fatal. As a result, many narcoleptics were very reluctant to drive.

During her work with narcoleptics, Dr. Black had begun experimenting with a device that could be used to keep them awake while driving. The device was quite simple: it was a small alarm, powered by a miniature battery, and could be inserted in an elongated plastic case that hooked over the driver's ear, much like a hearing aid. When the driver's head was erect, the device was silent, but as soon as the driver's head began to tip forward or backward, as it would if he or she were falling asleep, the alarm would sound a shrill tone directly into the ear. If the head did not return to an erect position within three seconds, the device would administer a small electric shock.

Her increasing disenchantment with medical practice coupled with the potential for her "Narcolarm," as she called the device, led her to resign from her position on the hospital staff and devote full attention to the invention. She obtained a patent for it and found an investor to provide the capital needed to produce, market, and sell the Narcolarm. In conjunction with her efforts to get her production and marketing activities under way, there were several questions that she thought important to answer. First, at her anticipated sales price of $10 per unit, how many Narcolarms would she need to sell to cover all of her costs? Second, if she wanted to earn a modest before-tax profit of, say, $60,000 in her first year of operations, how many units would she need to sell? These decisions were complicated by her assessment of the market for the Narcolarm. Dr. Black estimated that if the Narcolarm were priced appropriately, her annual sales could be on the order of 25,000 units. If this were the case, she wondered how much she would have to charge to cover all of her costs and how far this price was from her anticipated price of $10 per unit.

While pondering these matters, Dr. Black received a phone call from a local businessman who informed her that he was interested in manufacturing the electronic shock devices that were inserted in the Narcolarms. He told her that he would charge her a fixed amount of $7,500 per year for his work. Dr. Black calculated that by having the business-man's company manufacture the devices, she would be able to reduce her variable costs by $0.50 per unit.

Narcolarm's estimated annual costs were as follows:

	Fixed	Variable (per Unit)
Direct labor	$110,000	$2.30
Direct materials		5.90
Power	4,000	
Rental of plant and equipment	100,000	
Maintenance	20,000	0.20
Administration and general	66,000	0.10
TOTAL	$300,000	$8.50

Suggested Cases

Boston University Medical Center Hospital

Lakeside Hospital

Assignment

1. How many units must Narcolarm produce and sell to break even? How many units would the organization have to produce and sell to cover all costs and earn a profit before taxes of $60,000?

2. If sales of 25,000 units a year can be reached, how much must Dr. Black charge per Narcolarm to break even?

3. What price should Dr. Black use for a Narcolarm?

4. Based on cost considerations only, should Dr. Black accept the local businessman's offer?

5. In addition to cost information, what else should Dr. Black consider in her decision to accept or reject the offer?

6. What do you think of Dr. Black's venture?

Notes

1. Clearly there are complicating issues, such as severance pay and unemployment insurance. These factors would need to be included in a complete analysis.

CHAPTER 5

ACTIVITY-BASED COSTING

I n chapter 2 we looked at some of the basic decisions that are made in a full-cost accounting system: defining a cost object, determining cost centers, distinguishing between direct and indirect costs, selecting allocation bases for support center costs, choosing an allocation method, and allocating support center costs to mission centers.

The discussion in chapter 2 took us through what is called stage 1 of the cost accounting effort—to the point where all costs reside in mission centers. We also touched briefly on stage 2, where a mission center's costs are attached to the products that it worked on or delivered. In doing so, we identified the distinction between a process system and a job order system.

Stage 2 can be a tricky part of the cost accounting effort and, if not carefully designed, can produce misleading information. Unfortunately, many health care organizations, particularly hospitals, spend considerable time and effort selecting precise bases for allocating support center costs to mission centers in stage 1, but then take a simplistic approach to attaching a mission center's costs to its outputs in stage 2. This can produce inaccurate information about the full cost of each of the mission center's products.

Organization of the Chapter

This chapter discusses ways to improve stage 2 of the cost accounting effort. It begins with a discussion of health care's stage 2 challenge, and then provides a functional classification of manufacturing costs, discussing their applicability to health care. It next describes the concept of an overhead rate, using it as a segue to a discussion of activity-based costing. Finally, it introduces the idea that

LEARNING OBJECTIVES

On completing this chapter, you should know about

- Some additional cost accounting terminology

- Health care's stage 2 cost accounting challenge

- The concepts of activity-based costing and overhead cost drivers

- The distinctions among facility-sustaining, product-sustaining, batch-related, and unit-level activities in an activity-based costing system

- How to use multiple overhead rates to attach manufacturing overhead to products during stage 2

there is an important link between the measurement of costs in a full-cost accounting system and an organization's pricing policies or product cross-subsidization decisions.

Health Care's Stage 2 Challenge

To understand the importance of stage 2 of the cost accounting effort, begin by analyzing this problem:

PROBLEM

The renal dialysis unit of Lakeside Hospital had direct costs of $1,500,000 and allocated support center costs of $600,000, for full costs of $2,100,000. During the year in which it incurred these costs, it performed 6,000 dialysis treatments. What is the full cost of a dialysis treatment? What kind of cost system are you using (in terms of the types of cost systems discussed in chapter 2)?

ANSWER

Because the department's only product is a dialysis treatment, the costs can be attached to a treatment simply by dividing the total costs by the total number of treatments. As a result, the full cost of a dialysis treatment is $350 ($2,100,000 ÷ 6,000 treatments). This is a process system—one in which all output units worked on in the cost center are more or less identical.

But now consider a more complex example. The Radiology Department at Lakeside Hospital had direct costs of $2,900,000 and was allocated support center costs of $970,000, for total costs of $3,870,000. If we were to divide $3,870,000 by the total number of procedures the department conducted during the accounting period, we would have a meaningless average. The average would be meaningless because unlike the dialysis unit, the radiology department produces a heterogeneous mix of outputs: chest X-rays, joint X-rays, CT scans, magnetic resonance imaging, and so forth. This is clearly more like a job order system.

The department could rather easily develop a job ticket for each procedure that would record such items as technician labor and supplies (such as a contrast medium). These are all direct costs of the department and are contained in the $2,900,000 figure. Some of them are also direct costs of the procedures. That is, it is relatively easy to determine the technician time (and hence cost) as well as the cost of a contrast medium and any other supplies used for a given procedure.

But the job ticket doesn't completely solve our problems. What about the costs of the supervisor in the department who doesn't work on the procedures? Or the department's scheduling personnel? Or any of a variety of other people in the department who don't work directly on the procedures? These are all direct costs of the department—they are unambiguously associated with the department—but they are indirect costs with regard to any given procedure, and they will not show up on the job ticket. And yet, if we are to know the full cost of a given procedure, we must find a way to attach a portion of these costs to it.

And then there is the $970,000 in support center costs that were allocated to the department during stage 1. These costs are indirect with regard to both the department and its procedures, but we nevertheless must find a way to attach a portion of them to each procedure.

So, if the department conducted, say, 3,000 CT scans during the year, how should we go about attaching an appropriate portion of these various overhead costs to each CT scan to calculate the full cost of a scan? Answering that question is the subject of this chapter.

The Ratio of Costs to Charges

To address the question just posed, many health care organizations, especially hospitals, use a ratio of costs to charges (RCC). They take the sum of a year's charges for a mission center; compute the center's full costs for that year (that is, complete stage 1); and divide total costs by total charges to determine the RCC. They then determine the cost of any given product in that center by multiplying its charge by the RCC.

Although this approach gives a reasonably accurate full-cost figure for a large aggregation of products, it can be extremely misleading for any single one. Research has suggested that the RCC approach to determining a hospital's costs is about 95 percent accurate at the product line level and about 85 percent accurate for a diagnosis-related group (DRG).[1] Below that level of aggregation, its accuracy is questionable, and it is extremely unreliable for any single product or service provided by a mission center.

The following example illustrates how inaccurate the RCC method can be for a single product or service:

EXAMPLE

We wish to compare the costs of two ancillary tests between a teaching hospital and a community hospital. Assume that identical ancillary tests are conducted for a patient in both hospitals: one "simple" test and one "esoteric" test. Because the patients in the two facilities receive the same tests, there should be no difference in cost, unless of course one hospital is more efficient or has lower factor prices (such as wage rates) than the other.

Assume that the two hospitals are equally efficient and pay the same factor prices. If this is the case, there should be no cost differences between the two facilities. Thus the "true cost" of each test is the same in both hospitals.

For various reasons, however, the two hospitals use different "strategic markups," resulting in different charge structures, but these differences net out at the department level. That is, the *average* markup percentage is the same in each hospital's laboratory. Assume that we have the following data:

	True Cost	Average Markup	Strategic Markup (or Markdown)	Total Markup	Charge	RCC*
Teaching Hospital						
Simple test	$10.00	108.3%	+291.7%	400.0%	$50.00	0.20
Esoteric test	50.00	108.3%	−58.3%	50.0%	75.00	0.67
Department total	$60.00	108.3%	0.0%	108.3%	$125.00	0.48
Community Hospital						
Simple test	$10.00	108.3%	−8.3%	100.0%	$20.00	0.50
Esoteric test	50.00	108.3%	+1.7%	110.0%	105.00	0.48
Department total	$60.00	108.3%	0.0%	108.3%	$125.00	0.48

*Ratio of costs to charges = True cost ÷ Charge.

As a result, the reported costs (using the average RCC of 0.48) multiplied by the charge for each test are as follows:

	Simple Test	Esoteric Test
Teaching hospital	(0.48 × $50) = $24.00	(0.48 × $75) = $36.00
Community hospital	(0.48 × $20) = $9.60	(0.48 × $105) = $50.40

In short, when we compare the *true costs* of the four tests, we find that, as we would expect, the teaching hospital is no more expensive than the community hospital; that is, its use of resources is exactly the same. However, as shown here, the difference between the true cost and the RCC-based cost differs considerably:

	True Cost	RCC-Based Cost	Difference
Simple Test			
Teaching hospital	$10.00	$24.00	$14.00
Community hospital	$10.00	$9.60	$(0.40)
Esoteric Test			
Teaching hospital	$50.00	$36.00	$(14.00)
Community hospital	$50.00	$50.40	$0.40

In general, the use of RCCs will produce misleading information about the true cost of a given test or procedure. Therefore, it is not useful for determining the cost of the services received by a single patient or even a small group of patients.

Solving the Problem

Hospitals and other health care providers that wish to measure their costs more accurately—for competitive bidding purposes, better cost management, or any other reason—can learn a great deal from the cost accounting methodologies and techniques developed over the past twenty-five years or so in the manufacturing sector. To explore this issue, we first need to understand the typical way that costs are attached to products in a manufacturing organization that produces a heterogeneous mix of outputs.

A Functional Classification of Manufacturing Costs

Let's begin by defining some new cost accounting terminology. In a typical manufacturing environment (as we'll see later, much of what goes on in hospitals and other health care organizations falls into this general category), several elements make up the cost of the product. These are shown in figure 5.1 (using health care examples) and are discussed in the paragraphs that follow.

Direct Manufacturing Costs

Direct manufacturing costs consist of direct labor and direct materials. Direct materials (sometimes called raw materials) become part of the product; examples are steel, wires, upholstery, and plastic in an automobile. Direct labor comprises the individuals who lay hands on the product (or on the machines that produce the product). These people mix ingredients in an ice cream factory, tighten bolts in an automobile assembly plant, operate the robots in an electric motor manufacturing plant, and so on.

Cost Type	DESCRIPTION	EXAMPLES
Direct	These costs are unambiguously associated with the cost center where the cost objects are produced. They can be attached rather easily to any given cost object by using . . .	
Direct labor	. . . time and motion studies.	Technicians in a radiology department, nurses on an inpatient ward
Direct materials	. . . material usage studies.	Reagents in a laboratory; medical supplies on an inpatient ward
Other direct	. . . machine or equipment studies.	Depreciation on a piece of equipment that is used for a single cost object
Indirect		Material handlers , inspectors, supervisors
Indirect labor	These costs also are unambiguously associated with the cost center where the cost objects are produced, but they *cannot* be attached directly to a given cost object.	Cleaning solvents for machines, recordkeeping supplies
Indirect materials		Depreciation on the department's office computers
Other indirect		
Allocated support center costs	These costs are allocated to the cost center from the organization's support centers. They also cannot be attached directly to a given cost object.	Maintenance, laundry, or housekeeping costs that are allocated to the department

Figure 5.1 Manufacturing Cost Terminology

Indirect Manufacturing Costs

manufacturing overhead (MOH) Costs other than direct material and direct labor, such as indirect material, indirect labor, and other costs that are associated with the manufacturing effort but that cannot be associated directly with a product that is manufactured. Examples include utilities, depreciation, and taxes.

Indirect manufacturing costs, sometimes called *manufacturing overhead (MOH)*, consist of costs that are direct for the department but are not directly associated with a unit of output, plus the support center costs that were allocated to the department during stage 1. The first category of costs includes labor, materials, and some other costs not directly associated with a product. Indirect labor consists of a variety of people who are needed for the operation of a factory or department but who do not actually work on the product, such as supervisors, maintenance personnel, schedulers, and material handlers.

Indirect materials consist of two kinds of items: (1) those that are needed for the smooth operation of the department but that don't go into the product, such as cleaning solvents, rags, and paper supplies, and (2) those that go into the finished product but are so small that it is not worth keeping track of them separately, such as grease on ball bearings or glue in toys. Other indirect costs include equipment depreciation and the expenses associated with a variety of items needed to operate a factory, such as heat, electricity, maintenance, insurance, and rent.

The second category comprises the costs that were allocated to the mission center during stage 1 of the cost accounting effort. They include such items as central maintenance, property taxes, and building security.

In summary, a mission center's indirect manufacturing costs include (1) a variety of costs that are direct for the center but indirect with respect to the products it makes, and (2) the support center costs that are allocated to it during stage 1 of the full-cost allocation effort. The goal of stage 2 is to attach a fair share of these costs to each unit of output manu-factured in the mission center.

Applicability to Health Care

It's not too much of a stretch to see how these concepts can be applied to a health care setting. As in a factory, direct "manufacturing" costs comprise direct labor and direct materials. Direct materials include such items as pharmaceuticals, food, reagents in a laboratory, blood plasma in an operat-ing room, and contrast media in a radiology department. Direct labor costs are for the salaries and fringe benefits of the individuals who conduct the procedures in a radiology department, perform lab tests in the lab, operate on patients, care for them at the bedside, and so forth.

Indirect "manufacturing" costs in health care are similar to those in a factory. Examples of indirect labor involve people who schedule proce-dures in a radiology department, order medical supplies on a ward, sterilize instruments in an operating room, and so forth. Indirect materials may include drinking water in a ward, sutures for an operating room, and cleaning solvents in a lab. In addition, most hospitals and other health care organizations, unlike factories, include administrative, marketing, and other general items as part of their indirect manufacturing costs. These costs are contained in support centers and are allocated to mission centers during stage 1.

EXAMPLE

Consider the case of a hospital laboratory, which is a mission center—that is, it charges for its output (perhaps as a transfer price to other mission centers, such as surgery).[2] The tests it conducts are done in batches of, say, 10 to 100. In addi-tion to the direct costs of labor and materials, each batch of tests incurs two general categories of indirect costs:

1. Costs that are direct for the lab—that is, they are unambiguously associated with the lab—but indirect with respect to any given batch of tests, such as the salary of the lab's supervisor.
2. Costs that are allocated to the lab, such as housekeeping. Housekeeping services are provided to all cost centers (including the lab) by the house-keeping department, a support center. The lab is allocated its fair share of the housekeeping department's costs during stage 1.

If we wish to know the full cost of a batch of tests, we must find a way to attach a portion of both categories of indirect costs to it.

Some Terminology Cautions

As discussed in chapter 2, terminology in cost accounting can be confusing on occasion. Throughout this chapter, for example, the terms *manufacturing overhead* and *indirect manufacturing costs* mean the same thing. Accountants frequently use other terms synonymously too, such as *apply*, *allocate*, and *assign*. Many accounting terms tend to be used somewhat interchangeably in manufacturing organizations as well, and in every setting one must be careful to determine a term's precise meaning either from the context or by asking.

Computing a Product's Full Cost

To understand how we can attach indirect manufacturing costs to a product, let's look at the computation of a product's full cost under two scenarios: a process system and a job order system.

Process System

A process system typically is used when there is a continuous production activity or when all units produced are identical, which means it is not necessary to identify the costs associated with any specific product or batch of products. A company that produces only one product, such as artificial hips, in a particular plant would use a process system. So would a renal dialysis department, assuming all dialyses were more or less identical. A laboratory processing only complete blood counts (CBCs) also would be likely to use a process system. Shouldice Hospital in Canada, which performs only hernia operations, also could use a process system.

Clearly, it would not make sense to attach a job ticket to each artificial hip in a factory, or to each blood sample in a lab, because the actions of each worker in the manufacturing process are the same for any given item. If the batch of artificial hips or tests were small, however, containing, say, 100 units or so, we might attach a ticket to the batch and use a job order system. But if the batch contained several thousand units, we would simply keep track of the total costs incurred during the period when the hips were manufactured or the tests were processed, and then divide to get the cost per item.

Job Order System

As discussed in chapter 2, a job order system is used when each product is unique or when products are produced in batches and each batch is

BUZZARD GLEN HOSPITAL
EMERGENCY DEPARTMENT PATIENT ACTIVITY SHEET

Patient No. _30-033_   **Date/Time Arrived** _3 Aug 14: 1pm_   **Date/Time Left** _3 Aug 14: 6pm_

Presenting Condition _Laceration of left calf—3 inches long._

Activity	Labor	Materials	Overhead	Total
Initial treatment and blood work	$30	$25	$15	$70
Local anesthesia	20	15	10	45
Suturing of wound	60	5	30	95
Tetanus shot	10	20	5	35
Application of dressing	20	5	10	35
Instructions for follow-up care	10	0	5	15
Assisting patient to transport	10	0	5	15
Total	**$160**	**$70**	**$80**	**$310**

Figure 5.2 Job Ticket for Buzzard Glen Hospital

unique. Let's look at a job order system as it might function in the emergency department (ED) at Buzzard Glen Hospital. Assume that for each patient who enters the ED, the staff sets up a patient activity sheet (or a medical record). This is shown in figure 5.2 and is the equivalent of a job ticket in a manufacturing company. As tests and procedures are requisitioned for the patient, and as the professional staff cares for him or her, the staff members record the information, and the accounting staff later enters the appropriate cost information. When the patient is discharged, the activity sheet shows the treatment's cost.

It is unlikely that any ED keeps track of costs in exactly this way, but most do something similar. Doing so allows managers to determine whether the ED's costs were above or below the payment that the hospital received for the visit. It thus could determine the characteristics of those visits where costs were below the payment, and those where costs were not fully covered by the payment.

Using this medical record, let's examine the cost accounting issues involved. Although the meaning of the direct material and direct labor costs on the job ticket are pretty clear, the overhead is less so.

PROBLEM

Spend a few minutes studying the patient activity sheet in figure 5.2. How was the overhead calculated?

ANSWER

Overhead is 50 percent of the direct labor amount charged.

Although it is relatively easy in situations such as this to figure out *how* overhead was calculated, it is much more difficult to determine *why* this approach was used. We will cover this topic later in the chapter.

Unit Costs

With either a job order or a process system, the computation of unit costs is relatively easy. We add up the total costs and the number of units, and then we divide the two. In a job order system such as that shown for Buzzard Glen, where only one unit (the patient) is involved, we don't even need to divide. If a job order system is being used for batches of identical products, such as a batch of 100 CBCs, and the job ticket shows that the batch cost $2,000, it is a relatively simple matter to divide the number of units into the total cost and determine that each test cost $20.

The Overhead Rate

In Buzzard Glen's case, overhead was attached to a patient (a job) at a rate of $0.50 for every $1.00 of direct labor. Although this may appear to be an easy approach to overhead attachment, the determination of a rate can be complicated.

To understand the complexity involved in determining the overhead rate, assume that the emergency department at Buzzard Glen is one of several mission centers in the hospital and that $100,000 of the hospital's support center costs have been allocated to it during stage 1. The ED also has $200,000 in indirect costs—that is, costs that are direct for the ED but indirect for any given patient it treats. Together these two categories of costs make up the ED's "manufacturing overhead."

The ED now must find a way to attach a portion of this MOH to individual patients. In this instance, the ED chose to do so by using the rate of $0.50 of overhead for every $1.00 of direct labor. The questions we must answer are, "Why did it choose direct labor dollars as the basis?" and "How did it make the computation?"

The Basis

Just as it is important to select appropriate bases for allocating support center costs to mission centers, it is also important to use an appropriate basis to attach a mission center's MOH to its products (such as procedures in a radiology department or patients in an emergency room). Here, as with the allocation of support center costs, we are seeking a good cause-and-effect relationship. That is, we are attempting to answer the question, "What activity in the department drives the use of the department's MOH?"

In most instances, this is a difficult question to answer. Buzzard Glen effectively said that the activity was direct labor dollars. Other departments, particularly ones that are capital intensive, such as radiology, might use machine hours. Still others might use direct labor hours (as opposed to direct labor dollars). If management decides to use only one basis per mission center for attaching overhead to products, it must exercise considerable judgment in selecting the one that measures cause and effect as accurately as possible.

The Computation

Once we have selected the basis and know the total amount of overhead to be attached, we must determine the amount in the denominator of the ratio. The Buzzard Glen ED, for example, had $300,000 of manufacturing overhead ($100,000 of allocated support center costs plus $200,000 of indirect costs). The basis for attaching MOH is dollars of direct labor. Thus, to compute the rate, we need to know the total direct labor dollars that were used during the period. Because the rate the ED used was $0.50 of overhead for every $1.00 of direct labor, the ED must have used $600,000 of direct labor. (The budgeting process actually works the other way around: we estimate both manufacturing overhead and direct labor dollars for the period and then divide MOH by direct labor dollars to determine the overhead rate. We use that rate for each dollar of direct labor to attach MOH to the ER's patients (that is, its jobs).

PROBLEM

Assume the machining department in a company that manufactures surgical instruments is highly capital intensive and has $100,000 in MOH. The department has 5,000 direct labor hours for a total cost of $80,000, $5,000 of raw material costs, and 20,000 machine hours. How would you attach the $100,000 of MOH to the instruments worked on by the department? Specify the basis you would use, and compute the rate.

ANSWER

Because the department is highly capital intensive, it probably makes sense to attach MOH on the basis of machine hours. With $100,000 in MOH and 20,000 machine hours, the overhead rate is $5.00 ($100,000 ÷ 20,000) per machine hour. Thus, for every hour an instrument spends on a machine, it receives $5 of MOH.

Predetermined Overhead Rates

The process just described works when we can wait until the end of the accounting period to calculate overhead rates and attach overhead to products. In general, however, most manufacturing organizations use *predetermined* overhead rates, which are set as part of their budgeting process (discussed in chapter 9).

Advantages of a Predetermined Overhead Rate

The main advantage of a predetermined overhead rate is its ease of use. Overhead can be attached to products without undertaking a monthly (or more frequent) cost allocation effort, and financial statements can be prepared relatively quickly. This is important when managers are asked to use financial information as a basis for exercising cost control. In addition, organizations that use a cost-plus basis for pricing (such as manufacturers that make products to order, academic medical centers that seek research funding, and hospitals and medical groups that develop bids for managed care contracts) need a way to include overhead costs in a bid or to estimate overhead costs in a contract. A predetermined overhead rate can serve this purpose.

Disadvantages of a Predetermined Overhead Rate

The main disadvantage of a predetermined overhead rate is its potential lack of accuracy. Because the numerator (a department's overhead) and the denominator (the number of, say, machine hours) may vary from predetermined levels, the rate will not provide management with a completely accurate measure of the overhead actually used by a product. To understand why this is true, consider the following problems.

PROBLEM

Computex, a division of a large company, manufactures bedside data-entry terminals for use in hospitals. Computex's expected and actual production plans, and its expected and actual overhead costs for one year, are shown in the following table. (Note that column numbers and also formulas for the operations performed in the table are provided for reference. For example, column 3 is column 1 multiplied by column 2.)

Review the information in the table carefully. Which number is the predetermined overhead rate? What is the rationale for your choice?

	Number of Units Produced	Machine Hours per Terminal	Total Machine Hours	Overhead*	Overhead per Machine Hour	Overhead per Terminal Produced
	1	2	3 = 1 × 2	4	5 = 4 ÷ 3	6 = 5 × 2
Expected	5,000	2.0	10,000	$50,000	$5.00	$10.00
Actual	3,000	2.5	7,500	$41,250	$5.50	$13.75

*Overhead consists of allocated support center costs plus the costs of indirect labor, indirect materials, and plantwide depreciation.

ANSWER

The predetermined overhead rate is the $5 in column 5. It is based on the expected overhead amount in column 4 and the expected number of machine hours in column 3. Note that the predetermined overhead rate is per machine hour, not per unit of production (a terminal in this instance). This is usually the case. That is, the overhead rate is based on inputs to the production process rather than outputs. The reason is that the inputs, not the outputs, drive the costs. The tricky part, of course, is determining which inputs drive which costs.

PROBLEM

Given Computex's predetermined overhead of $5 per machine hour, how much overhead do you think was attached to all the products? Careful: this is a little tricky.

ANSWER

The amount of overhead attached to products was $30,000, computed by multiplying the 3,000 terminals actually manufactured by the *standard efficiency* of 2 machine hours per terminal by the *standard overhead* of $5 per machine hour. This compares with actual overhead of $41,250, meaning that overhead was $11,250 higher than expected ($30,000 versus $41,250).

PROBLEM

Why was attached overhead not equal to actual overhead?

ANSWER

Attached overhead, sometimes called *applied* or *absorbed overhead* (the terms are used interchangeably), was not equal to actual overhead because two numbers differed from those expected: (1) the number of machine hours, and (2) the actual overhead spending. Note that the number of machine hours used in the computation was based on the standard of 2 hours per terminal. Thus the attached overhead was calculated by applying the standard number of machine hours per terminal to the actual number of terminals manufactured.

Some people consider this difference between attached and actual overhead to be a disadvantage of predetermined overhead rates. They reason that such a difference does not exist in a system that does not use predetermined rates, and it thus adds an unnecessary complication to the accounting effort. However, a predetermined overhead rate coupled with some additional analytical techniques can produce useful managerial information about what are called *overhead variances*. For example, the $11,250 difference between the overhead attached to products and the actual overhead ($30,000 versus $41,250, respectively) is an important figure for Computex's managers if they wish to exert control over manufacturing costs. The difference can be divided among several different causes: volume changes, efficiency changes, and changes in unit costs. Techniques for computing these different variances are a little tricky, and beyond the scope of this text.[3] The main value of these variances is the information they provide for cost control. They are the result of two quite different forces:

- A volume variance arises because production volume was not as anticipated. Although there probably is little that a manufacturing manager can do about this, it nevertheless is a concern for senior management. If the entire MOH variance were due to volume changes, senior management would probably wish to have some discussions with the sales force or other "volume creators," rather than with the manufacturing manager. Of course, there is always the possibility that delays and breakdowns in the plant prevented the manufacturing manager from completing the orders placed by the sales force, and this possibility would need to be investigated also.

- Efficiency and unit cost (or spending) variances arise because actual overhead differed from what overhead should have been at the actual level of volume produced. If the variances are negative, they suggest that the individuals responsible for the various activities that make up overhead costs spent more than they should have. Although there may be good reasons for this, a large negative efficiency or spending variance nevertheless gives senior management an indication that some discussions need to take place with the manufacturing manager.

Absorption Costing in Health Care Organizations

The previously described approach to attaching mission center costs to the goods they make (or the services they provide) ordinarily is called *absorption costing*, in that costs are "absorbed into" the mission center's products. In a manufacturing company, MOH remains with the product until it is sold, at which point it becomes part of the cost of goods sold.

As indicated earlier, many manufacturing-like activities take place in a hospital (and in other health care organizations), such as processing tests in a laboratory or conducting procedures in a radiology department. Indeed, from a conceptual perspective, patients are in "inventory" while they remain in the hospital, and their costs accumulate in the same way as do those of products in a manufacturing company (although hospitals do not use a "cost of goods sold" account when they discharge a patient!).

As we have seen, the absorption process can be a little tricky. More important, it can give misleading results. Specifically, when a mission center uses only one overhead rate for the absorption process, the implicit assumption is that the unit of activity used in that rate (for example, machine hours or direct labor dollars) is what drives the use of all MOH. But MOH generally results from a more complex array of forces, with the result that absorption costing systems using a single overhead rate can give misleading information about a product's *real* use of MOH.

Activity-Based Costing

activity-based costing (ABC)
A costing system that uses multiple cost pools and overhead bases to attach manufacturing overhead to products. Considered to be more accurate than a method that uses a single rate,. ABC is especially useful when there is product diversity, cost diversity, or volume diversity.

A technique to correct this deficiency is called *activity-based costing (ABC)*. Instead of only one MOH cost pool, an ABC system uses several MOH pools, each with its own overhead rate. With ABC the goal is to make the resources in each cost pool as homogeneous as possible and then to identify the unit of activity that drives their use. As we will see, ABC has a great deal of applicability to service organizations in general and to health care organizations in particular.[4]

EXAMPLE

One company applied ABC to the costs of processing customer orders and making credit adjustment decisions. It discovered that the cost of processing small credit claims was almost as much as the cost of settling them. As a result, the company established a new policy that allowed sales representatives to approve on-site credit adjustments for small complaints.

A physician's office, an emergency department in a hospital, a freestanding laboratory, an independent radiology practice, and many other health care organizations might consider a similar analysis. Some of these organizations pursue the collection of small dollar items (such as a missed copayment) with the same vigor as they pursue unpaid claims of several hundred dollars or more. An ABC analysis might lead to a policy that allowed the collection department to write off claims that would cost more to collect than the amount that would be received.

EXAMPLE

An insurance company supplemented routine expense information from its regular accounting systems with cost sampling for different activities and tasks. Because most of the organization's costs were employee related, it focused these sampling efforts on gaining a clear picture of how employees spent their time. This allowed management to develop estimates of how much time was devoted to various activities and tasks, which helped management to adjust staffing needs for local offices based on each office's particular mix of activities. Such an approach would be applicable to a health insurance company or a health maintenance organization (HMO), and it might also be used in a variety of other health care settings, such as physician group practices.

Conditions for ABC

Earlier in the chapter we saw examples of organizations that used a single activity (or cost driver), such as a machine hour, to attach MOH to products. Although there are situations where a single rate is adequate, there are many where it is not.[5] In general, there is a need for multiple overhead pools and cost drivers when at least one of three factors is present: product diversity, cost diversity, or volume diversity.

Product diversity exists when different products use MOH in different proportions, such as when one product requires considerably more setup time than another. However, product diversity is important only when the costs of the different MOH activities are significantly different for different products; this is cost diversity. Finally, because some overhead activities are affected by the size of the batch being processed and others are not, *volume diversity* exists when the products are manufactured in batches of different sizes.[6]

product diversity
The condition that exists when different products use overhead-related services in different proportions: for example, when one product requires considerably more inspection time than another. Product diversity is important only when the costs of the different activities are significantly different.

When an organization uses multiple overhead rates, the analysis usually begins with the activities that cause the costs for one batch of products to differ from those for another batch. Each activity is then given its own overhead rate. If, for example, one type of product requires more setup time than another, the appropriate rate is something associated with setups. If a considerable amount of supervision is needed for one type of product but not for another, the appropriate rate is related to supervision hours. In this way, each overhead rate is used to measure a product's use of MOH.

volume diversity
The condition that exists when products are manufactured in batches of different sizes.

EXAMPLE

Consider a hospital's pathology laboratory. Some tests, such as CBCs, are processed in large batches using equipment that requires some setup time but relatively little direct labor. Other tests, such as frozen sections or hematoxylin and eosin stains, are handled individually, requiring some machine time but also considerable direct labor (as the stains are examined under a microscope) and perhaps some supervision time as well. The lab clearly has product and volume diversity, and it uses different overhead activities for different tests.

Establishing Multiple Second-Stage Overhead Rates

cost diversity
The condition that exists when the costs of different MOH activities are significantly different for different products

When product diversity, *cost diversity*, volume diversity, or a combination of these factors exists, there is a need for multiple overhead rates, or what are often called *multiple second-stage cost drivers*. The process for establishing them can be tricky. The details are discussed in many cost accounting texts and are beyond the scope of this book[7]; however, there are several important concepts worth noting. Some of these concepts were discussed in chapter 2, which emphasized the idea that different products use different kinds and amounts of resources. That is why we used different allocation bases for different support centers. Similarly, at the mission center level, four general categories of activities tend to influence the use of overhead:

- Facility-sustaining activities are the highest-order activities. They include building management, building repair and maintenance, security, and grounds maintenance.

- Product-sustaining activities ensure that products are produced according to specifications. They include process engineering, product specifications, engineering change notices, and product enhancements.

- Batch-related activities are performed each time a batch of products is manufactured. They include setting up machines, material movements, and inspections.

- Unit-level activities are tied directly to the number of units produced. They include direct manufacturing costs (such as those of direct labor and direct materials), plus utility usage, machine depreciation, and other activities linked directly to products.

Within each of these categories there usually are one or more cost pools. Once a mission center's activities have been grouped into homogeneous (or relatively homogeneous) cost pools, and once the cost pools have been classified into one of the four categories, the accounting staff can define and measure the unit of activity that causes a product to use each pool. On a conceptual level, the search is for an activity unit that reflects the demand of a product for each pool. For some pools, this is relatively easy; for others, it can be somewhat difficult.

EXAMPLE

One cost pool in a laboratory might be the labor and supervision time needed to set up some machines to run a test on several dozen or several hundred blood samples. In this case the appropriate cost pool would be everything associated with setting up the machines (such as cleaning and adjusting tolerances), and the appropriate activity unit for an overhead rate would be the number of setups. Each unit in a small batch of tests thus would get a larger share of the setup overhead than each unit in a large batch.

EXAMPLE

A radiology department might have a cost pool for its allocated building depreciation, housekeeping, maintenance, and other "facility-sustaining" costs. It might distribute these to the areas where different procedures are conducted, such as the MRI suite, on the basis of square feet. Each MRI would then receive its fair share of these costs based on the number of procedures performed. A predetermined overhead rate could be established by estimating the number of procedures to be performed during a given time period, usually a year.

PROBLEM

Classify each of the following overhead cost pools for a radiology department into one of the four categories just described. Identify a good basis for an overhead rate for each pool.

	Category	Basis
Indirect Labor		
Engineering (to adjust machine tolerances)		
Supervision (for all image processing relative to patient volume)		

	Category	Basis
Material handling (based on requisitions)		
Maintenance (based on breakdowns)		
General cleaning		
Inspection and quality control		
Indirect Materials		
Solvents (to clean machines after each procedure)		
Other		
Equipment depreciation		
Plantwide depreciation		
Utilities		
Insurance		

ANSWER

There is, of course, room for some disagreement about this classification. Here is one possible list:

	Category	Basis
Indirect Labor		
Engineering (to adjust machine tolerances)	Product sustaining	Adjustments
Supervision (for all film processing; relative to patient volume)	Unit level	Units
Material handling (based on requisitions)	Batch related	Requisitions
Maintenance (based on breakdowns)	Product sustaining	Maintenance hours
General cleaning	Facility sustaining	Hours or square feet
Inspectors and quality control	Batch related	Units
Indirect Materials		
Solvents (to clean machines after each procedure)	Batch related	Batches
Other		
Equipment depreciation	Unit level	Machine hours
Plantwide depreciation	Facility sustaining	Square feet
Utilities	Unit related	Machine hours
Insurance	Facility sustaining	Book value of assets

The key point here is not the "correct" classification of costs or the "precise" identification of a basis. That kind of judgment is, in general, a task for the accounting staff. Nevertheless, it is important for managers to be involved in the decision-making process because classification of activities in this way permits them to assess more thoroughly how products consume overhead resources. Moreover, by conducting this sort of analysis, management not only can be assured that the accounting system is measuring costs as accurately as possible but also can concentrate on controlling costs by controlling the cost drivers; that is, it can begin to focus on managing the activities that comprise the bases rather than costs, per se. It is this shift in thinking—from measurement to control—that is one of the most powerful benefits of an ABC system and, in particular, of multiple stage 2 overhead rates.

EXAMPLE

In one Internal Revenue Service office, the cost pools were (1) managing accounts; (2) informing, educating, and assisting; (3) ensuring compliance; and (4) "resourcing." The bases included volume and cycle time.[8] One could imagine a similar approach being used in a health insurance company or an HMO.

Done well, ABC also can be helpful for several cost accounting–related activities discussed in chapter 2, such as pricing and profitability analysis. Indeed, the use of ABC has led managers in many organizations to reverse their thinking on which products are the most profitable, and it can help senior management in many health care organizations to identify more clearly the nature and extent of cross-subsidization among its programs and services. When these sorts of benefits are achieved, the additional complexity and cost of using an ABC system would appear to be small by comparison.

EXAMPLE

Chrysler estimated that over a period of only a few years, its ABC system generated hundreds of millions of dollars in benefits by helping the company simplify product designs and eliminate unproductive, inefficient, or redundant activities. The benefits were ten to twenty times greater than the company's investment in ABC. The savings at some sites were 50 to 100 times the implementation cost.[9]

> A similar approach could be of enormous assistance to a hospital or a large academic health center, where there are no doubt a variety of inefficient or redundant activities. In one hospital, for example, an analysis of efficiency and redundancy in its admitting office revealed that there was no need for such an office at all!

A General Approach

The four categories of activities listed earlier provide a useful way to classify costs and to begin thinking about overhead bases. In a more general sense, the analytical effort consists of moving away from the traditional way of classifying costs—which is based largely on a line-by-line listing of such items as personnel, depreciation, maintenance, and the like—toward the activities that drive them. In a manufacturing setting, the bases are requisitions, setups, maintenance hours, machine hours, and so forth.

PROBLEM

Domino Labs is a freestanding facility that conducts two kinds of tests for nearby physician practices. Test 1 is ordered in large volumes and can be processed in large batches. Test 2 is ordered in much smaller quantities and is processed in smaller batches. In addition, to ensure quality for test 2, Domino must purchase the necessary reagents in small quantities.

Domino has a single facility where it conducts all its tests. Its major direct cost is labor, although each test also requires small amounts of reagents. However, there is a substantial amount of overhead in the lab's purchasing and material-handling activities. Many of these activities are highly automated, especially material handling. The expected direct costs for a single test of each type are as follows:

	Test 1	Test 2
Direct material	$0.50	$1.00
Direct labor	$3.00	$3.00
Other direct costs	$1.00	$1.00

Domino's budget for the upcoming year includes overhead of $1.32 million, which currently is attached to each test on the basis of machine hours. However, Domino's controller believes that this approach may be providing misleading information. She has developed the following analysis of the budgeted overhead costs:

Activity	Cost Driver	Number	Cost
Purchasing	Purchase orders (POs)	1,200 POs	$600,000
Material handling	Batches	1,800 batches	720,000
TOTAL OVERHEAD COSTS			$1,320,000

Budget data for producing the two tests throughout the upcoming year are as follows:

	Test 1	Test 2	Total
Tests conducted	800,000	200,000	1,000,000
Machine hours	400,000	100,000	500,000
Purchase orders	400	800	1,200
Batches	500	1,300	1,800

Using these data and the table that follows, determine the cost of one test of each type, first using the traditional approach of absorbing overhead based on machine hours, and then using an ABC approach.

	Traditional Approach		ABC Approach	
	Test 1	Test 2	Test1	Test 2
Direct material	$0.50	$1.00	$0.50	$1.00
Direct labor	3.00	3.00	3.00	3.00
Other direct	1.00	1.00	1.00	1.00
Overhead	?	?	?	?
TOTAL				

What accounts for the differences?

ANSWER

The overhead rate under the traditional approach is $1,320,000 ÷ 500,000 machine hours, or $2.64 per machine hour. Overhead for test 1 is calculated as follows:

400,000 machine hours × $2.64 per machine hour = $1,056,000

$1,056,000 ÷ 800,000 tests = $1.32 per test

Overhead for test 2 is calculated as follows:

100,000 machine hours × $2.64 per machine hour = $264,000

$264,000 ÷ 200,000 tests = $1.32 per test

Overhead under the ABC approach is calculated as follows:

Activity	Cost Driver	Budgeted Units	Total Cost	Unit Cost
Purchasing	Purchase orders	1,200	$600,000	$500 per PO
Material handling	Batches	1,800	$720,000	$400 per batch

	Production Data		Cost per Test	
	Test 1	Test 2	Test 1	Test 2
Purchase orders	400	800	$0.25[a]	$2.00[b]
Batches	500	1,300	0.25[c]	2.60[d]
TOTAL			$0.50	$4.60

[a] $500 per PO × 400 purchase orders = $200,000;
$200,000 ÷ 800,000 tests = $0.25 per test.
[b] $500 per PO × 800 purchase orders = $400,000;
$400,000 ÷ 200,000 tests = $2.00 per test.
[c] $400 per batch × 500 batches = $200,000;
$200,000 ÷ 800,000 tests = $0.25 per test.
[d] $400 per batch × 1,300 batches = $520,000;
$520,000 ÷ 200,000 tests = $2.60 per test.

Total costs can now be compared, as follows:

	Traditional Approach		ABC Approach	
	Test 1	Test 2	Test 1	Test 2
Direct material	$0.50	$1.00	$0.50	$1.00
Direct labor	3.00	3.00	3.00	3.00
Other direct	1.00	1.00	1.00	1.00
Overhead	1.32	1.32	0.50	4.60
TOTAL	$5.82	$6.32	$5.00	$9.60

The explanation for the differences is that, under the traditional approach, test 1 was absorbing a lot of the overhead that was more appropriately associated with test 2. With ABC, because test 2 required more purchase orders and had more batches, it received more overhead. As a result, assuming a constant markup in pricing its products, the laboratory would be charging more for test 1 and less for test 2 than is appropriate.

PROBLEM

An abbreviated cost report for a hospital is shown here:

| | Assigned Costs | Allocated Costs | Costs to Be Allocated | Allocations | | | | Full Cost |
| | | | | Depreciation (Square Feet) | Maintenance (Hours) | Housekeeping (Square Feet) | Administration (Salary Dollars) | |
	1	2 = 4 + 5 + 6 + 7	3 = 1+2	4	5	6	7	8 = 1+2
Support Centers								
Building depreciation	$1,200,000	$0	$1,200,000					
Building maintenance	950,000	105,000	1,055,000	$105,000				
Housekeeping services	300,000	154,555	454,555	95,000	$59,555			
Administration and general	1,300,000	381,605	1,681,605	156,000	158,250	$67,355		
Mission Centers								
Radiology	1,750,000	688,321		140,000	147,700	64,300	$336,321	$2,438,321
Laboratory	2,000,000	788,814		160,000	172,545	69,500	386,769	2,788,814
Dialysis unit	1,250,000	423,930		50,000	116,050	22,455	235,425	1,673,930
Inpatient care	7,000,000	959,723		350,000	158,250	165,600	285,873	7,959,723
Outpatient	2,250,000	889,212		144,000	242,650	65,345	437,217	3,139,212
Total cost	$18,000,000			$1,200,000	$1,055,000	$454,555	$1,681,605	$18,000,000

During the period covered by the cost report, the dialysis unit did 4,500 procedures, and radiology did 30,000 procedures. Thus, the average cost of a dialysis procedure was $371.98 ($1,673,930 ÷ 4,500), and the average cost of a radiological procedure was $81.28 ($2,438,321 ÷ 30,000).

The hospital wanted to know the cost of treating two patients, each of whom received two radiology procedures and three dialysis procedures. It concluded that each patient had the same cost, as shown here:

	Patient A			Patient B		
	Radiology	Dialysis	Total	Radiology	Dialysis	Total
Number of procedures	2	3	—	2	3	—
Cost per procedure	$81.28	$371.98	—	$81.28	$371.98	—
Total cost	$162.55	$1,115.94	$1,278.49	$162.55	$1,115.94	$1,278.49

What is your assessment of this analysis?

ANSWER

For dialysis, this analysis would be reasonably accurate. As discussed earlier, cost centers that produce a single product do not need an ABC system. In the dialysis unit, for example, the only product is a dialysis procedure, and because all dialysis procedures are roughly identical, the average cost per procedure is a relatively accurate number. By contrast, because the radiology department conducts a wide variety of procedures, an ABC approach would be needed to determine the different costs.

You are now ready to work on the practice cases for this chapter. Analyzing the Lincoln Dietary Department and Owen Hospital cases will help you sharpen your ABC skills. The Owen Hospital case deals with the problem just discussed, that is, the cost of the radiology procedures.

KEY TERMS

Activity-based costing (ABC)	Product diversity
Batch-related activities	Product-sustaining activities
Cost diversity	Unit-level activities
Facility-sustaining activities	Volume diversity
Manufacturing overhead (MOH)	

To Bear in Mind

1. Research has suggested that the RCC approach to determining a hospital's costs is about 95 percent accurate at the product line level and about 85 percent accurate for a DRG. Below those levels of aggregation, its accuracy is limited, and it is extremely unreliable for any single product or service provided by a mission center.

2. Activity-based costing is primarily concerned with the absorption of manufacturing overhead into products. Instead of using a single overhead rate, such as machine hours, to do this, ABC uses multiple rates, each of which is based on an activity that drives the use of the relevant overhead cost pool. Thus, two questions must be answered: "What are the overhead cost pools?" and "What activity drives the use of each pool?" The goal is to define each pool as a set of homogeneous resources (such as those required to carry out the purchasing function), and then to identify the activity that has a cause-and-effect relationship with the resources in that pool (such as purchase orders).

Test Yourself

1. Distinguish between stage 1 and stage 2 of the full-cost accounting effort. In which stage do most health care organizations need to do a better job than they currently do?

2. "If a mission center works on only one product, it does not need to worry about stage 2." Comment and explain your thinking.

3. Define direct and indirect manufacturing costs, and give examples of each. Be sure to specify the two categories of indirect manufacturing costs. What is another name for indirect manufacturing costs?

4. What is wrong with using a single overhead rate to attach manufacturing overhead to products? How can this problem be corrected?

5. What are the four general categories of activities that tend to influence the use of overhead? Give an example of an activity in each category.

Suggested Cases

Neighborhood Servings

Massachusetts Eye and Ear Infirmary

PRACTICE CASE A

LINCOLN DIETARY DEPARTMENT

The dietary department at Lincoln General Hospital produced breakfast, lunch, and dinner for its patients. Most meals were standard, but some patients needed special meals for which the department had to purchase special ingredients. Standard ingredients were used in large volumes, whereas special ingredients were used in very low volumes.

The department was located in the basement of the hospital, where it conducted all its activities. It "sold" its meals to the hospital clinical care departments at a transfer price equal to the full production cost plus a markup of 20 percent.

The department's budgeted costs broke down as follows:

Direct (raw) materials (meal ingredients)	$875,000
Direct labor (preparing and cooking the food)	1,145,000
Overhead (purchasing, material handling, quality control, and packaging)	1,533,000
TOTAL	$3,553,000

Exhibit 5A.1 shows the budgeted direct material and labor costs for the two types of meals. Exhibit 5A.2 shows a breakdown of the department's $1,533,000 of overhead costs, which at that time were allocated to each meal on the basis of the meal's direct material cost. Exhibit 5A.3 shows the budgeted meal data. As it indicates, the department expected to produce 300,000 regular meals but only 50,000 special meals. As it also indicates, having both regular and special meals placed some demand on the purchasing staff because the required purchase orders varied considerably in terms of the number of meals they would encompass.

The meals were produced in batches. Because of their ingredients, the special meals needed to be produced in small batches, in contrast to the regular meals, which could be produced in large batches. This affected quality control, because inspections were done by batch. Similarly, each batch needed to be set up: the material handlers needed to take the ingredients out of refrigeration and prepare them for cooking. The meals also were packed in batches for delivery to the floor.

At a recent management meeting, several nurses had noted that the cost of meals had been increasing steadily over the past few years. They emphasized that they were not concerned about the dietary department's 20 percent markup, which they knew was needed to cover the support center costs (mainly plant depreciation, administration and general, housekeeping, and laundry) that were allocated to the department. They also realized and accepted the fact that the special meals would cost more. In fact, most thought that the special meals were reasonably priced, perhaps half of what they might cost in another hospital. The nurses' main complaint was with the cost of the regular meals.

The manager of the dietary department agreed to look into the matter and present a report at the next monthly management meeting.

Assignment

1. Compute the department's predetermined overhead rate under the current system, and use that rate to determine the full cost and selling price of one regular meal and one special meal.

2. Compute the full cost and selling price for one regular meal and one special meal using an ABC approach.

3. What are the pros and cons of adopting the ABC system? Should the department adopt it?

EXHIBIT 5A.1   Direct Manufacturing Cost for One Meal

	Regular	Special
Direct material	$2.25	$4.00
Direct labor	$3.20	$3.70

EXHIBIT 5A.2   Budgeted Overhead Costs

	Cost Driver	Budgeted Units of Activity	Budgeted Cost
Purchasing	Purchase orders	620	$527,000
Material handling	Setups	36,000	720,000
Quality control	Batches	13,000	195,000
Packaging	Packaging hours	14,000	91,000
TOTAL			$1,533,000

EXHIBIT 5A.3   Production Data

Cost Driver	Unit of Activity	Regular	Special
Budgeted meals	Meals	300,000	50,000
Batch size	Meals in a batch	100	5
Setups	Setups per batch	2	3
Purchase order size	Meals in a PO	2,500	100
Packaging hours	Hours per 100 meals	4	4

PRACTICE CASE B

OWEN HOSPITAL

I don't believe we lost money on both those patients. I've talked with the attending physicians who treated them, and Peter ordered much simpler tests and procedures. He also didn't use the ICU [intensive care unit]. Megan ordered some complex tests and procedures, and kept her patient in the ICU for two days.

The speaker was Sheila Leddy, MD, chief of medicine at Owen Hospital. She was talking to Joe McCarthy, her departmental administrator, about the situation with two patients, each of whom had a discharge DRG that resulted in a payment of $5,600. The hospital records showed that the cost of care for each patient was $5,922. Having obtained the medical records, Dr. Leddy realized that the physicians who had treated these patients had ordered quite different tests and procedures and also had used the ICU differently. She continued:

> I've obtained some summary information from fiscal affairs. Here's an abbreviated cost report [exhibit 5B.1], and the data the folks in fiscal gave me that show what they call the cost per unit [exhibit 5B.2]. They put that information together with their information on the patients' use of tests, procedures, and bed days, and they came up with this ludicrous set of numbers that shows both patients cost exactly the same [exhibit 5B.3].
>
> The problem is that Peter's patient [patient 1] used pretty simple lab tests and X-rays, whereas Megan's [patient 2] used much more complex tests and procedures. I know this is not as precise as you might like it to be, but it should be good enough to see if I'm right that the information from fiscal affairs is pretty worthless. Please see if you can compute the costs when these differences are built in, and also figure out how to include the ICU costs, which, as far as I can tell, are lumped in with the costs for the DOM [department of medicine] overall.

In an effort to respond to Dr. Leddy's request, Mr. McCarthy discussed the costs in the pathology and radiology departments with his counterparts there, and obtained the information shown in exhibit 5B.4. He also did some research using hospital records and talked with the nursing staff in the department of medicine. The results of those activities are also shown in exhibit 5B.4. He explained:

> I've used round numbers since nothing is very precise, but I think I've come pretty close. In radiology and pathology, for example, they had done some time and motion studies to determine how much labor and supplies went into different tests and procedures. As you can see, in both departments they didn't get very sophisticated, but the distinction between simple and complex is probably good enough for our purposes.
>
> Getting department administrative costs was a little tricky, but I decided that if I multiplied the labor and material cost per unit by the number of units, I would get the total department direct costs that were also direct with regard to the test or procedure. Everything else must be administrative, or at least not directly associated with a test or procedure even though it's direct for the department.
>
> Inpatient care was a little more tricky, but not excessively so. I simply found as best I could all the department of medicine's costs that could be directly

associated with a day of stay; these included mainly nursing costs, but they also included costs associated with some other personnel and some supplies. I then divided them between the main ward and the ICU based on where nurses were spending their time and how many nurses were in each place on a typical day.

Housekeeping was a support center cost allocated to each department, so I didn't include it in the direct cost figure. The same was true for the other support centers on the cost report [exhibit 5B.1]. Instead, to figure out how much of a center's costs should be allocated within a department, I just extended the approach in the cost report. For example, in pathology, I did a rough measure of square footage and found that the simple tests took up about 30 percent of the space in the lab, whereas the complex tests took up about 70 percent. Of course, some space was used for other purposes, but I tried to divide it as fairly as I could between the two types of tests. I did the same for maintenance hours and salary dollars, although they were both easier, since there were maintenance records for all the machines and salary records for the technicians and other personnel.

I then did the same sort of thing for radiology and inpatient care. Again, there were some minor problems in assessing some of the costs, but nothing too difficult. However, as I say, I kept the numbers rounded since nothing is completely precise.

Mr. McCarthy knew he needed to work quickly with the data he had gathered, because Dr. Leddy was expecting a report by late afternoon.

Assignment

1. Using the data assembled by Mr. McCarthy, compute revised cost figures for the two patients. What assumptions, if any, did you need to make?

2. How valuable are the cost figures you computed? That is, how might Dr. Leddy use them for decision making? Be as specific as you can in identifying the kinds of decisions she might make with this new information—decisions related to pricing, profitability analysis, product cross-subsidization, product elimination, physician behavior, and so on.

3. How might you improve on the data Mr. McCarthy has gathered? That is, if you had the opportunity, what additional data would you gather, and with what goals in mind?

EXHIBIT 5B.1 Abbreviated Hospital Cost Report

	Direct Costs	Costs	Costs to Be Allocated	Allocations				Full Cost
				Depreciation (Square Feet)	Maintenance (Hours)	Housekeeping (Square Feet)	Administration (Salary Dollars)	
	1	2 = 4 + 5 + 6 + 7	3 = 1 + 2	4	5	6	7	8 = 1 + 2
Support Centers								
Building depreciation	$1,200,000	$0	$1,200,000					
Building maintenance	950,000	105,000	1,055,000	$105,000				
Housekeeping services	300,000	154,555	454,555	95,000	$59,555			
Administration and general	1,300,000	381,605	1,681,605	156,000	158,250	$67,355		
Mission Centers								
Radiology	1,750,000	688,321		140,000	147,700	64,300	$336,321	$2,438,321
Laboratory	2,000,000	788,814		160,000	172,545	69,500	386,769	2,788,814
Dialysis unit	1,250,000	423,930		50,000	116,050	22,455	235,425	1,673,930
Inpatient care	7,000,000	959,723		350,000	158,250	165,600	285,873	7,959,723
Outpatient department	2,250,000	889,212		144,000	242,650	65,345	437,217	3,139,212
Total cost	$18,000,000			$1,200,000	$1,055,000	$454,555	$1,681,605	$18,000,000

EXHIBIT 5B.2 Computing the Average Full Cost per Unit

	Full Cost	Number of Units	Cost per Unit
	1	2	3 = 1 ÷ 2
Mission Centers			
Radiology	$2,438,321	30,000	$81.28
Laboratory	2,788,814	150,000	$18.59
Dialysis unit	1,673,930	4,500	$371.98
Inpatient care	7,959,723	7,000	$1,137.10
Outpatient department	3,139,212	25,000	$125.57
Total cost	$18,000,000		

EXHIBIT 5B.3 Cost for 2 Patients

	Number of Units	Cost per Unit	Cost
Patient 1			
X-ray 1	2	$81.28	$162.55
Lab test 1	2	$18.59	37.18
Lab test 2	2	$18.59	37.18
Inpatient stay	5	$1,137.10	5,685.52
Outpatient visits	0	$125.57	0.00
Total			$5,922.44
Patient 2			
X-ray 1	2	$81.28	$162.55
Lab test 1	2	$18.59	37.18
Lab test 2	2	$18.59	37.18
Inpatient stay	5	$1,137.10	5,685.52
Outpatient visits	0	$125.57	0.00
Total			$5,922.44

EXHIBIT 5B.4   Information Obtained by Mr. McCarthy

	Labor and Material Cost per Unit[a]	Number of Units[b]	Percentage of Space Occupied[c]	Percentage of Maintenance Hours[d]	Percentage of Salary Dollars[e]
	1	2	3	4	5
Radiology					
Simple X-ray	$40.00	25,000	40%	20%	80%
Complex X-ray	$70.00	5,000	60%	80%	20%
Total		30,000			
Department administrative costs					$400,000
Pathology					
Simple test	$9.00	125,000	30%	40%	60%
Complex test	$16.00	25,000	70%	60%	40%
Total		150,000			
Department administrative costs					$475,000
Inpatient Care					
Ward	$700.00	6,000	30%	20%	70%
Intensive care unit	$1,600.00	1,000	70%	80%	30%
Total		7,000			
Department administrative costs					$1,200,000

[a]These figures were computed based on time and motion studies; they include both technician time and materials used.
[b]These figures were computed based on each department's records.
[c]These figures were obtained from hospital records and computed for areas in each department where units are produced.
[d]These figures were obtained from hospital records.
[e]These figures were computed based on each department's records.

Notes

1. Michael Shwartz, David W. Young, and Richard Seigrist, "The Ratio of Costs to Charges: How Good a Basis for Estimating Costs?" *Inquiry* 32 (Fall 1995): 476–481.

2. A transfer price is an internal charge between one department or program and another. Transfer prices are discussed in chapter 7.

3. For a discussion of the computational techniques, see David W. Young, *Management Accounting for Managers,* 3rd ed. (Cambridge, MA: Crimson Press, 2013).

4. Timothy D. West and David A. West, "Applying ABC to Healthcare," *Management Accounting* 22 (February 1997): 22–33; Don Lambert and John Whitworth, "How ABC Can Help Service Organizations," *CMA Magazine* 70 (May 1996): 24–28; Seema Pandey, "Applying the ABCs in Provider Organizations," *Healthcare Financial Management* 66 (November 2012): 112–116, 118, 120.

5. Robin Cooper, "You Need a New Cost System When . . . ," *Harvard Business Review,* January–February 1989, 77–82.

6. For a detailed discussion of these factors, see Robin Cooper, "The Rise of Activity-Based Costing—Part Three: How Many Cost Drivers Do You Need, and How Do You Select Them?" *Journal of Cost Management,* Winter 1989, 34–46.

7. One good source of additional information is Robert S. Kaplan and Steven R. Anderson, *Time-Driven Activity-Based Costing: A Simpler and More Powerful Push to Higher Profit* (Boston: Harvard Business School Press, 2007). Another good source, particularly the chapter titled "ABC in Service Industries," is Robin Cooper and Robert S. Kaplan, *Cost and Effect: Using Integrated Cost Systems to Drive Profitability and Performance* (Boston: Harvard Business School Press, 1998).

8. John B. MacArthur, "Cost Management at the IRS," *Management Accounting* 78 (November 1996): 42–47.

9. Joseph A. Ness and Thomas G. Cucuzz, "Tapping the Full Potential of ABC," *Harvard Business Review,* July–August 1995, 130–138.

CHAPTER 6

RESPONSIBILITY ACCOUNTING: AN OVERVIEW

An organization's accounting staff prepares financial statements for use by outsiders and cost analyses for use by line and senior managers. The accounting staff also undertakes ad hoc analyses of differential cost and revenue data for use in making alternative choice decisions. These analyses frequently are done in response to specific needs expressed by senior and line managers.

Preparing both routine reports and undertaking ad hoc analyses are accounting activities that assist managers in decision making. However, a third kind of accounting information assists in ongoing management. This is the information that is generated and provided to managers via the *responsibility accounting system*, or what sometimes is called the *management control system*. This information focuses on the costs, and sometimes the revenues, that are controllable by various managers and therefore are the responsibility of those managers.

In its broadest sense, a responsibility accounting system is concerned with *planning* and *controlling*, rather than *measuring*, an organization's resources. Clearly, measurement is important to planning and control, so the two cannot be completely divorced. Nevertheless, the focus in the remaining chapters of the book will be on planning and control.

Organization of the Chapter

The chapter begins with an analysis of the relationship between cost accounting and responsibility accounting, which allows us to distinguish between measurement and control. We then look at the various factors that

LEARNING OBJECTIVES

On completing this chapter, you should know about

- The relationship between cost accounting and responsibility accounting

- The definition of a responsibility center, the different responsibility center options, and the basis for choosing one type over another

- The four phases of the management control process, and the characteristics of each must be considered in the design and use of a good responsibility accounting system. We next turn to the question of the responsibility accounting structure, which consists of the organization's network of responsibility centers, and discuss the different types of responsibility centers, explaining the rationale for choosing one type over another. Finally, we turn to the topic of the management control process, breaking it into four separate phases: programming, budgeting, operating and measuring, and reporting. The chapter looks at each phase separately, discussing its characteristics and how it relates to the other phases.

Cost Accounting and Responsibility Accounting

The relationship between cost accounting and responsibility accounting rests in large part on the concept of resources. The cost accounting discussions in chapters 2 and 5 focused on measuring the resources expended for a particular endeavor (the cost object). Differential cost accounting, discussed in chapters 3 and 4, also focused on measurement, emphasizing the ways that costs change with changes in volume.

Responsibility accounting, by contrast, focuses on the managers who are responsible for controlling the use of those resources. The responsibility accounting system requires *senior management* to establish a network of responsibility centers. A *responsibility center* is an organizational unit headed by a manager who is charged with achieving some agreed-on financial results. The nature of these results depends on the kind of responsibility center. In addition, in many health care organizations, managers are also charged with achieving a variety of nonfinancial results, which will be discussed in later chapters.

It would be useful if the cost center structure (discussed in chapters 2 and 5) were also the structure for accumulating responsibility center information. Unfortunately, this is rarely the case. As we will see in this chapter and the next, a different accounting structure is needed.

The differences among full-cost accounting, differential cost accounting, and responsibility accounting are summarized in table 6.1. As this table indicates, differences exist in the type of information in each category. Differences also exist in the kinds of decisions made with the information, and in the main group responsible for determining the information's structure and format.

---

senior management
Collectively, the individuals at the top of the organization's hierarchy. They are responsible for seeing that the organization accomplishes its objectives. They generally formulate the organization's overall strategic directions, sometimes with assistance from line management.

responsibility center
An organizational unit headed by a manager charged with achieving certain agreed-upon results. From a responsibility accounting perspective, the number of people in the center is relatively unimportant. The key issue is determining how senior management will measure the group's financial performance. Senior management's goal is to design responsibility centers in such a way that the responsibility center manager is responsible for those activities over which he or she exercises a reasonable amount of control.

Table 6.1 Summary of Management Accounting Information

	Full-Cost Accounting	Differential Cost Accounting	Responsibility Accounting
Goal	Improving the full-cost system	Assessing cost (and sometimes revenue) behavior	Controlling costs
Primary Design Responsibility	Accounting staff	Accounting staff	Senior management
Information Used	Direct and indirect costs	Fixed, variable, semivariable, and step-function costs	Controllable costs and revenues
Key Activities	Choosing cost objects Assigning costs to cost centers Choosing allocation bases Allocating support center costs to mission centers Attaching mission center costs to cost objects	Analyzing cost behavior Analyzing contribution Making alternative choice decisions	Designing responsibility centers Selecting new programs Determining cost drivers Budgeting with cost drivers Reporting on results with cost drivers
Managerial Uses	Determining product line profitability Formulating strategic decisions (programs, facilities, personnel needed to support chosen product lines) Establishing prices	Offering a special price Outsourcing an activity Retaining or discontinuing an unprofitable program or product line	Using cost drivers to improve cost control Motivating key managers Measuring performance Assigning responsibility to controlling agents

EXAMPLE

Consider the cost of a day of inpatient care in a hospital. From a cost accounting perspective, we would add together the various resources that go into that day: room, board, nursing care, medications, and so on. From a responsibility accounting perspective, we are concerned with the individuals who control those resources. For example, physicians carry a major responsibility for the use of resources: they prescribe medications, decide on the level of nursing care, order tests and procedures, and determine a discharge date. A nursing director or supervisor, who establishes the staffing patterns of nurses, carries some responsibility. The director of housekeeping, who is responsible for the cost and quality of the cleaning effort, also bears some responsibility. And so on.

Designing a Responsibility Accounting System

The goal of a responsibility accounting system is to help ensure the effective and efficient use of an organization's resources. *Effectiveness* is about accomplishing what the organization wants to do. The more of an organization's objectives a department or a program accomplishes, the greater its effectiveness. *Efficiency* can be measured by a ratio of outputs to inputs—that is, the amount of output achieved per unit of input. Efficiency is measured without regard for whether the output was in support of the organization's objectives (although the goal usually is to accomplish the organization's objectives at a low cost). Thus, an organization can be effective without being efficient, and vice versa. Outputs usually are measured in terms of revenue (although, as will be discussed later, this is changing); inputs are measured in terms of expenses.

In practice, we find a wide variety of responsibility accounting systems in organizations. Sometimes these systems function well, and sometimes not. Sometimes the responsibility accounting system consists of highly formal procedures and regularly scheduled activities, and sometimes the procedures and activities are informal and sporadic. Sometimes the system requires a great deal of senior management's time, and sometimes senior managers are only marginally involved. Sometimes a great deal of decision-making autonomy is delegated to division, department, or program managers, and sometimes these *line managers* have limited authority over decisions concerning the use of resources.

These differences arise because the characteristics of a responsibility accounting system are determined in large measure by the amount of autonomy and flexibility that senior management wishes to give to lower-level managers. The amount of autonomy relates, in part, to the amount of stability or turbulence that exists in the organization's environment and how quickly the organization needs to respond to environmental changes. But it is also a matter of leadership style and trust.

Because of these differences, there is no easy way to specify the precise design of an organization's responsibility accounting system. As is the case with many principles of management, responsibility accounting principles are incomplete and occasionally contradictory. Moreover, because these principles are concerned with the behavior of people, the motivation of managers, and the role of information, they do not lend themselves easily to experimentation or "proof."

Despite these limitations, responsibility accounting principles provide a way of thinking about an important set of management problems, and consequently it is better for managers to consider them than to ignore

effectiveness
Accomplishing what the organization wants to do. The more of an organization's objectives a responsibility center accomplishes, the greater its effectiveness.

efficiency
Accomplishing something at a low cost. It can be measured by a ratio of outputs to inputs-that is, amount of output achieved per unit of input. Measures of efficiency do not consider whether the output was in support of the organization's objectives.

line manager
A person responsible for the day-to-day operations of a program or responsibility center. This is a person whose judgments are incorporated into the organization's plans, who must see to it that those plans are implemented, and whose performance is measured by the responsibility accounting system. Line managers are sometimes called operating managers.

them. In general, although there is no single correct way to design a responsibility accounting system, many managers have found that responsibility accounting principles are useful in designing systems to assist the organization with its planning and control activities.

Successful health care organizations operating in the same geographical area and competing for the same physicians, patients, managed care contracts, and other third-party payers often have very different responsibility accounting systems. Some use a very formal reporting process, providing managers at all levels with information pertaining to their activities, and expect close adherence to the financial objectives established in the equally formal budget formulation process. Others use the budget as a rough guide and look only at a manager's performance at the year's end to see if it is satisfactory. There are many more variations.

The idea that there is no "right" responsibility accounting system has come about both as a result of management researchers' direct observation of the activities of successful organizations and as part of a way of thinking about the design of an organization in general, called contingency theory. Contingency theory holds that the most suitable form for an organization is one that "fits" with the organization's environment, its general strategic thrust, and its senior managers' values. A similar fit must be attained for its responsibility accounting system.

What, then, is a responsibility accounting system? Equally important, what can be said about it that will assist managers of small and large health care organizations alike in thinking about both its design and its fit with their strategies and organizational structures?

At the most fundamental level, any system consists of a structure and a process. Structure is what the system *is*; process is what it *does*. When we study the system of the human body, for example, we study anatomy (its structure) and physiology (its process). Similarly, a responsibility accounting system can be thought of as having an anatomy and a physiology.

The Responsibility Accounting Structure

The structure of a responsibility accounting system can be assessed in terms of groups of individuals who work together to accomplish some portion of an organization's objectives. Generally, each group—a responsibility center—is led by a manager who has overall accountability for the group's performance. Responsibility centers may take a wide variety of forms. A regional sales office of a managed care plan is a responsibility center, as is a housekeeping department or a laboratory in a hospital or

revenue centers
A type of responsibility center whose manager's financial performance is measured in terms of the amount of revenue earned by the center—for example, a development office in a university or a sales office in an HMO.

standard expense centers
A responsibility center where financial performance is measured a flexible budget. In each reporting period, the budgeted variable cost per unit is multiplied by the actual number of units of output, to which the budgeted fixed costs are added. The result is a budget to which the center's actual expenses are compared for the purpose of measuring financial performance. Sometimes the unit of output is adjusted by type, such as the type of test in a laboratory.

discretionary expense centers
A responsibility center whose manager's financial performance is measured in terms of the total expenses incurred by the center regardless of how much output the center produces.

outpatient clinic. At the extreme, a single physician or visiting nurse might also be a responsibility center.

Except for the activities at the lowest levels of the organization, each responsibility center generally consists of an aggregation of smaller responsibility centers. Indeed, from the perspective of the responsibility accounting structure, an organization can be thought of as a collection, or network, of responsibility centers. As a result, the key question in designing the responsibility accounting structure is, "For what is each group responsible?" A significant activity for senior management is to design, coordinate, and control the work of these responsibility centers in such a way that individuals are held responsible for, and are able to manage, those activities over which they can exercise a reasonable amount of control. As we will see, this simple-sounding task can become quite tricky in practice.

Types of Responsibility Centers

There are five main types of responsibility centers: *revenue centers, standard expense centers, discretionary expense centers, profit centers*, and *investment centers*. The selection of the most appropriate type for a particular organizational unit is not always readily apparent. The principal factor guiding senior management's selection is the kind of resources it wishes the responsibility center manager to control.

Table 6.2 lists the five possible types of responsibility centers and the financial objectives of each. As it indicates, if a manager has considerable

Table 6.2 Types of Responsibility Centers and Their Financial Objectives

Type	Responsible for . . .	Examples
Revenue center	Revenue earned by the center	An HMO's regional sales office A medical center's development office
Standard expense center	Expenses per unit of output, with a flexible budget used to compute total allowable expenses for each period	A hospital's laundry or dietary department
Discretionary expense center	Total expenses incurred by the center regardless of the volume of output	An accounting department A corporate staff department
Profit center	Total revenue minus total expenses of the center	A medical school in a large university A clinical care department
Investment center	Total revenue minus total expenses of the center, computed as a percentage of the assets used by the center (that is, the center's return on assets)	A hospital or physician practice in an integrated delivery system

control over revenue, such as ordinarily is the case in a university development office or a regional sales office for an HMO, his or her department generally would be a revenue center. This is true even though the department incurs some expenses. That is, the manager's *performance* is evaluated in terms of revenue generation.

By contrast, if a manager has a great deal of control over his or her department's expenses but no ability to generate revenue, the department ordinarily would be an expense center. In this regard, an important distinction is between standard and discretionary expense centers. A standard expense center is an appropriate designation when a manager can control the expense per unit of output but not the number of units of output.

profit centers
A responsibility center whose manager's financial performance is measured in terms of the total revenues of the center minus its total expenses.

investment centers
A responsibility center whose manager's financial performance is measured in terms of the total revenues minus the expenses of the center, computed as a percentage of the assets used by the center-that is, the center's return on assets.

EXAMPLE

A hospital's laundry department might be a standard expense center. The department would be responsible for the expense per pound of laundry washed but not for total expenses, which would partly depend on the number of pounds washed (which are not under the department's control). The hospital's accounting staff would prepare a flexible (or performance) budget, which would use the actual volume of activity (pounds washed, in this example) and the standard (or budgeted) expense per unit of activity. The department's financial performance would then be measured by comparing its actual expenses to the expenses calculated in the flexible budget, rather than to those in a fixed budget.

The computation for the flexible budget can be made more precise by dividing the department's expenses into their fixed and variable components. With this method only the variable components are flexed; the fixed components remain at their budgeted levels as long as the volume is within the relevant range.

It is also possible to introduce a "mix factor" into the flexible budget. For example, if a hospital established its department of radiology as a standard expense center, it would need to incorporate procedure mix into the flexible budget. Unlike the units of output of a laundry department (pounds washed), not all units of output for a radiology department are identical, meaning that each is likely to have a different variable cost.

PROBLEM

A department of radiology had the following budget data for three procedures for a month:

Procedure	Variable Cost per Unit	Budgeted Units	Total Costs
A	$25	2,000	$50,000
B	$40	500	20,000
C	$60	1,000	60,000
Total variable costs			$130,000
Fixed costs			100,000
Total budget			$230,000

During the most recent month, the department had the following activity:

Procedure A	2,500 units
Procedure B	1,000 units
Procedure C	500 units

Prepare a flexible budget for the most recent month. Assume that the volume of all procedures was within the relevant range of the budgeted fixed costs.

ANSWER

The flexible budget would look as follows:

Procedure	Variable Cost per Unit	Actual Units	Total Costs
A	$25	2,500	$62,500
B	40	1,000	40,000
C	60	500	30,000
Total variable costs			$132,500
Fixed costs			100,000
Total budget			$232,500

A discretionary expense center, by contrast, is a department where there is no easily measurable unit of output, such as a human resources or accounting department. Under these circumstances, the department ordinarily would receive a fixed budget, negotiated with senior management but not linked to any units of output. The manager would be expected to adhere to this budget during the budgetary period (usually a year).

If a manager has reasonable control over both revenues and expenses, the center ordinarily would be a profit center. Over the past several years, many health care organizations have instituted profit centers in their clinical care departments as a way to give their physician chiefs of service incentives to both control expenses and generate additional revenues.[1] Some organizations have extended the profit center idea to support departments as well, such as laundry, housekeeping, dietary, and computer support services. These departments sell their services internally at agreed-on transfer prices (discussed in the next chapter) and are expected to break even.

Finally, it is possible that a manager also exerts some control over the acquisition and management of certain assets, such as machines, accounts receivable, or inventory. If this is the case, the manager could reasonably be expected to have control over the productivity of those assets in addition to the center's revenue and expenses. This would imply that the unit should be an investment center. The manager would then be responsible for the surplus earned in his or her center as a percentage of the center's assets—that is, the center's return on assets (ROA). Few health care organizations have taken this step, although the use of investment centers might be appropriate in such capital-intensive units as radiology departments, pathology labs, operating rooms, freestanding outpatient clinics, and hospitals in integrated delivery systems.

Role of Senior Management

Senior management weighs many factors in determining the best formal organizational structure, which is a prerequisite to designing the network of responsibility centers. Some of these factors include the most appropriate division of tasks, the duties of specialized staff units, the activities that should be the responsibility of line managers, the decisions that should be made at or near the top of the organization, and the decisions that should be delegated to lower levels.

In some organizations, senior management spends considerable time designing the formal organizational structure and then (mistakenly) delegates to the accounting staff the job of determining the network of responsibility centers to overlay on that structure. Or, worse, senior management fails to be explicit about the network of responsibility centers, leaving department heads and other managers to figure out the design for themselves based on discussions in budget meetings or other similar activities. Both approaches can leave the organization without a network of responsibility centers that supports and reinforces senior management's strategy. Moreover, under these circumstances, line managers will not know how their performance is being measured and may take actions that are not in the best interests of either their respective departments or the organization overall.

It is therefore important for senior management to think carefully about the design of the organization's responsibility centers, because all but very small organizations will have not just a network but a hierarchy of responsibility centers. The hierarchy ranges from sections or other small units at the lowest level to departments and, ultimately, divisions. Indeed, because units with some sort of responsibility exist in almost all organizations, the central question senior managers must ask is not whether there *are* responsibility centers, but whether their design facilitates the organization's ability to achieve its goals.

In addition, each responsibility center manager must be given adequate incentives to achieve his or her center's objectives. Therefore, in addition to selecting what it believes to be the most appropriate type of responsibility center for a given organizational unit, senior management also must consider the design of an appropriate motivation process to reward managers and their subordinates for good performance. This and several related issues are discussed in chapter 7.

The Design Process

In designing an organization's network of responsibility centers, senior management usually begins with the fundamental premise that the organization itself is an investment center. This is true for all organizations— for-profit and nonprofit. They all must obtain a sufficiently high ROA to help finance asset acquisition and replacement, provide the cash needed to support growth, and create reserves for a rainy day. In this regard, the only real distinction between a nonprofit organization and a for-profit one is that the latter must satisfy investors' need for an adequate financial return.[2] This means that the key structural design question in all but the tiniest of health care organizations is how to decentralize ROA responsibility among the various organizational units, such as programs, divisions, and departments.

To answer this question, we begin with the elements of the ROA equation and assess who controls each one. This assessment will help guide the responsibility center choices.

ROA is calculated as follows:

$$\textbf{ROA = Annual profit (or surplus)} \div \textbf{Assets}$$

Determining the assets that a particular responsibility center manager can control is usually difficult, because in some instances, assets are shared among two or more responsibility centers. For example, if the organization's cash is maintained centrally, it is virtually impossible to determine how much of it should be attributed to a given responsibility center. By contrast, many assets can be directly associated with a particular responsibility center. The machines in a radiology or pathology department are clearly within the province of the department. Accounts receivable probably can be linked to individual organizational units, as can inventories.

Once the assets associated with a responsibility center have been isolated, the next question concerns profit (or surplus). Let's begin with the basic equation:

Profit (or surplus) = Revenue — Fixed costs — Variable costs

As we saw in chapter 3, revenue is price multiplied by volume, variable costs are variable costs per unit multiplied by volume, and fixed costs do not depend on volume as long as they remain within the relevant range. These relationships allow us to unbundle the calculation:

Profit (or surplus) = (Price × Volume) — Fixed costs
— (Variable costs per unit × Volume)

Senior management can then determine which elements of this formula a given responsibility center manager can control, or which elements it *wants* that manager to control. That determination will help guide the decision about the kind of responsibility center the unit should be. In some instances, the ability of the manager to control certain elements of the equation is quite clear; in others, there is ambiguity. In still others, there is a choice to be made between two or more possible arrangements, either of which can be appropriate depending on other design choices.

EXAMPLE

Some universities designate their schools as profit centers, and each school is expected to achieve at least breakeven operations for each academic year. Others designate their profitable schools as revenue centers but budget their expenses as discretionary expense centers. In one university, the school of management was a revenue center, expected to generate revenue of $50 million a year. It was given an expense budget of $20 million, which did not increase automatically if revenue went up. This gave the dean considerably less latitude than if the school had been designated as a profit center with an expectation of earning a $30 million surplus. Indeed, it also did not give him any formal motivation to increase revenue above the $50 million target.

Aligning Responsibility and Control:
The Fairness Criterion

An important principle in designing responsibility centers is to align responsibility with control, or what is known as satisfying the "fairness criterion." It sometimes can be difficult, however, to determine which elements of the ROA formula a given responsibility center manager can control, or how to give a manager control over the elements that senior management wants him or her to control. As a result, senior management may spend considerable time debating the most appropriate responsibility center arrangement.

Overall, senior management must design the responsibility accounting structure in such a way that line managers have a level of control and decision-making authority that corresponds to their type of responsibility center. If this is not the case, these managers quite likely will feel that they are being held responsible for resources they cannot control. This can lead to considerable stress and frustration.

PROBLEM

Newport Medical Associates, a physician group practice, is part of Alston Health System, an integrated delivery system. Newport has been designated as a profit center. Its physician-manager is responsible for devising a marketing strategy to bring in new patients, and hence earn revenue. He also must control the group's expenses and make sure they do not exceed revenue. Each month approximately 20 percent of the administrative expenses of the health system are allocated to Newport. These expenses are allocated using bases of allocation that all those in the health system, including the physician-manager of Newport, agree are appropriate. Some bases use square footage, others use salary dollars, and others use work orders (for work by the building and grounds staff, for example). What problems do you think might arise with this arrangement?

ANSWER

Although the cost accounting system seems to be well designed, the responsibility accounting system is not. The distinction senior management must make here is between measurement and control. The cost accounting system appears to have done a good job of measuring Newport's fair share of the health system's administrative expenses. However, because Newport's physician-manager cannot control the allocated portion of the system's expenses, it is unfair to ask him to run Newport as a profit center. That is, although the allocation bases are appropriate for the full-cost accounting effort, the manager nevertheless is being held responsible for some expenses that he cannot control.

As we will see in chapter 7, there are techniques that can be used to give line managers, like the physician-manager in this example, greater control. At the moment, however, it is important to note only that by using the information from the full-cost accounting system for the responsibility accounting system, Newport has violated the fairness criterion.

The Responsibility Accounting Framework

Much of what goes on in a responsibility accounting system takes place in the context of the organization's overall strategic direction. More specifically, according to the late Robert N. Anthony of Harvard Business School, who is widely considered to be the "conceptual father" of responsibility accounting, managers engage in three different types of planning and control activities: strategic planning, task control, and management control.[3]

Strategic Planning

During the strategic planning process, senior management determines the organization's goals and the general nature of the activities needed to achieve them, frequently undertaking a SWOT (organizational Strengths and Weaknesses in comparison to environmental Opportunities and Threats) analysis. Because environmental opportunities and threats do not arise in orderly, predictable ways, strategic planning decisions are not made according to a prescribed timetable. As a result, the strategic planning process is irregular and unsystematic.

Task Control

At the other extreme from strategic planning is a set of activities used in carrying out the day-to-day operations of the organization, in particular the performance of specific tasks. Task control is the process of ensuring that these operations are carried out effectively and efficiently. Although task control will vary with the nature of any given organization's operations, it generally involves such activities as maintaining adequate levels of inventory, sending out invoices in a timely way, collecting accounts receivable and depositing funds, issuing paychecks, and so forth.

Many task control activities do not involve managers. If they are automated, they do not even involve humans, except to ensure that the activity is functioning properly and to deal with matters not included in the automated process. For example, many organizations with sizable inventories rely on bar codes, scanners, and a computer to place an order directly with the appropriate vendor whenever the quantity of an item in inventory decreases to a preset level.

Management Control

Management control sits between strategic planning and task control. It usually begins with the goals determined in the strategic planning process and focuses on how best to attain them. To this end, it addresses the programs (or product lines) that can help move the organization toward its strategic goals. It focuses on these programs' budgets, as well as on the budgets for other activities, such as information technology services. The *management control process* also is concerned with the collection of data and the design and preparation of reports that present those data to line managers and others so that they can assess whether their respective responsibility centers are meeting budgeted projections. Increasingly, the process also focuses on measuring and reporting a variety of nonfinancial items that line managers are expected to attain, such as patient satisfaction, process improvements, and employee training and development.

management control process
A sequence of activities that take place in four phases: programming, budgeting, operating and measuring, and reporting.

Unlike strategic planning, the management control process is regular and systematic, with predictable, repeated steps. And unlike task control, which may not directly involve humans, management control is fundamentally behavioral: it is an activity in which line managers interact with a variety of people in the organization, particularly other managers. In many organizations, line managers also interact with professionals, such as engineers, scientists, computer programmers, physicians, and nurses.

This balance between the optimal allocation of resources and the behavior of managers, professionals, and others means that the management control process is governed by the principles of both economics and social psychology. Not only are the principles found in these two disciplines quite different, but their relative importance to the management control process varies greatly in different situations.

Much of the management control process is informal. Meetings, ad hoc memoranda, and hallway and lunchtime conversations all can serve to influence how managers make decisions about the use of resources. Nevertheless, in most organizations there also is a more formal process. This formal process usually consists of a set of regularly scheduled activities in which decisions are made about the kinds and quantities of goods or services the organization expects to provide during an upcoming period of time and the resources needed to generate that output. During the year, records usually are kept on actual results (revenues, expenses, and nonfinancial metrics), and most organizations prepare regular reports on these results that managers can use as a basis for determining whether corrective action of some sort is needed.

Formal Management Control Activities

In most organizations, the regularly scheduled activities are considered to be a part of the formal management control process. They can be classified into four separate phases: (1) programming, (2) budgeting, (3) operating and measuring, and (4) reporting.

These phases recur in a regular cycle and build on each other, as indicated in figure 6.1. The remainder of this chapter discusses the four phases briefly. They are discussed in greater detail in subsequent chapters.

Programming

During the programming phase of the management control process, an organization makes a variety of decisions concerning both the kinds of new services, product lines, or programs it will begin to offer and the amount of resources it will devote to each. In general, as figure 6.1 indicates, these

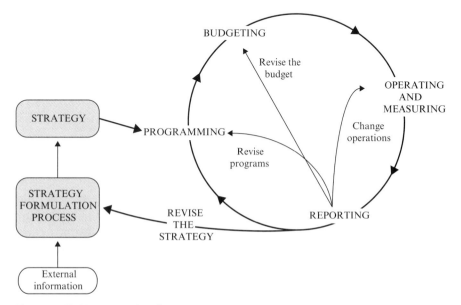

Figure 6.1 The Management Control Process

decisions are made in the context of the organization's strategy, coupled with whatever information is available about new opportunities, increased competition, new or pending legislation that might affect the organization's efforts, and a variety of similar considerations.

EXAMPLE

Overdale, a large visiting nurse association (VNA), is considering the addition of a home repair program. The program would do minor construction work for the agency's clients, ranging from small home repairs to somewhat larger projects, such as building a deck. Adding this program would require an investment of approximately $500,000 to convert some space, purchase the necessary materials, and buy the required equipment.

This example illustrates several important aspects of programming:

- The decision is a programming one, as it involves a new service, product line, or program.

- The decision is not easily reversible and thus requires careful analysis and consideration.

- The decision has two strategic components. First, the VNA believes that it can compete with smaller neighborhood home repair services and can convince its clients who use traditional VNA services (nurse visits, home health aide visits, and so forth) to buy home repair services as well. Second, the agency believes that it can recruit and manage people with the needed skills (certainly managing a carpenter is different from managing a nurse or home health aide).

- The decision entails a capital investment and therefore requires an analysis of the return on the proposed investment (a technique for calculating this return is discussed in chapter 8).

For these reasons, programming decisions generally are considered to have a long-range nature, and the programming phase of the management control process may look ahead by as much as five or ten years. The program planning document frequently is lengthy, describing each proposal in detail, estimating the resources necessary to accomplish it, and calculating the expected social and financial returns. The economic analysis may include benefits that are difficult to quantify, which complicates the decision. For example, in assessing Overdale's proposed home repair program, senior management must ask itself whether some people who use the program will be new to the VNA and will use one or more of the agency's health care services at some time in the future.

Because many of the benefits of new program proposals are difficult to quantify, and because line managers tend to be optimistic about their program proposals, there frequently is a "new program bias" in the programming phase. Senior management tends to counteract this bias by using its own staff to analyze proposals submitted by line managers. As might be imagined, there is occasional friction between staff and line managers, not to mention a political aspect to the entire process. Managing this friction and the political content so that the final result is a tough but realistic assessment of the proposal is perhaps one of the most challenging tasks that senior management faces.

Budgeting

In contrast to programming, which looks ahead several years, budgeting generally looks ahead only one year. It accepts service lines and programs as givens and attempts to determine the amount of revenue and expenses associated with each during the year. In many organizations, service lines and programs fall neatly into responsibility centers, such that each responsibility center manager can be charged with preparing a budget for each of his or her service lines or programs. Sometimes a program and a responsibility center are identical.

EXAMPLE

Woodruff Medical Center has several departments that are profit centers: medicine, surgery, OB-GYN, and pediatrics. Each department has one or more programs. For example, the pediatrics department has one program for Kawasaki syndrome, another for childhood immunizations, and a third for neonatal intensive care. OB-GYN has one program for in vitro fertilization, another for teenage pregnancy counseling, and a third for postmenopausal therapy.

In formulating the medical center's budget, senior management asks each program manager to develop a budget for his or her program. These program budgets are grouped into department budgets, and finally into a master budget for the medical center.

In this organization the programs fit neatly into responsibility centers, but in many organizations the fit is not so neat, and a more complicated budgeting process is needed. This frequently happens when programs cut across several responsibility centers.

PROBLEM

Excelsior Medical Center has an oncology program, a geriatrics program, a heart institute, and a research program. Its responsibility centers include not only programs but departments as well, such as medicine, surgery, and OB-GYN.

Each program uses one or more physicians from each of the departments, and physicians in each department are likely to divide their time among two or more programs. How do you think programs and departments are incorporated into the budget formulation process in this organization?

ANSWER

Budgeting here must balance the plans of program managers and those of department managers. Each program manager can specify how many physicians of what specialties are needed for his or her program, and each department manager can indicate how many physicians he or she wants in the department. But there must be a balance between the needs of the two.

Because of these differing kinds and levels of complexity, an organization must design its budgeting phase to meet its unique needs. Nevertheless, a good budgeting phase usually includes the following elements:

- A set of guidelines, including a timetable, that is developed by senior management and communicated to line managers. Establishing these guidelines is usually the first step in the phase.

- A participatory element that gives each line manager an opportunity to prepare a budget for his or her responsibility center and to discuss this budget with his or her superiors.

- A central staff (usually in the controller's office) that is responsible for coordinating the budgeting activities, attending to technical details, and occasionally providing analyses that serve as checks and balances against responsibility center managers' projections.

- A hierarchy of information that begins with the smallest responsibility center and accumulates budget information into progressively larger responsibility centers, eliminating excessive detail at each step in the hierarchy.

- A negotiation step during which, if necessary, each responsibility center manager has an opportunity to defend his or her budget against anticipated reductions or to otherwise argue why it should be retained as originally proposed.

* A final approval and sign-off by senior management, authorizing responsibility center managers at each level to carry out their agreed-on budget.

In general, this final approval constitutes a commitment between each responsibility center manager and his or her superior that the budget will be adhered to unless there are "compelling reasons" to change it. Compelling reasons include large and unanticipated changes in volume, a lengthy strike, fuel shortages and resulting large price increases, a fire in the main building, and any number of similarly significant or catastrophic events.

As anyone who has participated in a budgeting effort knows, there is a certain game-like quality to it. This, in part, is the reason senior management uses staff analyses to assess the information submitted by responsibility center managers. The intent is to eliminate any "slack" in the budget, so that the final budget estimates the future as realistically as possible. Overall, the budget for each responsibility center should be relatively difficult to attain, but attainable nevertheless.

EXAMPLE

A classic game-playing technique is to arouse or threaten to arouse public protest by suggesting that a popular or essential service must be eliminated to cut a manager's budget. In what is now known as "The Washington Monument Elevator Ploy," the manager of the Washington Monument proposed to reduce his budget by eliminating the elevator service. He knew that such a change would antagonize hundreds of thousands of visitors each year.

Another example, and one that actually was carried out, took place some years ago in New York City. New York's mayor at the time was asked to reduce spending to avoid bankruptcy. He responded by dismissing 7,000 police officers and firefighters and closing 26 firehouses. Many people believe he did this to inflame public opinion against budget cuts. It did in fact have this effect, and the order was reversed.[4]

Operating and Measuring

Once programs have been established and a budget has been agreed on, the organization begins operating during the budget year. This is, of course, an oversimplification, because all organizations except newly established ones operate continually. However, if some new programs have been approved, or if new funds have been made available for existing programs, it is quite likely that a variety of new or different operations will commence at the beginning of the new budget year.

From a responsibility accounting perspective, new or different types of operations have important implications. Specifically, if the budget is to be adhered to, managers must receive information that compares their responsibility centers' performance to budgeted objectives. Consequently, both new and ongoing activities must be measured. More specifically, financial and nonfinancial data must be collected and incorporated into the responsibility accounting system. The operating and measuring phase of the process, then, puts plans into place and measures the relevant inputs and outputs.

If the measuring activity is to be effective, the organization must have a well-developed accounting system. This system not only must keep track of revenues and expenses but also must permit the information to be used for four purposes:

- To prepare financial statements. Here, rules imposed on the organization by outside agencies (for example, the Financial Accounting Standards Board in the United States) govern how the information is to be organized and presented.

- To allocate support center costs to mission centers and attach each mission center's full costs to its products to determine the full cost of each of its cost objects.

- To prepare reports that measure the performance of responsibility center managers by comparing actual revenues, expenses, or both to budgeted ones.

- To prepare reports that assist senior management in evaluating the organization's programs and determining their overall financial impact, thereby helping to guide future programming decisions.

Although the information has multiple uses, it must be integrated. That is, even though data collected for one purpose may differ from those collected for another, and even though certain data elements will sometimes be reported in detail and sometimes in summary, in all instances the data must be reconcilable from one report to another. This requires careful and thoughtful design of the information coding structure at the outset and a cautious, systematic process for adding new data elements when the system is modified. Moreover, in designing and modifying the accounting system, the members of the organization's accounting staff (who usually design such systems) must be carefully managed to ensure that they are aware of the multiple uses of the information.

In general, the system is built on a financial base; that is, amounts are stated in monetary units, because these are generally the easiest to collect, maintain, and integrate with each other. Nevertheless, managers frequently wish to see a variety of nonmonetary measures, such as minutes per visit, number of patients per day, false-positive and false-negative percentages, patient satisfaction rates, the incidence of postoperative infections, injuries from falls, and so forth. These nonmonetary items also are part of the operating and measuring phase. Indeed, many health care organizations have begun to rely on a technique known as the *balanced scorecard* (BSC) to report on a variety of nonfinancial items that are important to their success. The BSC is discussed in chapter 11.

The operating and measuring phase is complicated by two factors. First, different managers in an organization make different kinds of decisions. Second, any given manager will make a variety of decisions depending on the particular circumstances he or she faces at various times in the operating year. These factors mean that the measurement aspect of the phase must be flexible and dynamic—in any growing or evolving organization, the information that senior and middle managers need will differ from one responsibility center to the next, and are likely to be changing constantly.

In this regard, it must be remembered that information itself is a resource. Like all resources, it has both a cost and a use to which it can be put. Senior management must constantly assure itself that its utility exceeds the cost of gathering, processing, and presenting it.

Reporting

The final phase of the management control process is the presentation of information to responsibility center managers. The information collected in the operating and measuring phase of the cycle is classified, analyzed, sorted, merged, totaled, and finally reported to these managers. The resulting reports generally compare planned outputs and inputs with actual ones, thereby allowing both responsibility center managers and their superiors to evaluate performance during the operating period. This information, along with whatever other information seems appropriate (from informal sources, industry analyses, and so forth), generally leads to one of three courses of behavior, as indicated in figure 6.1.

Changing Operations

If the responsibility center manager or his or her supervisor is not satisfied with the results shown on the reports, corrective action of some sort is needed. This action may include such activities as examining sources of supply in an attempt to obtain lower prices, asking supervisors about the use of overtime, speaking with nurses and physicians about patient satisfaction or dissatisfaction with the care they received, and so forth. Action may also include giving praise for a job well done; offering constructive criticism; reassignment; or, in extreme cases, termination.

Revising the Budget

In some instances, key aspects of the activities in a responsibility center are not under the manager's control. For example, the volume of inpatient days in a rehabilitation hospital may be determined by the hospital's referral personnel and their success in working with acute-care discharge planners. As a result, the manager of, say, the physical therapy department would have no ability to control volume, and the budget would need to be flexed to reflect the actual volume of patients served.

Similarly, if supply prices are the responsibility of the purchasing department, and if wage rates are determined by senior management in its negotiations with unions, managers of the affected responsibility centers will have little control over variations from the budget in these areas. Moreover, the effect of a strike or a natural disaster may mean that it is all but impossible for a responsibility center manager to meet the budget. In these instances some organizations will revise the budget.

EXAMPLE

In the wake of Superstorm Sandy in 2012, many hospitals and other health care providers in the Northeast needed to make significant changes in their budgets. Some changes reflected unexpectedly large increases in patients served, whereas others reflected unexpectedly large decreases.

Revising Programs

The responsibility center reports can also be used as a basis for program evaluation and revision. For any of a number of reasons, a programming decision might not have been optimal. The anticipated demand might not exist; competition might be stronger than originally thought; technological improvements might have made the program obsolete. In extreme situations, the reports may indicate not only a need to revise or discontinue one or more of the organization's programs but also a need to change the organization's strategy.

Because the reporting phase has this feedback characteristic, the loop shown in figure 6.1 is a closed one. As a consequence, the management control process tends to be rhythmic—it follows a pattern that is about the same every year. Managers learn this pattern and adjust their activities to it.

You are now ready to work on the practice case, Akron Public Health Department, which will give you an opportunity to think about an unusual responsibility center design. Appendix B at the end of the book contains a solution.

KEY TERMS

Discretionary expense centers	Profit centers
Effectiveness	Responsibility center
Efficiency	Revenue centers
Investment centers	Senior management
Line managers	Standard expense centers
Management control process	

To Bear in Mind

1. Do not confuse *is* with *should*. The first step in analyzing a responsibility accounting system is to determine the kind of responsibility center each organizational unit *is*, given the resources for which the manager is held responsible. You then need to assess the kind of responsibility center that the unit *should be* in terms of what its manager can control and what senior management wants him or her to control.

2. It is not enough to determine that a particular organizational unit is an expense center. You also must determine whether it is a discretionary or a standard expense center. The two are quite different.

Test Yourself

1. What are the key activities that managers engage in when designing and using a responsibility accounting system? What are the managerial uses of the system?

2. Define a responsibility center, and list the five types of responsibility centers.

3. What is the distinction between a discretionary expense center and a standard expense center? What is the importance of this distinction? Give an example of each type of responsibility center. What accounting technique is used in conjunction with a standard expense center?

4. What is the "fairness criterion"? Give an example of how it can be violated.

5. What are the four phases of the management control process? Briefly describe what happens in each phase and what kinds of actions managers might take place in that phase.

Suggested Cases

Franklin Health Associates

Penn State Geisinger Health System

Southern Seattle University Health System (A)

PRACTICE CASE

AKRON PUBLIC HEALTH DEPARTMENT

I made two pretty significant changes. First, I set up some labor-management committees, each consisting of shop supervisors, tradespeople, and a shop steward. Second, I created what I called "profit centers" to substitute for work standards in the bureau. The results were phenomenal.

The speaker was Anthony Edwin, director of the Bureau of Motor Equipment of the Akron Public Health Department. The bureau was responsible for maintaining the department's 1,000 vehicles. It had about 250 employees and an annual operating budget of about $8 million.

Background

Two years prior to Mr. Edwin's assuming the position of director, the bureau had used a series of negotiated work standards that covered practically every job, from rebuilding an engine to fixing a generator. At that time, according to a report of the city's financial control board, conditions in the bureau were chaotic. On an average day, over half the vehicles it was responsible for repairing were out of service, resulting in huge amounts of overtime pay for the drivers assigned to the remaining vehicles. Mr. Edwin commented:

I was placed in charge of the bureau almost immediately after the mayor received the report from the financial control board. I spent a few weeks discussing the problems with everyone from supervisors to mechanics. No one seemed happy. The mechanics thought that the work standards were demeaning, and the supervisors complained that the effort needed to enforce those standards was oppressive. Clearly, some sort of radical change was needed.

Rather than attempting to solve the problems himself, Mr. Edwin created eight labor-management committees, one for each of the facility's eight departments (called shops): transmission, axle and related, upholstery, radiator, exhaust system, brakes, electrical system, and engines. He commented:

> I gave the committees a mandate to solve problems, improve the quality of work life, and increase productivity. I instructed them to meet monthly with me to recommend improvements. Early on, it became apparent that committee members were concerned that if they suggested ways to improve productivity and their suggestions were implemented, management would subsequently adjust the work standards upward. So there was a lot of distrust. We seemed to be at an impasse. That was when the profit center idea occurred to me. Of course the idea took some selling, but in the end the committees accepted it.

The profit center plan had the following elements. First, management would no longer focus on work standards as they applied to specific jobs and individuals, and individual records of time spent on jobs would no longer be required. Instead, management would focus only on whether each shop as a whole was producing at an acceptable level. The "value" of output would be measured by what it would have cost to purchase the same items or services from outside vendors, and the total value of output for a period would be compared with the total cost of operating the shop.

The output values were determined by checking outside price lists or obtaining price quotes for specific jobs. If the electric shop repaired an alternator, for example, the shop would receive a credit equal to what it would cost to buy a rebuilt alternator from a private supplier. The costs included labor costs (salaries, fringe benefits, sick pay, vacations, and jury duty); material costs; depreciation of machinery; and other overhead costs. The difference between output values and cost was called "profit," and the eight shops were therefore called profit centers. Mr. Edwin reflected on the impact:

> This system provides a mechanism to measure productivity without threatening the individual workers. Labor has responded enthusiastically to this concept. In addition, employees in individual shops can now see how well they're doing compared to the private sector. Each shop has a large chart in a visible location, and a spirit of competitiveness has developed, further spurring their desire to increase efficiency. The combination of the "profit motive" and the elimination of threats has worked like magic.

Results

Within two years, the bureau was supplying 100 percent of the primary vehicles needed every day. Mr. Edwin commented:

I estimate that we have avoided over $3 million of overtime costs during the two years that this new system has been in place. Some people might consider this to be a somewhat soft number. Fine, but take a look at this table [see exhibit 6.1]. The productivity improvements speak for themselves.

As exhibit 6.1 shows, all profit centers except the engine shop reported an annualized profit. The situation in the engine shop illustrates the difficulty of measuring output. Initially, the shop's credit for rebuilt engines was the same as the cost to buy new engines because reliable data on the price of rebuilt engines were not available. As exhibit 6.1 indicates, productivity was less than 1.0, meaning that the city could have purchased new engines for less than it spent rebuilding them.

As a result of decisions made by the shop's labor-management committee, the engine shop doubled its productivity and appeared to be producing at a substantial "profit." However, once a database containing the outside price of rebuilt engines had been developed, and once all the shop's past reports were converted to the rebuilt values, the shop was again operating at a "loss." This led the labor-management committee to take further steps to increase productivity, including the discontinuation of unprofitable products and the transfer of personnel from support functions to line functions. A few months later, the engine shop's productivity factor had risen to 1.19.

The relatively low productivity in the brake shop had a different cause. Employees were still required to list the actual time it took to do each job, and they feared that if they consistently beat readily available industry-wide standards, management sooner or later would either require more work from them or track each person's daily performance. They therefore omitted certain jobs from their daily work sheet, thereby leaving their productivity factor at just above 1.0. According to Mr. Edwin, this problem was solved in a way consistent with his overall philosophy:

> After the reasons for the artificially low productivity figure became apparent, I convened some meetings between the labor-management committee and the entire shop's workforce. One result was to agree that employees would no longer need to list the actual time it took to do a job. A few months later, the report for the shop showed that productivity had risen to 1.30.
>
> More generally, I have found that getting labor involved in the running of an operation is not only exciting and rewarding but also extremely worthwhile in terms of improving productivity and service quality. Our experience belies the common notions that the government worker cannot be productive or that the output of a government operation cannot be measured.
>
> There is no simple formula for succeeding in the change from a traditional approach to the labor-management approach, and there should be no doubt that management's commitment to the process is a critical factor. But given a true desire to see it succeed and a willingness to spend the necessary amount of time and effort, it can work. The simple proof is what the bureau has achieved.

Assignment

1. What are the strengths and weaknesses of the system that Mr. Edwin developed for the bureau?

2. Records of performance by individuals or of costs for individual jobs were discontinued. Do you agree with this policy?

3. What recommendations, if any, would you make to Mr. Edwin concerning the system he has developed? How might you improve on it?

EXHIBIT 6.1 Profit Center Status Report

Profit Center	Number of Weeks from Inception to Present	Annualized (in Thousands of Dollars)		Profit (Loss)	Productivity Factor*
		Input	Output		
Transmission	37	$350	$716	$366	2.05
Axle and related	40	1,280	2,146	866	1.68
Upholstery	35	126	183	57	1.45
Radiator	36	263	438	175	1.67
Exhaust system	23	643	1,562	919	2.43
Brakes	30	494	534	40	1.08
Electrical system	37	603	717	114	1.19
Engines	43	1,272	822	(451)	0.65
TOTAL		$5,031	$7,117	$2,086	1.41

*This factor is calculated using the formula Output ÷ Input.

Notes

1. For an argument that such an approach can produce unintended consequences that are not in the hospital's best interest, see David W. Young, "Profit Centers in Clinical Care Departments: An Idea Whose Time Has Gone," *Healthcare Financial Management* 62 (March 2008): 66–71.

2. For details, see David W. Young, *Note on Financial Surpluses in Nonprofit Organizations* (Boston: Harvard Business School Publications, Product TCG307, 2013).

3. Robert N. Anthony, *The Management Control Function* (Boston: Harvard Business School Press, 1988).

4. For more information on budget ploys, see Robert N. Anthony and David W. Young, *Note on Budget Ploys* (Boston: Harvard Business School Publications, Product TCG303, 2012).

CHAPTER 7

DESIGNING THE RESPONSIBILITY ACCOUNTING STRUCTURE

Chapter 6 discussed some of the basic design issues in developing or reconfiguring a responsibility accounting structure. Among the challenging matters touched on in chapter 6 are the link between the responsibility center structure and the organization's motivation process; the development of appropriate transfer prices for intraorganizational transactions; and some of the informal matters that arise in the context of decentralizing responsibility in organizations that are large, complex, or both. This chapter addresses those issues.

Organization of the Chapter

The chapter begins with a discussion of some important matters that senior managers must consider if they are to make profit centers (or investment centers) work to the overall benefit of the organization, including some design complications in matrix-like organizations. Next, it takes up the general topic of motivation and presents some recent thinking on various ways to reward managers and others for good performance. The argument is made that one of the principal objectives in designing a responsibility accounting system is to attain congruence between the goals of individual responsibility managers and the organization's overall goals. A number of factors must be considered to attain this goal congruence, one of which is the design of the motivation process.

The chapter then addresses some specific situations to illustrate the difficult nature of determining appropriate transfer prices. Inadequate attention to this topic by senior management explains why many responsibility

LEARNING OBJECTIVES

On completing this chapter, you should know about

- Issues that senior management must consider if its organization's profit centers are to be most effective

- The relationship between the responsibility accounting structure and managers' incentives

- Transfer prices and their role in a responsibility accounting system

- How matrix-like organizational structures can complicate the design effort

- Issues to consider in designing an appropriate motivation process for an organization's employees

- Informal decision making and its influence on an organization's success

fairness

When a manager makes a good financial decision from the standpoint of achieving the goals of his or her responsibility center, the measurement and reporting system shows improved financial results. A lack of such fairness ordinarily means that the measurement system needs to be revised to distinguish between controllable and non-controllable items and that the manager's performance needs to be measured with regard to those items over which he or she exerts a reasonable amount of control.

transfer prices

The prices at which an intra-organizational transactions takes place. For example, in a hospital, the Department of Surgery purchases lab tests from the Clinical Pathology Department. Because both are departments of the same hospital, their transaction is intra-organizational. The transfer prices for such transactions can range from market price to variable costs. Transfer prices frequently are important elements of an organization's responsibility accounting system.

accounting systems fail to achieve the goal of encouraging managers to do what is in their organization's best interests. The chapter concludes with a brief discussion of some of the informal aspects that can influence the success of a given responsibility center design. In particular, it looks at how individuals in organizations gain power and influence outside the formal responsibility center network.

Making Profit Centers Work

If senior management designates an organizational unit as a profit center—as is happening in many health care organizations—it must pay careful attention to four important design considerations: (1) the *fairness* criterion, (2) the goal congruence criterion, (3) transfer pricing arrangements, and (4) the cross-subsidization policy.

The Fairness Criterion

As discussed in chapter 6, a profit center manager needs to be able to exert *reasonable* influence over both the revenues and the expenses of his or her center. (If the center is designated as an investment center, he or she also needs reasonable control over the assets included in measuring the center's performance.) This does not imply that the manager must have *complete* control over these items, for few if any responsibility center managers have this kind of control. However, a profit center manager should be able to exercise control over the center's volume of activity, work quality, variable costs, direct fixed costs, and (depending on market conditions) the prices charged. Stated somewhat differently, the manager of a profit center should perceive that the surplus (or deficit) reported for his or her unit fairly measures the unit's financial performance.

The Newport Medical Associates problem in chapter 6 illustrated a fairly typical violation of the fairness criterion. Recall that senior management had allowed the accounting staff to allocate some portion of actual overhead costs to the physician group practice. In so doing, it effectively had asked the group's manager to be responsible for some costs that he could not control.

This problem could have been avoided with two changes to the responsibility accounting system. First, *transfer prices* could be used to account for the costs of support centers that provide measurable units of service (such as the laundry department or the pharmacy). With transfer prices, those units could be "purchased" by the departments receiving them. Second, for departments where transfer prices are not feasible because there are no units of service (such as administration and general), senior management could have the accountants assign to a receiving center only the portion of the relevant overhead expenses that was agreed to in the budgeting phase of the management control process, rather than allocating a portion of the costs actually incurred (which the group practice could not control). These sorts of changes would have helped to satisfy the fairness criterion.

The Goal Congruence Criterion

The term *goal congruence* is borrowed from social psychology and describes the idea of aligning the goals of each responsibility center manager with the goals of the organization as a whole. Other terms, such as *aligning incentives*, often are used to describe the same idea. A lack of goal congruence is present when a responsibility center manager takes actions that improve his or her own center's performance but worsen the organization's overall performance. For example, if a laboratory is designated as a discretionary expense center (and therefore has a fixed budget regardless of the volume and mix of tests done), its manager may be reluctant to incur overtime costs even though test results may be badly needed by other responsibility centers.

goal congruence
Alignment between the goals of managers of individual responsibility centers and the goals of the organization overall. Goal congruence is an important consideration in designing a management control system, and a lack of it ordinarily results in behavior on the part of responsibility center managers that is not in the best interests of the organization as a whole. Its absence ordinarily means that some changes are needed in the nature of the organization's responsibility centers or its transfer pricing structure.

When senior management sees a need for cooperative actions among profit center managers, it can encourage them by designing the responsibility center structure in such a way that cooperation has a positive impact on each profit center's reported performance (or at least does not adversely affect it). In the example just given, converting the laboratory into a profit center and using transfer prices based on not only the kind of test ordered but also the time the request is made (during or outside of normal working hours), as well as on whether the test is ordered "stat" (immediately) or not, would help promote goal congruence.

In addition, some organizations have fostered cooperation with a policy that no profit center manager receives a bonus unless *all* profit centers meet or exceed their budgeted targets. In other organizations, profit performance is only one of several items considered in the motivation process, and a manager's bonus depends on good performance along several other dimensions as well. In all instances, the idea is to enhance goal congruence.

EXAMPLE

Some organizations outside of health care have begun to link bonuses and other rewards to a manager's performance on several nonfinancial measures as well as on financial ones. One company tied 60 percent of its executives' bonus dollars to financial performance (which consisted of a weighted average of five components: operating margins, return on capital, cost reduction versus plan, growth in existing markets, and growth in new markets). The remaining 40 percent was based on balanced scorecard (BSC) indicators concerning customer satisfaction, internal process improvements, and employee growth and development.[1] It is not too difficult to imagine a health care organization introducing several similar measures concerning the same three nonfinancial areas, all of which are important to its success—if not this year, then in the future. Doing so would greatly improve goal congruence.

Transfer Pricing Arrangements

As already suggested, transfer prices play an important role in many health care organizations where there are intraorganizational transactions. These sorts of transactions can exist between two profit centers in a relatively small organization or between two divisions in a large integrated delivery system (IDS). A transfer price is appropriate in a hospital when, say, a physician in the pediatrics department orders a test from the laboratory, or in an IDS when a physician in a group practice designated as a profit center admits a patient to one of the system's hospitals.

If there are internal transactions and no transfer prices, it is not appropriate to designate the unit providing the service as a profit center, because it has no ability to generate revenue (for example, an internal auditing department usually provides services without charge and therefore should not be set up as a profit center).

Arriving at a set of satisfactory transfer prices is one of the most complicated aspects of designing a responsibility accounting structure. Later in the chapter, we will look at some of the issues that senior management must consider in developing effective transfer pricing arrangements.

The Cross-Subsidization Policy

When an organization has profit centers, senior management must decide if there will be cross-subsidization among them. Profit centers that are independent, meaning that they (1) do not cross-subsidize each other, and (2) have managerial rewards linked to bottom-line performance, are, in effect, a series of small, stand-alone business units. This arrangement is sometimes referred to as "every tub on its own bottom," or ETOB.

If, for example, an integrated delivery system had an ETOB arrangement, each operating unit (such as a hospital or a physician group practice) would be an independent profit (or investment) center. Units that incurred a deficit would need to find a way to absorb it.

In contrast, if an organization engages in cross-subsidization, senior management must make certain that profit center managers with surpluses not only accept the fact that they are providing subsidies to profit centers with deficits but also understand the rationale for doing so. In addition, at budgeting time, senior management must see to it that all profit center managers buy into the forecasted subsidy amounts.

EXAMPLE

In many academic medical centers, "profitable" departments, such as cardiothoracic surgery and orthopedics, subsidize departments that incur deficits, such as pediatrics and psychiatry. Within a department of medicine, procedure-oriented subspecialties, such as gastroenterology, sometimes subsidize other subspecialties, such as endocrinology and infectious diseases, that have difficulty generating a surplus. In many departments, clinical care subsidizes education and unfunded research activities. When these sorts of cross-subsidization activities take place, senior management must make sure that everyone agrees that the subsidies are fair; it also must ensure that everyone's work is valued even if it does not generate a surplus. A comment made by a cardiothoracic surgeon in one large IDS, "I'm tired of subsidizing those lazy pediatricians," is indicative of a situation in which the cross-subsidization issues have not been fully resolved.

Design Complications

Determining an appropriate network of responsibility centers would be relatively easy if each service line (1) sold its services to the outside; (2) were staffed by personnel who worked for no other service line; and (3) were the responsibility of a manager who had reasonable control over hiring and other personnel decisions, as well as decisions on supply and material purchases. Under these circumstances, each service line most likely would be designated as an investment or profit center.

Unfortunately, most organizations do not have such a tidy formal structure. Many integrated delivery systems operate over large geographical areas, for example, and must consider this fact when designing their respective structures. Does such an IDS have one manager of home care with broad geographical responsibilities, or does it have several regional managers, each with responsibility for all programs in his or her region, including home care?

Matrix Organizations

In general, a separate formal structure is needed when responsibility for the success of a program or service line depends on more than one supporting functional unit. For example, the director of a heart institute in an academic medical center may draw on physicians from several different departments (such as medicine and surgery) who work in the institute. In addition, each physician may work in several programs and therefore have multiple program reporting relationships as well as a reporting relationship with his or her department chair. The result is a blurring of program and functional lines.

The blurring occurs because one set of managers is responsible for the programs and another is responsible for the functional units (or departments). This creates a need for a fit between the two lines of authority, usually resulting in a matrix organization, such as that illustrated in figure 7.1.

In this arrangement, each program manager is accountable for his or her program's success. Functional unit managers, in contrast, are held accountable for the skill mix and service quality in their respective units. In the example in figure 7.1, most employees would have a home base in a functional unit and would be "purchased" at a transfer price by one or more programs. Because program managers call on functional units for work to

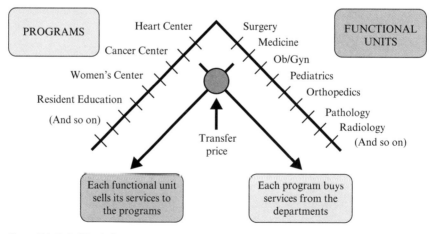

Figure 7.1 Typical Matrix Structure

be done in their programs, responsibility is divided between the functional units and the programs. The program managers, whose programs are likely to be designated as profit centers, would be responsible for the profitability of their programs. The functional units might be standard expense centers, with each unit manager responsible for recruiting personnel with the needed skill mix, and undertaking whatever training is required to meet the needs of the programs. In some instances, a functional unit specialist might be needed for a relatively short amount of time, such as for a clinical consult. In others, the functional specialist might spend the majority of his or her time working exclusively for a given program, such as an oncology center, or he or she may be spending considerable time in a "medical home."[2]

Complex Matrix Organizations

To understand how complex a matrix organization can become, consider the case of the department of mental health in a medium-size state government. The complexity, illustrated in figure 7.2, exists along several dimensions and affects the agency's responsibility accounting structure as well as the budgeting phase of the management control process. Some of those dimensions are the following:

- The agency does not generate revenues (which come from the state's income tax). It is therefore an expense center. Because its budget probably cannot be changed with changes in volume during the year, the agency is therefore a discretionary expense center.

- Resource allocation occurs along two dimensions. One is based on field operations and facilities, corresponding to the agency's functional structure (the left side of the matrix). The other is based on the agency's major programs, such as its community mental health centers (the right side of the matrix). The major programs correspond to appropriation accounts in the state's budget and are under the direction of the *account executives.*

- Both field operations and the major programs have several layers of responsibility. The field operations activity encompasses regions at the highest level, followed by facilities, and then units within the facilities. Each major program includes several subprograms (such as day treatment in a community mental health center).

- Overall program control is the responsibility of the account executives, who presumably cannot spend more than the amount allotted to their appropriation accounts. The programs cut across all regions, although not all regions or all facilities have all programs or all subprograms. As a result, one of the jobs of an account executive is to determine the

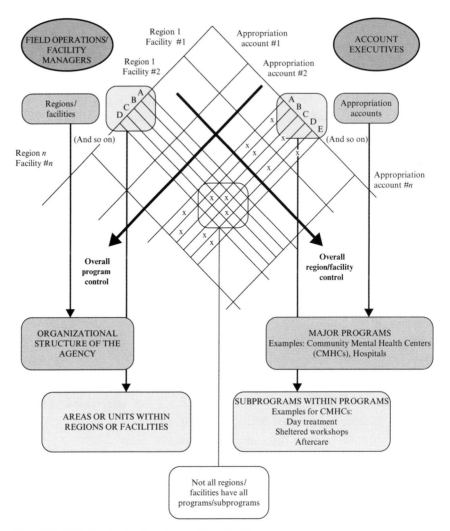

Figure 7.2 Matrix Structure in a Department of Mental Health

regions and facilities that can provide the most cost-effective service for each major program and its various subprograms.

* Control over activities in regions and facilities is the responsibility of the *field operations and facility managers*. They receive budgets from the account executives and must adhere to them while striving to meet the objectives of the programs and subprograms.

* Although the agency is a discretionary expense center, regional units could be established as standard expense centers, which would be appropriate because a unit manager has no control over the number or mix of individuals who need the unit's services. However, because the appropriation account budgets are fixed, the account executives

would need to ensure that increases in one region or facility were matched by decreases in other regions or facilities. Such an approach might provide greater motivation to unit, facility, and region managers to operate more effectively and efficiently.

Responsibility Centers and Motivation

As you might imagine given the discussion thus far, a responsibility accounting structure can provide a powerful motivating force for an organization's line managers. It is therefore extremely important for senior management to consider the incentives that underlie the structure. Indeed, unless there is a *motivation process* in place that bases a portion of a responsibility center manager's compensation on his or her center's performance, the type of responsibility center chosen is irrelevant.

motivation process
The set of rewards and (occasionally) punishments that managers receive based on their performance.

There is considerable disagreement about how to design a good motivation process. What motivates people to perform well in organizations and what role monetary compensation plays in rewarding superior performance are quite controversial. Despite the disagreements, one fact seems to stand out above all the rest: financial compensation is not everything. As Stanford's Jeffrey Pfeffer, who has studied the impact of compensation on performance, concludes in *The Human Equation*, "A challenging and empowering workplace often has a greater impact on employee behavior than monetary incentives."[3] This certainly is true for many health care professionals.

Harvard's Dorothy Leonard and Tufts's Walter Swap made a parallel argument in *When Sparks Fly*. They emphasized the importance of employees' passion for work that led them to lose the distinction between work and play. They gave the examples of 3M, where research and development (R&D) employees were allowed to use 15 percent of their time to pursue any individual project they wanted, and Hewlett-Packard, where R&D employees could set aside 10 percent of their time to work on individual projects. As a result, they argued, both 3M and Hewlett-Packard were among the most innovative companies in the world.[4] A similar approach might be appropriate for physicians (especially young ones) in academic medical centers.

Role of Contingent Compensation

Although these authors and others consider financial rewards to be of secondary importance, most observers tend to agree that financial rewards, when present, work best when they are in the form of contingent compensation. For example, when employees receive a share of their profit center's surplus through, say, a bonus, they are likely to work hard to keep costs low and to seek ways to increase revenues.[5]

In this regard, it is worthwhile to consider some well-established theoretical underpinnings related to motivation. For example, Abraham Maslow's classic "hierarchy of needs" begins with the most basic physical needs (such as food and clothing) at the bottom and rises to "self-actualization" at the top.[6] Of course, not all employees will see their jobs related to the same level in Maslow's hierarchy. Indeed, not all employees will be self-actualized, no matter what kind of motivation process senior management designs!

These differences exist because people are complex. In assessing their complexity, David McClelland has argued that most people have some combination of three motives: achievement (the need to seek tasks that will provide a sense of accomplishment), power (the need to be in charge of and influence others), and affiliation (the need to have social and interpersonal relationships).[7] An ideal motivation process would target each employee's mix of these three motives and align itself with them—a daunting task, indeed.

Overarching Themes

In light of these various theories, it is not surprising that so much has been written about the topic of motivation. Yet most managers would agree that no theory or combination of theories can eliminate the difficult (or perhaps impossible) task of designing a motivation process that both challenges and appropriately rewards each employee in an organization. There are, however, three basic themes that senior managers can use as they design (or redesign) their organization's motivation process.

1. *Rewards can be both extrinsic and intrinsic.* Other than financial rewards, extrinsic rewards can include praise, recognition, gold watches, and a variety of other nonfinancial items. Intrinsic rewards, by contrast, derive from within the employee and relate to how well he or she believes a task was performed. A good motivation process incorporates both types of rewards.

2. *Employees need feedback.* Regardless of the set of rewards and recognition activities that senior management uses, it needs to find ways to provide employees with feedback on their performance. Feedback allows employees to satisfy one or more of several needs, such as relating rewards to the effort they expended or comparing their rewards to an external standard of some sort.

3. *Procedural justice is important.* Employees need to believe that a fair process was used to determine the distribution of rewards among them.

Link to the Responsibility Accounting System

In addition to incorporating the three themes just listed, the motivation process must fit with the responsibility accounting system. Otherwise, it is likely that senior management will be sending mixed messages to employees or that there will be a lack of goal congruence. To the extent that employee attitudes, patient satisfaction, and operational performance are important, and are used as a basis for rewarding employees, senior management must build them into the incentive compensation portion of each responsibility center's budget. Moreover, if senior management wants profit center managers to engage in entrepreneurial behavior, the motivation process must provide appropriate rewards for the kinds of risks being taken, and the operating and measuring phase of the management control process must assign costs to profit centers in a way that managers perceive as fair.

Transfer Pricing Problems

The quest for fairness and goal congruence and the design of an effective motivation process can be impeded (if not totally torpedoed) by a poorly constructed set of transfer prices. Because a health care organization frequently has several responsibility centers that engage in transactions among themselves, the prices at which these transactions take place—the transfer prices—are important elements of the responsibility accounting structure.

EXAMPLE

In some hospitals, clinical care departments (such as medicine and surgery) have been established as profit centers, but there is no transfer pricing mechanism to account for the transactions between them and the hospital's clinical service departments (such as radiology and pathology). If there is no accounting for the costs of lab tests and radiological procedures used by the clinical care departments, these departments' costs are understated and their bottom-line performance looks better than it actually is. If the clinical service departments' costs are allocated to the clinical care departments, the clinical care departments have no ability to control those costs. In addition, the allocated costs will include any inefficiencies in the clinical service departments and thus may be higher than costs for the same services if they were purchased from outside the hospital. In this instance, the bottom-line performance of the clinical care departments will be worse than it otherwise might have been.

To illustrate how transfer prices can affect fairness and goal congruence, let's examine a relatively simple situation.

PROBLEM

The department chairs in an academic medical center (AMC) were being strongly encouraged to have their faculty use the AMC's photocopying facility for the reproduction of research papers and other photocopying needs. At a meeting of the department chairs, one chair reported that the cost of making 100 copies of a research paper was $20 more using the AMC's photocopying facility than it would have been if the work had been done at a private copy center located about one block from her department's offices.

This kind of situation arose several times a week in each department, totaling many thousands of dollars a year. At the request of the department chairs, the manager of the AMC's photocopying facility had prepared a detailed breakdown of the facility's costs for the 100 copies of the research paper:

Direct materials		$150
Direct labor		40
Variable overhead	$5	
Fixed overhead	20	25
Total costs		$215
Markup		22
Price		$237

The private copy center had proposed to do the same job (which would have been of the same quality and speed as at the AMC's photocopying facility) for $217. The chairs knew that the AMC's photocopying facility had the capacity to produce about 300,000 copies a week but was operating at a level of only about 250,000 a week.

What is the lowest price that the AMC's photocopying facility should charge for this job? What is the highest price that the department should pay? What should be done about the transfer pricing policy for the photocopying facility?

ANSWER

This is a relatively straightforward transfer pricing problem. The market price is known and is greater than the variable costs of the in-house entity. Quality and speed are similar for the two options, the fixed overhead costs of the in-house entity have been clearly identified, and the in-house entity has excess capacity.

Under this set of circumstances, it is possible to establish a transfer price that would promote fairness—in other words, that would give department chairs greater control over the costs for which they are being held responsible. To do so, the lowest price that a department should pay would be the photocopying facility's variable costs, as follows:

Direct materials	$150
Direct labor	40
Variable overhead	5
Total variable costs	$195

There frequently is some debate about the highest price that should be paid. The usual argument is that it should be the market price—$217 in this situation. If the transfer price were set at the market price, the AMC's photocopying facility would cover its variable costs and some, but not all, of its fixed overhead. However, by paying market price, the department would perceive the transfer price as "fair." The AMC also would be financially better off because no resources would flow to the private copy center.

If, for some reason, the private copy center's price were below the in-house facility's variable costs, an argument could be made that the lowest price the department should pay would still be the market price. Under these circumstances, however, there would be a clear signal to the AMC that its photocopying facility was being run inefficiently (or that the cost computations were in error). If the cost figures were accurate, the AMC would be better off eliminating its in-house facility and having the work done by the private copy center. This is because it would not incur any of the variable costs (which exceed the market price) and it possibly could eliminate some or all of the fixed overhead.

In this problem it was possible to determine the market price and to ascertain that all other factors (quality, turnaround time, and so on) were comparable. This is not always the case. If a market price is unavailable, or if there are differences in some of these other factors, the transfer pricing decision becomes more complicated. Moreover, it usually is much more difficult to identify fixed overhead, capacity is a bit more elusive, and comparable quality is rarely as clear.

Issues to Consider in Setting Transfer Prices

The resolution of transfer pricing problems is one of the most complicated aspects of designing a responsibility accounting system. In arriving at a transfer price, senior management typically chooses among market price, full cost, and marginal cost.[8] Different organizations use different options depending on a variety of considerations, including the availability of market price information and the effect of the choice on managers' motivation. Consequently, no option can be called the "right" option. Nevertheless, there are four basic issues that senior management must consider in establishing its transfer pricing policy: (1) autonomy versus central control, (2) rules of the game, (3) price consistency, and (4) standby capacity.

Autonomy versus Central Control

Assuming an in-house facility (such as a copy center) is not required for strategic reasons, senior management must decide how much autonomy it wishes to give to its individual managers. Will it allow selling units to set their own prices without intervention, or will it intervene to set prices? Will it allow purchasing units to go outside if they can get a better arrangement (in terms of price, quality, service, and so on) than internal selling divisions offer them?

If, on the one hand, senior management gives its selling units the autonomy to set prices at the level they choose and gives its purchasing units the autonomy to buy from the outside, it must be prepared to lose some intraorganizational transactions. The loss of these transactions may cause the organization's surplus to fall in the short run. Senior management must believe, therefore, that the increased autonomy will give managers the motivation to increase their surpluses and that the resulting increases will more than offset the short-run declines in the overall surplus caused by the use of outside purchases. If, on the other hand, senior management decides to intervene in managers' price setting and outside purchasing decisions, it must be prepared to engage in many of these interventions. It thus will need to design a process to address the frequent conflicts that arise between its managers.

Rules of the Game

The "rules of the game" must be clear. Managers must know their options at the beginning of the budget year. If they must buy from inside the organization, this needs to be well understood and agreed to. Many organizations have a rule that the transfer price must correspond to the market price. However, this approach is not always possible due to the unavailability of market price information for some internally provided goods and services. Under these circumstances, some other transfer pricing formula must be determined and incorporated into the budgeting phase of the management control process.

Price Consistency

When the price (or pricing formula) is established during the budgeting phase of the management control process and held constant throughout the budget year, a manager who is purchasing internally does not pay for inefficiencies in a selling unit that cause the unit's actual costs to exceed its budgeted ones. To allow selling units to pass along their inefficiencies to buying units would remove the incentive for them to control their costs, and would violate both the fairness and goal congruence criteria.

Standby Capacity

Transfer prices frequently are affected by the need for standby capacity. An in-house laboratory incurs some fixed costs simply by being "ready to serve" the clinical departments, for example. These costs can include both depreciation on the lab equipment as well as the costs of some technicians and other employees who must be present, perhaps on a twenty-four-hour-a-day basis and on weekends.

To deal with situations of this sort, some organizations establish a two-part transfer price. At the time budgets are prepared, each department that expects to use the in-house entity's services projects how much of the service it plans to use. This allows the selling unit to determine an appropriate level of fixed costs. Each buying unit then agrees to pay its fair share of those costs each month regardless of its use of the selling unit. That is, it agrees to pay the selling unit for being available when the department needs the service. Then, when the department uses the selling unit's services, it pays only the variable costs associated with the services used. Thus, one part of the transfer price is fixed each month, and the other part is variable, based on actual use of the selling unit's services.

Clearly, there can be many complications in adopting a two-part transfer price. Separating fixed and variable costs can be tricky. Determining a buying entity's fair share also can be complicated; some divisions may require continuous availability, for example, whereas others may not. And there also can be game playing in which some buying units deliberately underestimate their needs. These complications can be resolved, however, if senior management believes that a two-part transfer price will promote greater fairness, enhance goal congruence, or both.[9]

More generally, the key question is whether an organization's transfer pricing policies motivate managers to take actions that are in the best interest of *both* their individual responsibility centers *and* the organization as a whole. If so, the policies would seem to be appropriate. If not, senior management will need to consider modifications.

Relation to Informal Authority and Influence

Responsibility centers can be powerful forces in helping an organization achieve its strategy. No matter how carefully the responsibility centers are designed, however, *informal authority* and influence always will be present. Some of the considerations include unwritten rules concerning, for example, the decisions that a profit center manager may make independently, those that require a superior's approval, and those that require consultation with (but not necessarily approval of) higher-level managers. Moreover, senior management tends to give more autonomy to

informal authority
Influence that comes about for reasons other than a person's position in the formal organizational hierarchy.

subordinates whom they know well and whose judgment they trust. As a result, despite the presence of a variety of formal devices in an organization, some profit center managers may have considerably more authority and influence than others.

In addition, the responsibility center network links with the organization's *culture* and its conflict management processes. For example, dramatic cultural change would result from eliminating profit centers, centralizing revenue, and establishing a series of standard expense centers. Rapid cultural change also would result from shifting the organization's responsibility center structure from, say, an ETOB approach to one with cross-subsidization, or vice versa. In addition, profit center arrangements with cross-subsidization will almost certainly produce conflict about the appropriate sizes of the subsidies. This conflict will need to be managed, as will conflict about transfer prices.

Managing culture and conflict requires addressing these more informal factors and thinking about how they relate to the formal responsibility accounting structure. The result can help improve the functioning of the responsibility accounting system overall.[10]

Informal relationships often are described in terms of the power and influence that some people in an organization gain for reasons other than their position in the formal hierarchy or the kind of responsibility center they run. As John Kotter, one of the leading authorities on the subject, has observed, "A manager can be dependent in varying degrees on superiors, subordinates, peers in other parts of the organization, the subordinates of peers, outside suppliers, customers, competitors, unions, regulating agencies, and many others."[11]

Clearly, the lines on the organizational chart fall far short of depicting all of these relationships. In fact, as Kotter went on to observe, even the lines are not always reliable "because virtually no one in modern organizations will passively accept and completely obey a constant stream of orders from someone just because he or she is the 'boss.'" As Herbert Simon observed almost seventy years ago in the book that contributed to his winning the Nobel Prize for economics, "Authority is only one of a number of forms of influence. Its distinguishing characteristic is that it does not seek to convince the subordinate, but only to obtain his acquiescence. In actual exercise, of course, authority is usually liberally admixed with suggestion and persuasion."[12]

In short, although an organizational chart identifies the *formal authority* arrangements, and although these arrangements may be overlaid with a clear network of responsibility centers, both of these formal devices can and frequently do exclude many key decision makers. This is especially true

culture
The set of basic assumptions that underlies decision making in an organization.

formal authority
The influence that a manager derives from his or her position in the organizational hierarchy.

in team- and knowledge-based organizations, where authority is much more informal. For example, in some hospitals physicians who admit a large number of patients have a great deal of influence in organizational decision making, even though they may be independent practitioners and might not even appear on the organizational chart. Their influence comes in large measure from their ability, should they so choose, to admit their patients to another hospital and thus to cause a significant shift in the hospital's revenue stream.[13]

Similarly, in some academic medical centers, researchers have considerably more power than the organizational chart might indicate, because much of the organization's future depends on their successful endeavors. For example, a world-class researcher with a sizable National Institutes of Health grant may have considerable influence based on his or her ability to direct grant funds to alternative (but legitimate) uses.

In these situations, the physician's and the researcher's power derives in large measure from the uncertainty of their decisions. This idea was perhaps best illustrated by Michel Crozier in his classic study of organizational power and influence. Crozier identified low-level maintenance workers in a manufacturing plant as having a great deal of power due to their ability to control machine downtime—a critical success factor for the organization—and the uncertainty as to where they would deploy their efforts.[14]

As these comments suggest, an organization's informal decision-making processes generally are unwritten and frequently are somewhat mysterious. They encompass a network of interpersonal relationships that has important implications for management. Because they are unwritten, however, they usually are difficult to identify, and certainly hard to manage.

You are now ready to work on the practice case, Valley Hospital, which will give you an opportunity to determine some transfer prices and think about their implications. The solution to this case is in appendix B at the end of the book.

KEY TERMS

Culture	Informal authority
Fairness	Motivation process
Formal authority	Transfer prices
Goal congruence	

To Bear in Mind

1. The responsibility center structure overlaid on the organizational chart is senior management's *formal* way of assigning financial responsibility; it tells each manager the elements of the return on assets (ROA) formula for which he or she is responsible. To be successful, it needs to fit with the organization's strategy and, if properly designed, usually will include transfer prices.

2. Three concepts are key to having a successful responsibility center structure:

    - *Fairness.* Managers have the ability to exercise control over the elements of the ROA formula for which they are held responsible.

    - *Goal congruence.* Individual managers pursuing their units' best interests are simultaneously pursuing the organization's best interests.

    - *Motivation.* Managers are rewarded for doing a good job in achieving their goals, with rewards usually in the form of contingent compensation, although they sometimes can come in other ways.

Test Yourself

1. Define the goal congruence criterion. Why is it important for an organization to achieve goal congruence?

2. What is a transfer price? Give an example of a transfer price that might be incurred by a department of medicine in a hospital. Why, in terms of fairness and goal congruence, is it important to have a well-designed transfer pricing arrangement?

3. Describe the difference between an ETOB arrangement and a cross-subsidization arrangement for profit centers in an academic medical center. What kinds of problems do you think each type creates? Which type do you think predominates in academic medical centers? Why?

4. What is a matrix structure, and how might it look in an academic medical center? What role do transfer prices play in a matrix structure?

5. In designing a motivation process that incorporates contingent compensation, what are the three themes that senior management must keep in mind? Why is it important that the motivation process link to the responsibility accounting system?

Suggested Cases

Apogee Health Care

Converse Health System

National Youth Association

White Hills Medical Center

PRACTICE CASE

VALLEY HOSPITAL

First they tell me I'm running a profit center, which seems to be a good idea. Then they tell me to run the department as though it were a little business, which I like. Then they tell me that I have to buy lab tests at prices much greater than what I would have to pay to Biolab, despite the fact that Biolab can give me equally fast turnaround time and equal quality. Now what do I do?

Phyllis Martin, MD, director of the ambulatory care division of Valley Hospital, had received both good and bad news. The good news, which came several months ago, was that her division, along with most other divisions in the hospital, had been reorganized into a profit center. Each profit center had been given responsibility for its own bottom line, and profit center managers and their key staff members were to be paid annual bonuses based on the surpluses of their respective units. The bad news was that Dr. Martin had just been told that she had to purchase all her division's laboratory tests from the laboratory division, another profit center. She continued:

Here's a good example. We charge our patients $22 for a CBC [complete blood count], which typically is required in conjunction with a diagnostic workup. The $22 charge covers the time spent by nurses in my division assisting the patient; the processing of paperwork by our administrative staff; the supplies needed for the CBC (syringes, vials, and so on); and the time spent by our staff reporting the results to the patient. However, we don't have the capability to do the actual lab work needed to analyze the patient's blood. This I must "purchase" from somewhere else. I've been using the hospital's lab division, but I now find out that its price is totally unreasonable.

The laboratory division charged all the hospital's divisions $12 for a CBC. According to Joseph Goodman, the laboratory manager:

My price for a CBC is very reasonable. It is based on our variable costs of $4, which are mainly supplies and labor, plus $6 of our fixed costs, and only $2 of margin, which is a fair amount.

Dr. Martin's concern arose because her staff had found that they could purchase CBCs of comparable quality for $9.00 each from Biolab, a freestanding laboratory located nearby. By doing so, she could improve her division's bottom line considerably.

The conflict had reached the office of Sam Black, the hospital's chief financial officer. According to him:

> They keep talking about what's fair and what's not fair. A fair is a summer event with cows and baked goods! We have a hospital to run. If we let Phyllis buy her lab tests from Biolab, then we have to let our other profit centers buy from Biolab. What happens to our own lab at that point? It does only the expensive tests that the labs-in-a-box can't or won't do. Can you imagine what would happen to our per-test cost at that point, not to mention our vulnerability in the marketplace? Biolab could hold us up, and we'd have no recourse. You can't have a hospital without a lab, and you can't have a lab doing only the esoteric stuff.

Although Dr. Martin was sympathetic to both Mr. Goodman's and Mr. Black's points of view, she also felt quite strongly that there had to be a better solution to the problem.

> I understand where Joe's coming from. He runs a profit center too, and he and his staff get a bonus based on his department's bottom line. But his bonus shouldn't be at my division's expense. Each time we purchase a CBC, our profits decline by $3 from what they otherwise would be, and along with that our bonuses fall too.

Mr. Black knew that the conflict would not dissipate without some intervention from his office. He wondered what he should do and what the implications of his decision would be for the other departments in the hospital, such as radiology, that also were profit centers.

Assignment

1. Using the following structure, calculate each profit center's financial performance under the two options shown:

	Ambulatory Care Division	Lab Division	Hospital Overall
Option 1: Buy from hospital lab division			
Revenue			
Variable costs			
Contribution			

	Ambulatory Care Division	Lab Division	Hospital Overall
Option 2: Buy from Biolab			
Revenue			
Variable cost			
Contribution			

2. What problems, if any, are illustrated by your computations? Please be as specific as you can.

3. What should Mr. Black do about the conflict between Dr. Martin and Mr. Goodman over the price of a CBC? What should he do about the prices for other lab tests and other procedures (such as X-rays)?

Notes

1. Robert S. Kaplan and David P. Norton, *The Balanced Scorecard* (Boston: Harvard Business School Press, 1996). The BSC will be touched on again later in the book.

2. A medical home is an approach to providing comprehensive primary care that strives to allow better access to health care services, increase patient satisfaction, and improve overall health status. A medical home requires such resources as health information technology and appropriately trained staff to provide coordinated care through a team-based approach. The team-based approach involves specialists, hospitals, home health agencies, and nursing homes. A medical home demonstration project with the Group Health System in Seattle indicated that there were 29 percent fewer emergency room visits, 6 percent fewer hospitalizations, and total savings of $10.30 per patient per month over a twenty-one-month period. For details, see Robert J. Reid et al., "The Group Health Medical Home at Year Two: Cost Savings, Higher Patient Satisfaction, and Less Burnout for Providers," *Health Affairs* 29 (May 2010): 835–843.

3. Jeffrey Pfeffer, *The Human Equation: Building Profits by Putting People First* (Boston: Harvard Business School Press, 1998).

4. Dorothy Leonard and Walter Swap, *When Sparks Fly: Harnessing the Power of Group Creativity* (Boston: Harvard Business School Press, 2005).

5. Pfeffer, *The Human Equation*.

6. Abraham H. Maslow, *Motivation and Personality* (New York: Harper & Row, 1954).

7. David C. McClelland, "Business Drive and National Achievement," *Harvard Business Review* 40 (July–August 1962): 99–112.

8. Transfer pricing has been the subject of many articles and treatises in the accounting literature. One of the best management-oriented descriptions can be found in David Solomons, *Divisional Performance: Measurement and Control* (Homewood, IL: Irwin, 1965). This book is considered a classic in the responsibility accounting literature.

9. Solomons, *Divisional Performance*, contains a section on two-part transfer pricing. For an application of this idea to integrated delivery systems in health care, see David W. Young, "Two-Part Transfer Pricing Improves IDS Financial Control," *Healthcare Financial Management* 52 (August 1998): 56–65.

10. For additional discussion of the link between responsibility accounting and culture, see David W. Young, "The Six Levers for Managing Organizational Culture," *Business Horizons* 43 (September–October 2000): 19–28.

11. John P. Kotter, "Power, Dependence, and Effective Management," *Harvard Business Review*, July–August 1977, 128.

12. Herbert A. Simon, *Administrative Behavior*, 2nd edition (New York: Free Press, 1957), 151–152.

13. David W. Young and Richard B. Saltman, *The Hospital Power Equilibrium* (Baltimore: Johns Hopkins University Press, 1985).

14. Michel Crozier, *The Bureaucratic Phenomenon* (Chicago: University of Chicago Press, 1964).

CHAPTER 8

PROGRAMMING

Chapter 6 briefly described two aspects of planning in a responsibility accounting system: programming and budgeting. These represent long-range and short-range planning activities, respectively. In the programming phase of the management control process, senior management's decisions frequently involve investments in fixed assets that will be used over several years and that will result in some sort of financial "payback."

Programming decisions are sometimes called capital budgeting decisions and usually involve an analytical technique that recognizes the multiyear period over which the fixed assets will be used. We examine programming in this chapter and discuss operational and cash budgeting in chapters 9 and 10, respectively.

Organization of the Chapter

The chapter begins with an overview of the programming phase of the management control process, positioning it as a key activity in implementing an organization's strategy. Programming decisions that call for the purchase of a new asset (such as a new facility or new equipment) usually rely, in part, on one or more of three analytical techniques: payback period, net present value, and internal rate of return. Although there are instances when an organization may decide to purchase a fixed asset without undertaking a formal financial analysis, the use of one of these analytical techniques usually is an important aspect of a programming decision.

Next, we examine how organizations go about choosing a "discount rate" for the analysis. This segues into the issue of risk and how to deal with risk in assessing a capital investment proposal. The chapter concludes with a discussion of the political, behavioral, and other

LEARNING OBJECTIVES

On completing this chapter, you should know about

- The meaning of the terms *payback period, net present value*, and *internal rate of return* and their role in programming

- The issues involved in choosing a discount rate for assessing a capital project

- The impact of political and behavioral matters on the choice of capital projects

- The issues associated with undertaking a benefit-cost analysis, especially when it involves quantifying the value of a human life

considerations that can influence senior management's choice of a proposal, including ways that programming links to both an organization's culture and its conflict management processes. Appendix 8A at the end of the chapter discusses the concept of present value. Appendix 8B discusses some of the special programming issues that governmental organizations face in attempting to assess nonfinancial benefits, such as the impact of a proposal on society or on a class of individuals. It also discusses the tricky issue of valuing a human life.

It is important to note that this chapter provides only an introduction to the topic of programming. In some schools of management or programs in health care management, an entire course is devoted to the topic. A more extensive discussion of the topic can be found in most textbooks on corporate finance.[1]

Programming: An Overview

In the programming phase of the management control process, senior management makes a variety of long-term decisions concerning the organization's product lines, the new programs it will undertake, and the resources it will devote to each. As discussed in chapter 6, these decisions are made within the context of the organization's overall strategy, coupled with whatever information is available concerning new opportunities, increased competition, new or pending legislation that might affect the organization's efforts, and other similar matters.

In a large organization, such as an integrated delivery system, each division or service line may prepare its own strategic plan in which it defines its business elements, its competitors, and its competitive advantages and disadvantages. These plans establish a framework for the organization's programming activities. In some large organizations, there is a lengthy program planning document that describes each program proposal in detail, estimates the resources needed to accomplish it, and calculates the expected returns.

Capital Budgeting Techniques

Decisions about fixed assets involve multiyear commitments. A new piece of equipment, for example, usually will last for three to five years, sometimes longer. A new or renovated facility usually will last for fifteen to twenty years before substantial renovations are needed.

In making decisions with multiyear commitments, we must recognize that a financial benefit received at some point in the future is not worth as much as that same amount received today. This section discusses why this is so and introduces the notion of net present value, a technique that is frequently used to deal with the issues raised when we translate future financial benefits into today's terms.

Capital Investment Decision Making

A decision to purchase a fixed asset can have an important impact on an organization's financial statements in both the short run and the long run. In the short run, the purchase may affect cash management through either the use of cash to purchase the fixed asset or an increase in debt to finance its purchase. In the latter instance, assuming the debt is long term (that is, several years in duration); the short-term impact is mitigated somewhat, resulting in annual debt service outlays (principal and interest payments) rather than the large outlay of cash that otherwise would be necessary.[2] These matters are discussed in greater detail in chapter 10.

The long-run effect comes about as a result of the impact the new fixed asset has on annual cash flows. That is, the acquisition of a fixed asset—generally a piece of equipment but occasionally a new or renovated facility of some sort—will almost always result in some positive cash flow effects. These effects can come about as a result of either decreased operating expenses or increased contribution (incremental revenues minus incremental expenses). The period over which these cash flows will be received is known as the asset's *economic life* (as distinct from its *physical life*, which usually is much longer).

The decision to purchase a new fixed asset entails a variety of considerations that are difficult to quantify. In many organizations, strategic and competitive concerns, regulatory mandates, employee morale, union grievances, and the like play a role in such decisions. In addition, however, an important aspect of almost all capital investment decisions is financial feasibility. Determining financial feasibility consists of comparing the purchase price of the asset with the estimated future cash inflows that can be attributed to it. The three most common techniques used to make this comparison are *payback period*, *net present value*, and *internal rate of return*.

Payback Period

This technique consists of simply dividing the net investment by the estimated annual cash inflows it generates. The quotient is the number of years of cash inflows needed to recover the investment. The *net investment* generally is defined as the cost of the new asset plus installation costs, plus

payback period
The number of years needed to recover an investment. It is equal to the amount of the investment divided by the incremental annual cash flows resulting from the investment.

net present value
Gross present value less the amount of the investment needed to achieve it.

internal rate of return
The discount rate that will result in a net present value of zero.

disposal costs for the asset being replaced, minus any revenue received from selling that asset. Annual cash flows are the reduced expenses or increased contribution attributable to the new asset.

PROBLEM

Nido Escondido Hospital is considering the purchase of a $10,000 piece of equipment for its admitting office. The new equipment will replace an existing piece of equipment, which the vendor has offered to repurchase for $2,000. It will also result in labor savings of approximately $4,000 a year. How long will it take the hospital to "pay back" the investment?

ANSWER

The net investment amount is $8,000 ($10,000 − $2,000 for the old equipment). The labor savings of $4,000 a year constitute the cash inflows attributable to the investment. The resulting payback period is two years ($8,000 ÷ $4,000).

The main advantage of the payback period approach is simplicity; it frequently is used to gain a rough estimate of the feasibility of a particular investment opportunity. Its main disadvantages are that (1) it does not facilitate a comparison of the financial feasibility of two or more competing projects, and (2) it does not consider the time value of money.

Referring to the time value of money is another way of saying that a dollar saved one year from today is not as valuable as a dollar saved today, a dollar saved two years from today is worth even less, and so on. If the payback period is relatively short, as it was in the Nido Escondido Hospital problem, this is not a particularly serious limitation, but when assets have longer economic lives, the payback period technique is somewhat misleading.

Net Present Value

The net present value technique avoids the limitation of the payback period by incorporating the time value of money into the analysis. It does so, as its name implies, by calculating the *present value* (that is, the value in today's terms) of a proposal's future cash inflows. (If you do not understand the concept of present value, please work through appendix 8A at the end of this chapter before reading any further.)

A capital investment analysis using the technique of net present value has five steps:

1. Determine the estimated annual cash inflows that result from the new asset. These may be either increased contribution or decreased expenses, but they must result exclusively from the new asset itself and not from any activities that would have taken place apart from the investment.

2. Estimate the economic life of the new asset. This is not its physical life, but rather the period over which it will generate the cash inflows.

3. Determine the net amount of the investment: a combination of the purchase price, installation costs, and disposal costs for the old asset, minus any revenue received from the sale of the old asset.

4. Determine the required rate of return, sometimes called the *discount rate* (a technique for computing the discount rate is discussed later in the chapter).

discount rate
The interest rate used to compute the present value of a future stream of cash flows.

5. Compute the net present value according to the following formula:

Net present value = Present value of cash inflows

− Net investment amount

A variety of handheld calculators, as well as most spreadsheet software packages, have present value functions that can be used to make these computations. For our purposes here, we will use the present value factors contained in tables 8A.1 and 8A.2 in appendix 8A. Using the present value factor in these tables, the preceding formula looks as follows:

Net present value = (Cash inflows × Present value factor)

− Net investment amount

$$\text{or } NPV = (CF \times pvf) - I$$

Present value factors for one-time cash flows are contained in table 8A.1, and present value factors for steady annual cash flows are shown in table 8A.2. The present value factor lies at the intersection of the year row and percent column selected in steps 2 and 4.

PROBLEM

Nido Escondido Hospital has an opportunity to purchase some equipment that will result in labor savings of approximately $3,300 a year. The equipment has a purchase price of $12,000 (net) and is expected to produce the labor savings for five years. The hospital's board has decided that an acceptable project must have a rate of return of at least 8 percent a year. Is the proposed investment financially feasible?

ANSWER

The computations are as follows:

1.	Annual cash flows	=	$3,300
2.	Economic life	=	5 years
3.	Net investment amount	=	$12,000
4.	Rate of return	=	8%
5.	*NPV*	=	$(CF \times pvf) - I$
		=	($3,300 × 3.993) − $12,000
		=	$13,177 − $12,000
		=	$1,177

The investment therefore is financially feasible—that is, using a discount rate of 8 percent, the net present value of the annual cash flows is greater than the amount of the investment.

There are several important points to bear in mind about a net present value analysis such as this one. First, once we have determined our desired rate of return, a project that yields a net present value of zero or greater should be acceptable. That is, it is not important for the project to produce a net present value greater than zero because if this were the case, the implication would be that we should raise our desired rate of return.

Second, although an analysis of this sort appears to offer a great deal of precision, we should recognize that most of its significant elements are estimates or guesses and may be quite imprecise. Specifically, projected cash flows beyond a period of two to three years usually are not especially reliable, nor, in industries with a high rate of technological change, such as health care, is the economic life of an asset. We should thus be careful about attributing too much credibility to the precision the formula seems to give us.

Third, inflation is a factor. It is quite likely, owing to potential increases in wage rates, that labor savings from an investment will be greater five years from now than they are today. If we are to adjust our cash flows for the effects of inflation, however, we also should adjust the required rate of return to reflect our need for a return somewhat greater than the rate of inflation. By excluding an inflation effect from both the cash flow calculations and the required rate of return, we neutralize the effect of inflation and thus do not need to undertake the somewhat complex calculations that might otherwise be necessary.[3]

Finally, the financial analysis is only one aspect of the decision-making process. Clearly, there are many more considerations, including political and strategic ones. Managers must be careful not to let the financial analysis dominate a decision that has strategic consequences, even if those consequences cannot be quantified easily. In these instances, a manager's judgment and "feel" for the situation may be as important as the quantitative factors. Moreover, if a project is mandatory (for example, to meet required health and safety standards), its net present value is irrelevant.

In short, almost all capital budgeting proposals involve a variety of nonquantitative considerations that will influence the final decision. The use of net present value (or a related technique) only formalizes the quantitative part of the analysis. As a result, when we calculate net present value, we should be satisfied if it is fairly close to zero. If it is greater than zero, the project has a higher financial return than we require; if it is close to zero or even slightly negative, we should recognize that it is probably financially feasible and should turn to nonquantitative considerations to evaluate it further. Nonquantitative factors are discussed in detail later in the chapter.

Internal Rate of Return

The internal rate of return (IRR) method is similar to the net present value approach, but instead of using a required rate of return to make the calculations, we set the net present value equal to zero and calculate the *effective* rate of return for the investment. Although this method is slightly more complicated than the net present value approach, it has the advantage of giving an exact rate of return, rather than simply concluding that a proposed project meets (or fails to meet) the required rate of return. This in turn makes it easier to rank proposed projects in terms of their financial benefits. Because an organization may not have sufficient funds to undertake all desirable projects, the IRR approach can assist it to determine its financial priorities.

The IRR approach begins with the net present value (NPV) formula:

$$NPV = (CF \times pvf) - I$$

It then sets NPV equal to zero, so that

$$CF \times pvf = I$$

$$\text{or } pvf = I \div CF$$

Once the present value factor has been determined, it can be located in table 8A.2, in the row corresponding to the economic life of the project. The resulting rate of return can be determined from the column in which the present value factor is found. (As mentioned earlier, some calculators and spreadsheet programs have present value functions that compute the IRR easily, even when there are uneven cash flows.)

PROBLEM

Nido Escondido Hospital wishes to determine the IRR for the project described in the previous problem. What is it?

ANSWER

The computations are as follows:

$$pvf = I \div CF$$
$$pvf = \$12{,}000 \div \$3{,}300$$
$$pvf = 3.636$$

Looking at table 8A.2, in the row for five years (the economic life of the investment), we find a present value factor of 3.790 in the column for an interest rate of 10 percent and a present value factor of 3.605 in the column for an interest rate of 12 percent. Our project's IRR is therefore about 11 percent.

Tax Effects

For-profit organizations—such as some investor-owned hospitals, nursing homes, medical equipment manufacturers, dialysis centers, and the like—must consider the tax effects of a proposed project. That is, anytime a for-profit organization realizes some cost savings, the resulting increase in income before taxes will be taxed, and the organization will not receive the full effect of the savings. Similarly, depreciation serves as a tax shield, reducing the amount of taxes that would otherwise be paid. It does so by increasing the organization's expenses, which, other things being equal, reduces income before taxes.

The issue of tax effects is complicated and beyond the scope of this text. A good discussion can be found in almost any textbook on finance.

Selecting a Discount Rate

In the net present value example, we used a discount rate of 8 percent. A question that may have occurred to you is, "How does senior management determine this rate?" The discount rate clearly can have a significant impact on a project's financial feasibility. Therefore, the way it is determined is important to the decision-making process.

The approach used by many organizations, both for-profit and non-profit, begins with a calculation of the entity's *weighted cost of capital (WCC)*, which is discussed later on. The WCC is then incorporated into a computation of the *weighted return on assets*, which allows senior management to determine the rate of return that must be earned by the entity's fixed assets.

This approach is based on the fact that an organization must earn an overall return on assets (ROA) that is at least equal to its WCC if it is to remain financially viable. The approach entails several interrelated steps.

weighted cost of capital (WCC)
The weighted interest rate of all the sources used to finance an organization's assets. It uses the interest rate paid for each liability (such as a mortgage or bond) as well as the rate assigned to the organization's equity.

weighted return on assets
The weighted interest rate of all of an organization's assets. It uses the interest rate earned for each asset, and weights it by the percent of total assets that that asset comprises.

Step 1: Agree on an Interest Rate for Equity

The trickiest aspect of computing a WCC is choosing an interest rate for equity, which is a topic of ongoing debate in many nonprofit organizations. Although some people argue that equity in a nonprofit is essentially free, and therefore should be assigned a zero interest rate, most managers believe there is at least an opportunity cost for using equity.

Although managers may agree on the relevance of *including* an interest rate for equity, there is considerably less agreement about how to determine it. One argument is that permanently restricted equity (which may not legally be used for operating purposes) typically is invested in stocks, bonds, or similar instruments. If some of these funds are used for a particular project, there is a reduction in the amount available for investments, and hence an opportunity cost. This opportunity cost—the rate the organization is earning on its investments—is an appropriate rate to use for equity in computing the WCC. A similar argument can be made for the organization's unrestricted equity. Even though there is no legal impediment to its use for operating purposes, there nevertheless is an opportunity cost associated with its use.

Step 2: Determine the Interest Rates for Liabilities

Some liabilities, such as accounts payable, are usually interest-free, but short- and long-term debt instruments carry an interest rate that the organization must pay. For example, assume that the liability and equity side of a hospital's balance sheet is as shown in the following table, with the interest rates indicated (note that the organization has selected a rate of 10 percent for its equity):

Item	Amount	Interest Rate
Accounts payable	$3,000	0.0%
Accrued salaries	2,000	0.0%
Short-term note payable	10,000	9.0%
Total current liabilities	$15,000	
Long-term note payable	75,000	7.0%
Mortgage payable	150,000	6.0%
Permanently restricted equity	150,000	10.0%
Unrestricted equity	50,000	10.0%
Total liabilities and equity	$440,000	

Step 3: Compute the Weighted Cost of Capital

We next determine the percentage of the total liabilities and equity that each source represents; that is, its weight. We multiply its weight by its interest rate, and then add the resulting totals together. The calculations for the situation just given would look as follows, resulting in a WCC of 8 percent.

Item	Amount	Interest Rate	Weight	Weighted Interest Rate
Accounts payable	$3,000	0.0%	0.007	0.00%
Accrued salaries	2,000	0.0%	0.005	0.00%
Short-term note payable	10,000	9.0%	0.023	0.21%
Total current liabilities	$15,000			
Long-term note payable	75,000	7.0%	0.170	1.19%
Mortgage payable	150,000	6.0%	0.341	2.05%
Permanently restricted equity	150,000	10.0%	0.341	3.41%
Unrestricted equity	50,000	10.0%	0.114	1.14%
Total liabilities and equity	$440,000		1.000	8.00%

Step 4: Use the WCC to Determine the Rate of Return Needed for Fixed Assets

If an organization's overall ROA is not at least equal to its WCC, it is paying more to finance its assets than it is earning on them. In effect, it is atrophying. This gives rise to the need to compute a weighted return on assets.

The need for a weighted ROA arises because not all assets earn a return. Accounts receivable and inventory, for example, do not earn a return. It thus is necessary to determine how much the property, plant, or equipment assets (that is, the ones involved in capital investment decision making) must earn if the overall ROA is to be equal to the WCC. To do this, we . . .

1. Start with a breakdown of the assets, and compute their weights.

2. Determine the returns of all *except* the property, plant, and equipment (PP&E) account. Current assets other than investments usually do not earn anything, for example. Assume, for the purposes of these computations, that all cash is invested and earns 10 percent.

3. Insert the WCC percentage as the total weighted return on assets, and determine the interest rate for PP&E that must be attained to achieve it. In effect, the return needed for PP&E is the unknown percentage needed to have the overall ROA equal the WCC.

The result, shown here, is a need for PP&E to earn 16.5 percent. This figure sometimes is called the *hurdle rate*—the rate that a project must meet or exceed if it is to be acceptable on financial grounds alone.

hurdle rate
The discount rate that a capital project must demonstrate in order to be acceptable financially. It can be determined by computing the return on fixed assets that is needed in order for the organization's return on assets to equal its weighted cost of capital.

Item	Amount	Interest Rate	Weight	Weighted Interest Rate
Cash	$11,000	10.0%	0.025	0.25%
Accounts receivable	77,000	0.0%	0.175	0.00%
Inventory	100,000	0.0%	0.227	0.00%
Prepaid expenses	$46,000	0.0%	0.105	0.00%
Total current assets	234,000			
Noncurrent assets				
Property, plant, and equipment	206,000	16.5%	0.468	7.73%
Total assets	$440,000		1.000	8.00%

There are three issues associated with this approach:

- We must consider that some new PP&E projects will not yield a 16.5 percent return. Repairs and renovations, for example, probably will lead to very little in terms of additional cash flows (although there may be some savings in maintenance). This means that we will need to find some projects that give us much more than 16.5 percent.

- This analysis is based on a weighted cost of capital of 8 percent. As we undertake additional borrowing, and as our composition of liabilities changes, our weighted cost of capital will change. This means that our required ROA also will change. As a practical matter, these changes ordinarily will be rather small, and therefore of little consequence.

- To include the effects of the changes just mentioned, some organizations will use a *forecasted* WCC; that is, senior management will determine the magnitude of the additional debt the organization plans to put on its balance sheet and also whether it will have additional equity from contributions, grants, or operating surpluses. It then uses the expected interest rate the organization will pay on the additional debt, combined with the other interest rates, to calculate its forecasted WCC. This becomes the figure that management uses to determine the hurdle rate for the upcoming year's capital investment proposals (which are the ones that will result in new assets' going onto the balance sheet).

Once these financing decisions have been made, the organization can choose its capital investments up to the limit set by the combination of debt and equity. In this regard, it is important to note that although net present value and IRR techniques are useful in making these determinations, they do not assist the organization in deciding how much additional debt it can carry on its balance sheet or whether additional equity is needed. These matters are discussed in chapter 10.

Incorporating Risk into the Analysis

Capital investment proposals are not risk-free. They involve future cash flows, and senior management must recognize that the future may not be as anticipated. This element of *risk* needs to be incorporated into the analysis. If risk is not considered explicitly, then a very risky proposal might be evaluated in the same way as one that has a high probability of success.

risk
The possibility that a proposed capital investment project will not yield the return that its proponents suggest it will.

There are several ways to incorporate risk into an analysis. With all of them, an increase in risk reduces the net present value of a proposal. A common approach is to adjust the discount rate upward to compensate for increased risk. The problem with this approach is that there is no easy way to establish a meaningful risk scale or to otherwise make appropriate adjustments to the discount rate. Statistical techniques are available for incorporating the relative riskiness of a project into an analysis,[4] but they require analysts to estimate the probabilities of possible outcomes, a task that can be quite difficult.

Another approach is to discount heavily any projected cash flows beyond some predetermined period, such as five years. The hurdle rate is used as the discount rate for all cash flows in, say, the first five years of a proposed project, and a higher rate is used for all subsequent years. Some organizations even exclude all cash flows beyond a certain number of years. In all instances, the reasoning is that the uncertainty of cash flows is greater the further out the projections. Although this approach tends to bias decisions in favor of projects with short payback periods, many organizations in industries experiencing rapid technological change (such as health care) believe that using short payback periods is justified.

A third approach gives greater weight to projections of cost savings than to projections of additional financial contribution. When a particular technological improvement, such as a new piece of equipment, has demonstrated its ability to produce certain cost savings in other organizations, senior management reasons that projections of similar cost savings in their own organization are quite reliable. In contrast, a projection that a given investment will result in new business, and hence additional financial contribution, is far more uncertain. Such factors as patients' willingness to use the new service, competition, third-party payment policies, and so forth will affect a new investment's return. Some organizations therefore use a lower discount rate for projects with cost savings than for ones that are expected to yield additional financial contribution.

In summary, when we consider the following formula, the only reasonably certain amount is the investment:

$$NPV = (CF \times pvf) - I$$

Cash flow estimates and economic lives can be highly speculative. Senior management can incorporate adjustments for uncertainty by shortening the economic life or raising the required rate of return, but in all instances there are no guarantees that the future will be as anticipated.

Nonquantitative Considerations

Net present value or IRR computations are only one aspect of a capital investment decision. As mentioned earlier, most organizations include *nonquantitative factors* in their decision-making processes. These factors may include quality improvements, the need to offer a full range of services, requirements by regulatory agencies (such as the Occupational Health and Safety Administration or the Environmental Protection Agency), and political and behavioral matters. Of these, the last is perhaps the least well understood.

nonquantitative-factors
Elements other than a financial analysis that affect senior management's decision about whether to approve a capital investment proposal.

For a variety of reasons, some line managers are viewed more favorably than others. They may have the ear of senior management. Or they may run an organizational unit (such as an oncology center) that is seen as key to the organization's future. They may simply be more articulate or more forceful than some of their colleagues. Or, in the case of chiefs of service in academic medical centers, they may have been promised a "dowry" when recruited.[5] As a result they may receive a favorable decision on a proposed project that has a much lower IRR than a proposed project in another organizational unit whose manager is not seen in such a favorable light. In short, it would be naive to assume that the sort of financial analysis described in the previous section is totally deterministic. Nevertheless, in most organizations such an analysis is an important ingredient in the decision-making process, and in some it is given considerable weight.

Link to Strategy

Programs and product lines are among the most readily observable aspects of an organization's strategy. Because of this, line managers need to understand the link between their unit's activities and the organization's overall strategic direction. Moreover, if an organization's strategy is to evolve over time because of shifting environmental opportunities and threats and changing organizational strengths and weaknesses, senior management must find ways to monitor and manage the organization's programs and product lines so that they remain consistent with, and supportive of, the evolving strategy. Thus, although many large organizations have decentralized considerable decision-authority to their divisions, most of them stipulate that large programming decisions require the approval of senior management. Their reasoning is that if these decisions are not carefully considered, they may lead the organization in strategic directions that are different from those desired by senior management.

Exhibit 8.1 is an example of a worksheet developed by a multihospital system in its effort to assess the impact of different capital investment proposals on strategic goals. As it indicates, the hospital system was attempting to measure the impact of a capital investment proposal on three stakeholder groups: physicians, its community, and employees. An important question was, "What will happen if . . . ?" That is, what will happen if the proposal is accepted, and what will happen if it is not accepted?

EXHIBIT 8.1   Example of a Qualitative Evaluation

A. Physician Impact

Will this project have an effect on the physicians' attitude toward the hospital?
Yes _____ No _____

(If no, proceed to Part B. If so, enter information about the extent of the impact, circle two answers below (one for non-acceptance and one for acceptance), and explain.)

What is the scope of impact on the physicians?

___ a. One or two physicians will be affected.
___ b. The majority of the physicians in a hospital service will be affected.
___ c. A substantial portion of the medical staff will be affected.

Explain your answer in a memorandum.

Not Accepted

−4   The affected physicians will move their practices to other hospitals.
−3   The affected physicians will tend to reduce their practices at the hospital.
−2   The affected physicians will be disgruntled and will discuss the lack of the expenditure or project in the community and with other physicians.
−1   The affected physicians will be aware of the lack of support for the project, and will be less likely to believe that the hospital is maintaining a proper level of patient care.
0   No effect

Accepted

+1   The affected physicians will be aware of the expenditure or project and will be satisfied that the hospital is maintaining a high level of patient care.
+2   The affected physicians will be very impressed and will discuss the expenditure or project favorably in the community and with other physicians.
+3   The affected physicians will moderately increase their practices at the hospital.
+4   The affected physicians will move their practices to the hospital.

B. Community Impact

Will this project have an effect on the community attitude toward the hospital?
Yes _____ No _____
      (If no, proceed to Part C. If so, circle two answers below: one for non-acceptance and one for acceptance, and explain.)

Not Accepted

−4   Intense and widespread negative reaction in the community will result in a severe blow to the hospital's image.
−3   A widespread negative effect on the hospital's general image and reputation will result.
−2   The hospital's image will be damaged among certain groups in the community.
−1   The attitudes of a few people will be negatively affected.

Accepted

+1   Relatively few people will be positively affected.
+2   Some community groups will be favorably impressed.
+3   A widespread positive effect on the hospital's image and reputation will result.
+4   Significant and widespread positive community reaction will contribute significantly to the hospital's reputation.

C. Employee Impact

Will this project have an effect on the attitude of the hospital's personnel?
Yes _____ No _____
   If yes, circle two answers below: one for non-acceptance and one for acceptance, and explain your answers.

Not Accepted

−4   Major and widespread negative impact on employee morale and attitude toward the hospital.
−3   Widespread disappointment with the hospital and some negative effects on the hospital's image among employees.
−2   A limited group of employees (one or two departments) will react negatively.
−1   Relatively few employees will be disturbed.
0   No effect

Accepted

+1   Relatively few employees will know about the decision but they will be pleased.
+2   A limited group of employees will be very pleased.
+3   Nearly all employees will be pleased.
+4   Major and widespread positive impact with long-term effects on employee attitude toward the hospital will result.

Source: This exhibit is a modified version of an assessment tool described in *Hospital Progress.* Copyright © by the Catholic Hospital Association. Reprinted with permission.

More broadly, programming can be an especially important tool for senior management to use to influence the organization's culture, that is, the basic assumptions that underlie decision making.[6] Specifically, the constraints on programming that senior management establishes and the way it distributes the "programming purse" can have a profound impact on line managers' understanding of what is acceptable and unacceptable in the organization. This in turn can help either to maintain or to change the organization's culture.

Link to Conflict Management

As mentioned in chapter 6, many of the benefits of new program proposals are difficult to quantify, and line managers (especially profit and invest-ment center managers) tend to be quite optimistic about their program proposals. As a result, there tends to be a bias in capital investment proposals toward new programs. In particular, many proposals tend to overestimate revenues, and others may tend to underestimate costs.

Senior management can counteract this bias by using its own staff to analyze the proposals. When this happens, there can be considerable friction between the planning staff and line managers. One of the most challenging tasks senior management faces in programming is designing a conflict management process to deal with this friction, so that each proposal receives a tough but realistic analysis.

You are now ready to work through the practice case for this chapter. The first two assignment questions are largely mechanical, but the remaining questions ask you to consider some fairly tricky issues, including power and influence.

KEY TERMS

Discount rate	Payback period
Hurdle rate	Risk
Internal rate of return	Weighted cost of capital (WCC)
Net present value	Weighted return on assets
Nonquantitative factors	

To Bear in Mind

1. Although many capital investment proposals are based on a solid financial analysis, line managers tend to be optimistic. Clearly, no one will submit a proposal with a negative net present value; senior management must therefore apply a "reality check" to the underlying assumptions. In most instances the culprit is optimistic revenue projections. For this reason, proposals with net present value computations based on cost savings generally have greater credibility, especially if the cost savings have been verified with other organizations that have made a similar investment.

2. It is not sufficient to approve a capital investment proposal. Senior management then must follow up to make sure the proposal is implemented as planned. Many capital investment proposals that were based on labor savings, for example, never actually realized the savings. This happened because senior management did not follow up in the operational budgeting phase of the management control process to

make sure that the savings specified in the program proposal were incorporated into the line manager's operating budget.

Test Yourself

1. Describe the differences between the payback period technique, the net present value technique, and the internal rate of return technique for programming (or capital budgeting). Which technique or techniques use a hurdle rate?

2. How should an organization compute its weighted cost of capital? What is the most difficult part of this process?

3. In addition to computing a weighted cost of capital, what else must an organization do to determine its hurdle rate? Why is it important for the organization's investments in fixed assets to meet or exceed this hurdle rate?

4. What are some ways that risk can be incorporated into a programming decision? How can statistical techniques help with risk assessment? Why might they be misleading?

5. What kinds of factors other than financial ones might be included in a programming decision?

Suggested Cases

Yoland Research Institute

Green Valley Medical Center

Disease Control Programs

PRACTICE CASE

ERIE HOSPITAL

Christian Larson, MD, chief of cardiology at Erie Hospital, was contemplating the proposal recently submitted to him by Francesca Michaels, MD, the head of the cardiac catheterization lab. Dr. Michaels's request was for the purchase of some new equipment for activities currently performed on less-efficient equipment. The purchase price was $300,000, delivered and installed.

Background

Erie Hospital was a nonprofit, university-affiliated medical center whose physicians practiced in a number of specialties and subspecialties. A 350-bed institution located on the shores of Lake Erie in Cleveland, Ohio, it had been in existence for some forty years. Although it treated patients with a variety of problems, its distinguishing specialty was cardiology, where it prided itself on having the latest in technology and up-to-date services and facilities. Because of the rapid changes taking place in the field of cardiology, maintaining the hospital's cutting-edge position required constant upgrading of its facilities and equipment.

In recent years, third-party payers, especially managed care organizations, had placed increasing pressures on the hospital's bottom line. Although some of Erie's equipment and facilities were used for research and could be purchased with grant funding, items used for clinical purposes had to be financed exclusively from patient care revenues. Because of the increased financial pressures, the hospital was taking a hard look at all proposals for capital equipment designated for patient care.

The Request

In the case of Dr. Michaels's request, the equipment was for patient care purposes. No grant funds were available, and hence the cost would need to be financed from patient care revenues. Dr. Michaels had worked closely with the equipment manufacturer to determine the potential benefits of the new equipment, however, and she estimated that compared with the existing equipment, it would result in annual savings of $60,000 in labor and other direct costs. She also estimated that the proposed equipment's economic life was ten years.

The hospital had recently borrowed on a long-term note to finance another project. Paul Hershenson, the vice president of fiscal affairs, had informed Dr. Larson that because of this, he was certain the hospital could obtain additional funds at 12 percent, although he would not plan to negotiate a loan specifically for the purchase of this equipment. He did feel, however, that an investment of this type should have a return of at least 20 percent, even though the hospital paid no taxes. The hospital's capital structure (debt and equity) is shown in exhibit 8.2.

EXHIBIT 8.2   Weighted Cost of Capital

	Percentage of Total	Average Interest Rate	Weighted Interest Rate
Debt	40.0%	12.0%	4.8%
Equity	60.0%	0.0%	0.0%
Total	100.0%	12.0%	4.8%

There were three complications. First, the existing equipment was in good working order and probably would last, physically, for at least fifteen more years.

Second, this request was for what Dr. Michaels called "even better equipment" to replace some equipment purchased two years ago and using the same economic life and dollar amounts to compute the NPV. Dr. Michaels had informed Dr. Larson that the new equipment would render the existing equipment completely obsolete, with no resale value.

Third, at a recent board meeting, the chairman of the hospital's finance committee had discussed some inconsistencies between Erie's capital structure and the 20 percent rate of return that Mr. Hershenson was recommending. Specifically, he had pointed out that Erie's equity consisted of donations and other gifts that were essentially free—that is, they involved no interest charges. As a result, he thought the proper discount rate to use for capital investment proposals was not 20 percent, as suggested by Mr. Hershenson, but only about 5 percent.

The Decision

Although funds could be obtained to finance the purchase of Dr. Michaels's proposed new equipment, Dr. Larson and Mr. Hershenson were both concerned about the mistake made two years ago and wanted to be sure that a similar mistake was not being made this time. Mr. Hershenson also was not certain that Dr. Michaels's request was justifiable.

Assignment

1. What is the net present value of Dr. Michaels's proposal? Use a discount rate of 20 percent and then use a discount rate of 5 percent. What is the proposal's internal rate of return?

2. What is the appropriate discount rate to use? Why?

3. If the hospital decides to purchase the new equipment for Dr. Michaels, a mistake has been made somewhere, because good equipment bought only two years ago is being scrapped. How did this mistake come about? What should be done?

4. What nonquantitative factors should the hospital consider in making this decision? How important are they? Would it make a difference if the proposal were for new technology rather than for replacement of existing technology, or if it were for new technology with the same dollar amounts but in the laundry department? Why?

Appendix 8A: The Concept of Present Value

The concept of present value rests on the principle that money has a time value. That is, a dollar received a year from today is worth less than a dollar received today. The following problems illustrate the concept.

PROBLEM

In return for a loan, a colleague offers to pay you $1,000 one year from today. How much would you lend her today?

ANSWER

Presumably, unless you were a good friend or somewhat altruistic, you would not lend her $1,000 today. Because you could invest your $1,000 and earn a return on it over the course of the year, you would have more than $1,000 a year from now. If, for example, you could earn 10 percent on your money, you could invest your $1,000 and have $1,100 in a year. Similarly, if you had $909 and invested it at 10 percent, you would have (in rounded figures) $1,000 a year from today.

Thus, if your colleague offers to pay you $1,000 a year from today and you are an investor expecting a 10 percent return, you would lend her only $909 today. Given a 10 percent interest rate, $909 is the *present value* of $1,000 received one year hence.

PROBLEM

Now, how much would you lend your colleague if she offered to pay you $1,000 two years from today?

ANSWER

Here we must incorporate the concept of compound interest—that is, the fact that interest is earned on previously received interest. For example, at a 10 percent rate, $826 loaned today would accumulate to roughly $1,000 in two years, as shown by the following computations:

$$\$826 \times 0.10 = \$83 \text{ (rounded)}$$

$$(\$826 + \$83) \times 0.10 = \$91 \text{ (rounded)}$$

$$\$826 + \$83 + \$91 = \$1,000$$

In this situation, therefore, you would be willing to lend your colleague $826.

PROBLEM

The previous problem consisted of a promise to pay a given amount two years from today, with no intermediate payments. Another possibility to consider is the situation in which your colleague offers to pay you $1,000 a year from today and another $1,000 two years from today. How much would you lend her now?

ANSWER

We now must combine the analyses in each of the two previous problems. For the $1,000 received two years from now, you would lend her $826, and for the $1,000 received one year from now, you would lend her $909. Thus the total you would lend would be $1,735.

The process of making these calculations is simplified by present value tables. Two abbreviated tables are included at the end of this appendix. Table 8A.1 is the table we would use to determine the present value of a single payment received at some specified time in the future. For instance, we could determine the answer to the first problem in this appendix by finding the factor at the intersection of the column for 10 percent and the row for one year hence; this factor is 0.909. Multiplying 0.909 by $1,000 gives us the $909 we would lend our colleague. Similarly, if we look at the intersection of the column for 10 percent and the row for two years hence and multiply the factor of 0.826 by $1,000, we arrive at the answer to the second problem: $826.

Table 8A.2 is used for even payments received over a given period. Looking at table 8A.2, we can see that the present value for a payment of $1 received each year for two years at 10 percent is 1.735. This figure multiplied by $1,000 comes to the $1,735 that we calculated in the third problem earlier. We can also see that 1.735 is the sum of the two amounts we located on table 8A.1 (0.909 for one year hence, and 0.826 for two years hence). Thus table 8A.2 simply sums the various elements in table 8A.1 to facilitate calculations.

These computations are greatly simplified when one uses the present value function on a calculator or in a spreadsheet package. The data need

Table 8A.1 Present Value of $1

Years Hence	1%	2%	4%	6%	8%	10%	12%	14%	15%	16%	18%	20%	22%	24%	25%	26%	28%	30%
1	0.990	0.980	0.962	0.943	0.926	0.909	0.893	0.877	0.870	0.862	0.847	0.833	0.820	0.806	0.800	0.794	0.781	0.769
2	0.980	0.961	0.925	0.890	0.857	0.826	0.797	0.769	0.756	0.743	0.718	0.694	0.672	0.650	0.640	0.630	0.610	0.592
3	0.971	0.942	0.889	0.840	0.794	0.751	0.712	0.675	0.658	0.641	0.609	0.579	0.551	0.524	0.512	0.500	0.477	0.455
4	0.961	0.924	0.855	0.792	0.735	0.683	0.636	0.592	0.572	0.552	0.516	0.482	0.451	0.423	0.410	0.397	0.373	0.350
5	0.951	0.906	0.822	0.747	0.681	0.621	0.567	0.519	0.497	0.476	0.437	0.402	0.370	0.341	0.328	0.315	0.291	0.269
6	0.942	0.888	0.790	0.705	0.630	0.564	0.507	0.456	0.432	0.410	0.370	0.335	0.303	0.275	0.262	0.250	0.227	0.207
7	0.933	0.871	0.760	0.665	0.583	0.513	0.452	0.400	0.376	0.354	0.314	0.279	0.249	0.222	0.210	0.198	0.178	0.159
8	0.923	0.853	0.731	0.627	0.540	0.467	0.404	0.351	0.327	0.305	0.266	0.233	0.204	0.179	0.168	0.157	0.139	0.123
9	0.914	0.837	0.703	0.592	0.500	0.424	0.361	0.308	0.284	0.263	0.225	0.194	0.167	0.144	0.134	0.125	0.108	0.094
10	0.905	0.820	0.676	0.558	0.463	0.386	0.322	0.270	0.247	0.227	0.191	0.162	0.137	0.116	0.107	0.099	0.085	0.073
11	0.896	0.804	0.650	0.527	0.429	0.350	0.287	0.237	0.215	0.195	0.162	0.135	0.112	0.094	0.086	0.079	0.066	0.056
12	0.887	0.788	0.625	0.497	0.397	0.319	0.257	0.208	0.187	0.168	0.137	0.112	0.092	0.076	0.069	0.062	0.052	0.043
13	0.879	0.773	0.601	0.469	0.368	0.290	0.229	0.182	0.163	0.145	0.116	0.093	0.075	0.061	0.055	0.050	0.040	0.033
14	0.870	0.758	0.577	0.442	0.340	0.263	0.205	0.160	0.141	0.125	0.099	0.078	0.062	0.049	0.044	0.039	0.032	0.025
15	0.861	0.743	0.555	0.417	0.315	0.239	0.183	0.140	0.123	0.108	0.084	0.065	0.051	0.040	0.035	0.031	0.025	0.020

Table 8A.2 Present Value of $1 Received Annually for *N* Years

Years N	1%	2%	4%	6%	8%	10%	12%	14%	15%	16%	18%	20%	22%	24%	25%	26%	28%	30%
1	0.990	0.980	0.962	0.943	0.926	0.909	0.893	0.877	0.870	0.862	0.847	0.833	0.820	0.806	0.800	0.794	0.781	0.769
2	1.970	1.941	1.887	1.833	1.783	1.735	1.690	1.646	1.626	1.605	1.565	1.527	1.492	1.456	1.440	1.424	1.391	1.361
3	2.941	2.883	2.776	2.673	2.577	2.486	2.402	2.321	2.284	2.246	2.174	2.106	2.043	1.980	1.952	1.924	1.868	1.816
4	3.902	3.807	3.631	3.465	3.312	3.169	3.038	2.913	2.856	2.798	2.690	2.588	2.494	2.403	2.362	2.321	2.241	2.166
5	4.853	4.713	4.453	4.212	3.993	3.790	3.605	3.432	3.353	3.274	3.127	2.990	2.864	2.744	2.690	2.636	2.532	2.435
6	5.795	5.601	5.243	4.917	4.623	4.354	4.112	3.888	3.785	3.684	3.497	3.325	3.167	3.019	2.952	2.886	2.759	2.642
7	6.728	6.472	6.003	5.582	5.206	4.867	4.564	4.288	4.161	4.038	3.811	3.604	3.416	3.241	3.162	3.084	2.937	2.801
8	7.651	7.325	6.734	6.209	5.746	5.334	4.968	4.639	4.488	4.343	4.077	3.837	3.620	3.420	3.330	3.241	3.076	2.924
9	8.565	8.162	7.437	6.801	6.246	5.758	5.329	4.947	4.772	4.606	4.302	4.031	3.787	3.564	3.464	3.366	3.184	3.018
10	9.470	8.982	8.113	7.359	6.709	6.144	5.651	5.217	5.019	4.833	4.493	4.193	3.924	3.680	3.571	3.465	3.269	3.091
11	10.366	9.786	8.763	7.886	7.138	6.494	5.938	5.454	5.234	5.028	4.655	4.328	4.036	3.774	3.657	3.544	3.335	3.147
12	11.253	10.574	9.388	8.383	7.535	6.813	6.195	5.662	5.421	5.196	4.792	4.440	4.128	3.850	3.726	3.606	3.387	3.190
13	12.132	11.347	9.989	8.852	7.903	7.103	6.424	5.844	5.584	5.341	4.908	4.533	4.203	3.911	3.781	3.656	3.427	3.223
14	13.002	12.105	10.566	9.294	8.243	7.366	6.629	6.004	5.725	5.466	5.007	4.611	4.265	3.960	3.825	3.695	3.459	3.248
15	13.863	12.848	11.121	9.711	8.558	7.605	6.812	6.144	5.848	5.574	5.091	4.676	4.316	4.000	3.860	3.726	3.484	3.268

only be entered and the appropriate buttons pushed or functions selected to obtain the present value amount.

Appendix 8B: Special Programming Issues in Governmental Organizations[7]

Nonprofit and governmental organizations frequently go beyond the techniques discussed in the chapter to undertake a benefit-cost analysis. The underlying concept is the obvious one: that a program should not be undertaken unless its benefits exceed its costs. This is not a new idea. Certain government agencies, such as the Bureau of Land Reclamation, have made such analyses for decades; proposals to build new dams, for example, frequently were justified on the grounds that their benefits exceeded their costs.

Interest in benefit-cost analysis grew rapidly in the 1960s when the US Department of Defense applied it to problems for which no formal analysis previously had been attempted. During this time, a variety of promotional brochures, journal articles, and proposals implied that benefit-cost analysis did everything, including "taking the guesswork out of management." As a result of this burgeoning interest, nonprofit organizations began to apply benefit-cost analysis to all sorts of proposed programs. When these efforts produced mixed results, public policy experts began to question the merits of the approach.

Although there is no doubt that many benefit-cost analyses have produced questionable results, others have led to more informed decisions. To ensure useful results, decision makers should consider two essential points:

- Benefit-cost analysis focuses on those aspects of a proposal that can be expressed quantitatively. Because there is no important problem for which all relevant factors can be reduced to numbers, benefit-cost analysis never provides a complete answer. Not everything can be quantified, and no one should expect a benefit-cost analysis to do so. Analyses claiming to have quantified everything are dubious.

- To the extent that managers or analysts can express some important factors in quantitative terms, they should do so. This narrows the area where the decision maker must exercise judgment. Thus, although the need for judgment is not eliminated, it can be reduced.

In short, the issue is not whether benefit-cost analysis is a panacea or a fraud, for in general it is neither. Rather, the issue is to define the circumstances under which it is likely to be useful. This appendix discusses some of the relevant factors.

EXAMPLE

Several years ago, the federal government began to support local transportation for the disabled. Because the US Department of Transportation (DOT) then subsidized local bus and subway lines, its natural inclination was to finance the modification of buses to provide lifts that would permit easy wheelchair access. The extra capital and maintenance costs of such equipment turned out to be huge, and use was not high because people with disabilities had no way to get from their homes to the buses. As a result, the cost per passenger was high—$1,283 per trip in Detroit, for example. Subsequently, the DOT decided to provide transportation by vans that picked up people with disabilities at their door and took them directly to their destination. This was both more convenient and less expensive—between $5 and $14 per passenger trip in most cities that tried it.[8]

A focus on the goal of transporting people with disabilities, rather than modifying existing modes of transportation, might have avoided the costly installation of lifts in buses. Moreover, speculating on alternative ways of reaching the goal could also have produced a more effective solution.

Clarifying Goals

The benefits in a benefit-cost analysis must be related to an organization's goals; there is no point in undertaking such an analysis unless all involved managers agree on these goals. That is, the purpose of benefit-cost analysis is to suggest the best alternative for reaching a goal. The formulation of goals is largely a judgmental process, and various members of management and various staff people may have different views of the organization's goals. Unless these groups reconcile their views, line managers will find it difficult to think about programs that are designed to reach senior management's goals.

Just as it is important to agree on goals, it is also important to make sure that the goals are reasonable and achievable, and that the program being proposed will help attain them.

EXAMPLE

Some years ago, when locusts threatened the crops of many African nations, the US Agency for International Development and other international aid agencies responded with a fleet of aircraft that helped bomb crops with millions of liters of pesticides. A few years later, a report by the Office of Technology Assessment said that the campaign may have been a wasted effort. It concluded, "Massive insecticide spraying . . . tends to be inefficient in the short-term, ineffective in the medium term, and misses the roots of the problem in the longer term." Moreover, the study suggested that the justification for the entire operation may have been flawed because locusts were not as big a threat as had been thought.[9]

Proposals Susceptible to Benefit-Cost Analysis

Benefit-cost analysis rests on two general principles: (1) management should not adopt a program unless its benefits exceed its costs, and (2) when there are two competing proposals, the one with the greater excess of benefits over costs is preferable. To apply these principles, we must be able to relate benefits to costs.

Economic Proposals

Many proposals in health care organizations include estimates of benefits and costs in monetary terms and thus are similar to capital budgeting proposals in for-profit companies. A proposal to convert the heating plant of a hospital from oil to gas involves the same type of analysis that would be used in any organization. Conversely, for problems that have nonfinancial) effects, analysts have difficulty making monetary estimates of benefits. Frequently, because benefits are so elusive, analysts cannot make a reliable estimate at all.

Alternative Ways of Reaching the Same Objective

Even if benefits cannot be quantified, a benefit-cost analysis is useful when there is more than one way to achieve a given objective. If each of several alternatives could achieve the objective, then management ordinarily will prefer the lowest-cost one. This approach has many applications because it does not require that the objective (or benefit) be stated in monetary terms or even be quantified. Instead of measuring the degree to which each alternative meets the objective, we need only determine that any of several proposed alternatives will achieve it, and then choose the least costly one.

Equal-Cost Programs

If competing proposals have the same total costs but one produces more benefits than the other, it ordinarily is the preferred alternative. This conclusion can be reached without measuring the absolute levels of benefits. Analysts often use such an approach to determine the best mix of resources in a program. The approach requires only that benefits be expressed comparatively, not numerically.

Different Objectives

A benefit-cost comparison of proposals that are intended to accomplish different objectives is likely to be worthless. An analysis that attempts to compare funds to be spent for primary care with funds to be spent for cardiovascular surgery, for instance, is not worthwhile. Such an analysis would require assigning monetary values to the benefits of each program, a task that is all but impossible.

Nevertheless, because funds are limited, policymakers must recognize that an opportunity cost is associated with any given program. Although experienced managers may have an intuitive feel for the opportunity costs within their organizations, relatively few of them have sufficient experience or skill to make trade-offs across organizations, particularly when those organizations have disparate goals and clients. Nor are there many managers with the authority to make such trade-offs. A reduction in funding for public health programs, for example, does not necessarily mean that those funds will be available for social welfare programs.

Causal Connection between Costs and Benefits

Many benefit-cost analyses implicitly assume that there is a causal relationship between incurring costs and achieving benefits—that is, that spending X dollars produces Y benefits. Unless a causal connection actually exists, a benefit-cost analysis is fallacious.

EXAMPLE

A government agency with a job training program defended the program with an analysis indicating that it would lead participants to get new jobs. The new jobs would increase their lifetime earnings by $25,000 per person. Thus, the $5,000 average cost per person trained seemed well justified. However, the assertion that the proposed program would indeed generate these benefits was completely unsupported; it was strictly a guess. There was no plausible link between the amount requested and the projected results.

A Benefit-Cost Way of Thinking

Because of the difficulty of quantifying benefits, benefit-cost analysis is feasible for only a small portion of decisions, which tend to be well-structured, administrative-type problems. Nevertheless, a "benefit-cost way of thinking" is useful for a great many problems. One characteristic of competent managers is their ability to evaluate program proposals, at least in a general way, by comparing the expected benefits and costs. They may not be able to quantify the relationship, nor do they need to do so in many instances, but they can readily distinguish factors that are relevant from those that are not.

Overreliance on the Benefit-Cost Approach

Benefit-cost thinking also can be carried to extremes. If senior management rejects all proposals that do not display a clear causal connection between costs and benefits, line managers may be reluctant to submit innovative program proposals. A primary characteristic of many new, experimental—and promising—schemes is that there is no way of estimating a benefit-cost relationship in advance. Undue insistence on benefit-cost analyses, therefore, can result in approval of only overly conservative programs. The risk of failure of an innovative proposal may be high, but it is frequently worth taking a chance on a risky proposal if an organization wishes to serve its clients in the best way possible.

Quantifying the Value of a Human Life

In their analyses of proposed programs, public health program managers frequently encounter the question of the value of a human life. This question arises because some programs—such as automobile safety, accident prevention, drug control, and medical research—are designed to save or prolong lives. In these programs, the value of a life is a relevant consideration in measuring benefits.

Analysts are often squeamish about attaching a monetary value to a human life because there is a general belief in our culture that life is priceless. Nevertheless, such a monetary amount often facilitates the analysis of certain proposals. In a world of scarce resources, it is not possible to spend unlimited amounts to save lives.

There are, of course, circumstances in which society devotes significant resources to saving a specific life, as when hundreds of people, supported by helicopters and various high-tech devices, are brought together to search for a child who is lost in the woods. In most situations, however, the focus is not on saving a single life but rather on saving the lives of a class of people (such as motorcyclists or cancer victims) or on valuing a life that already has been lost (such as in cases of litigation for medical malpractice). There are four general approaches used for such an analysis, each of which presents difficulties.

The Earnings Approach

This approach discounts the expected future earnings of the person (or persons) affected by the program; this discounted present value presumably represents the person's economic value to his or her family or to society. Sometimes this approach deducts the person's food, clothing, shelter, and other costs from the earnings to find the net value of his or her life.

This approach frequently is used in litigation having to do with "wrongful deaths." It is relevant to cases involving deceased persons, automobile accidents, industrial pollution, or the release of toxic chemicals.

EXAMPLE

The US General Accounting Office (GAO) reported on a study that determined the average lifetime cost of a firearm injury. The data used in the study included actual dollar amounts spent for hospital and nursing home care, physician and other medical professional services, drugs and appliances, and rehabilitation. The study concluded that injuries without hospitalization cost $458 per person; those requiring hospitalization cost $33,159 per person. The average lifetime cost of a firearm fatality was $373,520, which the GAO called "the highest of any cause of injury." Using annual figures for injuries and deaths attributable to firearms, the GAO concluded that the estimated lifetime costs for accidental shootings was close to $1 billion a year.[10]

As this example illustrates, the problems in applying the earnings approach include the difficulty of (1) estimating the amount of future earnings and related costs, (2) choosing an appropriate time period, and (3) selecting a discount rate. Perhaps more important, the earnings approach tends to discriminate against people with relatively low expected lifetime earnings, such as the elderly, homemakers, members of minority groups, schoolteachers, ministers, artists, and retired college professors.

The Societal Willingness Approach

This approach computes the value of a life in terms of society's willingness to spend money to prevent deaths. The development and enforcement of occupational safety regulations and building codes might be based on benefit-cost comparisons, for instance, but this is rarely the case. Instead, spending decisions for many of these programs frequently are based on emotional arguments or political posturing.

EXAMPLE

In the early 1990s, the state of Oregon wanted to change its Medicaid program so that it would cover more poor residents but offer fewer services. The state ranked 1,600 medical procedures according to costs, benefits, and patients' "quality of well-being." Under the scheme, immunizations ranked higher than treatment for gallstones and depression, and cosmetic surgery and sex-change operations fell in the lowest rank. The state drew a horizontal line through the list, with funding to be provided for procedures above the line and denied for those falling below it. Because Medicaid rules required the funding of "all medically necessary" services, the state needed a federal waiver to implement the plan. In 1992, a presidential election year, the waiver was denied based, in part, on the argument that the plan valued some human lives more than others and that such a valuation was unfair.[11]

The Insurance Approach

This approach seeks to measure the value people place on their own lives as indicated by, say, the amount they are willing to spend on life or disability insurance or by risk premiums they earn in hazardous occupations. This implies that these individuals' decisions are based on economic considerations, but many other considerations may be involved as well.

EXAMPLE

At one time, the exposure standard for benzene was 10 parts per million, averaged over an eight-hour workday. At this rate, one benzene worker would die of benzene-related cancer every third year. According to the Occupational Safety and Health Administration, a standard of 1 part per million would have eliminated the risk, but would have cost $100 million annually for the 30,000 workers who were exposed to benzene. One analyst asked the following questions: "Would each of the 30,000 benzene workers be willing to pay $3,333 a year (his or her share of the $100 million) to eliminate the risk? If not, would the $100 million be better spent in a highway-improvement or cancer-screening program that could save more than one life every third year?"[12]

Similarly, Merril Eisenbud, a member of the Three Mile Island Advisory Board and former chairman of the North Carolina Low-Level Radioactive Waste Management Authority, criticized some states' regulations concerning the design of low-level radioactive waste disposal sites. He argued that some states, in response to public pressure, require more protection than is specified by the Nuclear Regulatory Commission. According to Eisenbud: "The additional protection involves expenditures of more than $100 million over the life of a facility, which is the equivalent to many trillions of dollars per premature death averted!"[13]

The Lives-Saved-per-Dollar Approach

A "lives-saved-per-dollar" approach may be a useful way of choosing between alternative proposals even when it is not possible or feasible to measure the value of a life. Specifically, the alternative that saves the most lives per dollar spent generally is considered preferable from an economic viewpoint. The Federal Highway Administration uses this approach in ranking the attractiveness of various highway safety alternatives. Such an analysis is limited to judging whether a particular program saves more lives per dollar spent than other lifesaving or life-prolonging programs. It does not compare costs with monetary benefits.

In short, despite its limitations, a benefit-cost approach may show that a proposal is outside a reasonable boundary in either direction—that it is obviously worthwhile or obviously not worth the associated costs from an economic standpoint. Unfortunately, this does not guarantee either its acceptance or rejection.

EXAMPLE

Studies of the effect of a 55-mile-per-hour speed limit showed that the benefits may not be worth the costs. Benefits were lives saved. Costs could be measured in terms of the additional time taken to reach a destination. Even when time was valued at low amounts per hour, and lives were given a high value, the costs exceeded the benefits in most of these studies. Nevertheless, this speed limit persists in many states.

Summary

Managers frequently must choose between two or more competing programs. When this happens, an attempt to quantify both benefits and costs usually can assist in the decision-making effort.

When two or more proposals have roughly the same benefits, the comparison is relatively easy because only costs need to be calculated. It is similarly easy when competing proposals have the same costs but one clearly produces more benefits than the other. The decision becomes complicated when benefits and costs extend over several years (as is the case with almost all proposed new programs (especially those in the pubic health arena), or when competing proposals have both different benefits and different costs.

Benefits and costs frequently cannot be expressed easily in monetary terms. This happens, for example, when managers attempt to incorporate risk into the analysis, because risk is inherently difficult to measure. It also happens when managers attempt to quantify the value of a human life and include that in the analysis. In addition, a variety of other nonquantitative considerations are part of almost every proposed program. In all instances, managers must be careful not to allow the quantitative factors to dominate the decision. They need to recognize that their judgment occasionally must override the results of the quantitative analysis.

Notes

1. The May 2013 issue of *Healthcare Financial Management* (volume 67, issue 5) contains some interesting and potentially useful articles on programming strategies and alternative methods of financing.

2. It is worth noting that the depreciation expense associated with a new fixed asset is not a cash outlay. Indeed, to include depreciation in the computations would be to double-count the investment (which is the source of the depreciation). However, depreciation can have cash flow implications for organizations

whose reimbursement is partially cost based, as is the case for some health care organizations. In many such situations, depreciation is a reimbursable expense, which means that it results in cash inflows. Depreciation also can have cash flow implications for organizations that are taxed on their earnings, as some health care organizations are. For further discussion on this point, see William O. Cleverly, James O. Cleverly, and Paula H. Song, *Essentials of Health Care Finance*, 7th ed. (Sudbury, MA: Jones and Bartlett Learning, 2010).

3. This assumes equal rates of inflation in investment earnings and cash flows. If the rates are unequal, then there is a need to increase the discount rate by an amount equal to the opportunity cost of invested funds and to increase the cash flows each year by an amount equal to their inflation rate. The cash flows then are discounted back to present value using the new discount rate. Depending on the assumed rates, the resulting net present value can make an investment look either more or less attractive than it does when inflation is excluded from the analysis.

4. One tool to do this is @Risk, an Excel add-on.

5. A dowry is a (usually) large sum of money that is promised to an incoming chief of service. It most often is used for capital equipment or other programming purposes. For details, see David W. Young and Richard B. Saltman, *The Hospital Power Equilibrium* (Baltimore: Johns Hopkins University Press, 1985).

6. For a discussion of culture, see Edgar H. Schein, *Organizational Culture and Leadership*, 2nd ed. (San Francisco: Jossey-Bass, 2010).

7. This appendix has benefited from discussions and information exchanges with the late Professor Robert N. Anthony, who was deeply involved in benefit-cost analyses when he served as controller for the Department of Defense in the 1960s.

8. Alice L. London, "Transportation Services for the Disabled," *GAO Review* 21 (Spring 1986): 21–27.

9. Ann Biggons, "Overkilling the Insect Enemy," *Science* 249 (August 1990): 621.

10. US General Accounting Office, *Accidental Shootings: Many Deaths and Injuries Caused by Firearms Could Be Prevented*, Report to the Chairman, Subcommittee on Antitrust Monopolies, and Business Rights, Committee of the Judiciary, US Senate, Washington, DC, March 1991. The study cited by the GAO was Dorothy P. Rice, Ellen J. MacKenzie, and Associates, *Cost of Injury in the United States: A Report to Congress* (San Francisco: Institute for Health and Aging, University of California and Injury Prevention Center, The Johns Hopkins University, 1989).

11. Health One® and Deloitte & Touche, *Managing Care and Costs: Strategic Choices and Issues; An Environmental Assessment of U.S. Health Care, 1991–1996* (Minneapolis: Health One Corporation, 1991).

12. From Steven E. Rhoads, "Kind Hearts and Opportunity Costs," *Across the Board*, December 1985.

13. Merril Eisenbud, "Disparate Costs of Risk Avoidance," *Science* 241 (September 1988): 1277–1278.

CHAPTER 9

OPERATIONAL BUDGETING

A s long as there are scarce resources with alternative uses, an organization will face financial constraints. Most deal with these constraints during the budgeting phase of the management control process. In contrast with programming, which looks ahead several years, budgeting generally is for a single year. Ordinarily it uses the new programs or product lines that emerged from the programming phase, along with existing programs and product lines, and attempts to determine the revenues, expenses, and, sometimes, nonfinancial (or programmatic) outcomes associated with each.

In some organizations, programs fall neatly into responsibility centers, and each responsibility center manager prepares a budget for each of his or her unit's programs. Alternatively, it also is possible that each program is a separate responsibility center, generally a profit center. When neither of these arrangements is possible, a more complex, matrix-like structure may be needed, such as that discussed in chapter 7.

It is important for the budgeting phase to fit with the organization's responsibility center structure and strategy. To accomplish the latter, line managers must budget for nonfinancial as well as financial goals and objectives. Senior management then can link each responsibility center's activities to the organization's overall strategic direction.

Most organizations have two budgets. The operating budget, discussed in this chapter, focuses on revenues and expenses on an accrual basis and is used as one aspect in measuring the performance of line managers. The cash budget, discussed in chapter 10, projects the cash inflows and outflows associated with both ongoing operations and financing; it is used by the controller or treasurer to help manage the organization's cash.

LEARNING OBJECTIVES

On completing this chapter, you should know about

- The organizational context in which operational budgeting takes place

- The budgeting context, which includes the organization's cost structure, strategic success factors, organizational structure, and motivation process

- The components of the operating budget and the mechanical aspects of formulating it

- Some frequent budgeting misfits, or areas where operational budgeting does not fit well with other aspects of the organization

Organization of the Chapter

The chapter looks at operational budgeting through several lenses. The discussion begins with the nature of the operating budget and the broad context in which budgeting takes place, distinguishing between the behavioral and mechanical aspects of budgeting. It then looks at the components of the operating budget and the steps involved in formulating a budget. The appendix at the end of the chapter discusses some budgeting "misfits," or areas where the budgeting phase may be poorly aligned with other organizational activities.

General Nature of the Operating Budget

It is during the budgeting phase of the management control process that an organization sets out its plans for the upcoming year and attaches monetary amounts to its various activities and programs. In addition, in many organizations, the budget is used as a central aspect of measuring managerial performance. This combination means that the budgeting phase has both behavioral and mechanical aspects.

Relationship between Programming and Budgeting

In concept, operational budgeting follows programming but is separate from it. Ideally, the budget is a "fine-tuning" of an organization's programs for a given year, incorporating the final decisions on the amounts to be spent for each program. The budget also specifies the organizational units that are responsible for carrying out each program. In most organizations, however, there is no clean separation between programming and budgeting. Even organizations that have a well-developed programming phase occasionally discover circumstances during the budgeting phase that require revisions of programming decisions. In organizations that do not have a clearly defined programming phase, many programmatic decisions are made as part of the budgeting phase.

Despite this overlap, these two types of activities have different characteristics, and it is therefore useful to think about them separately. Programming decisions usually include rough estimates of the associated revenues and expenses. Budgeting, by contrast, requires careful estimates of revenues and expenses, and a budget usually is formulated within the context of estimated available resources.

Because a budget is a plan against which actual performance is compared, senior management must be certain that it corresponds to individual responsibility centers. As such, it provides a basis for measuring the performance of responsibility center managers. If a program is to be used as the basis for performance measurement, senior management generally must designate it as a separate responsibility center. Otherwise, responsibility for many of a program's elements may be too diffused throughout the organization to permit the measurement of any given manager's performance.

EXAMPLE

Consider a hospital with a teenage substance abuse program. To be successful, the program may need contributions from the departments of pediatrics, psychiatry, internal medicine, and social work. If the program were not set up as a responsibility center, each department no doubt would do its best to provide the services within its capabilities, but those services would not be coordinated. As a result, it would be difficult to measure the performance of the program's manager.

Instead, the program could be established as a profit center in a matrix-like organization, such as that shown in figure 7.1 (in chapter 7). The result might be as shown in figure 9.1. In this arrangement, the manager of each program would "purchase" the services of people in each of the departments at a transfer price. Under these circumstances, one goal in the budgeting phase of the management control process would be to have managers agree on (1) the transfer prices, (2) the estimated amount of time to be purchased from each department, and (3) the expected results from the services provided by the departments.

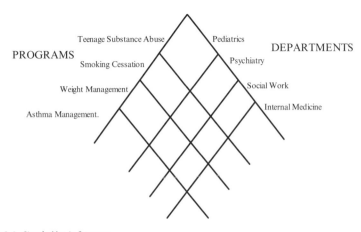

Figure 9.1 Simple Matrix Structure

Contrast with Manufacturing Companies

Budgeting is perhaps more important in a health care organization than in a manufacturing company due largely to contrasting cost structures. In a manufacturing company, many costs are engineered. The amount of labor and the quantity of materials required to make a unit of output are determined within close limits by design and engineering specifications. By contrast, in most health care organizations, many costs are discretionary—the amount to be spent per discharged patient (a hospital's "output unit") varies widely depending on decisions by program managers, physicians, and other professionals. Many of these decisions are made during the budget formulation phase of the management control process.

EXAMPLE

Many hospitals have developed "clinical pathways" for patients with different diagnoses or diagnosis-related groups (DRGs). A clinical pathway is like an engineered cost in that it specifies the ideal mix of resources for a "typical" patient with a given diagnosis: length of stay, laboratory tests, radiology procedures, physical therapy sessions, and so forth. However, unlike in a manufacturing company, where the products of any given type are identical, all patients are not the same. Senior management must therefore be willing to accept some deviation from the standard. How much of a deviation, under what circumstances, and for what kinds of patients are topics that must be addressed during the budgeting phase. More specifically, as figure 1.8 (in chapter 1) indicated, although it may be relatively easy to budget for the modal case, a hospital also must consider the impact of outliers.

Managerial Context for the Operating Budget

Budgeting clearly has mechanical aspects. Revenue forecasts must be made, the associated expenses must be estimated, and the resulting surplus or deficit must be calculated. For organizations to use the budget as a managerial tool, however, they must view it from a broader perspective than just its mechanics. We will look first at this contextual perspective, and then use it as a basis for discussing the mechanical side of budgeting.

budget monitoring
One aspect of the reporting phase of the management control process. It compares actual results to budgeted ones.

In this regard, it is important to emphasize that the management control process has both a *budgeting* phase and a *reporting* (or *budget monitoring*) phase. In this chapter, the emphasis is on budgeting.

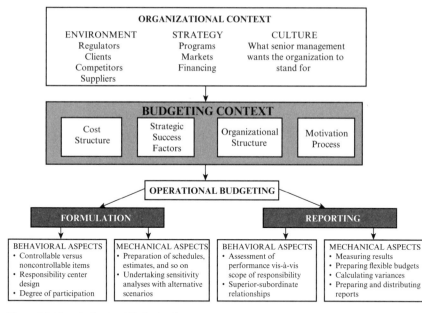

Figure 9.2 Organizational and Budgeting Contexts

Nevertheless, to put budgeting in context, we need to look at both phases. Doing so allows us to view budgeting's *mechanical aspects* and *behavioral aspects* in a more holistic context. Moreover, both phases exist in a broad organizational context, which explains why different organizations have different budgeting and reporting activities. This idea is shown schematically in figure 9.2 and explained in the paragraphs that follow.

Organizational Context

The *organizational context* for budgeting can be viewed in terms of environment, strategy, and culture. In most instances, these factors serve to constrain certain budgeting decisions.

Environment

If, on the one hand, an organization operates in a highly regulated environment, such as that of a public utility, its budgeting phase must be geared in part to the needs of the regulatory agencies and the constraints they place on its decision making. If, on the other hand, it operates in a more competitive environment, as do many health care organizations, it will need to eliminate as much "slack" as possible. By contrast, if an organization is the sole provider (or one of only a few providers) of a particular service, it may not need to pay much attention to its budget, perhaps using it as a rough guide only.

mechanical aspects
The part of the budgeting phase that makes calculations and ultimately computes the resulting surplus or deficit.

behavioral aspects
Elements of the budgeting phase of the management control process that consider how line managers are to be involved in formulating the budget.

organizational context
A framework for budgeting that can be viewed in terms of environment, strategy, and culture. In most instances, these factors serve to constrain certain budgeting decisions.

Strategy

An organization's strategy will also have a great deal to do with the way it prepares its budget. A home health agency operating in a rural area that focuses on assisted living and uses many unskilled employees is likely to prepare its budget differently than would a similar agency located in an urban area that focuses on nursing and physical therapy visits and uses highly trained professionals. Shouldice Hospital in Canada, whose strategy is to offer only one service—hernia operations—will prepare its budget quite differently than would an academic medical center with several "centers of excellence."

Culture

Finally, an organization's culture influences its budget. If, for example, a medical school values a highly collegial atmosphere among its faculty, it is likely to budget differently than a medical school that thinks of its faculty as "hired help." Moreover, senior management's choice about the nonfinancial information it will include in the budget can have an important impact on the organization's culture.

EXAMPLE

A health maintenance organization (HMO), a physician group practice, or any other health care organization that collects and regularly reports on information about patient satisfaction, and holds line managers and care providers responsible for achieving certain threshold scores, can expect to have a culture that places a greater emphasis on patients than that of an organization that does not collect and report such information.

Many health care organizations have extended this idea to the use of a balanced scorecard (BSC). A typical BSC measures several metrics in each of four areas: (1) customer (or patient) satisfaction, (2) employee growth and development, (3) internal process improvements, and (4) financial performance.[1]

Budgeting Context

budgeting context
A set of considerations that flows from the organizational context and consists of four features that influence and constrain how the budget is prepared.

The *budgeting context* flows from the organizational context and consists of four features that influence and constrain how the budget is prepared: cost structure, strategic success factors, organizational structure, and motivation process.

Cost Structure

An organization's cost structure influences its budget largely in terms of the split between fixed and variable costs. For example, a visiting nurse association that believes it is important to have a full-time, salaried labor force will have a different cost structure from that of an agency that chooses to use many part-time, hourly workers. Full-time, salaried labor generally can be considered a fixed cost, whereas part-time, hourly labor can be thought of as a variable cost.

Strategic Success Factors

Most organizations have two or three factors that are crucial to their success. For an HMO, hospital days per 1,000 enrollees is important. For many home health agencies, the number of visits per nurse per day is significant. How the organization deals with these factors relates directly to its budget.

PROBLEM

The Pleasant Street Home Health Agency charges $100 per visit and has a staff of 50 nurses. Nurses make an average of 6 visits a day. Senior management believes that it will be possible to increase the average to 6.1 visits a day (about a 1.7 percent increase) per nurse over the course of the next year. By how much will budgeted revenue change with this increase?

ANSWER

Revenue will change by $120,000. Calculations are as follows:

Change in average visits per nurse $(6.1-6.0) = 0.1$

Number of workdays in a year $= 240$

Number of nurses $= 50$

Revenue per visit $= \$100$

Change in revenue $(0.1 \times 240 \times 50 \times \$100) = \$120,000$

Organizational Structure

The way the organization is structured also will influence how it goes about formulating and monitoring its budget. Recall from chapter 7 that some health care organizations are organized into departments, whereas others are organized into product (or service) lines or are program based. Others have a matrix-like structure. Budget formulation will differ across these various types, especially if transfer prices are used for intraorganizational transactions.

PROBLEM

Return to the matrix organization shown in figure 9.1. How should program managers prepare their respective budgets? How should department managers prepare theirs?

ANSWER

Program managers must forecast not only how many hours of service they will need from each of the departments but also what level of expertise they will need. These hours will be purchased from the departments at a transfer price (which will differ depending on the level of expertise used). Department managers will use this revenue to pay the employees in their departments who work for the programs. If there are not enough employees to meet the needs of the program managers, the department managers will need to recruit additional staff. If there are more employees than the program managers need, department managers will need to resize their respective departments or incur a deficit.

Motivation Process

Some organizations pay bonuses to key line managers. Others encourage line managers to behave in an entrepreneurial way and provide extra budgetary resources to those who are successful. There is therefore a link between the motivation process and the way the budget is formulated. Indeed, in many organizations the budget is used along with actual results as a major performance evaluation tool. When this is the case, managers' annual bonuses, salary increases, and promotions may be closely linked to how well they performed against their respective budgets.

Budget Formulation

The budget formulation phase flows from these two contexts (organizational and budgeting). As indicated earlier, it has both mechanical and behavioral aspects. Although they are related, let's look at them separately.

Mechanical Aspects

budget drivers
An activity or measure that can be managed and that can cause an organization's net income to increase or decrease.

All budgets have a mechanical component, in which schedules, estimates of revenues, hours of service, unit costs, and the like are agreed on. In the last thirty years or so, the use of spreadsheet technology has greatly facilitated the mechanical side of budget formulation. Managers can incorporate key *budget drivers* into a spreadsheet program in such a way that "what if?" scenarios can be tested for their budgetary implications.

Moreover, when spreadsheets are used, decisions made in budget meetings about reductions (or increases) can be incorporated into individual managers' budgets quickly and easily.

Behavioral Aspects

If a budget is to be useful as a management tool, its formulation must be more than a purely mechanical exercise, with arbitrary reductions across line items when the first pass leads to unacceptable bottom-line results. Indeed, if the budgeting phase is to be useful for managers at all levels in the organization, it must assist them in making a commitment to achieving a set of agreed-on results. Because the surplus or deficit in a health care organization does not fully measure performance, these results need to be both financial and nonfinancial in nature. In most instances, if managers are to commit themselves to achieving both the financial and nonfinancial results, they must have some degree of participation in setting the budgeted targets, and they must be held accountable only for those items over which they can exert a reasonable degree of control.

EXAMPLE

In preparing its annual budget, a rehabilitation hospital that had designated its programs (for example, the spinal cord injury program) as profit centers, asked its program managers to budget for both revenues and expenses. As might be expected, each program presented a budget with a surplus (even though most had incurred deficits the previous year). The finance committee of the board then asked the program managers to indicate which budget drivers they expected to change to achieve the surplus, and by how much. The budget drivers that the program managers specified were case mix, volume, payer mix, reimbursement rates, resources per case, variable cost per resource unit, and fixed costs.

Once this activity had been completed, the committee asked the program managers to determine the milestones associated with each budget driver and to time-phase them. For example, one milestone was to recruit and hire some nurses from abroad, which would relieve the need to use comparatively expensive agency nurses. Other milestones included such activities as obtaining visas and work permits, arranging for transportation, finding housing, and engaging in training activities. Each program manager was then asked to stipulate the resources needed for each milestone and to take responsibility for achieving the milestones. In undertaking these activities, the finance committee had injected a significant behavioral component into what otherwise might have been a mechanical (and optimistic) exercise in budget formulation.

Reporting Results

The mechanical side of reporting on (or monitoring) the budget consists of measuring the same elements as were used to formulate it and structuring the information in a way that is useful for program and department managers in taking action to deal with problems. Reports are then distributed to managers on a regular basis or as needed.

EXAMPLE

Returning to the rehabilitation hospital example given previously, an important part of monitoring the budget was using milestone reports. By reviewing the monthly milestone report, the board's finance committee was able to learn of milestones that were not achieved by the target date, and thus had advance notice that some budgetary goals might not be achieved. The committee then was able to work with the program managers to determine what sorts of corrective action would be needed to bring the budget back in line.

Components of the Operating Budget

In all but the simplest of organizations, the mechanical side of preparing the operating budget is performed in contexts discussed earlier. It also is conducted in light of the decisions that senior management has made about the organization's responsibility centers. For example, a profit center manager will build his or her budget differently than will a standard expense center manager, whose budget will be different still from those of managers who run discretionary expense centers. These budgets in turn will be quite different from those of managers of revenue centers. In general, however, the mechanical aspects of preparing the operating budget consist of addressing three factors: revenues, expenses, and *nonfinancial measures* (sometimes called programmatic measures).

Revenues

The general purpose of a health care organization is to provide as much service as it can with available resources. In some health care organizations, such as a public health agency or a managed care plan, the total amount of revenue in any given budget year is, for all practical purposes, confined within quite narrow limits. The goal in preparing the operating budget is therefore to decide how best to spend it.

Most managers would agree that the budgeting phase should anticipate revenues first, and then estimate the related expenses. This policy
provides a bulwark against arguments, often made by highly articulate and
persuasive people, that an organization should undertake a program even
though it cannot afford it.

Discipline Required for a Revenue-First Policy

Carrying out a revenue-first policy requires considerable discipline in two
respects. First, it requires a careful and prudent estimate of total revenues
from all sources, including patient copayments, gifts, grants, contracts,
third-party payments, and endowment earnings. Once this figure has been
established, it is locked in.

Second, it requires a commitment to engaging in cost cutting if the
first approximation of the budget indicates a deficit or an insufficient
surplus.[2] Although the least painful course of action is to anticipate additional sources of revenue, this is highly dangerous. If the original revenue
estimates were made carefully, all feasible sources were included. New
ideas that arise subsequently may produce additional revenue, but frequently the evidence that they will do so is not strong. If the additional
revenue does not materialize, financial problems will result. The safer
course of action is to take whatever steps are necessary to reduce expenses.

Exceptions to the Revenue-First Policy

A policy that budgeted revenue should set the limit on expenses is not
applicable under some of the conditions discussed in the following
paragraphs.

Discretionary Revenues

In some organizations, senior management may be able to increase revenues by, for example, intensifying its fundraising efforts so as to increase
gifts and donations. This idea of "spending money to make money" is the
health care counterpart of a for-profit company's marketing activities. To
the extent that this practice is valid, it is appropriate to speak of discretionary revenues as well as discretionary expenses.

Such opportunities are not of major significance in many health care
organizations, however. Ideally, the organization has already incorporated
into the budget all the fundraising devices it can think of, and managers
must take the revenues from such efforts as a given.

Anticipated Grant Revenues

Some organizations, such as universities and research institutions, include
anticipated contract or grant revenues in their budgets. This is because

they frequently apply for contracts or grants but do not learn whether they will be awarded them until well into the fiscal year. If the budget were prepared only on the basis of *known* revenues, key professional staff might be laid off, they might obtain employment elsewhere, and they might be unavailable when the contract or grant is awarded. Some organizations thus decide to incur deficits in anticipation of receiving these awards. Such a strategy is risky and clearly can be sustained only if awards of sufficient magnitude are received.

Short-Run Fluctuations

When managers expect short-run revenue fluctuations around an average, it is appropriate to budget for the average amount of revenue rather than for a specific level of revenue anticipated in a given year. In some years expenses may exceed revenues, and in others revenues will exceed expenses. Over time, the two should net out. This strategy must be carefully managed, of course, to make sure the organization can weather the bad times.

A Promoter

On occasion, the amount of revenue available can be increased by a dynamic individual. The governing board then may authorize an operating budget with a deficit in anticipation of the new resources this person will bring in. Such a decision obviously is a gamble. If it works, the organization may be elevated to a higher plateau. If it doesn't, painful cutbacks may be needed to bring expenses back in line with revenues.

Hard and Soft Money

Assuming a reasonably consistent pattern of patient flows from one year to the next, a health care organization can count on a certain amount of patient care revenue; this is considered to be *hard money*, or money that is relatively certain to be received. Income from endowment investments is also hard money. It is prudent to make long-term commitments, such as tenured faculty appointments, when they will be financed with hard money. By contrast, revenue from annual gifts or grants for research projects is *soft money*. In an economic downturn, gifts may drop drastically and grantors may decide not to renew their grants. Managers must be careful not to make long-term commitments to activities that will be financed with soft money.

line-item format
A way of presenting a budget that classifies expenses by function, such as salaries and wages, rather than by programs. Contrasts with program format.

Expenses

There are two general formats for the expense portion of the budget. The traditional format, called the *line-item format*, focuses on such expense elements as wages, fringe benefits, supplies, and other similar resources.

The other format, called a *program format*, focuses on programs and program elements. The contrast between the two for a public health department is shown in Table 9.1.

The program format permits a decision maker to judge the appropriate amount of resources for each activity. It also permits senior management

program format
A way of presenting a budget that classifies expenses by program (such as community mental health), rather than by function. Contrasts with a line-item format.

Table 9.1 Line-Item and Program Budgets for a Public Health Department (in Thousands of Dollars)

	Last Year Actual	This Year Budget
Line-Item Format		
Wages and salaries	$4,232	$4,655
Overtime	217	72
Fringe benefits	783	861
Retirement plan	720	792
Operating supplies	216	220
Fuel	338	410
Uniforms	68	70
Repairs and maintenance	340	392
Professional services	71	0
Communication	226	236
Vehicles	482	450
Printing and publications	61	65
Building rental	447	450
Other	396	478
TOTAL	$8,597	$9,151
Program Format		
Community health and prevention	$2,677	$2,845
Emergency preparedness	1,610	1,771
Environmental health	470	482
Family health and nutrition	320	347
Health care safety and quality	182	180
Health information, statistics, research, and evaluation	680	704
Infectious disease prevention, response, and service	64	70
State Laboratory Institute	86	92
Public health hospitals	1,427	1,530
Substance abuse services	236	260
Regional offices	563	560
General administration	282	310
TOTAL	$8,597	$9,151

to match planned spending with measures of each activity's planned outputs. It is important to note, however, that although the focus of this format is on programs, there almost always is a line-item listing of the various expense elements within each program.

Nonfinancial Measures

nonfinancial measures
Information on planned outputs, usually consisting of process and results measures. Some organizations commit themselves to specific output targets for each program.

The third component of the operating budget is information on planned outputs. Output (or nonfinancial) information usually consists of process and results measures.[3] Some organizations commit themselves to specific output targets for each program as part of the budgeting process. When this happens, these nonfinancial measures become important ingredients in the budget.

Steps in Formulating the Operating Budget

Although every organization formulates its operating budget somewhat differently, most have an annual timetable that includes five steps.

Step 1: Disseminating Guidelines

Senior management usually begins the process by distributing a set of guidelines for managers to follow in preparing their budgets. These guidelines include dates when various documents are due. Sometimes managers are asked to submit a partial budget (such as a revenue budget) before preparing the remainder of their budget, and sometimes they are asked to submit only a complete budget.

If approved programs exist, the budget should be consistent with them. This does not necessarily mean that the budget should contain only approved programs, which can frustrate operating managers. Indeed, desirable innovations may come to light if managers are permitted (or even encouraged) to propose activities that are not among the approved programs. These activities should be clearly distinguished from the approved programs, however, and operating managers should understand that the chances for approval of new programs during the budget formulation phase are slight. Otherwise, senior management may be downgrading the programming phase of the management control process.

Senior management also must make sure that operating managers are aware of any other constraints that exist, such as a requirement that the budget not be for more than 105 percent of the prior year's budget. Constraints also can be quite detailed, such as stipulations that the budget be consistent with (1) senior management's assumptions about wage rates and other input prices, (2) the conditions under which new employees may be recruited, (3) the number of employees who may be promoted, or (4) expected productivity gains—or a combination of these.

In addition, there often are guidelines about the format and content of the proposed budget. These are intended to ensure that the budget estimates are submitted in a fashion that both facilitates analysis and permits the comparison between actual and planned performance.

Step 2: Preparing Revenue Budgets

For managers of profit centers, the first step usually is to prepare a revenue budget. Doing so provides the organization with some reasonable assurance that anticipated revenues are based on the market. If expenses were estimated first, there could be a tendency to assume that the amount of revenue would be high enough to cover them, which might be unrealistic.

In preparing the revenue budget, the manager of each profit center in a large organization may ask his or her revenue center managers to estimate their revenues for the year. If a profit center is responsible for several programs, the profit center manager may ask each program manager to estimate the revenues for his or her program.

Sometimes revenue estimates are reviewed and evaluated by senior management's staff to ensure that they are realistic in light of general economic conditions, competitive forces, capacity constraints, and so forth. In large, complex organizations, revenue budgets contain considerable detail on exactly what types of services or goods will be sold, to whom, in what quantities, and where. These projections may go through divisional management for approval before being sent to senior management.

Step 3: Preparing Expense Budgets for Profit and Standard Expense Centers

Each program's expense budget usually is constructed by beginning with the volume and mix estimates used for the revenue budget and attaching variable cost elements to the units. The results are multiplied to give total variable costs, after which the appropriate step-function costs and fixed costs are added. In the case of a standard expense center, although no revenues are received (unless there are transfer prices), the manager still will need to estimate expenses by beginning with the anticipated volume and mix of the center's outputs.

EXAMPLE

In a hospital's dietary department, the total variable cost for food can be estimated by using the average variable cost per meal, multiplied by the average number of meals served a day, multiplied by 365 days in the year. If the variable cost is different for each meal (breakfast versus lunch and dinner), a mix factor will be needed. To this total can be added the step-function costs of the department's kitchen and service personnel, various nonfood supply costs, and the department's fixed costs (such as dietitians).

In a hospital's social service department, if the number of cases can be predicted, the budget for social worker salaries can be obtained by using a standard workload factor (cases per social worker) multiplied by the average salary of a social worker. If there are different levels of social workers (MSW versus BA, for example), a mix factor will be needed, with the possibility that each level will have a different workload factor. To this total can be added the fixed costs of the department.

Step 4: Preparing Expense Budgets for Discretionary Expense Centers

The manager of each discretionary expense center prepares a budget for the center's expenses. Because these expenses are unrelated to volume or mix of outputs, the budget is a fixed amount, based on assumptions about the kinds and amounts of activities that staff members will need to engage in during the year. For example, if litigation is pending, the budget for legal services might be higher this year than it was last year. Or if there are plans to undertake a major revision of the management information system, the budget might be higher. Similarly, if activities that took place last year won't take place this year, the corresponding budget should be reduced.

Step 5: Preparing the Master Budget

The various profit center budgets are assembled to determine the forecasted contribution to standard and discretionary expense centers for the year. Standard and discretionary expense center budgets are then subtracted to give the overall surplus. This budget usually is taken to the board of directors for approval.

If the master budget is not approved (usually because the surplus is not sufficiently high, but sometimes because some flaws in forecasts are identified), it may be returned to one or more responsibility center managers for reworking. For reasons discussed earlier, profit center managers usually are not permitted to adjust their revenue forecasts. Instead, they (and sometimes standard and discretionary expense center managers) must reduce their expenses. A reduction in expenses can be achieved by lowering either step-function or fixed costs, or by reducing variable costs per unit, but ordinarily not by assuming a different volume or mix of output.

Figure 9.3 shows how these various pieces might be brought together for a hospital operating in a DRG payment environment. As it indicates, clinical care departments (such as surgery and medicine) forecast the number and mix of patients they will serve, classified by DRG, as well as the payer mix (for example, Blue Cross versus Medicare) and each payer's price for each DRG. They also forecast the resources they will use to treat each case, such as the average length of stay (LOS), radiology procedures, laboratory tests, and so forth. And they forecast the resources they will need from the patient service departments, such as laundry, housekeeping, medical records, and dietary.

In this example, the *clinical service departments* (such as radiology) and *patient service departments* (such as dietary) are standard expense centers.[4] They compute their variable costs and arrive at a transfer price for each of their services. The transfer price for each service is combined with the resources needed by the clinical care departments to treat each case, which leads to the budgeted variable cost per DRG. After each clinical care department's step-function and fixed costs are subtracted, the result is its contribution to the hospital's surplus.

From the sum of the contributions from all clinical care departments, the hospital subtracts the step-function and fixed costs of its clinical service and patient service departments, which gives the contribution to the administrative service departments (which are discretionary expense centers). The result, after deducting the expenses of these departments, is the hospital's surplus (or deficit).

Use of Models

Operational budgeting can benefit from a model that describes the underlying variables and the relationships among them. Such a model need not be complicated, and frequently can be prepared with a relatively simple spreadsheet. Table 9.2 shows how a model might be designed for the budgetary activities described in figure 9.3. The categories have been simplified (only two payers, for example, only four DRGs, and only three service departments), and the numbers are hypothetical. It would be rather easy, however, to increase the number of payers, DRGs, service departments, and so forth, and to insert actual numbers.

PROBLEM

Spend a few minutes studying tables 9.2a and 9.2b, focusing on DRG A. How was the revenue of $1,121,000 (shown on the third page of the table) computed? How was the $650 variable cost of nursing for this DRG computed? How was the total variable cost of $192,680 computed? Careful: there is a rounding error with this last one (your computations should total $192,640).

ANSWER

Revenue of $1,121,000 was computed as follows:

$$\text{Payer 1: } 60 \text{ cases} \times \$7,350 \text{ per case} = \$441,000$$
$$\text{Payer 2: } 100 \text{ cases} \times \$6,800 \text{ per case} = \$680,000$$
$$\$441,000 + \$680,000 = \$1,121,000$$

The $650 for DRG A was computed as follows:

$$60 \text{ nursing minutes per day} \times \$0.50 \text{ per nursing minute} = \$30 \text{ per day}$$
$$10 \text{ supply units per day} \times \$3.50 \text{ per unit} = \$35 \text{ per day}$$
$$10 \text{ days} \times (\$30 + \$35) = \$650 \text{ per case}$$

Total variable cost of $192,680 was computed as follows:

$$\$1,204 \text{ variable cost per case} \times 160 \text{ cases (60 with Payer 1 and 100 with Payer 2)}$$
$$= \$192,640 \ (\$192,680 \text{ with the rounding error})$$

Once the full number of payers, DRGs, service departments, and the like have been included, the consequences of budgeting decisions can be seen in terms of their impact on the hospital's surplus. If the surplus is too small, or if there is a deficit, the options available (other than increasing prices, changing payer mix, changing case mix, or increasing volume) are the following: (1) change the treatment patterns for a given case type; (2) decrease the variable cost per resource unit; (3) decrease step-function or fixed costs (or both) in clinical care departments, clinical service departments, or patient service departments; or (4) decrease costs in administrative service departments. With a properly designed spreadsheet, the impact on the hospital's surplus of the various options can be explored rather easily.

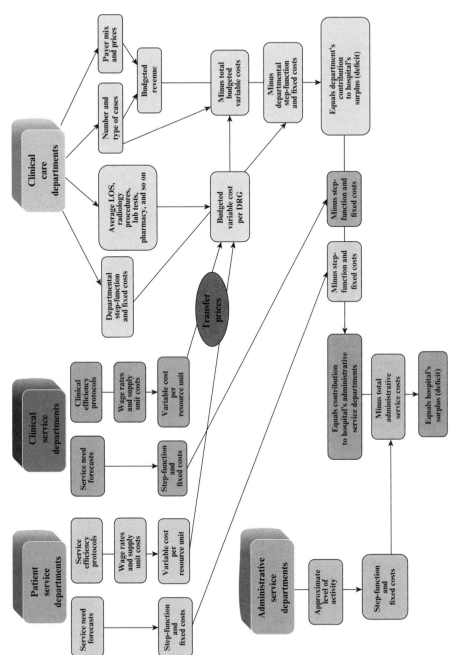

Figure 9.3 Budgeting in a Hospital

Table 9.2 Spreadsheet Model for a Hospital Budget

	Case Mix				
	DRG A	**DRG B**	**DRG C**	**DRG D**	**Total**
FORECAST REVENUE					
DEPARTMENT #1					
PAYER #1					
Forecast number of cases	60	200	100	50	
Expected revenue per case	$7,350	$1,430	$2,020	$7,650	
Total Revenue	$441,000	$286,000	$202,000	$382,500	$1,311,500
PAYER #2					
Forecast number of cases	100	50	300	150	
Expected revenue per case	$6,800	$1,500	$3,000	$7,400	
Total Revenue	$680,000	$75,000	$900,000	$1,110,000	$2,765,000
TOTAL REVENUE					$4,076,500
DEFINE CLINICAL PATHWAYS	DRG A	DRG B	DRG C	DRG D	
Resources from Clinical Service Departments					
No. of patient days per case	10	5	6	12	
No. of x-rays per case	5	1	2	3	
No. of CBCs per case	10	5	3	12	
Resources from Patient Service Departments					
No. of meals per case	30	15	18	36	
No. of pounds of laundry per case	15	7.5	9	18	
No. of medical records per case	1	1	1	1	
STEP FUNCTION AND FIXED COSTS AT THIS VOLUME AND MIX					
Step-function costs (e.g., nursing)					$1,000,000
Fixed costs (e.g. departmental administration)					1,500,000
TOTAL STEP AND FIXED COSTS AT THIS VOLUME AND MIX					$2,500,000
DETERMINE VARIABLE COST PER RESOURCE UNIT					
CLINICAL SERVICE DEPARTMENTS	DRG A	DRG B	DRG C	DRG D	
CLINICAL EFFICIENCY PROTOCOLS					
No. nursing minutes per patient day	60	40	50	40	
No. technician minutes per x-ray	40	40	40	40	
No. technician minutes per CBC	20	20	20	20	
No. units of nursing supplies per patient day	10	3	5	8	
No. units of supplies per x-ray	3	3	3	3	
No. units of supplies per CBC	4	4	4	4	
WAGE RAGES AND UNIT SUPPLY COSTS					
Cost per minute for nurses	$0.50	$0.50	$0.50	$0.50	
Cost per minute for x-ray technicians	$0.20	$0.20	$0.20	$0.20	

Table 9.2 (*Continued*)

	Case Mix				
	DRG A	**DRG B**	**DRG C**	**DRG D**	**Total**
Cost per minute for lab technicians	$0.20	$0.20	$0.20	$0.20	
Cost per unit for nursing supplies	$3.50	$3.50	$3.50	$3.50	
Cost per unit for x-ray supplies	$5.00	$5.00	$5.00	$5.00	
Cost per unit for CBC supplies	$2.00	$2.00	$2.00	$2.00	
VARIABLE COST (TRANSFER PRICE) PER RESOURCE UNIT IN CLINICAL SERVICE DEPARTMENTS					
Patient day	$65	$31	$43	$48	
X-Ray	$23	$23	$23	$23	
CBC	$12	$12	$12	$12	
PATIENT SERVICE DEPARTMENTS	**DRG A**	**DRG B**	**DRG C**	**DRG D**	
SERVICE EFFICIENCY PROTOCOLS					
No. minutes per meal	10	10	10	10	
No. minutes per pound of laundry	1	1	1	1	
No. minutes per medical record	5	5	5	5	
No. units of ingredients per meal	5	5	5	5	
No. units of laundry supplies per pound	3	3	3	3	
No. units of supplies per medical record	2	2	2	2	
WAGE RAGES AND UNIT SUPPLY COSTS					
Cost per minute for meals	$0.25	$0.25	$0.25	$0.25	
Cost per minute for laundry	$0.15	$0.15	$0.15	$0.15	
Cost per minute for medical records	$0.30	$0.30	$0.30	$0.30	
Cost per unit for dietary supplies	$1.50	$1.50	$1.50	$1.50	
Cost per unit for laundry supplies	$0.30	$0.30	$0.30	$0.30	
Cost per unit for medical record supplies	$1.00	$1.00	$1.00	$1.00	
VARIABLE COST (TRANSFER PRICE) PER RESOURCE UNIT IN PATIENT SERVICE DEPARTMENTS					
Meals	$10	$10	$10	$10	
Laundry	$1	$1	$1	$1	
Medical Records	$4	$4	$4	$4	

ESTIMATE SERVICE DEPARTMENT STEP AND FIXED COSTS AT FORECASTED VOLUME			
CLINICAL SERVICE DEPARTMENTS	**STEP**	**FIXED**	**TOTAL**
Nursing	$350,000	$700,000	$1,050,000
Radiology	250,000	800,000	1,050,000
Laboratory	320,000	600,000	920,000
Total			$3,020,000
PATIENT SERVICE DEPARTMENTS	**STEP**	**FIXED**	**TOTAL**
Dietary	$180,000	$600,000	$780,000
Laundry	100,000	400,000	500,000
Medical Records	150,000	300,000	450,000
Total			$1,730,000

(*Continued*)

Table 9.2 (*Continued*)

CALCULATE VARIABLE COST/CASE	DRG A	DRG B	DRG C	DRG D	
From Clinical Service Departments					
Nursing	$650	$153	$255	$576	
Radiology	115	23	46	69	
Laboratory	120	60	36	144	
From Patient Service Departments					
Dietary	$300	$150	$180	$360	
Laundry	16	8	9	19	
Medical Records	4	4	4	4	
TOTAL VARIABLE COST PER CASE	$1,204	$397	$530	$1,171	
COMPUTE THE SURPLUS (DEFICIT) FOR EACH CLINICAL CARE DEPARTMENT					
Revenue	$1,121,000	$361,000	$1,102,000	$1,492,500	
Minus Variable Costs	192,680	99,219	211,980	234,280	
Equals Contribution to Step and Fixed	$928,320	$261,781	$890,020	$1,258,220	$3,338,341
Minus Step and Fixed Costs					2,500,000
Equals Contribution to Clinical and Patient Service Step and Fixed Costs					$838,341
COMPUTE CONTRIBUTION TO HOSPITAL OVERHEAD					
Contribution from Clinical Care Departments (assumes 10 with same contribution)					$8,383,413
Minus Step and Fixed Costs of Clinical Service Departments					3,020,000
Minus Step and Fixed Costs of Patient Service Departments					1,730,000
Equals Contribution to Hospital Overhead					$3,633,413

ESTIMATE ADMINISTRATIVE SERVICE COSTS	STEP	FIXED	TOTAL
Legal	$250,000	$300,000	$550,000
Human Resources	300,000	600,000	900,000
Fiscal Affairs	300,000	850,000	1,150,000
Total			$2,600,000

COMPUTE HOSPITAL'S CLINICAL SURPLUS (DEFICIT)	
Contribution to Hospital Overhead	$3,633,413
Minus Estimated Administrative Costs	2,600,000
Equals Hospital's Surplus (Deficit)	$1,033,413

Important Features

The multistep process described in figure 9.3 and table 9.2 is only a rough guide to what actually happens in most organizations, and there are many variations on the general theme. Regardless of the specific approach an organization takes, however, there are several important features of this process:

- *Senior management is heavily involved.* Senior management sets the tone for the process and is involved in budget meetings with key managers. It does not turn the budgeting process over to the controller, but instead relies on the controller to assemble the information and conduct any needed analyses.

- *The timetable remains roughly the same each year.* It is adhered to closely so that managers and others who are involved know what to expect and when.

- *Corporate staff analyses are used as checks.* They are conducted principally by personnel in the controller's office and are designed to verify (or contradict) forecasts by responsibility center managers and their personnel. When a staff analysis contradicts a forecast, neither is allowed to dominate decision making. Instead, areas of disagreement are identified, discussed, and resolved. Where corporate staff and operating managers cannot resolve their differences, senior management makes the final decisions.

- *There is a negotiation phase.* Each operating manager has an opportunity to present his or her case to senior management and defend the forecasts.

- *The final budget represents a serious commitment by senior management.* Senior management commits to achieving the budgeted level of surplus, usually with the stipulation that nothing short of highly unusual circumstances can result in a budget revision. Highly unusual circumstances can include acts of nature (such as floods) or unforeseeable events (such as fires or prolonged strikes).

- *Within operating units or programs, budgets also represent serious commitments.* Sometimes these commitments differ from senior management's commitment. For example, managers of standard expense centers are expected to adhere to budgeted levels of unit variable costs and total fixed costs, but not to total costs, because total costs will be affected by the volume and mix of output (which is not under their control). Revenue center managers, in contrast, are expected to adhere to budgeted revenue forecasts. They may be allowed to change the volume and mix of resource inflows (such as contributions, contracts, grants, and so on) as long as total revenue forecasts are met.

Related Organizational Aspects

Several organizational aspects have a bearing on the operational budgeting phase. Most of these are applicable to health care organizations, even if only in a minor way.

Expense Creep

There is a tendency for the costs in support centers (such as human resources, dietary, and housekeeping) to creep upward. Because of this, staff analysts need to make special efforts to detect and eliminate unnecessary increases in these costs. If unit costs or ratios can be calculated, comparisons can be made with similar numbers in other responsibility centers or with external benchmarks.

This problem is particularly troublesome in responsibility centers whose output cannot be measured easily, such as a human resources department. Under these circumstances, it can be extremely difficult for supervisors to measure the effectiveness of resource use.

Behavioral Issues

The negotiation phase of the budget formulation effort tends to be a zero-sum undertaking in many organizations, with each budgetee negotiating for a larger share of the fixed budget pie. When resources are not abundant, such an arrangement generally produces a great deal of conflict and game playing.

EXAMPLE

One study of budget game playing identified five major activities: (1) understated volume estimates, (2) undeclared or understated price increases, (3) undeclared or understated cost reduction possibilities, (4) overstated expenses (such as for research), and (5) undeclared shifts in a program's mix. A principal reason for game playing given by one manager was that senior management did not have the time to check every number. So, one strategy was to 'pad' everything, with the hope that 50 percent of the cushions would be left after the plan reviews.

Conflict and game playing can be mitigated somewhat if there is a culture with some well-established norms. In some organizations, these norms include (1) trust between supervisors and their subordinates; (2) an assumption of competence, goodwill, and honesty on everyone's part; (3) a recognition that disagreements do not mean threats; (4) a spirit of openness and sharing of information; (5) a willingness by senior management to allow subordinates to develop their own solutions to budget-related problems; and (6) confidence on the part of everyone in the computations and other work of staff analysts.[5]

Role of Professionals

The attitudes of professionals is a particularly important factor in health care organizations. In a hospital, for example, the budgetee may be a physician, and another may be a nonclinical hospital administrator. Physicians are primarily interested in maintaining or improving the quality of patient care, enhancing the status of the hospital as perceived by their peers, and increasing their own prestige. Their interest in the costs that are involved generally is secondary. By contrast, hospital administrators are primarily interested in costs, although they realize that costs must not be so low that the quality of care or the status of the hospital is compromised. Thus, the two parties may weight the relevant factors considerably differently.

Toward More Effective Budgeting

Appendix 9A in this chapter discusses seven budgeting misfits, or areas where the budgeting phase of the management control process does not fit well with other organizational activities. As this appendix illustrates, most health care organizations require budgeting activities that are more sophisticated than those they currently have in place. In designing these new activities, they will need to consider four factors:

- The budgeting phase must incorporate case and service mix estimates so that the volume of each case or visit type becomes the driving force in formulating the budget. These estimates can be converted into dollar amounts by applying standard resources per case or visit and standard efficiency per resource unit.

- The reporting (or budget monitoring) phase must involve computing the variances between budgeted and actual expenditures by cost driver so that managerial action to correct an overall variance can be targeted toward its causes.

- Budget formulation and reporting must include nonfinancial as well as financial objectives.

- Budget formulation and reporting also must incorporate key line managers, professionals, and other employees in the decision-making process, who then must be rewarded for good performance.

Although somewhat costly and time consuming to develop initially, improved budgeting and reporting activities ultimately can have important benefits for an organization's responsibility accounting system. Moreover, they can be relatively inexpensive to operate on an ongoing basis.

You now are ready to work on the practice case for this chapter. The Los Reyes Hospital case gives you some practice in building a budget using cost and revenue drivers. A solution is in appendix B at the end of the book.

KEY TERMS

Behavioral aspects	Mechanical aspects
Budget drivers	Nonfinancial measures
Budgeting context	Organizational context
Budget monitoring	Program format
Line-item format	

To Bear in Mind

1. Seek the drivers. Almost all organizations have a relatively small number of activities that drive their overall budget—on both the revenue side and the expense side. When a budget is built using cost drivers, line managers can make budget modifications by focusing on the drivers rather than by making arbitrary decreases in expense line items.

2. Carefully consider the behavioral aspects. In general, operational budgeting is closely linked to the organization's culture and the way it rewards managers for good performance. Not surprisingly, operational budgeting frequently engenders considerable conflict among line managers and between line managers and corporate staff. These conflicts can be beneficial in terms of eliminating budgetary slack, but they must be carefully managed if they are to foster enhanced organizational performance.

Test Yourself

1. What is the difference between programming and budgeting? How do the two activities relate to each other?

2. What are the elements of the managerial context for the operating budget?

3. What is a revenue-first policy? Why should an organization have one?

4. How might a hospital use budget drivers to build its budget? How should it incorporate its payer mix into the budget?

5. What are the five steps that organizations follow in preparing their operating budget?

Suggested Cases

Bandon Medical Associates (A)

Centro Italiano Sviluppo

Lomita Hospital (A)

North Lake Medical Center

Rush Presbyterian–St. Luke's Medical Center

Sonsonala (A)

Southern Seattle University Health System (B)

PRACTICE CASE

LOS REYES HOSPITAL

Preparing this budget requires many assumptions that I'm not the least bit qualified to make. If the hospital is to have something that's realistic, I'm going to have to involve the physician chiefs and a few other key managers. The real question is how best to do that.

Alex Cohn, the chief financial officer of Los Reyes Hospital, was commenting on the frustration he felt as he began the process of preparing the hospital's budget for the upcoming fiscal year. As a first step in the process, he had requested some basic information from each of the hospital's clinical departments and service departments. He continued:

In reviewing this information I realized that I just couldn't make many of the budgeting decisions in a sensible way. So I thought I would ask the clinical and service departments to help. However, I know that I'll encounter some resistance in doing that because these people have never been involved in budgetary decision making before. I thought it might make sense to show them how they could become involved in a way that takes advantage of their expertise. I only hope that I'm not creating a monster!

Potential Managerial Roles

To demonstrate the potential role for physician chiefs and service department managers in formulating the hospital's budget, Mr. Cohn chose four case types in the department of medicine and four hospital service departments as the building blocks for a sample budget. He felt that if he could demonstrate a better approach to budgeting for these four case types and four departments, he then could expand his idea to cover the rest of the hospital.

The four case types were DRG 089 (simple pneumonia and pleurisy, age greater than seventeen); DRG 014 (specific cerebral vascular disorders except transient ischemic attack); DRG 096 (bronchitis and asthma, age greater than seventeen); and DRG 140 (angina pectoris). The departments he chose were routine care (that is, the hospital stay itself), radiology, laboratory, and pharmacy.

Financial Information

Mr. Cohn used the information he had obtained from his meetings and conversations with the chief of medicine, Maria Delgado, MD, to determine how many cases of each type she expected the physicians in her department would treat during the upcoming year and how many units of service she expected each case would use from each of the four service departments.

Because most of the hospital's contracts for care used a diagnosis-based form of payment, he then discussed the expected revenue the hospital would receive for each case type with his manager of contracting. The results of his information-gathering efforts are contained in exhibit 9.1.

Mr. Cohn met next with the heads of the four service departments to discuss and agree on their variable expenses. Because the hospital had just completed a lengthy and extensive study of the breakdown between its fixed and variable expenses, this information was readily available. Mr. Cohn determined that the variable expenses were as follows:

Day of routine care	$250
Radiology film	$25
Laboratory test	$15
Pharmacy unit (for example, a prescription)	$5

The final step in Mr. Cohn's analysis was to determine the fixed costs of the department of medicine. This information was also readily available because of the study that had been completed. He concluded that the department would have fixed costs totaling $1,950,600 for the upcoming year.

Mr. Cohn then asked his staff assistant to use this information to prepare a budget for the department of medicine for these four case types and the four service departments. He realized that this budget would not show the complete operating activities for the department of medicine because the department treated many additional case types. Nevertheless, he felt confident that if he could present the information to Dr. Delgado in an easily understandable form, she would see its value and would be willing to use the same process for completing the budget for the remaining cases in her department.

EXHIBIT 9.1 Budget Data

DRG	Expected Number of Cases	Expected Revenue per Case	Expected Days of Routine Care per Case	Expected Radiology Films per Case	Expected Laboratory Tests per Case	Expected Pharmacy Units per Case
089	300	$6,000	9	5	10	55
014	200	6,500	11	6	10	20
096	100	5,000	7	4	3	12
140	50	3,000	4	1	5	21

Assignment

1. Prepare a budget for the department of medicine for the four case types shown in exhibit 9.1. Organize your figures so that Dr. Delgado will find them understandable and useful. Try to set up a spreadsheet to calculate the budget and make it as formula driven as possible. This will allow you to easily test your assumptions as you answer question 2.

2. Assuming Dr. Delgado and Mr. Cohn are unhappy with the bottom line of this budget, what options are available to change it? Which of these options seem the most feasible to implement?

3. What problems do you think Dr. Delgado and Mr. Cohn will encounter in attempting to expand this budgeting effort to the rest of the department of medicine? What should be done about those problems?

4. What problems do you think Mr. Cohn will encounter in attempting to expand this effort to the rest of the hospital? What should be done about those problems?

Appendix 9A: Budgeting Misfits

The budgeting phase of the management control process not only is an integral part of an organization's responsibility accounting system but also is an essential ingredient in its success. But the utility of the budgeting phase depends to a large extent on its fit with a variety of other organizational elements. For this reason, the failure of the budget to play a useful role in some organizations might be assessed in terms of the misfits that follow.

Misfit 1: Between the Cost Structure and Budget Formulation

Budget formulation frequently is not built around the organization's cost structure. For example, many hospitals are reimbursed by the public sector (or third-party payers) via a per-discharge rate, based on the patient's DRG. Although the rate is designed to cover three types of costs—fixed, step function, and variable—it ordinarily is based exclusively on volume: the number of discharges of each DRG. Because fixed costs and a portion of step-function costs are time based (that is, dependent on the passage of time, not on volume), there is a misfit between the cost structure and the budget.

The resolution of this dilemma consists of holding managers responsible only for those costs over which they exercise reasonable control. Although some fixed costs are controllable during a budgetary period, many others are not. They exist because the organization has committed itself to being "ready to serve," and they will continue to exist even if the organization provides no units of service. A hospital emergency room, for example, must always be prepared to admit patients.

By contrast, most variable costs (and some step-function costs) *are* controllable, but only on a per-unit basis. As a result, although a manager can be asked to control variable costs per unit, he or she cannot be expected to control total variable costs. Total variable costs are affected by volume, which frequently is outside the manager's control.

Misfit 2: Between the Cost Structure and the Reporting Phase

In the reporting phase, a misfit exists when the budget-related reports do not adequately specify the reasons underlying a variance between budgeted and actual figures. Although accounting techniques, such as flexible budgets and variance analysis, have been developed to distinguish among these different cost drivers, they are not always used. As a result, managers frequently find it difficult to determine the reasons behind a deviation between budgeted and actual performance. Flexible budgets and variance analysis are discussed in chapter 11.

Misfit 3: Between Strategic Success Factors and Budget Formulation

Most organizations are able to identify one or two factors that are crucial to their success. Serious misfits can occur when these critical success factors are excluded from budget formulation. For example, for an HMO, a critical success factor is hospital days per 1,000 enrollees. Many HMOs have encountered serious financial problems when their hospitalization rates per 1,000 enrollees have exceeded budgeted levels.

Misfit 4: Between the Organizational Structure and Budget Formulation

Many organizations have a product line or service line structure, and many departments within an organization are organized into subdepartments. If the budget does not fit this structure, managers who make decisions that can affect the budget will not have appropriate budgetary responsibility. Situations of this sort can exist between, say, the support departments in a hospital (housekeeping, laundry, and the like) and the mission departments (such as medicine, surgery, obstetrics, and outpatient). Problems can occur, for example, when a mission department's costs are affected by the costs in several support departments but no transfer prices have been established. As a result, managers of support departments have minimal incentives to control their departments' costs.

Misfits also can occur when budgetary units either overlap or fall between organizational units. This situation can occur when the budget for a department has been disaggregated into some sections but not into others, or when budgetary categories do not correspond to a department's sections or other organizational units.

EXAMPLE

The department of medicine at Arlmont Hospital comprises several sections: general internal medicine, endocrinology, gastroenterology, and cardiology. Each section is managed by a chief of the specialty, and the department itself is under the direction of the chief of medicine. The budget report, which contains both budget and actual cost data, is prepared monthly and contains direct cost information classified into salaries, supplies, and depreciation. The information is broken down by ward, including two adult medicine wards. Each section chief is asked to prepare a budget and assist the hospital in its cost containment efforts. However, until the cost data are classified by section rather than by ward, the section chiefs will lack the requisite information to prepare and monitor a budget.

Misfit 5: Between Nonfinancial Goals and Budget Formulation

Organizations that engage in program budgeting have the opportunity to be explicit about any lack of congruence between strategic objectives and financial constraints. By so doing, they can address this lack of congruence during the budget formulation phase, making trade-offs as needed. Alternatively, issues concerning the congruence between financial and strategic objectives may be resolved by default, as happens when budget cuts are necessary but managers do not have sufficient information to determine which product or service lines are most successful in meeting the organization's overall goals. As a result, movement toward strategic objectives can be impeded.

Misfits of this sort can be corrected by expanding the operational budgeting phase to include a component in which department managers are asked to specify strategic objectives and commit to attaining them in addition to the financial objectives of the budget.

Misfit 6: Between the Motivation Process, Programming, and Budget Formulation

Although managers and other professionals in most health care organizations appear to derive some motivation from nonfinancial sources, the budget can play a role in providing them with incentives to work toward the organization's strategic objectives. To the extent that managers are committed to strategic objectives that are not financially feasible, for example, or are encouraged to develop new program ideas that are then thwarted during programming or budgeting, there is a misfit between the organization's motivation process and the programming and budgeting phases of its management control process.

Even worse is the situation in some organizations where the budget is seen as a hurdle to overcome rather than an integral part of the planning process. In these instances, line managers view budget formulation not as a useful management activity, but rather as an annual ritual akin to filing one's tax return. Under such circumstances, budget formulation is at best divorced from an organization's motivation process; at worst, it is inconsistent or incompatible with it.

Misfit 7: Between the Budgeting and Reporting Phases

There also is the possibility of a misfit between the budgeting and reporting phases of the management control process. Even if line managers have made strategic and financial commitments and are prepared to take them seriously, the entire process is weakened, and perhaps incapacitated, if the organization's reports do not provide information that is complete (in other words, that allows managers to assess the extent to which they are meeting their commitments); accurate; and timely. Yet the reports in many health care organizations take so long to arrive that the information is of little use to managers when it becomes available. Moreover, even reports that are timely frequently do not provide sufficient detail on the reasons underlying a budget variance. Managers thus find it quite difficult to assess the action that should be taken to correct a problematic situation. This topic is discussed more fully in chapter 11.

Notes

1. For an overview of the BSC, see Robert S. Kaplan and David P. Norton, *The Balanced Scorecard* (Boston: Harvard Business School Press, 1996). For an application of the BSC to health care, see Noorein Inamdar, Robert S. Kaplan, Marvin Bower, "Applying the Balanced Scorecard in Healthcare Provider Organizations," *Journal of Healthcare Management* 47 (May–June 2002): 179–196; William N. Zelman, George H. Pink, and Catherine B. Matthias, "Use of the Balanced Scorecard in Health Care," *Journal of Health Care Finance* 29 (Summer 2003): 1–16; Mehmet C. Kocakülâ and A. David Austill, "Balanced Scorecard Application in the Health Care Industry: A Case Study," *Journal of Health Care Finance* 34 (Fall 2007): 72–99.

2. A considerable body of literature addresses both the rationale for having a surplus in a nonprofit organization and techniques for computing the appropriate amount. For details, see David W. Young, *Note on Financial Surpluses in Nonprofit Organizations* (Boston: Harvard Business School Publications, Product TCG307, 2013).

3. For a discussion of output measurement, see David W. Young, *Note on Performance Measurement in Nonprofit Organizations* (Boston, Harvard Business School Publications, Product TCG311, 2013).

4. This is a somewhat tricky issue. When a hospital is operating in a DRG payment environment, especially (but not necessarily) when its prices are bundled, its payers do not pay separately for radiology, the laboratory, or any of a variety of departments that historically charged for their services (and hence would be candidates for designation as profit centers). However, in many physician group practices, or in hospital outpatient departments, imaging and laboratory services are billed for separately, thereby creating a revenue stream and the potential for designating these departments as profit centers. The focus in this section of the book is on building a budget for a hospital operating in a DRG environment, and hence treating its clinical service departments as standard expense centers. However, if the hospital used transfer prices for internal services, then these departments could be established as profit centers, with the idea that they would "break even" on internally provided services, but could earn a profit through services provided to outpatients. To do this properly, the hospital would need to use a two-part transfer price (discussed in chapter 7).

5. For additional discussion of game playing in budgeting, see Robert N. Anthony and David W. Young, *Note on Budget Ploys* (Boston: Harvard Business School Publications, Product TCG303, 2012).

CHAPTER 10

THE CASH BUDGET

Moving from preparing the capital and operating budgets to preparing the cash budget requires an understanding of both financial accounting and financial management. The former is concerned with the meaning of items on the balance sheet, the income statement, and the statement of cash flows. The latter focuses on the ways managers can affect these items. In particular, financial management is concerned with the choices managers make about (1) the use of debt or equity to finance assets, (2) the structure of debt, (3) the size of net income (or surplus), and (4) the management of growth. This chapter focuses on these items with the ultimate objective of relating the capital budget that emerged from the programming phase of the management control process (discussed in chapter 8) and the operating budget (discussed in chapter 9) to cash forecasts. Indeed, the cash budget is closely linked to the programming phase, as initiating a new program frequently entails acquiring some new fixed assets or making other investments that will require cash without an immediate receipt of revenue.

Organization of the Chapter

The chapter begins with a brief overview of a balance sheet and the link between the dual-aspect concept of accounting and cash management. This is followed by a discussion of two important cycles (and a subcycle of each) that organizations must manage if they are to assure themselves that they have sufficient cash on hand to meet daily obligations. The chapter then discusses three concepts that are important to an understanding of a cash budget: debt structure, leverage, and the role of profit (or surplus). The chapter concludes with a brief discussion of the statement of cash flows, the formal accounting

LEARNING OBJECTIVES

On completing this chapter, you should know about

- Two cash-related cycles—the operating cycle and the financing cycle—that an organization must manage if it is to make sure it has enough cash on hand to meet its obligations

- The role of an organization's debt structure in cash management

- The advantages and disadvantages of leverage, including the distinction between financial risk and business risk

- The role of profit (or surplus) as a financing mechanism for the fixed assets and working capital needed to support organizational growth

- The statement of cash flows and what it measures

statement that shows how an organization has managed its cash during a given accounting period.

It is important to note that, as with chapter 8, the discussion in this chapter is at an introductory level. The topics are covered in greater depth in books on finance.

Link to the Dual-Aspect Concept

dual-aspect concept
The accounting concept that is represented by the fundamental accounting equation: Assets = Liabilities + Equity. Assets are what an organization owns or has claim to, liabilities are funds owed to outsiders, and equity represents the combination of contributions from owners (or donors) and retained earnings.

The *dual-aspect concept* of accounting is represented by this fundamental accounting equation:

$$\textbf{Assets} = \textbf{Liabilities} + \textbf{Equity}$$

The left side of the equation indicates what an organization owns or has claim to, and the right side indicates how these items were financed. In most organizations, some portion of the assets has been financed with debt (liabilities), and some portion with equity.[1] In this regard, two issues that an organization must address are how much debt it should have on its balance sheet and what the term (repayment period) of each debt instrument should be. To examine these issues, let's use the balance sheet shown in table 10.1 for Homecare, the organization that was discussed in chapter 2.

Note that Homecare has three liabilities on its balance sheet: (1) accounts payable, which is debt that is owed to its vendors; (2) interest payable, which is interest on the debt that has been incurred but has not yet been paid to the lender; and (3) a note payable, which is the amount of

Table 10.1 Balance Sheet for Homecare, as of January 31 (in Thousands of Dollars)

Assets		Liabilities and Equity	
Cash	$8,200	Accounts payable	$3,000
Supplies inventory	3,500	Interest payable	50
Total current assets	$11,700	Total current liabilities	$3,050
		Noncurrent liabilities:	
		Note payable	5,000
		Total liabilities	$8,050
Noncurrent assets:			
Equipment (net)	5,900		
		Contributions	$10,000
		Retained earnings	(450)
Total assets	$17,600	Total liabilities and equity	$17,600

principal that it owes to the lender. The accounts payable usually are due within a month, and it is quite likely that the interest payable is due soon also. Because the note payable is noncurrent, we know that it is due over one year from the date of the statement, but we don't know exactly when.

Knowing when the note payable is due would be useful because we would like to know if Homecare will have at least $5,000 in cash at that time. If it does not, it will be unable to repay the debt. More generally, managers must be extremely concerned with their organization's cash flow. If an organization runs out of cash, it is in serious trouble: among other things, employees and vendors cannot be paid, which jeopardizes the organization's ability to continue with its normal operations.

Cash-Related Cycles

The amount of cash on hand is affected by two cycles: the *operating cycle* and the *financing cycle*. The former is concerned with day-to-day operations, the latter with longer-term financing.

The Operating Cycle

An organization clearly needs to have enough cash on hand to pay bills, meet payroll, and provide for many other operating activities that require cash. This need gives rise to the concept of the operating cycle, which is the cycle that all organizations must manage to ensure that there will be sufficient cash on hand to meet their daily needs. The operating cycle is shown schematically in figure 10.1.

As the figure indicates, if we assume for the moment a start-up situation, operations begin with the purchase of some inventory. In a manufacturing organization, this ordinarily is the raw materials inventory. If we were manufacturing wheelchairs, for example, we would purchase steel, rubber, leather, and various other parts, including such small items as nuts and bolts. Inventories differ in merchandising organizations (such as a hospital's gift shop), where no manufacturing takes place, and in service organizations (such as a primary care clinic), where no goods are sold. Even service organizations typically need an inventory of supplies, however. A hospital needs medical and surgical supplies, pharmaceuticals, scrubs, blood plasma, and a variety of other "raw materials."

Vendors generally do not require cash on delivery of the materials, which results in an account payable being created (or increased) by the same amount as the asset called inventory. Eventually, however, the organization's vendors must be paid in cash. At that time, there will be some "cash out"—cash that is paid to the vendors.

operating cycle
A set of activities that consist of purchasing inventory, using it in the production of goods or delivery of services, generating revenue from the sales of those goods and services, and collecting the associated accounts receivable.

financing cycle
A set of activities that consist of borrowing to finance fixed assets, purchasing the fixed assets, generating revenue from the use of those assets, and using the collection of accounts receivable to repay both the principal and interest on the debt.

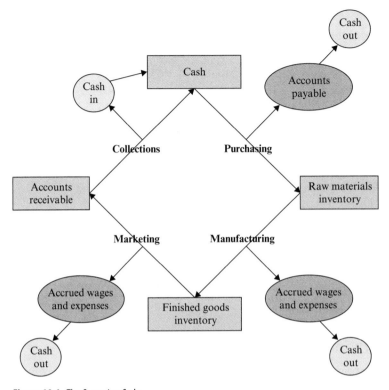

Figure 10.1 The Operating Cycle

In a manufacturing organization, the raw materials inventory is used up in the course of making the products, resulting in a finished goods inventory, which subsequently is shipped to customers. This, of course, requires some marketing and sales activities. In a service delivery organization, such as a hospital, raw materials (as defined earlier) also are used up as care is provided to patients.

In carrying out these and other activities, an organization incurs some expenses, such as salaries and wages for its employees. Because some employees are paid biweekly and others are paid monthly, wages are not paid out immediately in cash, which can give rise to an account called *accrued wages*—the equivalent of an account payable, but for employees. The organization's value-adding activities also give rise to some other expenses that do not result in immediate cash payments, which are called *accrued expenses*. Eventually, however, these too must be paid in cash. Of course, many expenses, such as rent and utilities, are paid in cash at almost the same time that they are incurred.

Similar activities take place in merchandising and service organizations. Goods are sold in a merchandising organization, and services are provided to customers in a service organization. Although the inventories are not transformed into finished goods as they are in a manufacturing company, they nevertheless must be purchased, with the associated cash payment frequently taking place before they are resold or used.

When the goods or services are sold, the organization earns revenue. However, in many organizations—particularly those that sell on credit (as most do)—the revenue is not received in cash immediately. Instead it takes the form of an *account receivable*. Only when accounts receivable are collected does the organization actually receive cash.[2] At that point, the operating cycle begins again.

EXAMPLE

Walmart uses point-of-sale technology, along with uniform product codes, to update its inventory every time it makes a sale. When the inventory of a product reaches a predetermined level, the system automatically places an order with the appropriate vendor. In this way, Walmart is able to manage each of its stores' unique inventory needs based on that store's customer buying patterns. A hospital, a physician group practice, or an integrated delivery system could manage its inventories (pharmaceuticals, medical supplies, and so on) in a similar way.

The Financing Cycle

Cash is paid out for activities other than operations. When, for example, an organization purchases some equipment, it ordinarily must make the payment in cash. In some instances, it will finance this acquisition with borrowing, such as a bank loan. Eventually, however, these borrowings must be repaid, and generally some interest payments must be made as well. These payments, called debt service, include both principal payments (to reduce the debt) and interest payments (which represent the expense associated with using the lender's funds). These relationships are shown schematically in figure 10.2.

As this figure indicates, borrowing can increase an organization's cash (as can the receipt of contributed capital from an equity offering or contributions from donors). Although, as figure 10.1 indicates, some borrowing can consist of accounts payable and accrued wages, we usually include only more formal debt in the category called *borrowing*. This category includes lines of credit, notes payable, bonds, capital leases, mortgages, and various other kinds of formal debt.

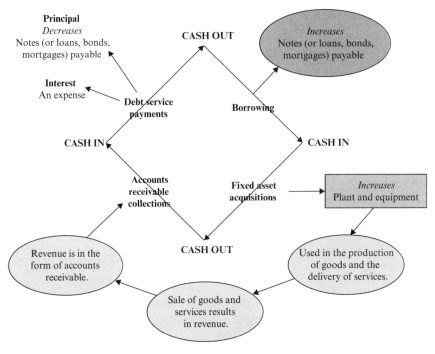

Figure 10.2 The Financing Cycle

Lines of credit tend to be used to finance seasonal cash flow problems associated with accounts receivable and inventory. Otherwise, the cash from borrowing ordinarily is used to purchase noncurrent (or fixed) assets, such as plant and equipment. The fixed assets are used in manufacturing and selling the organization's goods or in delivering its services. Even small organizations, such as a home health agency, need some fixed assets, such as desks, chairs, computers, and photocopying equipment.

As figure 10.2 indicates, the fixed assets, along with some operating cycle activities, are used to produce and sell the organization's goods and services. These sales provide revenue, which, as before, usually is in the form of accounts receivable and eventually is collected in cash. The cash received from the collection of accounts receivable can then be used to make debt service payments.

Managing this financing cycle is one of the most difficult tasks facing an organization. Senior management must make sure that there is enough cash on hand to purchase the fixed assets needed to produce the organization's goods or deliver its services. But senior management also must worry about the timing of the cash inflows from the sale of goods or services in relation to the timing of the required debt service payments. Having a debt service payment required before the cash is available to make it can create serious problems with an organization's lenders.[3]

The Revenue Cycle

An important aspect of managing the operating and financing cycles is addressing what has been called the *revenue cycle*.[4] In a hospital, the revenue cycle typically begins with the negotiation of payment rates with a managed care plan or other insurer. Then, when a patient calls to schedule an inpatient or outpatient service, he or she is registered, and the hospital collects some financial information (such as the name of the insurer, the nature of the policy, and so on).

When the patient arrives for care, a copayment may be collected. For inpatient care, many hospitals use a case manager to work with the insurance company to ensure that the patient's care is appropriate and that the hospital will be paid based on the terms of the contract. When the patient is discharged, the medical record is coded and the insurance company is billed. In addition, depending on the terms of the contract, the patient may be responsible for a portion of the final bill. Under these circumstances, two bills are sent out and collected: one from the insurer and one from the patient.

The revenue cycle does not end when the bills are paid (that is, when accounts receivable are collected). Many insurance companies, such as Medicare, periodically audit the hospital's finances to determine if the data were recorded correctly. If not, there may be a denial of all or a portion of the payment. Thus, part of managing the revenue cycle is making sure that data are recorded accurately and that the bills that are sent are appropriate under the terms of the contract.

In short, the revenue cycle comprises contract negotiations, payer relations, patient scheduling, patient registration, case management, coding, billing, collecting, and denial management. Cash inflows in the operating and financing cycles must therefore be thought of in a much more sophisticated way than as simply the collection of accounts receivable.

revenue cycle
A set of activities that typically begins with the negotiation of payment rates with a managed care plan or other insurer, registering patients, collecting some financial information, billing insurers and patients, collecting accounts receivable, and assuring the data were recorded correctly.

Financial Accounting versus Financial Management

Liabilities (such as an account payable) can delay the outflow of cash and accounts receivable can delay the inflow of cash. Nevertheless, all accounting-related activities in an organization eventually have an impact on cash. Although financial accounting measures the inflow or outflow of resources regardless of whether they are in cash, the organization's managers must pay careful attention to the associated cash flows.

debt structure
The mixture of short- and long-term liabilities on an organization's balance sheet. By matching the term of the debt to the life of the asset, a company's principal payments on the debt will be equal to the asset's depreciation, and, other things equal, its cash flows will be the same as its surplus (or deficit) on an accrual basis.

As the discussion so far has illustrated, making sure there is enough cash on hand is not always easy. Indeed, recognizing the existence of an operating cycle and a financing cycle and developing expectations for the amount of cash needed to make one complete rotation through each is an important managerial task. In some organizations, this analysis precedes the programming and budgeting phases of the management control process. It creates constraints on the amount of funds available for capital expenditures in the programming phase, and it establishes expectations for the overall profit (or surplus) figure in the budgeting phase. In other organizations, it follows the programming and budgeting phases and uses them as a guide to the amount of short- and long-term borrowing that must take place. In still others, the three activities may be run in parallel: decisions about the capital budget (that emerge from the programming phase) and overall profit figure (that is forecasted during the budgeting phase) are followed by an analysis of the cash-related implications, which may reveal a need to rework one or both budgets.

Key Cash Management Concepts

In managing the operating and financing cycles, there are three important financial management concepts to bear in mind: (1) *debt structure*, (2) *leverage*, and (3) the role of profit (or surplus).

Debt Structure

An important financial management maxim relating to the financing cycle is that the term of a debt instrument (such as a note) should match the life of the asset that it is financing. To understand this idea, consider the following problem.

? PROBLEM

Homecare does all its business on a cash basis. All sales are in cash, and all expenses are paid in cash, except depreciation. Depreciation is (as always) a noncash expense. As part of its programming activity, Homecare was deciding whether to purchase a replacement asset for an old piece of equipment at a cost of $300,000. The new asset would have a ten-year economic life and zero residual value. During the year, Homecare expected to have revenue of $200,000 and expenses other than depreciation of $130,000. The new asset would not change these items.

Assume that Homecare has decided to purchase the replacement asset. Prepare a pro forma (projected) income statement for the company in the space provided (ignore taxes). Next to the income statement column, show the cash inflows and outflows from each item, including the equipment purchase. By how much will Homecare's cash balance decline unless it finds some source of funds other than those from normal operations?

	Income Statement	Cash Flows
Revenue		
Expenses other than depreciation		
Depreciation		
Total expenses		
Surplus (deficit)		
Equipment purchase		
TOTAL		

ANSWER

Homecare's income statement and cash flows would look as follows:

	Income Statement	Cash Flows
Revenue	$200,000	$200,000
Expenses other than depreciation	130,000	(130,000)
Depreciation*	30,000	0
Total expenses	$160,000	
Surplus (deficit)	$40,000	
Equipment purchase		(300,000)
TOTAL		$(230,000)

*$300,000 ÷ 10 years = $30,000 per year.

As this answer indicates, although Homecare expects to earn a $40,000 surplus, its cash balance will decline by $230,000.

PROBLEM

Assume that Homecare has decided to finance the entire amount of the equipment purchase with debt. Annual interest payments will total $20,000 in cash. Everything else is the same as before. The income statement and cash flow analysis before the principal payments would look as follows:

	Income Statement	Cash Flows
Revenue	$200,000	$200,000
Expenses other than depreciation*	150,000	(150,000)
Depreciation	30,000	0

	Income Statement	Cash Flows
Total expenses	$180,000	
Surplus (deficit)	$20,000	
Equipment purchase		(300,000)
Receipt of note payable		300,000
TOTAL		$50,000

*Expenses are $20,000 more than before due to the inclusion of interest on the loan.

How would you structure Homecare's debt to make the company's cash flows identical to its surplus? That is, assuming equal principal payments each year, what should the term of the loan be?

ANSWER

If Homecare obtained a note with a term of ten years (the same as the life of the asset), its principal payments would be identical to the amount of depreciation on the asset, resulting in the following figures:

	Income Statement	Cash Flows
Revenue	$200,000	$200,000
Expenses other than depreciation	150,000	(150,000)
Depreciation	30,000	0
Total expenses	$180,000	
Surplus (deficit)	$20,000	
Equipment purchase		(300,000)
Receipt of note payable		300,000
Payment of first year's principal		(30,000)
TOTAL		$20,000

In short, by matching the term of the debt to the life of the asset, an organization's principal payments on the debt will be equal to the asset's depreciation, and, other things being equal, its cash flows will be the same as its surplus (or deficit) on an accrual basis. Although this may seem like a relatively simple concept, it is quite easy to slip into situations where the two are not matched.

leverage
A measure of the amount of debt relative to equity on an organization's balance sheet. Allows an organization to own more assets than would be possible if it relied only on its own equity. This, in turn, allows it to deliver more services or to produce more goods than otherwise would be possible, and therefore to earn more revenue.

Leverage

Many organizations use debt to finance some of their fixed assets. In so doing, they are creating *leverage*, which is defined as follows:

$$\text{Leverage} = \text{Assets} \div \text{Equity}$$

To understand this relationship, you should note that, according to the dual-aspect concept (Assets = Liabilities + Equity), if an organization had

Table 10.2 Examples of Leverage

Situation 1:		
No debt	Assets = Liabilities + Equity	
	1,000 0 1,000	
Leverage = 1,000 ÷ 1,000 = 1.0		
Situation 2:		
Debt of $500	Assets = Liabilities + Equity	
	1,500 500 1,000	
Leverage = 1,500 ÷ 1,000 = 1.5		
Situation 3:		
Debt of $1,000	Assets = Liabilities + Equity	
	2,000 1,000 1,000	
Leverage = 2,000 ÷ 1,000 = 2.0		

no debt whatsoever, its assets and equity would be equal and its leverage ratio would be 1.0. As the organization begins to rely on debt to finance its assets, the ratio increases. Table 10.2 illustrates this phenomenon with a simple example, beginning with a balance sheet in which assets equal equity, and moving to a situation in which assets are double equity. As can be seen, the leverage ratio increases to a level of 2.0 under these circumstances.

Advantages and Disadvantages of Leverage

As table 10.2 shows, leverage allows an organization to own more assets than would be possible if it relied only on its own equity. The organization is, in effect, using debt as a "lever" to expand its asset base. This in turn allows it to deliver more services or produce more goods than otherwise would be possible, and therefore to earn more revenue.

Leverage does not come without some drawbacks. Borrowed funds must be repaid, and generally there is an interest expense. Organizations that rely heavily on borrowed funds spend considerable time and effort predicting and managing the financing cycle shown in figure 10.2 so as to ensure sufficient cash on hand to meet their debt service obligations.

Financial Risk versus Business Risk

The appropriate degree of leverage can be assessed, in part, in terms of the *financial risk* it creates as compared with the organization's overall *business risk*. Financial risk and leverage are synonymous. Other things being equal, the higher an organization's leverage, the higher its debt service obligation, and the greater the risk that it will be unable to meet this obligation (that is, the greater its financial risk).

financial risk
Synonymous with leverage. Other things being equal, the higher an organization's leverage, the higher its debt service obligation, and the greater the risk that it will be unable to meet this obligation, that is, the greater its financial risk.

business risk

Refers to the predictability or certainty of an organization's cash flows. Organizations that have a high degree of uncertainty about their cash flows have a relatively high business risk. Organizations that have a high degree of certainty about their cash flows have a relatively low business risk.

Business risk, by contrast, refers to the predictability or certainty of an organization's cash flows. Organizations that have a high degree of uncertainty about their cash flows have relatively high business risk. A good example of an organization with high business risk is a farm, where product availability and cost are greatly influenced by unpredictable climatic conditions. A good example of an organization with low business risk is a popular fast food restaurant located in a busy urban area. The farm would face a great deal of uncertainty from one year and even one month to the next about its annual cash flows, whereas the fast food restaurant would be almost completely certain of its cash flows.

The relationship between financial and business risk is illustrated in figure 10.3. As the figure indicates, an organization with low business risk can have fairly high financial risk. Assuming it has structured its debt properly (namely, that it manages the financing cycle so that its cash flows can support its debt service obligations), the relative certainty of its annual cash flows gives it reasonable assurance that it will be able to meet these obligations as they come due each year.

By contrast, an organization with high business risk generally would find it unwise to have high financial risk. Because debt service obligations remain constant each year, the organization could quite easily find itself in a situation whereby its cash flows were not sufficient to meet these obligations because of events largely outside its control.

The Role of Profit (or Surplus)

Economists frequently cite profit as a fundamental characteristic of capitalism. According to them, it motivates, measures success, and rewards. Indeed, economists see an adequate profit as a legitimate cost of operating an organization. Indeed, excess profits (those greater than a "normal" return) provide an impetus for new organizations to enter a market. In the economists' purely competitive model, excess profits entice new

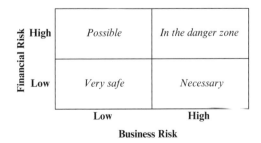

Figure 10.3 Business Risk versus Financial Risk

organizations to enter a market and increase the supply of goods and services. This process continues until prices fall to a level at which all organizations can earn a normal profit. At that point, the market is in equilibrium.

The managerial view of profit is somewhat different. For managers, profit not only provides a return for the owners of an organization but also finances fixed asset acquisitions and growth. In fact, a basic financial management maxim is that an organization should finance its fixed assets with some combination of long-term debt and equity. Contributed capital (from shareholders in a for-profit organization or from donors in a nonprofit one) and retained earnings are the only two sources of equity. Thus, for an organization with high business risk, equity is the preferred form of financing the growth of fixed assets.

Profit and Fixed Assets

This financing role of profit is important. Large health care organizations, such as hospitals, frequently add to plant capacity, purchase new and more sophisticated equipment, and upgrade their facilities. These large fixed assets require large amounts of financing from debt or equity. Even such small health care organizations as community health centers or nursing homes—which must add office equipment, computers, and other small fixed assets as they develop and grow—have fixed asset financing needs. Moreover, any organization wishing to remain in a steady state must provide for asset replacement, and, because of inflation, the replacement assets ordinarily cost more than the original ones.

Organizations could avoid the need for profits (beyond those necessary for dividend payments and stock options in for-profit firms) by relying exclusively on long-term debt. In general, however, this is not an adequate approach, especially for organizations with high business risk. For these organizations, equity is the only prudent source of additional funds. If a nonprofit organization is unable to obtain contributions to finance new or replacement assets (and few donors wish to have their contributions used to replace a worn-out asset), its only other source of equity is retained earnings (which come from surpluses).

Profit and Growth

An organization experiencing growth in revenues requires increasing amounts of cash to finance the growth in its current accounts (mainly accounts receivable and inventory). For example, because of the time lag inherent in collecting accounts receivable, an organization that is both

Table 10.3 Cash Needs Associated with Growth

	Month					
	1	2	3	4	5	6
Income Statement (All Items in Thousands of Dollars)						
Revenue	100	102	104	106	108	110
Expenses	100	102	104	106	108	110
Surplus	0	0	0	0	0	0
Cash Flow (All Items in Thousands of Dollars)						
Cash collections[a]	96	98	100	102	104	106
Cash payments[b]	100	102	104	106	108	110
Change in cash	(4)	(4)	(4)	(4)	(4)	(4)
Cumulative change	(4)	(8)	(12)	(16)	(20)	(24)

[a]Collections are from revenue earned two months earlier that went into accounts receivable.
[b]Cash payments are the same as expenses, due to assumption 3.

growing and extending credit to its customers has an increasing amount of cash tied up in accounts receivable. Moreover, as illustrated in figure 10.1, organizations that require a sizable inventory must have enough cash available to support operations during the time between acquiring inventory, using it or selling it, and collecting the associated accounts receivable.

Figure 10.1 illustrated a start-up situation. In a growing organization, the problem is exacerbated because the replacement inventory ordinarily is larger than the one used up and thus requires more cash than that coming from accounts receivable collections. Similarly, with growth, new accounts receivable are greater than collected ones. Thus, if an organization uses debt to finance its growth-related operating needs, its indebtedness will expand indefinitely.

Table 10.3 illustrates this scenario with a situation in which there is no profit. It shows the effect of revenue growth on cash that arises only out of the time lag in collecting accounts receivable. Additional cash requirements may result from the growth of inventory and other current assets (such as prepaid expenses) or from vendor pressures to expedite the payment of accounts payable. Consider the following assumptions when reviewing the table:

1. Growth in revenue and expenses of approximately 2 percent a month

2. Accounts receivable collection lag of two months

3. All expenses paid immediately

4. No growth in inventory or other current items

As the figure indicates, under the circumstances shown there is a constant need for cash. Consequently, if managers use debt to finance their cash needs, they will not be able to repay the debt unless the growth rate slows or they take other measures (such as accelerating the collection of accounts receivable or delaying the payment of accounts payable) to lessen their need for cash. Therefore, in such cases, managers generally consider debt to be an undesirable alternative.

Options other than debt exist for an organization facing this sort of scenario. The five that have the greatest impact are (1) slowing growth, (2) shortening the accounts receivable collection period, (3) shortening the inventory holding period, (4) extending the period for paying accounts payable, and (5) generating equity via either a surplus or additional equity contributions (such as stock sales in a for-profit entity and contributions in a nonprofit). Managers in this type of situation who rely on debt instead of one or more of these options ordinarily will encounter difficulties because they will not be able to repay the debt until they invoke one of the options. As the "cumulative change" row in table 10.3 indicates, unless one of the options is invoked, the negative cash (that is, the debt requirement) will expand indefinitely.

In general, organizations do not like to slow their growth, and if an organization is in line with industry standards, it may not be able to shorten its accounts receivable collection period or inventory holding time, or to lengthen its accounts payable payment period. Thus, for most organizations, the only feasible solution to the growth dilemma is to earn a profit (or surplus).

In the simplified example in table 10.3, surplus figures equivalent to the amounts in the "change in cash" row would avoid the cash shortages. This is shown in table 10.4, which has the same assumptions as table 10.3. Note that with a surplus of $4,000 per month, there is no change in cash. The surplus could be attained either by increasing revenue or by decreasing expenses. Here we did it by decreasing expenses.

Making the Forecasts

With an understanding of the concepts of debt structure, leverage, and the role of profit, forecasting cash needs is conceptually simple. An analyst must estimate how each account on the financial statements will look under different sets of assumptions. In practice, however, the forecasting task can become tricky. In particular, there are two situations that complicate the effort: business growth and product line changes.

Table 10.4 Using Income to Finance Growth-Related Cash Needs

	Month					
	1	2	3	4	5	6
Income Statement (All Items in Thousands of Dollars)						
Revenue	100	102	104	106	108	110
Expenses	96	98	100	102	104	106
Surplus	4	4	4	4	4	4
Cash Flow (All Items in Thousands of Dollars)						
Cash collections	96	98	100	102	104	106
Cash payments	96	98	100	102	104	106
Change in cash	0	0	0	0	0	0
Cumulative change	0	0	0	0	0	0

Growth

Almost all organizations (including those in health care) desire growth. Yet, as discussed earlier, growth must be carefully managed, especially with regard to the required cash needs. Indeed, growing organizations must develop accurate forecasts of the implications of their growth plans for both their operating and financing cycles. The sort of analysis shown in table 10.4 usually can suffice for analyzing the operating cycle, although it frequently must be expanded to include inventory and payables in addition to receivables. To extend the analysis to the financing cycle requires incorporating fixed asset acquisitions and debt service payments into the computations. Clearly, these computations can become complicated depending on senior management's assessment of such factors as leverage and business risk.

Product Line Changes

The need for financial forecasts frequently arises in the context of a decision to expand or eliminate a product line. Expanding a product line requires an assessment of the incremental fixed assets that will be required and the incremental returns that are expected as a result, as was discussed in chapter 8. All of these assumptions must be included in the operating budget. Once preliminary programming decisions have been made and the first pass at the operating budget is complete, senior management must estimate the resulting impact on cash and assure itself that the needed cash will be on hand to support both operating and financing activities.

The Statement of Cash Flows

Senior management's decisions concerning all of these activities, including how it has managed cash in general, are reported formally on the *statement of cash flows*, or the SCF. The SCF, which is one of the three basic financial statements (the income statement and the balance sheet being the other two), explains, in an organized way, the changes that took place between two balance sheets, focusing on how all the changes ultimately affected the cash account. The SCF therefore can be a powerful tool for understanding the kinds of cash-related decisions an organization's managers have made during an accounting period.

An example of an SCF is contained in table 10.5. It is shown in two acceptable formats: direct and indirect. In practice, an SCF can be quite complex, but no matter how complex, it always shows totals for three types of activities that give rise to the receipt or use of cash: operating, investing, and financing.

statement of cash flows
One of the three basic financial statements (the other two are the income statement and the balance sheet). It explains, in an organized way, the changes in cash that took place between two balance sheets. It classifies the changes into operating, financing, and investing activities.

Operating Activities

As already discussed, an organization uses cash during normal operations to purchase inventory, pay wages, and pay other operating expenses (for example, rent, cleaning, and utilities). As shown in figure 10.1, although an organization can delay some payments to vendors by charging purchases (that is, using accounts payable), eventually it must make these payments in cash. At the same time, although the organization is earning revenue, most of it usually is entered into accounts receivable and is collected in cash sometime later.

Because of the timing differences among these and other activities, it is possible that an organization will show a surplus (or profit) on its income statement but be paying out more in cash for its inventory and operating expenses than it is collecting from its accounts receivable. When this happens, the cash on hand will decrease. Note that net income or surplus on the SFC (shown in the indirect method in table 10.5) was $9,800,000, and yet cash decreased by $8,900,000.

Similarly, if an organization is selling off finished goods inventory items that were manufactured some time ago, it could be realizing cash inflows with minimal or no cash outflows. If the goods are being sold at a deep discount, perhaps to reduce obsolete inventory, the organization might show a loss on its income statement and yet an increase in its cash balance.

Table 10.5 Two SCF Formats, for the Year Ending December 31 (in Thousands of Dollars)

Direct Method		
Cash flows from operating activities:		
Cash received from customers		$155,000
Cash paid to suppliers and employees	$133,000	
Interest paid	7,400	
Income taxes paid	6,500	146,900
Net cash flow from operating activities		$8,100
Cash flows from investing activities:		
Acquisition of plant and equipment		(15,000)
Cash flows from financing activities:		
Payments on mortgage		(2,000)
Net increase (decrease) in cash		$(8,900)
Cash at beginning of year		10,100
Cash at end of year		$1,200
Indirect Method		
Surplus (deficit)		$9,800
Adjustments to reconcile to cash provided by operating activities:		
Depreciation	$9,000	
Increase in accounts receivable (net)	(7,000)	
Increase in inventory	(2,000)	
Increase in accounts payable	300	
Decrease in salaries and wages payable	(2,000)	(1,700)
Net cash flow from operating activities		$8,100
Cash flows from investing activities:		
Acquisition of plant and equipment		(15,000)
Cash flows from financing activities:		
Payments on mortgage		(2,000)
Net increase (decrease) in cash		$(8,900)
Cash at beginning of year		10,100
Cash at end of year		$1,200

Investing Activities

Organizations frequently are investing in fixed assets. These purchases result in an immediate cash outflow with the expectation that the assets will be used in the future to generate revenues, and ultimately a surplus. Ordinarily, however, several years of surpluses (and the associated cash inflows) are needed to recover the cash outflows that occurred when the assets were purchased.

It is possible, of course, to be *disinvesting*—that is, to be selling fixed assets. A fixed asset sale usually takes place when an organization upgrades its equipment, but it also could take place if a particular line of business were discontinued, resulting in a need to dispose of the fixed assets associated with it. In general, however, investing activities use up an organization's cash rather than generate it.

PROBLEM

Return to the Homecare situation discussed in the subsection on debt structure. Use the data from the answer to the final problem in that subsection in conjunction with the two SCF formats shown in table 10.5 and see if you can prepare an SCF for Homecare. Use the format shown here and assume that the revenues and expenses are the same for years 1 and 2, but that the equipment was purchased and the loan was obtained in year 1.

Direct Method	Year 1	Year 2
Cash flows from operating activities:		
Cash received from customers		
Cash paid to suppliers and employees		
Other (interest)		
Net cash flow from operating activities		
Cash flows from investing activities:		
Cash flows from financing activities		
Net increase (decrease) in cash		

Indirect Method	Year 1	Year 2
Net income		
Adjustments to reconcile to cash provided by operating activities:		
Net cash flow from operating activities		
Cash flows from investing activities:		
Cash flows from financing activities:		
Net increase (decrease) in cash		

ANSWER

The two statements would look as follows:

Direct Method	Year 1	Year 2
Cash flows from operating activities:		
Cash received from customers	$200,000	$200,000
Cash paid to suppliers and employees	(130,000)	(130,000)

Direct Method	Year 1	Year 2
Other (interest)	(20,000)	(20,000)
Net cash flow from operating activities	$50,000	$50,000
Cash flows from investing activities:		
Equipment purchase	(300,000)	0
Cash flows from financing activities:		
Receipt of note payable	300,000	0
Principal payment on note	(30,000)	(30,000)
Net increase (decrease) in cash	$20,000	$20,000

Indirect Method	Year 1	Year 2
Net income	$20,000	$20,000
Adjustments to reconcile to cash provided by operating activities:		
Add back depreciation*	30,000	30,000
Net cash flow from operating activities	$50,000	$50,000
Cash flows from investing activities:		
Equipment purchase	(300,000)	0
Cash flows from financing activities:		
Receipt of note payable	300,000	0
Principal payment on note	(30,000)	(30,000)
Net increase (decrease) in cash	$20,000	$20,000

*Depreciation is added back because it is a noncash expense that was included in the computation of net income. Because of this, net income, other things being equal, understates the increase in cash from operations. Adding back depreciation corrects for this understatement. Of course, in most organizations, a variety of other items also affect operating cash, such as a change in accounts receivable or inventories.

Financing Activities

Frequently, as discussed earlier, organizations compensate for the large cash outflows associated with the purchase of fixed assets by borrowing all or a portion of the necessary funds. On occasion, a for-profit organization may issue some new stock. When any of these sorts of events takes place, the financing activity will result in some cash inflows during the year, with an expectation that profits (and cash inflows) in subsequent years will generate the cash needed to repay the loan or pay dividends to shareholders. Payments of the principal on the loan, as well as payments of dividends to for-profit shareholders, are financing outflows.

As you might expect, by carrying out investing and financing activities concurrently, an organization may be able to borrow the funds needed to purchase some assets and then use the profits it earns from the use of those assets to pay the principal on a loan. Indeed, many organizations, including health care organizations, operate in exactly this way.

You are now ready to work through the practice case for this chapter, Gotham Meals on Wheels. Try to put your analysis on a spreadsheet so that you can test the impact of various assumptions about growth rates, collection periods, and so forth.

KEY TERMS

Business risk	Leverage
Debt structure	Operating cycle
Dual-aspect concept	Revenue cycle
Financial risk	Statement of cash flows
Financing cycle	

To Bear in Mind

1. One of the most important decisions that senior management must make is how much leverage they wish their organization to have. This financial risk needs to be balanced against the organization's business risk. Once the amount of leverage has been determined, a manager also must be concerned with debt structure—that is, with matching the term of the debt with the life of the asset it is financing.

2. Even small nonprofit organizations need a surplus. The surplus provides an ongoing source of equity, which allows the organization to replace its fixed assets as they wear out and to expand its fixed asset base. Profits also provide a source of financing for growth in current assets, such as accounts receivable and inventory—growth that typically is associated with an expansion of the business.

Test Yourself

1. What is the difference between the operating cycle and the financing cycle? How are these cycles similar? What role does the revenue cycle play in each?

2. Explain the meaning of the expression "match the term of the debt to the life of the asset it is financing."

3. Define leverage. What is its value to an organization? Under what circumstances might an organization not want to increase its leverage?

4. What is the role of a surplus in a nonprofit organization (or profit in a for-profit one)?

5. What is the statement of cash flows? What can one learn from it?

Suggested Cases

Boise Park Health Care Foundation (B)

Brookstone Ob-Gyn Associates

Menotomy Home Health Services

Sonsonala (B)

PRACTICE CASE

GOTHAM MEALS ON WHEELS

We're a success! And if our projections for the next six months are accurate, we'll have earned enough to rent facilities in Newburytown and double our service area. My only concern is whether we'll have enough cash on hand.

The speaker was Ethan McCall, executive director of Gotham Meals on Wheels, on seeing that his March surplus had reached $2,000. With that, Mr. McCall set about predicting how his cash would change in accordance with his projected growth in volume of activity. Although March had been a good month, cash had been falling since December, and he was concerned about making sure he had enough on hand to purchase supplies and meet payroll for the remainder of the year.

Background

Gotham Meals on Wheels was a nonprofit agency that specialized in preparing and delivering nutritious, appetizing meals to homebound people. Its clientele included many elderly people and individuals with AIDS who, because of the debilitating nature of their disease, were unable to leave their home and did not have enough strength to prepare their own meals. Convinced that there was a market for a specialized meal service and supported by a $25,000 grant from a local foundation, the agency had begun operations in early October.

To ensure that it would not run short during any given month, the agency prepared its meals one month in advance and froze them. By basing production on the following month's anticipated sales, the agency had found that it could assure its clients of uninterrupted service. All the costs associated with these meals were paid in the month in which production took place.

Another advantage of freezing the meals was that they could be delivered in bulk to each client. The meals were easily stored in the freezer compartments of clients' refrigerators. From the agency's perspective, freezing the meals and delivering several of them at a time had allowed it to keep its transportation costs at a minimum. Clients seemed to have no complaints about the food's being frozen, and many had in fact written Mr. McCall to tell him how much they enjoyed the meals.

Sales Results

There had been no sales in October. November sales had been 325 meals, and December sales had been 450 meals. Mr. McCall had expected that 500 meals would be sold in January and that sales would increase by 250 meals per month after that through the end of the year. Thus, by May, sales would be 1,500 meals, and by September they would reach 2,500 meals.

Because of the relatively low volume of sales, the first two months had been somewhat difficult, and the agency had run small deficits in both October and November. But in December it had earned a surplus that was enough to erase the October and November deficits. The balance sheet as of December 31 is shown in exhibit 10.1.

Mr. McCall's exuberance was due to sales for January through March's having been on target, and 1,250 meals' having been produced and frozen for delivery in April.

Financial Data

The ingredients and labor needed to produce each meal cost the agency $7. In addition, the agency incurred some monthly administrative costs, such as rent, that were not directly associated with the meals. These costs had grown from only $300 in October, when Mr. McCall had used his own home to produce and freeze the November meals, to $1,400 in November and December, and to $1,600 in January. In February and March they had reached $2,000 and were expected to remain at that level for the rest of the year. Mr. McCall commented:

> These monthly costs are what my accountants call "fixed costs." They are incurred whether or not we sell any meals at all. I think we've finally reached the point where we can grow without having them increase. By contrast, the $7 is a variable cost for each meal. We incur it only when we produce the meals. We sell all our meals at a price of $11 each.

Because many of the agency's clients were on a limited income, Mr. McCall did not insist on immediate payment. Instead, he billed the clients monthly. Because of some office inefficiencies, the bills usually were not sent out until a month after the meals had been delivered, and most clients took a full month to pay their bills. So, for example, bills for January meals were sent in February, and payment was not received until March. All clients were extremely conscientious about paying on time, however, and none exceeded the thirty-day time limit for payment.

EXHIBIT 10.1   **Balance Sheet as of December 31**

Assets		Liabilities and Equity	
Cash	$12,975	Contributed capital	$25,000
Accounts receivable	8,525	Retained earnings	0
Inventory	3,500		
Total assets	$25,000	Total liabilities and equity	$25,000

Assignment

1. Prepare actual balance sheets, operating statements, and statements of cash flows for October through March, and pro forma statements for April through September. Be sure you reconcile equity, accounts receivable, and inventory for each month, beginning in November. Also, for each account, use the basic formula:

   Beginning balance + Additions − Reductions = Ending balance

   Set up a spreadsheet containing the balance sheets, the operating statements, and the statements of cash flows in such a way that they are all interconnected. That is, try to make the spreadsheet as formula driven as possible, using only the number of meals, the variable cost per meal, the per-meal price, and fixed costs as the drivers.

2. What problems, if any, does the organization have? Please be as specific as you can, clearly identifying the *causes* of any problems you identify. What options are available to address these problems?

3. What advice would you give Mr. McCall?

Notes

1. For an introduction to financial accounting and financial accounting statements in a nonprofit context, see David W. Young, *Note on Financial Accounting in Nonprofit Organizations* (Boston: Harvard Business School Publications, Product TCG301, 2012). For a more detailed introduction to financial statements, see David W. Young, *Primer on Financial Accounting* (Cambridge, MA: Crimson Press Curriculum Center, 2008).

2. A particularly important aspect of managing the operating cycle (as well as the financing cycle) is accurately estimating the accounts receivable that actually will be collected. Many third-party payers use what are called "contractual allowances" to effectively reduce the amount they pay to below what was billed.

In other instances, if a patient is billed, he or she may not be able to pay the bill at all, and a "bad debt" expense is incurred. In forecasting cash inflows and outflows as part of the operating cycle, an organization needs to be certain to use *net* accounts receivable: the amount it estimates it actually will collect.

3. For some thoughts on ways to finance capital projects, see the following articles: Caryl E. Carpenter and Patrick M. Bernet, "How the Choice of Issuing Authority Affects Hospital Debt Financing Costs," *Healthcare Financial Management* 67 (May 2013): 80–84; and Daniel K. Zismer, James Fox, and Paul Torgerson, "Financing Strategic Healthcare Facilities: The Growing Attraction of Alternative Capital," *Healthcare Financial Management* 67 (May 2013): 92–99.

4. The Healthcare Financial Management Association defines the term *revenue cycle* as "all administrative and clinical functions that contribute to the capture, management, and collection of patient service revenue." For details, go to www.hfma.org/GSASearch.aspx?id=4482&searchterms=revenue%20cycle.

CHAPTER 11

MEASURING AND REPORTING

As we saw in chapter 6, responsibility accounting systems have both structure and process. Of particular importance in regard to process is the rhythmic flow of activities in four separate but integrated phases: programming, budgeting, measuring, and reporting. Chapters 8 and 9 discussed programming and operational budgeting. This chapter discusses measuring and reporting.

Organization of the Chapter

The chapter begins with an overview of the measuring and reporting phases of the management control process. It then moves to a discussion of some measuring techniques, particularly flexible budgeting and variance analysis, and a discussion of the criteria for a good reporting phase.

We then turn to the topic of measuring and reporting nonfinancial performance, an issue that is taking on increasing importance in many organizations. In health care, in particular, the measurement and reporting of quality has been a concern for many years, but more recently patient satisfaction, employee growth and development, and internal process improvements have emerged as important nonfinancial matters.

The Measuring Phase

Among other things, managers are paid to make decisions. Ordinarily an informed decision is better than an uninformed one. The difference, of course, is information. For this reason, the measuring and reporting phases of the management control process are critical aspects of the design effort; these are the phases in which managers' needs and accountants' skills merge. Managers must be

LEARNING OBJECTIVES

On completing this chapter, you should know about

- The meaning of the term *flexible budget* and the role of a flexible budget in a responsibility accounting system

- The technique of variance analysis and the different types of variances that can occur

- The uses and limitations of variance analysis and the relationship between variance analysis and the reporting phase

- The criteria for a reporting phase that can communicate action-oriented information to managers

- Some of the issues involved in measuring nonfinancial information and programmatic performance

able to communicate their information needs to the accounting staff; otherwise, the accounting staff will not be able to design a measurement system that captures the appropriate information. Similarly, the accounting staff must attempt to meet managers' information needs even if the resulting reports are not ones they would have designed on their own.

Aligning Responsibility with Control

An important assumption that underlies the measuring and reporting phases of the management control process is that all costs in an organization are controllable by someone. As chapters 6 and 7 discussed, ideally the system is designed so that each manager is held responsible only for those costs (and sometimes revenues) over which he or she exercises a reasonable degree of control. However, if managers are to control costs (and revenues), they must receive information pertaining to their respective responsibility centers in reports that are both useful and timely. This may mean augmenting the cost collection process, or it may mean simply that data already being collected for full-cost accounting or other purposes should be restructured for responsibility accounting purposes. In all instances, the way information is presented on the reports sent to a responsibility center manager is an important aspect of the responsibility accounting system.

Measuring Techniques

flexible budgeting
A technique that re-calculates a budget based on the actual volume and mix of output. It is used as a first step in computing variances, and isolates the impact of volume and mix on a responsibility center, allowing the manager to isolate labor, and material variances. It is especially important for a standard expense center where the manager has limited or no ability to control volume and mix.

In the context of measuring revenues and costs, two techniques stand out as particularly important: *flexible budgeting* and *variance analysis*. Both have been used extensively in the for-profit world and, used judiciously, can be quite helpful to managers in health care organizations as well.

Flexible Budgeting

The technique of flexible budgeting assists managers in isolating the effects of volume (and sometimes mix) differences between budgeted targets and actual results. In standard expense centers, for example, managers are expected to control the department's fixed costs and the variable cost per unit of output, but not the number or kinds of output units. As a result, they exercise little control over *total* variable costs. A flexible budget adjusts for volume (and sometimes mix) differences prior to measuring a manager's performance.

A flexible budget contrasts with a fixed budget, which does not adjust for volume or mix changes. A fixed budget typically is used in a discretionary expense center, where the manager is held responsible for spending no more than the originally agreed-on amount each month (or other reporting period).

A flexible budget classifies a responsibility center's expenses into their fixed and variable elements. The resulting budget is expressed as a cost formula that uses agreed-on fixed and step-function costs and agreed-on variable cost per unit. An expected level of volume is specified in the budget to make sure the fixed and step-function costs are within relevant ranges. The budget is then flexed each month (or other reporting period) by applying the actual volume of activity to the cost formula. The result is a budget that measures the responsibility center manager's performance with regard to the items that he or she can control. It is sometimes called a *performance budget*.

PROBLEM

The manager of Tanglewood Dentistry, a large dental group practice, estimated that 2,000 patients would need exams and cleanings each month. She estimated that each would take approximately half an hour of a dental hygienist's time, at an hourly rate of $20. Other costs associated with an exam and cleaning were supplies, electricity, and water, which totaled about $2 per cleaning. The monthly fixed and step-function costs associated with the exam and cleaning activity were $8,000. The result was the following budget:

Hygienist cost (1/2 hour at $20 per hour)	$10
Other variable costs	2
Variable costs per procedure	$12
Estimated number of procedures	2,000
Variable cost budget	$24,000
Fixed costs	8,000
Total budget	$32,000

During the reporting period, 2,500 patients had an exam and cleaning, and the total costs of the department were $40,000.

Prepare a flexible budget for Tanglewood and analyze the organization's performance.

ANSWER

A flexible budget for the department would look as follows:

Actual number of procedures	2,500
Variable costs per procedure	$12

Variable cost budget	$30,000
Fixed cost budget	8,000
Total budget	$38,000
Less: Actual costs	40,000
Spending variance	$(2,000)

Although it would initially appear that there was a budget overrun of $8,000 ($32,000 − $40,000), in fact only $2,000 was a "spending" overrun. The remaining $6,000 can be attributed to the volume change, which the manager could not control.

The flexible budget does not answer all the important questions. In the Tanglewood problem, we might still have some questions about the negative $2,000 spending variance. Among the possible explanations for this variance are that, compared to what was budgeted, Tanglewood experienced one (or more) of the following: (1) a higher hygienist wage rate, (2) higher per-unit supply costs, (3) more hygienist time per procedure, (4) more supply usage per procedure, (5) use of different kinds of supplies, or (6) higher fixed costs.

Once we know which of these factors was the cause, we can explore the issue further. If, for example, more hygienist time than budgeted was used per exam and cleaning, we need to know why. Had some new hygienists been hired who required training and thus were slower than anticipated? Or did patients require more complex exams and cleanings, resulting in the need for more time to complete the procedures? Or perhaps patients arrived late and scheduling was disrupted, slowing the hygienists down. And so on. Although accounting techniques cannot answer all questions of this sort, the technique of variance analysis can enhance our ability to examine the possibilities.

Variance Analysis

variance analysis
A technique that computes the difference between budgeted and actual financial results in terms of different causes, such as case mix, volume, resources per case, and cost per resource unit.

Variance analysis is an accounting technique that permits a close examination of the difference between budgeted and actual information, thereby allowing us to break the difference into categories that are useful for managerial action.

In most organizations, the variance between budgeted and actual performance can be explained by one or more of five factors:

• Volume (number of units of activity)

• Mix of units of activity

• Revenue per unit of activity (selling price)

+ Rates paid for inputs (such as labor wages and cost per unit of raw materials)

+ Usage and efficiency of inputs (usage of raw materials and efficiency of labor, for example)

Variance analysis allows us to determine how the total change between budgeted and actual amounts is divided among these factors.

Ordinarily the variance for each factor is considered separately. The three reasons for taking this approach are that (1) each variance typically has a different cause, (2) different variances usually involve different responsibility center managers, and (3) different variances require different types of corrective action. Thus, if responsibility for different factors has been assigned to different responsibility center managers, variance analysis allows senior management to help each manager determine the kinds of corrective action that might be taken.

A Graphic Illustration

Variance analysis can be illustrated most easily with a graph. Consider labor costs, for example. Total labor costs for a given employee or category of employees can be calculated by multiplying the number of hours worked by the wage rate per hour. For instance, assume that an organization's labor budget is $1,600, resulting from an estimate of 100 hours of work at $16 per hour. Graphically, this can be represented by a rectangle with the vertical axis indicating the wage rate and the horizontal axis indicating the number of hours, as follows:

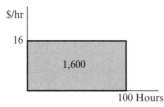

Assume now that the actual labor costs for the period in question were $2,400. A typical budget report might compute the variance as follows:

Item	Budget	Actual	Variance
Labor costs	$1,600	$2,400	$(800)

Although the report shows an $800 negative variance—that is, actual expenses were greater than budgeted ones—it does not indicate why the variance occurred. More specifically, in this instance it does not tell us whether the cause was a higher wage rate than anticipated, more hours than anticipated, or some combination of the two.

If the variance were solely the result of a higher wage rate, it could be represented graphically as follows:

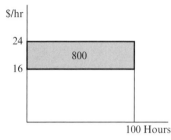

If it were a result solely of more hours than budgeted, it could be represented as follows:

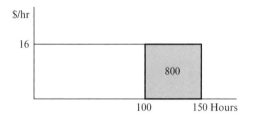

Finally, if the variance were a result of both a higher wage rate and more hours, it would be represented as follows (the exact proportions would depend on the actual amounts of each factor):

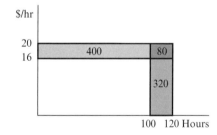

Note that in this last instance, the small rectangle shown in the upper-right corner of the graph represents the combination of both the rate (or wage) variance and the use (or hour) variance. This combination variance sometimes is referred to as the gray area, in that it cannot be assigned to either the higher rate or the higher use, but rather to the combined effect of the two. In this instance, then, $400 of the total variance is attributed to the higher wage rate, $320 to the greater number of hours, and $80 to their combined effect.

For ease of calculation, the combination effect ordinarily is included in the rate variance (here the labor wage variance). Not only does this approach simplify the calculation and presentation of information, but also it seems reasonable because whoever is responsible for the rate variance is responsible for it over as many units (hours in this case) as actually were used. This means that the $80 combination effect would be added to the $400 to give a $480 labor rate variance.

Given this approach, the budget report might look as follows:

Item	Budget	Actual	Variance
Labor costs	$1,600	$2,400	$(800)
Labor rate (wage) variance			$(480)
Use variance			$(320)

The managerial utility of this report comes directly from the fact that different managers are responsible for different elements of a total variance. In aligning responsibility with control, it is important to designate the portion of the total variance that is attributable to each individual manager. Senior management can then discuss the reasons for the variances with the managers responsible for controlling them.

In this context, it is important to emphasize that a negative variance should not be used as a club. Rather, it should be the first step in diagnosing the reasons why actual costs diverged from the budgeted ones, and in discussing the underlying causes with the appropriate managers. The goal is to determine where corrective action might be taken to bring costs back in line with the budget. Similarly, as we will see, a positive variance is not necessarily a cause for celebration. It does suggest, however, that there were some improvements in operations that might be examined for possible transfer to other operating units.

Calculating Variances

The accounting technique used to calculate a variance follows two relatively simple rules, with slight differences depending on whether the calculation is for a revenue or an expense variance.

Expense Variances

Other things being equal, when actual expenses exceed budgeted expenses, an organization's financial condition has worsened—that is, its surplus is lower than budgeted. Conversely, when actual expenses are below budgeted expenses, the organization's financial condition has improved. A worsened condition is represented by a negative number, and an improved condition by a positive number, leading to the following rules:

1. For an expense variance related to use, subtract the actual use from the budgeted use and multiply the result by the budgeted rate. If actual

use exceeds budgeted use, the result will be a negative number; if actual use is below budgeted use, the result will be positive.

2. For an expense variance related to rate, subtract the actual rate from the budgeted rate and multiply the result by actual use. If the actual rate exceeds the budgeted rate, the result will be a negative number; if the actual rate is below the budgeted rate, the result will be positive.

We can express these rules with formulas:

$$\text{Use:} (U_b - U_a) \times R_b$$

$$\text{Rate:} (R_b - R_a) \times U_a$$

In these formulas, U is *use*, R is the *rate*, and the subscripts a and b stand for *actual* and *budgeted*, respectively.

Revenue Variances

When actual revenue exceeds budgeted revenue, the organization's financial condition has improved—that is, other things being equal, its surplus is greater than expected. Conversely, when actual revenue is below budgeted revenue, the organization's financial condition has worsened. Again, a worsened condition is represented by a negative number, and an improved condition by a positive number, resulting in the following rules:

1. For a revenue variance related to volume, subtract budgeted volume from actual volume and multiply the result by budgeted selling price. If actual volume exceeds budgeted volume, the result is a positive number; if actual volume is below budgeted volume, the result is negative.

2. For a revenue variance related to selling price, subtract budgeted selling price from actual selling price and multiply the result by actual volume. If the actual selling price exceeds the budgeted selling price, the result is a positive number; if the actual selling price is below the budgeted selling price, the result is negative.

We can also express these rules with formulas:

$$\text{Volume:} (V_a - V_b) \times P_b$$

$$\text{Selling price:} (P_a - P_b) \times V_a$$

Here, V stands for *volume*, P stands for *selling price*, and the subscripts a and b stand for *actual* and *budgeted*, respectively.

Making the Computations

Let's return to the example of the $800 negative variance and perform the calculations according to these rules and formulas. Because there are no revenue variances in this instance, we need to calculate only the expense variances.

PROBLEM

Calculate the expense variances in the example of the $800 variance, using the formulas given earlier. It is important that you make your own calculations before looking at the analysis that follows. Variance analysis can be a little tricky, and making these calculations will help you understand it.

ANSWER

The expense variances can be calculated as follows:

Use Variance	(Budgeted hours	− Actual hours)	×	Budgeted wage rate	
	$(U_b$	− $U_a)$	×	R_b	
	(100	− 120)	×	$16	= $(320)
Rate (Wage) Variance	(Budgeted wage rate	− Actual wage rate)	×	Actual hours	
	$(R_b$	− $R_a)$	×	U_a	
	($16	− $20)	×	120	= $(480)

Graphically, the calculations look as follows:

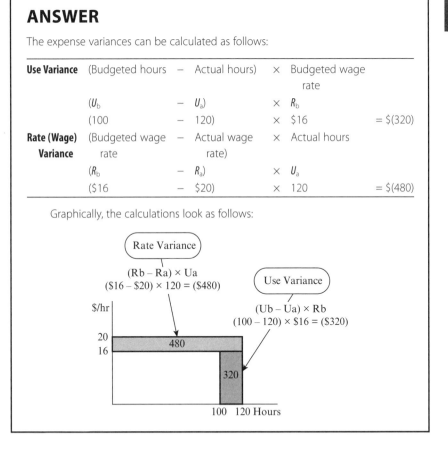

Although this problem involves only two items, the technique also can be used when several items have variances. When volume is involved, for example, a flexible budget can be prepared first, and the remaining variances can be calculated using the actual level of volume. Let's look at this more complicated situation with another example, this time using materials instead of labor.

PROBLEM

The Haskell Hospital Laundry uses such materials as detergent, bleach, and water. Its budgeted and actual material costs are as follows:

	Pounds of Laundry	Materials Used per Pound	Direct Material Cost per Unit	Total Cost
Budget	7,000	10 oz.	$0.20 per oz.	$14,000
Actual	6,000	12 oz.	$0.25 per oz.	$18,000

The laundry manager is interested in obtaining a better understanding of the reasons behind the budget overrun. As a first step, prepare a flexible budget for the department.

ANSWER

The flexible budget is prepared by changing the volume from its budgeted to its actual level while holding everything else at budgeted levels. We then can determine what the budget would have been if we had known volume in advance. This budget then can be compared to actual results, as follows:

	Pounds of Laundry	Materials Used per Pound	Direct Material Cost per Unit	Total Cost	Variances
Original budget	7,000	10 oz.	$0.20 per oz.	$14,000	
Flexible budget	6,000	10 oz.	$0.20 per oz.	12,000	$2,000
Actual	6,000	12 oz.	$0.25/oz.	18,000	(6,000)
TOTAL					$(4,000)

Note that the volume variance (Original budget − Flexible budget) is a favorable $2,000 ($14,000 − $12,000). That is, if the laundry had known its volume in advance, it would have budgeted $12,000 rather than $14,000. To calculate the flexible budget, we held all other factors at the original budgeted levels (10 ounces per pound and $0.20 per ounce), so this $2,000 positive variance is due exclusively to the lower volume. It is favorable because it reduces expenses, which, other things being equal, improves the hospital's surplus.

As discussed earlier, in most variance calculations, an unfavorable (or negative) variance—that is, one that lowers the organization's surplus—is shown in parentheses. A favorable (positive) variance is not enclosed in parentheses. Sometimes, unfavorable variances are labeled "UF" and favorable variances are labeled "F."

The spending variance (Flexible budget − Actual) is an unfavorable $6,000 ($12,000 − $18,000), caused, as we can see from the data, by using 2 additional ounces of material per pound of laundry and paying $0.05 more per ounce. The combined result of the positive volume and negative spending variances is a total unfavorable variance of $4,000.

PROBLEM

We now can calculate the reasons for the laundry's spending variance. As discussed, a portion of this variance is due to higher use (12 ounces versus 10 ounces per pound), and a portion is due to a higher rate ($0.25 per ounce versus $0.20 per ounce). Please make the calculations, using the formulas provided earlier, before looking at the solution that follows.

ANSWER

The expense variances can be calculated as follows:

Use	=	$(U_b - U_a)$	×	R_b	×	V_a		
	=	$(10 - 12)$	×	$\$(0.20)$	×	6,000	=	$\$(2,400)$
Rate	=	$(R_b - R_a)$	×	U_a	×	V_a		
	=	$(\$0.20 - \$0.25)$	×	12	×	6,000	=	$\$(3,600)$

Note that to obtain the total variance in each instance, we multiplied the unit variances by the actual volume of output—that is, the volume used in calculating the flexible budget. More generally, once we have prepared the flexible budget and determined the volume variance, we then use the actual volume for all remaining computations.

As this problem demonstrates, variance analysis can help managers to understand why actual expenses deviated from budgeted ones. In the case of Haskell Hospital, we now can see that the hospital saved $2,000 in expenses as a result of washing fewer pounds of laundry, but its expenses increased by $3,600 because of higher prices than anticipated for raw materials and by $2,400 because of a greater use of raw materials per unit of output (a pound of laundry in this example).

Mix Variances

The volume variance computed in the Haskell Hospital problem assumed that every unit of volume had the same variable expense associated with it (which is pretty reasonable for a laundry). In many situations, however, different types of goods and services have different unit variable expense amounts. When this is the case, and when the budgeted and actual proportions of the various types of goods or services differ, an output mix variance develops.

There also can be input mix variances with such items as raw materials and labor. For example, an input mix variance can happen if a responsibility center manager uses a different combination of raw materials from that budgeted, or if the actual skill mix of labor differs from the budgeted one. Techniques for calculating output and input mix variances are contained in most cost accounting textbooks.

If an organization does not calculate separate mix variances, the output mix variance automatically becomes part of the volume variance, and the input mix variance typically becomes part of the rate variance (assuming the different types of raw materials or different skill levels for labor have different rates).

EXAMPLE

In a hospital, an output mix variance would result from a change in the hospital's case mix (such as relatively more coronary artery bypass surgery cases than influenza cases). An input mix variance would come about if there were a change in the mix of services used to treat a given case type (such as different kinds of radiological procedures or laboratory tests ordered for each patient undergoing coronary artery bypass surgery). A second type of input mix variance would take place if the manager of, say, the radiology department used a mix of technicians (highly experienced versus inexperienced, for instance) that differed from the budgeted mix (assuming, of course, that the two types of technicians were paid different hourly rates).

Managerial Uses of Variances

An important feature of variance analysis is the ability it gives senior management to link managerial responsibility to changes in revenues and costs. By way of summary, table 11.1 lists the variances discussed earlier and identifies in general terms who controls each of them.

As this table suggests, operating managers ordinarily do not control the volume or mix of services provided by an organization for its patients (or customers), nor do they usually set wage rates for employees or control the rates paid for raw materials and other expense items. Variance analysis permits senior management to focus attention on each individual item and the managers who can control it.

Simply identifying the separate variances is not enough, however. Senior management needs to know why a variance arose. It also needs to know what steps are under way to correct unfavorable variances. Thus, by separating the overall variance between budgeted and actual results into its individual components, senior management is in a better position to

Table 11.1 Types of Variances and Controlling Agents

Variance Type	Controlling Agents
Volume variances	Marketing department, senior management, the environment (depending on the organization)
Output mix variances	Marketing department, senior management, the environment (depending on the organization)
Selling price variances	Senior management, the marketing department, responsibility center managers (depending on who sets or negotiates prices)
Raw material price variances	Purchasing department, responsibility center managers (who might order more or less costly raw materials than budgeted)
Wage rate variances	Senior management (which negotiates union contracts), responsibility center managers (who make job offers)
Raw material use variances	Responsibility center managers
Labor efficiency variances	Responsibility center managers
Input mix variances	Responsibility center managers

discuss potential corrective actions with the appropriate responsibility center managers.

Limitations of Variance Analysis

Variance analysis can highlight the reasons for a deviation between budgeted and actual financial performance, and it can do so in terms of volume, rate, use, and mix. However, it cannot explain *why* a particular organizational unit was more or less efficient than budgeted or *why* volume was higher or lower than anticipated. As a result, variance analysis can be a useful tool for senior managers seeking to ask the right questions and to identify the lower-level managers to whom those questions might be addressed. Like many other accounting techniques, however, it should be considered only a means to assist managers in learning more about the activities of their organization, not an end in itself.

In using variance analysis to inform managerial action, it is important to recognize that few variances can be interpreted independently from all others. A negative material use variance, for example, may have arisen because the purchasing department bought some raw materials of lower-than-anticipated quality. If the purchasing department spent less than budgeted on these purchases, it would have had a positive rate variance to show for its efforts. But this positive rate variance could have had negative "downstream" consequences in other departments.

In sum, identifying a negative expense variance (rate or use) can be extremely valuable: it can help management identify areas where operating improvements can take place, and it can also allow them to see the financial consequences of their corrective actions. Used in a club-like way, however, this same information can be quite threatening and may even lead to unproductive conflict or reduced cooperation among managers.

The Reporting Phase

Once appropriate data have been collected and the necessary variances calculated, a key task is to structure and present those data so that managers receive useful information. Moreover, if reporting is to be effective in providing responsibility center managers with the information they need to run their respective departments successfully, it must meet certain criteria.

Timeliness

The information must arrive on a timely basis. "Timely" in this context does not necessarily mean quickly, but rather appropriately with respect to the managerial action that may be necessary. In some instances, monthly reports that arrive within a few days of the end of each month may be required; in others, it may be acceptable for the monthly reports to arrive within a week or two after the end of the month. Similarly, daily, weekly, quarterly, or annual reports may be necessary, and each will have an appropriate time lag between the effective date of the information it contains and the date by which that information must be received by the managers who must act on it.

Hierarchy of Information

Information must be available at various levels of aggregation, from highly summarized to highly detailed. In general, not all managers at all levels in the organization will need to have the same level of detail in the information supplied to them. The manager of all the hospital's laboratories, for example, most likely would not want detailed efficiency information for each technician in each laboratory, but he or she might want information about the efficiency of different sections within the labs. Usually the information on the lab sections would appear at a second level in the hierarchy, so that it would not impede the manager's reading of more highly summarized information.

Because of these differing managerial needs, a good reporting system typically has several levels of detail:

- *A highly summarized level,* used only by senior management, generally organized according to divisions, programs, service lines, or departments.

- *A breakdown into sections or subdepartments within a division, program, service line, or department,* used primarily by managers of these units and available to senior management for reference.

- *A breakdown into activities (such as diagnosis-related groups [DRGs]) within sections or subdepartments,* used primarily by section or subdepartment managers and available to higher-level managers for reference.

- *A transaction-by-transaction listing of both personnel and supplies,* used for in-depth reference. This level contains the building blocks for all the previous levels (and for both financial accounting and full-cost accounting systems).

Obviously the levels of detail must be tailored to each organization and its needs. For smaller organizations, where management is intimately aware of each responsibility center's activities, a highly summarized level and a transaction level may be all that are needed. As potential problems are identified, senior management can discuss them with the individuals involved, using transaction information as necessary to answer questions. For larger organizations, all four (or even more) levels may be needed.

Figure 11.1 contains an example of the way information might be structured in an integrated delivery system (IDS), focusing on the system's inpatient division for the more detailed examples. This figure illustrates five levels of information, each of which disaggregates the information "above" it. For example, the inpatient care division is shown as a single line in the first-level report, a report designed for senior management. In the second-level report, the product lines of the division, such as women's health, oncology, and cardiology, are broken out.

The product lines are broken into regions in the third-level report, and the regions into facilities in the fourth-level report. Finally, the fifth-level report breaks each facility into its individual products.

With a report of this sort, the variance in a division's surplus or deficit can be traced down through the organizational hierarchy to locate its source or sources in product lines, regions, facilities, and individual products.

In reviewing this report, note the "drill-down" capability. The first-level report shows that division 2 (inpatient care) had a year-to-date negative profit variance of $2,590 (everything is in thousands). This amount is broken down into product lines in the second-level report, which shows that cardiology had a $620 negative year-to-date profit variance. This $620

A. First-Level Report: Division Summary (for Senior Management)

	Actual		(Over) or Under Budget	
Division	June	Year to Date	June	Year to Date
Division 1	$ 21,110	$ 120,030	$ (315)	$ 35
Division 2—inpatient care	24,525	147,280	(710)	(2,590)
Division 3	11,235	70,570	(125)	(210)
TOTAL	$ 56,870	$ 337,880	$ (1,150)	$ (2,765)
Controllable overhead	27,120	161,970	320	1,130
TOTAL SURPLUS (DEFICIT)	$ 29,750	$ 175,910	$ (830)	$ (1,635)

B. Second-Level Report: Division 2 — Inpatient Care. Product Line Summary (for Division Vice President)

	Actual		(Over) or Under Budget	
Product Line	June	Year to Date	June	Year to Date
Oncology	$ 5,340	$ 35,845	$ (625)	$ (1,380)
Cardiology	3,310	19,605	(30)	(620)
Women's health	3,115	18,085	90	(135)
Orthopedics	5,740	33,635	(65)	(640)
Pediatrics	7,020	40,110	(80)	185
TOTAL SURPLUS (DEFICIT)	$ 24,525	$ 147,280	$ (710)	$ (2,590)

C. Third-Level Report: Cardiology Regional Breakdown (for Product Line Manager)

	Actual		(Over) or Under Budget	
Region	June	Year to Date	June	Year to Date
Region 1	$ 895	$ 5,400	$ 119	$ 75
Region 2	1,030	7,000	176	(50)
Region 3	760	4,500	(160)	(350)
Region n	625	2,705	(165)	(295)
TOTAL SURPLUS (DEFICIT)	$ 3,310	$ 19,605	$ (30)	$ (620)

D. Fourth-Level Report: Cardiology Region 1, Facility Breakdown (for Regional Manager)

	Actual		(Over) or Under Budget	
Facility	June	Year to Date	June	Year to Date
Facility 1	$ 245	$ 1,300	$ (35)	$ (65)
Facility 2	300	1,775	20	120
Facility 3	150	780	35	165
Facility n	200	1,545	99	(145)
TOTAL SURPLUS (DEFICIT)	$ 895	$ 5,400	$ 119	$ 75

E. Fifth-Level Report: Cardiology Product Breakdown (for Facility Manager)

	Actual		(Over) or Under Budget	
Facility 1	June	Year to Date	June	Year to Date
Product A—stress testing	$ 90	$ 560	$ (25)	$ (50)
Product B—catheterizations	75	350	(20)	(80)
Product C—valve replacements	45	280	15	95
Product D—CABGs	35	110	(5)	(30)
TOTAL SURPLUS (DEFICIT)	$ 245	$ 1,300	$ (35)	$ (65)
Facility 2				

(And so forth)

Figure 11.1 Reporting Hierarchy for an Integrated Delivery System (in Thousands of Dollars)

negative variance is broken down into regions in the third-level report, which shows that region 1 had a $75 positive variance. The $75 positive variance is broken down by facilities in the fourth-level report, which shows that facility 1 had a $65 negative variance, which is then divided among the various product lines in the fifth-level report. As a result, senior management and line managers have the capability to examine in close detail the causes of a variance between the overall budgeted surplus and the actual surplus.

A similar report for the department of mental health in a state government is shown in figure 11.2. This is for the same agency shown in the matrix structure in figure 7.2. The basic format is the same as that in figure 11.1 but has been tailored to fit the matrix structure. Note also that because the agency has no revenue, this report contains direct expenses only, whereas the IDS report showed the surplus (or deficit).

In general, several factors are central to a decision concerning the appropriate number of summary levels and their content: (1) the managerial time associated with using the reports, (2) the kinds of actions that can be taken based on the reports, (3) the amount of responsibility given to individuals at different layers in the organization, and (4) the cost of preparing the reports. A careful weighing of these factors is essential in the design of an effective and usable set of reports.

Relevance and Accuracy

A good reporting process is characterized by the presence of relevant and accurate information. Although the term *accurate* needs no elaboration, the term *relevant* is slippery. Many reports contain a great deal of information that is of marginal or no use to managers receiving them, and yet certain crucial information is missing entirely. A good example is year-to-date information, which generally is of some use to a manager but often is not included on a set of reports. By contrast, if an organization has a highly seasonal pattern of operations, year-to-date information may be of little use unless adjusted for seasonality.

Unit cost information is another example of information that may be of little use. If a manager has no control over volume, then total unit cost information (which includes both fixed and variable costs) is of almost no value and indeed may be misleading. The relevant information would be either the controllable or the variable cost per unit, which presumably is not affected by volume and therefore includes costs that can be controlled by the manager.

Figure 11.3, an abbreviated report for Spenser Rehabilitation Hospital (SRH), illustrates relevance. This report is similar to figures 11.1 and 11.2,

A. First-Level Report: Appropriation Account Summary (for the Commissioner)

Appropriation Account	Actual		(Over) or Under Budget	
	June	Year to Date	June	Year to Date
5041 Psychiatric Hospitals	$ 210,110	$ 1,233,030	$ (3,555)	$ 3,980
5051 Community Mental Health Centers	24,525	147,280	(710)	(2,590)
5061 State Schools for the Retarded	102,235	736,570	(125)	(2,110)
TOTAL DIRECT EXPENSES	$ 336,870	$ 2,116,880	$ (4,390)	$ (720)

B. Second -Level Report: 5051 Community M.H. Centers, Subprogram Summary (for Account Executive)

Subprogram	Actual		(Over) or Under Budget	
	June	Year to Date	June	Year to Date
Crisis intervention	$ 5,340	$ 35,845	$ (625)	$ (1,380)
Psychiatric day care	3,310	19,605	(30)	(620)
Aftercare	3,115	18,085	90	(135)
Outpatient counseling	5,740	33,635	(65)	(640)
Administration	7,020	40,110	(80)	185
TOTAL DIRECT	$ 24,525	$ 147,280	$ (710)	$ (2,590)

C. Third-Level Report: Psychiatric Day Care, Regional Breakdown (for Account Executive)

Region	Actual		(Over) or Under Budget	
	June	Year to Date	June	Year to Date
Region 1	$ 895	$ 5,400	$ 119	$ 75
Region 2	1,030	7,000	176	(50)
Region 3	760	4,500	(160)	(350)
Region n	625	2,705	(165)	(295)
TOTAL	$ 3,310	$ 19,605	$ (30)	$ (620)

D. Fourth-Level Report: Psychiatric Day Care, Region 1, Facility Breakdown (for Field Operations Managers)

Facility	Actual		(Over) or Under Budget	
	June	Year to Date	June	Year to Date
Facility 1	$ 245	$ 1,300	$ (35)	$ (65)
Facility 2	300	1,775	20	120
Facility 3	150	780	35	165
Facility n	200	1,545	99	(145)
TOTAL	$ 895	$ 5,400	$ 119	$ 75

Figure 11.2 Reporting Hierarchy for a Department of Mental Health. Program Analysis (in Thousands of Dollars)

E. Fifth-Level Report: Psychiatric Day Care Region 1, Line-Item Breakdown (for Field Operations and Facility Managers)

Facility 1	Actual		(Over) or Under Budget	
	June	Year to Date	June	Year to Date
Org. Code A—nursing	$ 90	$ 560	$ (25)	$ (50)
Org. Code B—social work	75	350	(20)	(80)
Org. Code C—maintenance	45	280	15	95
Org. Code D—administration	35	110	(5)	(30)
TOTAL	$ 245	$ 1,300	$ (35)	$ (65)
Facility 2				
(And so forth)				

Figure 11.2 (continued)

FIRST-LEVEL REPORT: PRODUCT LINES
For the Board and Senior Management

Expense Surplus (Deficit)	Actual		Over or (Under) Budget		Revenue				Contribution Margin		
	This Month	Year to Date	This Month	Year to Date			Volume and Mix				Unit
					Price	Payer Mix	Revenue	Expense	Net	Utilizat ion	Cost
Inpatient-Weberg	$2,110	$12,030	$(315)	$35							
Inpatient-SRH	24,525	147,280	(710)	(2,590)	$(50)	$(320)	$150	$(90)	$60	$(250)	$(150)
Outpatient	1,235	7,570	(125)	(210)							
Research	1,180	7,045	95	75							
Education	3,590	18,960	(235)	245							
Ambulance	4,120	25,175	160	(320)							
Development	2,245	13,680	180	(160)							
Administration	3,630	22,965	(70)	(730)							
TOTAL	$42,635	$254,705	$(1,020)	$(3,655)							

SIXTH-LEVEL REPORT: DRG ANALYSIS BY PHYSICIAN AND COST CENTER
For Physician Chiefs and Physicians
Spinal Cord Injury
DRG 1

	Actual		Over or (Under) Budget		This Month's Variance Analysis						
	This Month	Year to Date	This Month	Year to Date	Lab	Radiology	Pharmacy	Physical Therapy	Routine Care	Other	Total
Physician 1	$245	$1,300	$(35)	$(65)	$10	$(50)	$20	$50	$(50)	$(15)	$(35)
Physician 2	300	1,775	20	120							
Physician 3	150	780	35	165							
Physician 4	200	1,545	99	(145)							
TOTAL	$895	$5,400	$119	$75							

Figure 11.3 Reporting Hierarchy for Spenser Rehabilitation Hospital, First and Sixth Levels (in Thousands of Dollars)

but it has a more detailed variance analysis, breaking variances down by several budget drivers. Note that at the senior management and board level, the report shows the reasons why a product line has not achieved its targeted surplus. The $710 negative variance for the month for inpatient-SRH, for example, is a result of lower prices ($50 negative), a worsened payer mix ($320 negative), an improved contribution margin ($60 positive), worsened utilization ($250 negative), and higher unit costs ($150 negative).

Similarly, lower-level managers, such as physician chiefs of service, can examine their units' performance for a given DRG. Note that physician 1 had a $35 negative variance for the month, due mainly to using more radiology ($50), routine care ($50), and other ($15) than budgeted. He or she came in below the budget in the lab ($10), pharmacy ($20), and physical therapy ($50).

Behavioral Factors

Reports such as those shown in figures 11.1, 11.2, and 11.3 permit senior and line managers to drill down very deeply into the organization's activities if they wish to do so. These reports can assist managers in understanding the underlying reasons for a variance, which can in turn help them determine the corrective actions that might be taken.

For the reports to be effective, corrective action must be a priority. It is not sufficient simply to prepare and distribute reports. Unless senior management communicates to managers at the various organizational levels its expectation that the reporting system will be used as a basis for taking action, the system will have little value.

Senior management can take any number of steps to communicate its intent, including holding regular meetings to discuss the reports, requiring follow-up memos from line managers, and even making telephone calls and participating in hallway conversations. Conversely, if senior management ignores the reports, line managers probably will too.

Measuring and Reporting Nonfinancial Information

In addition to reporting on financial performance, the management control process entails measuring and reporting on nonfinancial performance. Indeed, the objectives of all nonprofit organizations—especially those in health care—extend beyond the satisfaction of annual revenue or financial surplus targets to encompass a wide variety of nonfinancial objectives.

Nonfinancial objectives in health care organizations tend to fall into four general categories: (1) improving the quality of care; (2) avoiding unneeded care; (3) enhancing patient satisfaction; and (4) fostering improved job satisfaction and performance for physicians, other professional staff, and other employees. Indeed, when nonfinancial objectives become an important aspect of an organization's strategy, the measuring and reporting phases of the management control process must be modified to accommodate them.

Most nonprofit organizations have a continuum of output measures. The continuum ranges from relatively unmeasurable but highly meaningful indicators of performance to easily measurable but not terribly meaningful ones. The three categories involved—*social indicators, results measures,* and *process measures*—suggest the nature of the dilemma. With the first category, almost all health care organizations would agree that their principal objective is to have an impact on the health status of the communities they serve. But it is extremely difficult to measure a community's health status, and even if health status were measurable, identifying a causal link between the activities of a particular organization in the community and the community's health status would be an all but impossible task.

Just as social indicators are difficult to determine and measure, process measures are rather easy to quantify. The number of procedures performed, outpatient visits completed, newsletters produced, inpatient days provided, and the like are relatively easy to measure and report. Unfortunately, they say little about whether the organization is having an impact on its community.

Thus, most health care organizations focus on the category of results measures. The challenge to managers at all levels in an organization is to design a set of objectively measurable indicators of performance. These nonfinancial objectives then can be established during the budgeting phase of the management control process so that they can be measured and reported at regular intervals during the budget year. Some examples of such measures are shown in table 11.2.

Developing and measuring nonfinancial results as well as financial ones implies that managers need to receive reports in each category. To

social indicators
Measures related to the impact an organization has on society at large

results measures
Measures related to an organization's goals.

process measures
Easily quantifiable measures, such as outpatient visits completed, that say little about whether the organization is accomplishing its objectives.

Table 11.2 Measures of Nonfinancial Performance

Area	Positive Measures	Negative Measures
Quality of care	HEDIS (Healthcare Effectiveness Data and Information Set) scores Percentage of clinical pathways implemented	Hospital-acquired condition rates Postsurgical infection rates
Prevention	Primary care capacity utilization Percentage of children receiving immunizations	Preventable inpatient admissions Preventable emergency room use
Patient satisfaction	Percentage of positive survey results Percentage of health maintenance organization (HMO) reenrollment	Percentage of complaints
Employee satisfaction and growth	Percentage of positive survey results Percentage of promotions	Absenteeism rate Turnover rate

the extent feasible, these reports should be combined so that managers can determine the resources being consumed in attaining various nonfinancial results. And like financial reports, nonfinancial reports must provide line managers with accurate, timely, and useful information.

Criteria for Good Nonfinancial Reports

In attempting to develop a useful set of nonfinancial reports, managers may find it helpful to consider four interrelated issues. These issues are illustrated in table 11.3, a nonfinancial report for a medical school.

1. *Alignment of responsibility and control.* The report is divided into areas of responsibility. Marketing and recruitment, for example, is one such area, whereas student performance, program performance, and alumni satisfaction are three separate responsibility areas. Although it may not be possible to assign a specific person to each area, these nevertheless are areas where different individuals can take action. The head of the admissions office would be expected to take action concerning marketing and recruitment, for example, and the program director would have responsibility for student performance. The residency placement and development offices presumably would have responsibility for alumni satisfaction related to residency placement and alumni contributions.

2. *Relationship between outputs and inputs.* Outputs could be related to inputs in several areas. It would be possible, for example, to determine the cost per admitted applicant, the cost per course, or the cost per graduate. In the last two cases, tuition might be used as a surrogate for cost, and the program's performance per tuition dollar could be calculated.

3. *Role of nonfinancial objectives.* Although not all output measures relate directly to nonfinancial objectives, several do. Presumably the program is interested in attracting well-qualified students. To the extent that its yield (entering students as a percentage of admitted students) is high (assuming it is admitting only well-qualified students), it is doing its job. Similarly, it is likely that the program is interested in retaining only well-qualified students, and two items help to measure this: (1) how many well-qualified students (B+ average or better) leave (a negative measure), and (2) how many less-than-well-qualified students (C− average or below) leave. Finally, it is likely that the program is interested in placing its students appropriately and having them satisfied with their education. The area of alumni satisfaction addresses this issue.

Table 11.3 Program Performance Report Framework: Commonwealth Medical School

Indicator	Year 1	Year 2	Year 3	Year 4	Year 5
Marketing and Recruitment					
1. Number of inquiries to school					
2. Number of applications sent out					
3. Number of applications received					
4. Application rate ($= 3 \div 2$)					
5. Number of accepted applicants					
6. Admission rate ($= 5 \div 3$)					
7. Number of matriculants					
8. Yield ($= 7 \div 5$)					
9. Average GPA for matriculants					
10. Average MCAT for matriculants					
Student Performance					
11. Grade distribution					
A/A−					
B+/B/B−					
C+/C/C−					
Below C−					
12. Overall GPA					
13. Number of students with B+ average or better leaving program during year 1					
14. Percentage of matriculants ($= 13 \div 7$)					
15. Number of students with C+ average or worse leaving program in year 1					
16. Percentage of matriculants ($= 15 \div 7$)					
17. Number of students completing program					
18. Percentage of matriculants ($= 17 \div 7$)					
19. Number of graduates					
20. Percentage of matriculants ($= 19 \div 7$)					
Program Performance					
21. Average instructor rating					
22. Number of graduates attaining first-choice residency program					
23. Percentage of graduates ($= 22 \div 19$)					
24. Physicians in private practice after 10 years					
25. Percentage of graduates ($= 24 \div 19$)					
26. Physicians in academic medical centers after 10 years					

(Continued)

Table 11.3 *(Continued)*

Indicator	Year 1	Year 2	Year 3	Year 4	Year 5
27. Percentage of graduates ($= 26 \div 19$)					
Alumni Satisfaction					
28. Number of graduates making annual financial contributions to school					
29. Percentage of graduates ($= 28 \div 19$)					
30. Median gift per graduate					
31. Number of gifts of $500 or more					
32. Percentage of graduates ($= 31 \div 19$)					

spidergram

A reporting technique that presents results in a way that can be easily viewed in terms of their relationship to the minimum acceptable level and the desired goal.

balanced scorecard (BSC)

A technique that measures both non-financial as well as financial performance. Non-financial measures typically are clustered into three categories: customer satisfaction, internal process improvement, and employee growth and development.

nonfinancial measures

Data that indicate the success (or lack thereof) of a program in meeting an organization's goals.

4. *Changes over time.* By setting up a five-year series of comparisons, both the program manager and senior management can see how the program is changing over time. They could supplement this five-year series with a set of targets, enabling them to measure the program's performance both over time and with respect to the targets.

Figure 11.4 illustrates another way of reporting nonfinancial performance, called a *spidergram*. In this report, the organization, a hospital, is looking at four broad areas of performance: customer service, growth, financial performance, and internal processes. It has developed several measures of each and can use the report to tell at a glance where it is meeting—or failing to meet—its goals. On this report, the outer circle is the goal, the inner circle is the minimum acceptable score, and the jagged line measures actual performance. This report is designed for the hospital's board. Within each broad area of responsibility, the relevant managers would receive modified versions appropriate to that area.

Linking Nonfinancial to Financial Performance

Nonfinancial performance, although frequently not tied directly to an organization's financial performance, usually has an important relationship to it over time. That is, improvements in such areas as patient satisfaction, operational processes, and employee capabilities will generally lead to improved financial performance, although perhaps not immediately.

The now-well-known *balanced scorecard (BSC)* was developed in recognition of these linkages.[1] Senior managers of organizations using a BSC are required to think about the kinds of *nonfinancial measures* that are useful and how they interrelate—both to each other and, eventually, to overall organizational performance.[2]

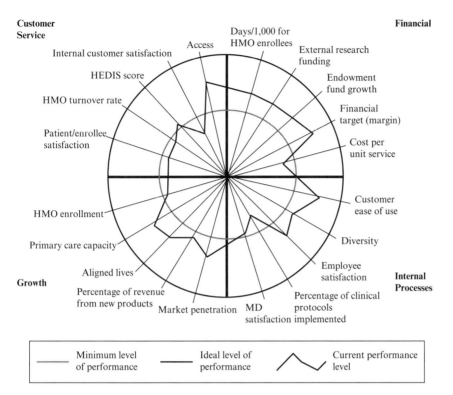

Figure 11.4 Example of a Spidergram
Source: David W. Young, *Management Control in Nonprofit Organizations,* 9th ed. (Cambridge, MA: Crimson Press, 2012), 286.

You should now work through the two practice cases for this chapter. Oak Street Nursing Home will give you some practice in preparing a simple flexible budget and calculating some variances, including some revenue variances. El Conejo Family Planning Clinic is somewhat more complicated and focuses on expense variances. The solutions are in appendix B at the end of the book.

KEY TERMS

Balanced scorecard (BSC)	Results measures
Flexible budgeting	Social indicators
Nonfinancial measures	Spidergram
Process measures	Variance analysis

To Bear in Mind

1. In most instances, an analysis of variances should begin with a flexible budget. The question you are seeking to answer is: "What would actual financial performance have been if only the volume and mix of outputs had differed from their budgeted amounts?" Holding everything constant except these two items and recalculating the budget (that is, preparing a flexible budget) can be revealing, even in a profit center. Managers can see how much of the total variance was due to volume and output mix changes alone. The next step is to compute all subsequent variances using the actual (rather than the budgeted) volume and mix of outputs.

2. Nonfinancial objectives have always been important in health care organizations, but they often have been excluded from the responsibility accounting system. If they are to be taken seriously by an organization's managers and professionals, however, senior management must modify the reporting phase of the management control process to accommodate them. Although a spidergram is a useful way to present both nonfinancial measures and the related financial measures, it provides only a broad overview. The reports also need to enable managers to drill down to understand the details underlying a problem shown on the spidergram.

Test Yourself

1. What is the purpose of a flexible budget? How does it contrast with a fixed budget? When is it most appropriately used?

2. What is variance analysis? How does it relate to a flexible budget? When is it most appropriate to use this technique? Give some examples of what it might measure.

3. What are the key characteristics of a good reporting process?

4. What are some of the major categories of nonfinancial information? Give an example in each category of an item that might be measured.

5. What is a spidergram? For what is it used?

Suggested Cases

Bandon Medical Associates (B)

Franklin Health Associates (B)

Lomita Hospital (B)

Los Reyes Hospital (B)

Spruce Street Shelter

United Medical Center

PRACTICE CASE A

OAK STREET NURSING HOME

The Oak Street Nursing Home was a small organization located in a popular resort town. Relatively healthy and ambulatory patients from other nursing homes could go there for short periods, which allowed them to accompany their children on vacations to the town. The home charged a nominal fee for a night's stay. The following budgeted and actual figures were available:

	Actual	Budget
Number of person nights	10,000	12,000
Revenue	$750,000	$720,000
Expenses	735,000	684,000
Income	$15,000	$36,000

Assignment

1. Explain the reasons for the $30,000 difference between budgeted and actual revenue, using appropriate revenue variances.

2. Prepare a flexible budget for the nursing home's expenses. Use this budget and the revenue variances to reconcile the difference between budgeted and actual income figures.

3. What additional information would you like to have to explain the difference between the budgeted and actual income figures?

PRACTICE CASE B

EL CONEJO FAMILY PLANNING CLINIC

Juana Ramirez, the director of finance of El Conejo Family Planning Clinic, recently had received a memorandum from the chair of the finance committee of the clinic's board of trustees. The memorandum, which also had been sent to all department heads, expressed concern that the results of the year's operations were considerably worse than budgeted.

One reason for this problem was that third parties had lowered their rate for one of the clinic's most significant visit types, but there appeared to be some other explanations as well. Ms. Ramirez had been asked to analyze the reasons for the poor performance, meet with the relevant department heads, and make a presentation at the next board meeting concerning the clinic's performance.

In reviewing the budgeted and actual results, Ms. Ramirez discovered that almost all of the clinic's variation from its budget could be attributed to four visit types and four services. For simplicity, she decided to base her presentation on these only.

Exhibit 11B.1 contains the original budget for these four visit types: IUD, first visit; oral contraceptive, first visit; special follow-up (when problems existed with the contraceptive or contraceptive method); and routine follow-up. It also shows the budgeted variable expenses per visit for the four services: physician care, nursing care, medical supplies, and laboratory tests.

EXHIBIT 11B.1   Original Budget

	IUD 1st Visit	Oral Contraceptive 1st Visit	Special Follow-Up	Routine Follow-Up	Total
Overall Budget					
Number of visits	3,000	2,000	1,000	500	6,500
Price per visit	$200.00	$100.00	$125.00	$40.00	
Total revenue	$600,000	$200,000	$125,000	$20,000	$945,000
Variable expenses per visit	$165.00	$75.00	$110.00	$10.00	
Total variable expenses	$495,000	$150,000	$110,000	$5,000	$760,000
Contribution	$105,000	$50,000	$15,000	$15,000	$185,000
Total fixed expenses					100,000
Surplus					$85,000
Variable Expense Detail					
Physician Care					
Average number of minutes per visit	30	10	15	5	
Average wage per minute	$1.00	$1.00	$1.00	$1.00	
Total expense per visit	$30.00	$10.00	$15.00	$5.00	

EXHIBIT 11B.1 *(Continued)*

	IUD 1st Visit	Oral Contraceptive 1st Visit	Special Follow-Up	Routine Follow-Up	Total
Nursing Care					
Average number of minutes per visit	30	20	30	10	
Average wage per minute	$0.50	$0.50	$0.50	$0.50	
Total expense per visit	$15.00	$10.00	$15.00	$5.00	
Medical Supplies					
Average number of units per visit	3	1	2	0	
Average expense per unit	$25.00	$25.00	$25.00	$25.00	
Total expense per visit	$75.00	$25.00	$50.00	$0.00	
Laboratory Tests					
Average number of tests per visit	3	2	2	0	
Average expense per test	$15.00	$15.00	$15.00	$15.00	
Total expense per visit	$45.00	$30.00	$30.00	$0.00	
Total Average Variable Expenses Per Visit	$165.00	$75.00	$110.00	$10.00	

As exhibit 11B.1 indicates, the clinic was paid on a per-visit basis. Its anticipated revenue for each visit type is shown in this exhibit, as is the anticipated use of services and the variable expense per unit for each service for each visit type. The total variable expenses per visit for each visit type was calculated using these estimates. The revenue and total variable expense per visit were then multiplied by the anticipated number of visits to give total revenue and total variable expenses by visit type. The latter was deducted from total revenue to give the contribution to fixed expenses from each visit type. The fixed expenses were then deducted from the total contribution to give a total budgeted surplus of $85,000 for the accounting period.

(Continued)

Ms. Ramirez asked her staff assistant, Anthony Loch, to use the actual data for the period, shown in exhibit 11B.2, as the basis for a report on results for the year. This report was to contain a complete breakdown of the reasons why the clinic's actual surplus diverged from the budgeted one. The report would be submitted to the clinic's chief executive officer, and Ms. Ramirez would use it for her presentation to the board of trustees.

EXHIBIT 11B.2   Actual Results

	IUD 1st Visit	Oral Contraceptive 1st Visit	Special Follow-Up	Routine Follow-Up	Total
Overall Results					
Actual number of visits	2,750	2,200	1,000	600	6,550
Actual price per visit	$200.00	$90.00	$130.00	$40.00	
Total fixed expenses					$100,000
Variable Expense Detail					
Physician Care					
Average number of minutes per visit	25	5	20	10	
Average wage per minute	$1.20	$1.20	$1.20	$1.20	
Nursing Care					
Average number of minutes per visit	40	30	25	5	
Average wage per minute	$0.60	$0.60	$0.60	$0.60	
Medical Supplies					
Average number of units per visit	4	2	2	0	
Average expense per unit	$21.00	$21.00	$21.00	$21.00	

EXHIBIT 11B.2 *(Continued)*

	IUD 1st Visit	Oral Contraceptive 1st Visit	Special Follow-Up	Routine Follow-Up	Total
Laboratory Tests					
Average number of tests per visit	5	3	5	0	
Average expense per test	$16.00	$16.00	$16.00	$16.00	

Mr. Loch began by using the data from exhibit 11B.2 to compute the actual financial results for the period (exhibit 11B.3), which showed that instead of earning a surplus, the clinic actually had incurred a deficit of $218,300. Then, reasoning that the clinic had essentially no control over the number or type of visits, he also prepared a flexible budget (exhibit 11B.4), which showed that $750 of the difference was due exclusively to the change in the number of visits in the clinic. Using similar reasoning, he prepared an analysis of the variance due to the changes in the third-party reimbursement rates (shown at the bottom of exhibit 11B.4), which showed that $17,000 of the difference was a result of these rate changes.

EXHIBIT 11B.3 Actual Results with Calculations

	IUD 1st Visit	Oral Contraceptive 1st Visit	Special Follow-Up	Routine Follow-Up	Total
Overall Results					
Actual number of visits	2,750	2,200	1,000	600	6,550
Actual price per visit	$200.00	$90.00	$130.00	$40.00	
Total revenue	$550,000	$198,000	$130,000	$24,000	$902,000
Actual variable expenses per visit	$218.00	$114.00	$161.00	$15.00	

EXHIBIT 11B.3 *(Continued)*

	IUD 1st Visit	Oral Contraceptive 1st Visit	Special Follow-Up	Routine Follow-Up	Total
Total variable expenses	$599,500	$250,800	$161,000	$9,000	$1,020,300
Contribution	$(49,500)	$(52,800)	$(31,000)	$15,000	$(118,300)
Total fixed expenses					100,000
Surplus					$(218,300)

Variable Expense Detail

Physician Care

	IUD 1st Visit	Oral Contraceptive 1st Visit	Special Follow-Up	Routine Follow-Up	Total
Average number of minutes per visit	25	5	20	10	
Average wage per minute	$1.20	$1.20	$1.20	$1.20	
Total expense per visit	$30.00	$6.00	$24.00	$12.00	

Nursing Care

	IUD 1st Visit	Oral Contraceptive 1st Visit	Special Follow-Up	Routine Follow-Up	Total
Average number of minutes per visit	40	30	25	5	
Average wage per minute	$0.60	$0.60	$0.60	$0.60	
Total expense per visit	$24.00	$18.00	$15.00	$3.00	

Medical Supplies

	IUD 1st Visit	Oral Contraceptive 1st Visit	Special Follow-Up	Routine Follow-Up	Total
Average number of units per visit	4	2	2	0	
Average expense per unit	$21.00	$21.00	$21.00	$21.00	
Total expense per visit	$84.00	$42.00	$42.00	$0.00	

Laboratory Tests

	IUD 1st Visit	Oral Contraceptive 1st Visit	Special Follow-Up	Routine Follow-Up	Total
Average number of tests per visit	5	3	5	0	

EXHIBIT 11B.3   (*Continued*)

	IUD 1st Visit	Oral Contraceptive 1st Visit	Special Follow-Up	Routine Follow-Up	Total
Average expense per test	$16.00	$16.00	$16.00	$16.00	
Total expense per visit	$80.00	$48.00	$80.00	$0.00	
Total Average Variable Expenses Per Visit	$218.00	$114.00	$161.00	$15.00	

EXHIBIT 11B.4   Flexible Budget and Related Variances

	IUD 1st Visit	Oral Contraceptive 1st Visit	Special Follow-Up	Routine Follow-Up	Total
Overall Budget					
Actual number of visits	2,750	2,200	1,000	600	6,550
Budgeted price per visit	$200.00	$100.00	$125.00	$40.00	
Total revenue	$550,000	$220,000	$125,000	$24,000	$919,000
Budgeted variable expenses per visit	$165.00	$75.00	$110.00	$10.00	
Total variable expenses	$453,750	$165,000	$110,000	$6,000	$734,750
Contribution	$96,250	$55,000	$15,000	$18,000	$184,250
Total fixed expenses					100,000
Surplus					$84,250

(*Continued*)

EXHIBIT 11B.4 *(Continued)*

	IUD 1st Visit	Oral Contraceptive 1st Visit	Special Follow-Up	Routine Follow-Up	Total
Revenue Volume Variance					
Actual visits − Budgeted visits	(250)	200	0	100	
Budgeted price per visit	$200.00	$100.00	$125.00	$40.00	
Variance	$(50,000)	$20,000	$0	$4,000	$(26,000)
Expense Volume Variance					
Budgeted visits − Actual visits	250	(200)	0	(100)	
Budgeted expense per visit	$165.00	$75.00	$110.00	$10.00	
Variance	$41,250	$(15,000)	$0	$(1,000)	$25,250
Contribution Margin Variance					
Revenue volume variance + Expense volume variance	$(8,750)	$5,000	$0	$3,000	$(750)
Revenue Price Variances					
Actual price per visit − Budgeted price per visit	$0.00	$(10.00)	$5.00	$0.00	
Actual number visits	2,750	2,200	1,000	600	
Revenue price variance	$0	$(22,000)	$5,000	$0	$(17,000)

Having analyzed and explained only $17,750 of the $303,300 total difference between budgeted and actual performance, Mr. Loch met with Ms. Ramirez to show her the results of his work. Ms. Ramirez explained to Mr. Loch that he needed to look into such matters as physician and nurse productivity and wage rates, medical supply costs, and laboratory costs. She asked Mr. Loch to assess these other possible reasons why actual results diverged from the budget, and to prepare a variance analysis that would explain each of those reasons.

Assignment

1. Be sure you understand how exhibits 11B.3 and 11B.4 were prepared. Do you agree with Mr. Loch's analyses so far?

2. Besides changes in the number of visits and the reimbursement rate per visit, what are the other possible reasons why actual results diverged from budget?

3. Calculate the variance associated with each of the reasons you gave in question 2. How, if at all, might this information be used in managing the clinic? How might it be used by the clinic's administration? By the chief of medicine? By the director of nursing?

4. What information concerning visits, costs, and revenues would you suggest the chief of medicine and the director of nursing see on a regular basis? Why?

Notes

1. For a discussion of the balanced scorecard, see Robert S. Kaplan and David P. Norton, *The Balanced Scorecard* (Boston: Harvard Business School Press, 1996). See also Robert S. Kaplan and David P. Norton, *Alignment: Using the Balanced Scorecard to Create Corporate Synergies* (Boston: Harvard Business School Press, 2006).

2. Much has been written about the applicability of the BSC to health care. See note 1 in chapter 9 for some relevant sources.

CHAPTER 12

IMPLEMENTING A NEW RESPONSIBILITY ACCOUNTING SYSTEM

The value of the concepts that form the basis of responsibility accounting systems lies in their applicability to real-world situations and problems. Designed properly, a responsibility accounting system can help facilitate improved organizational performance. The design effort requires assessing how a responsibility accounting system fits into its broader organizational context. This chapter addresses that idea and also discusses ways to overcome some of the difficulties that organizations encounter in implementing changes in their responsibility accounting system.

Organization of the Chapter

The chapter begins with an overview of the criteria for a good responsibility accounting system, followed by a list of some of the specific characteristics of a good system. The responsibility accounting system is then positioned in an organizational context as one of seven cross-functional activities (or processes). The chapter concludes with a discussion of some ways to manage an effort to introduce a new or redesigned responsibility accounting system.

Criteria for a Good Responsibility Accounting System

The criteria that characterize a good responsibility accounting system can be grouped into three categories: structural, process, and behavioral.

Structural Criteria

Senior management must ensure that the organization's responsibility centers are well designed and fit with the

LEARNING OBJECTIVES

On completing this chapter, you should know about

- The criteria for a good responsibility accounting system and some of the key characteristics of such a system

- The context in which the responsibility accounting system exists, comprising, in addition to the management control process, the activities of strategy formulation, conflict management, motivation, authority and influence, patient (or client) management, and cultural maintenance

- The questions that senior management needs to address to be certain that the responsibility accounting system is well designed

- The issues involved in managing an effort to introduce a new or redesigned responsibility accounting system

authority structure. "Well designed" means that (1) managers are held responsible only for those factors over which they exert a reasonable degree of control (the fairness criterion), and (2) a managerial decision that is good for a given responsibility center also is good for the organization overall (the goal congruence criterion).

Process Criteria

The responsibility accounting system should have a management control process that follows a rhythm consisting of four phases: programming, budgeting, measuring, and reporting. The programming phase should ensure that new programs and product lines fit with the organization's overall strategy and that the objectives for each product line or program are clearly spelled out.

The budgeting phase should identify the relationship between each responsibility center and the organization's product lines or programs, as well as the financial and nonfinancial expectations for each responsibility center. As a result, each manager is held accountable for both attaining the dollar amounts budgeted for his or her responsibility center and achieving certain nonfinancial results as well.

During the measuring phase, the accounting staff should collect data relating to revenues, expenses, and nonfinancial objectives as identified in the budgeting phase. The staff generally will need to organize expense data differently for budgeting and reporting purposes than for cost accounting purposes, and these differences should be incorporated into the measuring phase. Where appropriate, flexible budgets and variances should be calculated.

During the reporting phase, both financial and nonfinancial results should be made available to managers. The information should (1) be timely, accurate, and relevant to the responsibility center; (2) distinguish between controllable and noncontrollable items; and (3) contain information of varying levels of detail appropriate to the managers who will be using the reports.

Behavioral Criteria

Perhaps the most important behavioral criterion for a responsibility accounting system is that it is taken seriously by senior and line managers. Senior management's active participation in both budgeting and reporting is necessary if mid- and lower-level managers are to take the management control process seriously. In addition, if the responsibility accounting system lacks fairness or goal congruence, senior management must commit itself to making whatever modifications are needed to move the system closer to achieving these criteria.

Finally, to the extent that managers participate in the programming and budgeting phases of the management control process, their participation should be an integral part of those phases. When this is the case, their commitment to the programming and budgeting decisions can serve the organization's needs.

Key Characteristics of a Good Responsibility Accounting System

A health care organization that is performing in accordance with the criteria just given usually displays several specific characteristics:

* It has a strong governing body. Some members of this body spend considerable time examining program and budget proposals before they are submitted to the full board. Members of the governing body also analyze formal reports on performance and informal communication from patients and others on how well the organization is doing.

* The governing body is careful not to infringe on the prerogatives of management. It ensures that the chief executive has full authority to execute policies and that his or her decisions are supported by the board. It also ensures that his or her compensation is appropriate.

* Line managers have the authority to use their judgment (within certain strategic and ethical limits) in running their respective responsibility centers and in accomplishing budgeted results.

* The responsibility accounting system contains two principal account classifications: one structured in terms of programs, the other in terms of functions. This system frequently has a matrix-like structure.

* Responsibility centers are selected based on senior management's assessment of the resources that a manager can control, so that managers are held responsible only for those resources over which they exert a reasonable amount of control.

* When two or more responsibility centers engage in intraorganizational transactions, senior management makes sure that there is an appropriate set of transfer prices to facilitate the management control process.

* There is a programming phase in the management control process that is used for generating ideas for new programs or capital expenditures, analyzing these ideas, reaching decisions on them, and incorporating the results into ongoing operations.

- Budgeting is viewed as an important part of the management control process. The annual operating budget is derived from the approved programs, and responsibility for carrying out the programs is assigned to individual responsibility centers.

- There are measuring and reporting activities that help ensure that actual spending is kept within the limits specified in the approved budget—unless there are compelling reasons to depart from the budgeted amounts.

- Senior management devotes considerable attention to developing satisfactory nonfinancial measures. It recognizes that although many such measures are of limited validity, they are better than nothing. There is also a constant search for improved measures.

- Despite the fact that many people, especially professionals, dislike the idea of accountability, which is associated with the measurement of results, senior management proceeds with such measurements. All levels of management, including senior management, are involved in monitoring performance.

- Managers of each responsibility center receive regular comparisons between budgeted and actual revenues, expenses, and nonfinancial results. Reports containing this information are made available in a timely way and are designed to highlight significant information. Where appropriate, variances between planned and actual spending are isolated by cause, such as volume, mix, price, efficiency, or a combination of these.

- Senior management holds meetings with immediate subordinates to discuss results, variances, and planned corrective actions. It expects these individuals to hold similar meetings with their subordinates, and so on down the line.

The Responsibility Accounting Context

Given these criteria, we now can put the responsibility accounting system into a somewhat broader context. Specifically, one rarely if ever finds a single aspect of a responsibility accounting system in isolation. Indeed, the responsibility accounting system by necessity is part of, and is influenced by, an organization's broader set of management activities. One such activity is strategy formulation, because an organization's strategy can be expected to influence its financial and nonfinancial goals. Another activity relates to conflict management, because organizational (as distinct from interpersonal) conflict frequently arises in regard to such matters as the best programs to adopt, the best approaches to patient management, and the selection of an appropriate set of nonfinancial objectives. A third activity concerns the ways senior management uses compensation packages and other mechanisms to reward line managers for good performance.

Beyond these activities, senior management uses recruitment, training, and severance in an effort to maintain the organization's culture, and it gives considerable thought not only to how formal authority and influence flow within the organization but also to how this flow affects the organization's "management" of its patients (or clients).

Overall, the organization needs to attain a fit among these various *cross-functional activities*. To move toward or strengthen this fit, senior management must address a wide variety of matters. It must, for example, assure itself that the strategy formulation activity is addressing the organization's environment, including regulatory and competitive forces. In conjunction with engaging in strategy formulation, senior management must be sure that the programming phase of the management control process is leading to programs that support the full range of services needed to achieve the organization's strategy.

cross-functional activities
Seven activities (or processes) that interact in an organization and must be coordinated. They comprise strategy formulation, patient (or client) management, authority and influence, conflict management, cultural maintenance, motivation, and the management control process.

Other management activities tend to flow from these two and in many instances can also influence them. For example, some of the strategic decisions that senior management makes will be influenced by the kinds of information it receives from the reporting phase of the management control process. Similarly, depending on its design, the motivation process can encourage professionals to propose new programmatic endeavors or, more generally, to act in the best interest of the organization overall. Or it can discourage them from doing so.

In sum, as it designs or modifies its responsibility accounting system, senior management must make sure that the organization has

- A *management control process* that is consistent with the organization's strategy and provides appropriate information to managers who are involved in the strategy formulation process

- A *strategy formulation process* in which the information from the management control reports, along with a variety of other information— some of which is ad hoc—is used to examine the wisdom of the organization's strategy and modify it if circumstances warrant doing so

- An *authority and influence process* that involves an appropriate network of responsibility centers and that fosters collaborative decision making when necessary, especially between administrative staff and clinical professionals

- A *motivation process* that provides appropriate rewards for managers whose behavior is in the best interest of both their own responsibility centers and the organization overall

- A set of *conflict management processes* that addresses and helps resolve the many kinds of conflict that can arise in the course of achieving the organization's strategy

- A *cultural maintenance process* that helps create a set of common values across the organization and a set of basic assumptions that underlie all decision making in the organization

- A *patient (or client) management process* that helps the organization to attract the kinds of patients that are consistent with its strategy and to provide them with appropriate services at appropriate times, in an appropriate location

Each of these processes is important in and of itself, but perhaps most important, as the interconnections in figure 12.1 indicate, these various cross-functional activities must also fit with one another. They then can reinforce each other and, collectively, help ensure that the organization's patients are receiving appropriate, timely, coordinated, and cost-effective services.[1]

The following list presents the kinds of questions that senior management might ask in conjunction with each of these activities. As this list indicates, for a health care organization to achieve its strategy, senior management must take action on several related fronts: planning, organizational, and informational:

Strategy Formulation

- Do strategic decisions have significant senior management involvement, or are they a result of individual groups' acting independently?

- Does the reporting phase of the management control process provide information that is helpful for strategy formulation? If not, how can it be modified to do so?

Patient (or Client) Management

- How does a patient initially come into contact with the organization?

- What decisions are made about how that person will (or will not) be served? Who makes those decisions?

- What activities are needed to discharge a patient? Who makes the discharge decision? In consultation with whom?

- Is care delivered at the most appropriate site, by the most appropriate people, with the most appropriate resource mix?

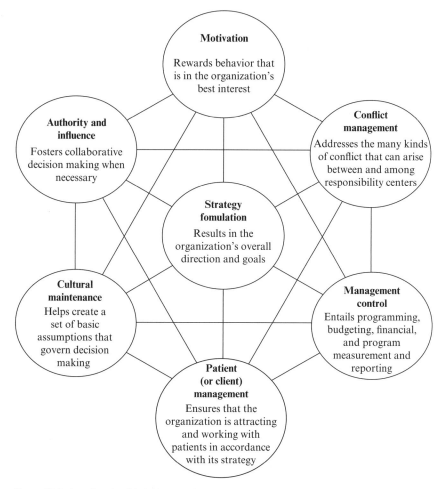

Figure 12.1 Cross-Functional Activities in an Organization

Cultural Maintenance

- What kinds of middle management decisions would be unacceptable to senior management?

- What kinds of decisions would be supported readily by senior management?

- How do recruitment, training, promotion, and severance, plus the motivation process, help maintain the culture?

Authority and Influence

- What kinds of responsibility centers have been established? Do they meet the fairness and goal congruence criteria?

- Does the flow of authority and influence foster collaborative decision making where needed?

- What formal mechanisms exist for professionals (such as physicians) to influence decision making in the organization?

Motivation

- If there is an incentive compensation system, is it part of the budgeting phase so that budgets incorporate it?
- How deeply into the organization does the incentive compensation system go? Should it go deeper?

Conflict Management

- Where are the potential sources of conflict in the organization? Who typically is involved?
- What formal mechanisms are in place (such as permanent or ad hoc committees) to manage conflict? Do they manage it appropriately?

Management Control

Programming

- How is the decision made to begin a new program? To change or eliminate an existing program?
- Does the programming phase lead to programs that reinforce the organization's strategy?
- How are requests for capital expenditures addressed? Do accepted requests move the organization toward its strategy?

Budgeting

- What are the organization's key success factors, and how are they incorporated into the budget? Are results in these areas linked to the motivation process?
- What kinds of drivers are used to build the budget?
- If there is cross-subsidization among programs and responsibility centers, how are the subsidies determined?
- Have transfer prices been established? If so, are responsibility center managers allowed to purchase from outside the organization if they think the transfer prices are too high? If not, how is fairness achieved?

Financial Measuring and Reporting

- How are costs and revenues measured and reported to key managers?
- Does the accounting system measure fixed and variable costs for different mixes of patients in different programs? Does it compute the relevant variances?

- Do the resulting reports help managers assess their financial performance against the budget in ways that assist them in taking corrective action when necessary?

Nonfinancial Measuring and Reporting

- How are programmatic and other nonfinancial results (quality, patient satisfaction, and so forth) being measured?

- How do financial and nonfinancial measuring and reporting relate to each other? Are managers able to assess the financial implications of a decision to improve nonfinancial performance?

Managing the Change Effort

It's one thing to want to take action to address one or more of the issues in the preceding list, but it's quite another to achieve the desired results. If senior management wishes to modify one or more of the activities shown in figure 12.1, how does it go about the change effort? In his article "Leading Change," Harvard's John Kotter, an authority on *change management*, describes eight steps that senior management must take.[2] Although these steps may seem self-evident and intuitive, Kotter's article has the ominous subtitle "Why Transformation Efforts Fail," suggesting that change efforts frequently are unsuccessful.

> **change management**
> The way an organization goes about implementing changes to its responsibility accounting system.

The eight steps discussed in his article are (1) establish a sense of urgency, (2) form a powerful guiding coalition, (3) create a vision, (4) communicate the vision, (5) empower others to act on the vision, (6) plan and create short-term wins, (7) consolidate improvements and produce still more change, and (8) institutionalize new approaches. Clearly, this effort is not easy.

Resistance to the Change Effort

At least some, perhaps many, people in an organization are likely to resist senior management's efforts to implement changes in the responsibility accounting system. How senior management deals with these individuals will depend partially on its preferred management style. Some CEOs embrace resisters and attempt to work with them, whereas others attempt to ride roughshod over them. Regardless of its style, the senior management team must recognize that line managers' and others' commitment to the change effort can be classified into one of four categories identified by Martin Charns of Boston University and shown in figure 12.2.

Generally when senior management establishes its powerful guiding coalition (step 2 in Kotter's eight steps), it selects the coalition's membership

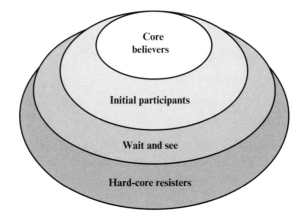

Figure 12.2 Commitment to Change
Source: Adapted, with permission, from an exhibit prepared by Martin Charns.

from among the core believers and perhaps the initial participants. That is, the change effort frequently begins with the inner circle in figure 12.2 and moves to the outer one. However, some managers will try to bring the "wait and see" people and the hard-core resisters into the effort early on, either as members of subcommittees focused on specific issues or as sources of concern.

There is no clear answer to the question of how to deal with the hard-core resisters. On the one hand, they may be resisting the change for good reasons, and their views may be important, perhaps even constructive. On the other hand, they may fear that the changes, once implemented, will have a negative impact on their careers, their incomes, their power in the organization, or some other matter of personal concern to them.

Dealing with Resistance

Kotter and his colleague Leonard Schlesinger have discussed six methods for dealing with resistance to change: (1) education and communication, (2) participation and involvement, (3) facilitation and support, (4) negotiation and agreement, (5) manipulation and co-optation, and (6) explicit and implicit coercion.[3] As they discuss, senior management must attempt to fit the method to the need in light of each method's advantages and disadvantages.

Short-Term Wins

It is easy to say that senior management should plan and create short-term wins (Kotter's step 6), but it is much more difficult to determine in advance

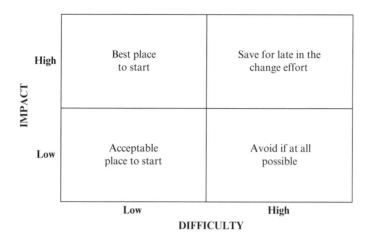

Figure 12.3 Impact versus Difficulty
Source: Prepared by Martin Charns.

what those wins might be. To assist senior management with this selection effort, Charns has developed the two-by-two matrix shown in figure 12.3. To create some short-term wins, senior management most likely needs to start with efforts that fall in the low-difficulty column, preferably in the high-impact row. In one successful change effort, for example, senior management simply made sure that all the facility's clocks were running on time, an easy and perhaps seemingly low-impact item. Yet because unreliable clocks had been a source of considerable employee dissatisfaction, taking this step had a high impact on morale. Subsequent tasks were much easier as a result. Despite such examples of success, it is amazing how many change efforts still begin in the lower-right quadrant of figure 12.3.

Consolidating and Moving Forward

In most organizations the hard-core resisters cannot be left out of the change effort indefinitely. Sooner or later they must be either incorporated into the effort or encouraged to leave the organization. Assuming the goal is to incorporate them, there are several matters that the senior management team must consider as it consolidates and moves forward (step 7 in the Kotter model). Some of the steps senior management should take to address these matters are the following:

1. Find out the specific reasons for the resistance.
2. Determine whether anything can be done to address these concerns, and at what cost.

3. Identify someone in the organization (perhaps a core believer) who can meet with the hard-core resisters and attempt to convince them to accept the change.

4. Decide if it is worth the effort (expense and angst) for the organization to attempt to convince the hard-core resisters to accept the change. If not, assist these people in moving into another organizational unit where they will not be significantly affected by the change.

You are now ready to analyze the practice case for this chapter. Hillside Hospital allows you to think about both the appropriate design of a responsibility accounting system as well as the steps needed to implement the needed changes.

KEY TERMS

Change management   Cross-functional activities

To Bear in Mind

1. It is not enough to know what the ideal responsibility accounting system or cross-functional activities should look like; senior management also must determine how it will make that ideal a reality. In this regard, the list of questions given in this chapter can serve two purposes: (1) it can help senior management determine those activities most in need of redesign, and (2) it can facilitate an assessment of the difficulty that senior management may encounter when it begins to initiate a change effort.

2. Some of the guidelines in this chapter on managing change may be helpful in avoiding pitfalls and in enlisting the support of key people in a change effort. Nevertheless, a change effort can be, and often is, a painful and frustrating endeavor.

Test Yourself

1. What are three important characteristics of a good responsibility accounting system?

2. Describe the responsibility accounting context. Why is it important?

3. What are Kotter's eight steps to change?

4. What are Kotter and Schlesinger's six methods for dealing with resistance to change?

5. Where is the best place to begin a change effort?

Suggested Cases

Centuria Health System

Easter Seal Foundation of New Hampshire and Vermont (A)

Fletcher Allen Health Care

Omega Research Institute

Priority Health System

The Robert Wood Johnson Medical School

PRACTICE CASE

HILLSIDE HOSPITAL

> This has been one of the ugliest things I've ever done—all the personal abuse, just for following the damn rules the university sent down. It is the closest I've come to quitting my job.

In September, Richard Wells, chief of medicine at Hillside Hospital in Chicago, announced that all full-time doctors in the department of medicine were required to join the department's group practice plan, called the Medical Practice Plan (MPP), or leave the hospital premises. In his eight years as chief, Dr. Wells had initiated numerous changes in the department, but never one as controversial as the MPP.

Dr. Wells had established the MPP two years earlier to serve two purposes. First, it was intended to regulate each physician's professional income to comply with Kent Medical School's salary regulations, and second, it would augment the department's income with funds not otherwise attainable. In addition, Dr. Wells was convinced that the department of medicine, as an academic department of Kent Medical School, needed guidelines to ensure a standard of excellence:

> I think this has to be done in any academic institution. Doctors here are supposed to provide ongoing patient care, carry on research, and teach. Now if you're at all good as a physician, your private practice will skyrocket, and your research and teaching will lose out. It's fun and lucrative to practice medicine, but in a teaching hospital you have other responsibilities, too.

Background

The department of medicine was a clinical department of the 85-year-old Hillside Hospital in Chicago. Hillside had been a teaching affiliate of Kent Medical School since its inception. In its many years as a teaching hospital, Hillside had demonstrated a firm commitment to teaching and research as well as patient care. Insisting that the three were interdependent and together enhanced the quality of medical care, Hillside's medical staff had distinguished itself among hospital teaching staffs. Hillside had become the most popular hospital among Kent medical students, and it attracted graduates of the top medical schools for its 175 intern and resident slots.

As part of the teaching hospital, Hillside's clinical departments were subject to the medical school's guidelines. These guidelines, which primarily stressed the school's commitment to scholastic achievement, had had little effect on the school's clinical departments. Dr. Wells explained:

> For years, we'd had what you'd call a gentleman's agreement with the medical school. It gave the department a modest budget and paid doctors something for their teaching and research. Other than that, doctors could work for the hospital and carry on a private practice, making about as much money as they wanted. There was some innocuous stipulation in our agreement allowing doctors to make as much money as "didn't interfere with their scholarly activities."

When Kent began to feel the financial constraints besetting most academic institutions and was unable to continue supporting its clinical departments, it altered the agreement, asking that patient fees support hospital clinical departments. The school also issued a salary regulation statement, from which the following is excerpted:

> Total Compensation paid to full-time members of the Faculty of Medicine may not exceed the level set for each individual in the Appointments and Compensation Requirements for the Faculty of Medicine at Kent University. The member's total income is equal to the sum of his/her Academic Salary plus Additional Compensation plus Other Personal Professional Income and may not exceed twice the member's Academic Salary.
>
> Each Clinical Department head shall be responsible for maintaining the records and reporting the income of all full-time members of the Department . . . Fees earned that are in excess of an individual's compensation level must be reported and disposed of as directed by the institution responsible for setting the level of compensation in consultation with the Dean of the Medical School.
>
> Inasmuch as the System has been adopted by the faculty and approved by the Kent Corporation, it is understood that no Faculty member may continue in the full-time system unless he/she is in full conformity with the system and the procedures designed to implement it.

According to Dr. Wells, it was difficult for him (and other department chairs) to abide by those regulations:

> The new guidelines caused quite a commotion, as you can imagine. Doctors were critical of the policy because they now had to report their salaries—something they'd never had to do before.
>
> When I asked people in my department for income disclosures, some of them tried everything to get around the rules. They were giving me their salaries after taxes and expenses—and it was unreal what they were calling "expenses." They were, of course, making just what they had been before. And it was becoming clear to me that I couldn't enforce the regulation.

Meanwhile, the department of medicine's revenue, which was derived from the hospital and grants, was not meeting its needs. Some physicians joined Dr. Wells in his concern about the department's financial problems. Eleanor Robinson, associate director of the department of medicine, explained:

> We were finding the department had needs, mostly of an academic nature, that we didn't have the money to support. Occasionally, we'd want to send residents to meetings or postgraduate education programs but couldn't afford to. Or someone would need financial assistance for a small research project that wasn't covered by long-term National Institutes of Health grants, and the money just wasn't there.

The Medical Practice Plan

Responding to these administrative and financial problems, Dr. Wells decided to establish a faculty practice plan. He intended to structure it as a department fund that would pool physicians' professional fees and pay them salaries according to Kent's regulation. Any surplus of fees would be retained by the department for its use.

The MPP was organized as an educational and charitable trust fund with nonprofit, tax-exempt status. Although the hospital and medical school became the MPP's beneficiaries, the department maintained total responsibility for its policies and budget. Dr. Wells commented:

> I watched the department of anesthesia at Memorial Hospital form a practice plan through their hospital about eight years ago. Everything goes into the hospital, and the hospital gives the group a yearly budget. The chief is now having difficulty getting a rundown from the hospital on the department's finances when he knows the department is making money. If he wants another anesthetist, he has to justify it to the hospital. I don't want to crawl to the hospital for what I need if I've got the space. So I chose not to do that.

Dr. Robinson, who aided in administering the MPP, added:

> We generally agreed that patient income for the department's use should be administered outside of the hospital budget, mainly because we didn't want

our money to be used to subsidize other departments. We hadn't had problems with the hospital, but it was a preventive measure.

The MPP offered members a salary in accordance with the medical school's guidelines plus benefits and a conditional overage expense account. As an incentive, salaries were graded down from the guideline ceiling with increases based on yearly evaluation meetings between Dr. Wells and the doctor concerned. Dr. Wells explained:

> A physician's salary is a function of his or her overall contribution to the department plus academic rank. What the medical school gave us is a maximum for each position. At the evaluation conferences, I decide, with the doctor, where he or she falls on that scale. In reality, we're all pretty close to our maximums, but it's an incentive to get the work done.
>
> It's important to realize, though, that salaries don't reflect the patient fees generated by the doctor. If a physician has a steady practice and generates an average income in patient fees but is an invaluable teacher or researcher, he or she might be promoted academically and hence be paid more than another physician whose best skills are in seeing patients.

Dr. Wells acknowledged that this could also be a disadvantage:

> There's a practical problem with tying salaries to academic ranks. It isn't always possible for people to do all three things equally well. If they don't do the academics, their salaries suffer. For example, we have some super cardiologists—absolutely super—but they don't have time to write academic papers. Their salaries are stuck at their academic ranks, whatever happens.
>
> But this is an academic hospital, and if doctors are interested in making money, they shouldn't be here. They should move up the street where they can make as much money as they want.

The MPP's benefits were health, life, malpractice, and long-term disability insurance, plus a tax-deferred annuity program. These were benefits that had previously been purchased with members' after-tax dollars. Thus, the MPP sought both to maximize members' income potentials within the context of the Kent ceiling and to offer tax advantages.

If a doctor generated more income than double his or her academic salary, he or she received an overage account for professional expenses. Fifty percent of a doctor's surplus income was to be credited to him or her to cover such expenses as subscriptions, books, and conference travel. According to the by-laws of the MPP, however, overage money could not be converted into salary. The remaining surplus income was to be used for department expenses.

The department would collect supplemental income from "chief-service patients." Prior to the MPP, these were patients who did not have a private physician, and hence were the responsibility of the chief resident. Because they were admitted to the hospital without a private physician, the medical services they received did not qualify for reimbursement.

When the department established the MPP, it employed the senior chief resident as the group's "junior-staff physician," and all of his or her patients were considered to be patients of the professional practice plan. The MPP could then bill for these patients on the basis of its provider status. As a result, the MPP collected fees that were not available when each doctor maintained an independent practice.

Governance and Membership

The MPP was governed by a board of trustees. The five-member board was responsible for MPP policies and approving loans and budgets. The board members were Dr. Wells, who held a permanent position; two trustees appointed by him; and two trustees elected by the department. In addition, Dr. Wells would hold periodic meetings for all MPP members.

By winter, there were four members of the MPP: the junior-staff physician, Dr. Wells, and two other young physicians. Critical of the MPP's organization and planning methods, four or five doctors opposed joining. Melvin Jefferson, who had been a cardiologist at Hillside for 10 years, was the most vocal about his position:

I was not going to join the MPP until I knew exactly what was being proposed. A number of important issues were left extremely vague. The reasons for establishing the MPP were even vague, in my mind at least, and our meetings did little to clarify the specifics. Some of the important issues, especially reconciling salaries, faculty rank, and academic and financial contributions to the department, were unresolved. I don't think these things had been thoroughly thought out, and yet we were being asked to join. So a few other doctors and I refused to join until we knew more about the details.

In the spring the following year, Dr. Wells asked all physicians to join the MPP. A few doctors who had verbally committed themselves to joining the MPP but had postponed doing so became members. But because attitudes in the department continued to differ, Dr. Wells decided membership had to be mandatory for all full-time academic physicians. He explained:

Membership had to be a prerequisite for remaining in the department, because I knew what was going to happen. I had a few nice guys, resigned to the idea of the MPP, carrying the department. And there were these other fellows, you know, friends of everyone; they'd been here a long time and didn't want to join. Some of them were earning significant compensation. Others, their friends, were toeing the line.

I knew that some people wouldn't go along with it, and maybe for good reasons. You have to be realistic about the specialty you're talking about; if cardiologists and gastroenterologists can make big bucks, how can you keep them down on the farm? In another one of our divisions, everyone is leaving. They're moving down the street to private offices. They're good specialists, and it's too bad we're losing them, but if they're interested in making money, that's where they should be.

At the announcement of mandatory participation, every physician was forced to make a decision. Ben Lewis, head of the gastroenterology division, explained his decision to join the MPP:

> We were told by Dr. Wells that the department was not in compliance with the medical school's guidelines. He told us that we had to change our system to comply, and that if we didn't, we'd have to leave.
>
> I said fine. I trusted Dr. Wells totally, I admired him greatly, and I liked my work. I was willing to change, even though I knew the financial and emotional costs. I knew the financial cost because I subtracted the guideline figure from my current compensation, and that was my loss. The emotional cost, loss of independence, is harder to evaluate and still troubles me.
>
> It makes you wonder why people stay here. Why do they? I guess it's because they like Dr. Wells. I think that's the main reason everyone stays. He's created a good faculty and a relatively favorable environment.

Other physicians, however, were still opposed to the MPP. Dr. Jefferson, the most reluctant to join, explained that his reticence stemmed from his impression of the MPP's operating structure:

> In thinking about the MPP earlier, I'd had exalted goals in mind. I thought we could use it to make a more unified and cohesive department of medicine. We could spread the patient care experience to the younger physicians and improve the department academically by removing some of the economic motivations. Somehow the MPP got sidetracked into an instrument whose sole purpose was to collect chief-service fees for the department, which resulted in a lot of divisiveness.
>
> For example, look at the method of remuneration as initially spelled out: a salary based on academic rank and an extremely modest fringe benefit package. That left the question of overages and benefits essentially unresolved. We were being asked to sign a document involving a significant financial decision that could theoretically involve making considerably less money than before, without having the specifics spelled out. We were just told that "no one would be hurt."
>
> I also thought it was absurd to erect a gigantic administrative superstructure. If the purpose was simply to conform to the medical school's guidelines and earn a little extra money for the department, we didn't need this whole organization with a billing office and everything else. I think we should have started small and built up; the fact is, we just don't have any big earners who can support an entity of this size.

From Dr. Wells's perspective, the MPP had by then become

a tremendous can of worms. I had physicians philosophizing about everything. You should have heard them. All upset because of their "loss of control." It wasn't loss of control at all, it was loss of money. The absurd part of it was that a lot of those people weren't losing money. Believe me, doctors can be a difficult bunch to work with.

Unfortunately, there's no uniformity in the way clinical departments interpreted the guidelines, so doctors could point to other departments and claim that they weren't complying the way we were. They were right, particularly in this school, because the dean is afraid to interfere too much in the autonomy of the hospitals.

The Billing System

At the outset of the MPP, Dr. Wells intended to have all members' billing managed by a central billing office. He had hired a business manager to administer billings, collections, and reports for members. He planned that each doctor would submit a daily "activity sheet" to the business office, detailing services rendered, patients' names, and fees.

However, because many present and future MPP members opposed the centralized billing plan, Dr. Wells postponed implementing it. Instead, on joining the MPP, each doctor had the choice of centralized billing through the business office or using the previous system wherein secretaries billed for doctors' private practices. Given the choice, half the physicians chose central billing and half chose to remain with the old system. Ann Miller, the business manager, explained:

Doctors really hold a spectrum of opinions on billing; some don't care at all about their bills, whereas others want to see and discuss every one. I think some doctors don't like the business aspect of medicine—they prefer not having to handle it. The others don't like not having control of it. They feel removed from their practice if they don't see the bills go out.

The doctors who continued to bill privately were to submit duplicate bills and their monthly collections to the business office. But most doctors never sent their duplicate bills, leaving the office with incomplete billing information. Ms. Miller was forced to establish a bill-receipt record system, posting bills and receipts simultaneously and trying to reconcile them. She said:

It was a crazy system, and we knew it. But what could we do? Physicians set their own fees, and we had no idea what they were. At the end of the month they would send us money with a record of patients' names and amounts paid. So we'd record that amount as billed and paid.

But it was no way to run a business office. For example, one day a doctor brought in $25,000 in checks, just like that. We hadn't expected it at all. We never had any idea of our accounts receivable or collection rates.

Ms. Miller added that centralized billing had developed its own complications:

Our main problem was that the information we received varied immensely from doctor to doctor. We didn't provide them with a formal activity sheet, so the doctors used their own systems of recording. As you can imagine, we were receiving dissimilar information from all of them.

From what they gave us, my three assistants would compile standard data sheets, which was unbelievably time consuming. On top of that, we were billing for five doctors, collecting and recording for 11 doctors, and preparing individual monthly reports for them. It was taking us three weeks to do just the monthly reports.

It was also becoming obvious to Dr. Wells that the MPP billing had to be uniform and managed by a central system:

Finally, I'd had it. The only efficient way to collect money for so many people was through one system. It had to be cheaper and more accurate, plus it would keep everyone honest. I figured that if collections changed at all, they should increase because one office was handling all the data.

Many physicians, however, disagreed with Dr. Wells on this issue, including Dr. Lewis:

I felt all along that it was crucial that we do our billing independently. Very simply, no one is more interested in collections than the person who worked for them: I can do it better because I care.

Second, there are complications in people's billings, which can be settled only by the doctor. If a patient is on welfare and can't pay, I'd know enough to drop the bill after one attempt to collect. Now, I'm never sure what the billing office charged or if they understand my intention.

Sometimes people come in and say, "Doctor, I've been in here three times, and I haven't received a bill yet. Why?" I'd have to say, "I don't know," which makes me feel foolish. When my secretary did billing, I'd just step out, ask her, and get the answer. Now, with the business office all the way over in Talbot, geographically remote from the department, it is very difficult to know what the current situation is.

In January, the MPP hired a company to manage its billings. The company was to receive billing and payment information from the business office and process it by batches into claims and collections. It would apply claims and collections to physicians' balances and maintain a continual record of the MPP's financial status. The company agreed to produce monthly printouts, by provider, so that doctors would have accurate records of their respective accounts. Nevertheless, the company never produced the information. Ms. Miller explained:

We had a terrible time with that company. The first problem was they never produced any reports according to doctor. We kept asking, and they kept agreeing, but they never gave us anything useful.

By the time we realized we weren't going to get that out of them, we had a more serious problem: they had dropped $30,000 in payments from the records. They just hadn't applied it to any accounts, so although we had the money, we didn't know which accounts, that is, doctors, it belonged to. That meant that the collection rates we had manually calculated were also meaningless. We got rid of the company then, but I'm afraid it was too late.

Some doctors, affected by these errors, were already furious. With minimal billing information and wide fluctuations in collection rates, doctors blamed the centralized billing system. In an attempt to trace the problems, Dr. Robinson studied the collection data. After analyzing patient mix, payer class, and service mix, she reached no conclusion:

I felt that centralized billing should, if anything, improve collections, but that wasn't our experience. Of course, with our other computer problems, the issue became more complicated because our information was incomplete.

Nevertheless, I think we have to separate questions of administrative efficiency from problems with the system itself. This is difficult to do, but we can't treat them all as one big problem with the billing system. Of course, we also have to consider that when physicians send their bills to a collection office, they feel like they're losing control. That's the motive for doing the billing ourselves.

Dr. Wells considered the billing problem to be one of administrative oversights:

Obviously there were problems with that company, but I don't see why this would be inherent to all centralized billing systems. I've discussed the problem with other groups, and our experience is atypical. It happened, though, and we can't explain it.

There's also the issue of overhead; doctors are seeing it now like never before. They can see costs that the hospital and department formerly paid, like secretaries, coming directly out of the MPP, and they're not pleased.

Other physicians, including Dr. Lewis, who had become an elected member of the board of trustees, maintained their opposition to the billing system. He commented:

I've been against centralized billing from the start, and I think time has borne me out. For one year, I've worked with no idea of what my collections have been. As a result, I don't know my overage, or if I even have one. If I submit receipts, I don't know if they'll be covered.

I got some information for a few months last year, and according to that, my collections had fallen by 33 percent. Yet Dr. Wells calls this a more efficient system.

This method must be costing us more. My secretary still prepares the background information on bills and sends that to the billing office to finish.

She might as well do the whole thing. It's unnecessary and inefficient to involve that whole office.

Dr. Jefferson thought that the system was, for him, less efficient than his previous one:

Last year I tried to get some information about my collections and was appalled at how little they'd collected and how little they knew. They couldn't even give me records on patient payments. I did find out, though, that overhead was about 19 percent of my salary. We all agreed that this was excessive.

Dr. Lewis added that in his opinion, the controversy over billing methods and other administrative matters was indicative of problems inherent in the MPP's overall administrative policies:

What happened with billing is typical of the way the MPP is run. I like and respect Dr. Wells, but our finances are in shambles because he isn't interested in them and doesn't have the necessary skills. For example, look at what happened with the billing company that he and Ms. Miller engaged.

What it comes down to is that the MPP is really Dr. Wells. It reflects his personality, plus he controls the majority of votes. Of the five board members, three are Dr. Wells and his two appointments, giving him three-fifths of any vote—it would be impossible to beat him. Not that there has been a showdown, but the fact is, he's playing with a loaded deck. It's okay as long as you like him and trust him, but it makes for an uncertain future.

Evaluation

By late winter, all 14 full-time physicians at Hillside had joined the MPP. Five doctors had left the department in the previous two years for reasons both related and unrelated to the MPP. Some joined the staffs at other hospitals, and others left to establish independent private practices. Dr. Wells gradually filled their positions with physicians who joined the MPP when they joined the department.

Although opinions in the department still differed on some aspects of the MPP, there were also points of general agreement among members. One such area concerned the MPP's effect on the department's economic condition. Dr. Robinson commented on it:

One of the most important results of the MPP has been the increased revenue generated for the department. It remains to be seen whether any of this is from the changes in the billing system, but collecting chief-service patient fees has certainly helped us financially.

Before the MPP, the department was stretching to take care of the usual expenses. In the past few years, we've not only covered our usual costs but also been able to pay for postgraduate education and extend interest-free loans to residents. We even lent travel money to a resident so that his family could go to England with him when he was studying there.

The problems in the MPP were really administrative and business problems. People here are devoted to academic pursuits, so they're not concerned about who is generating the most income—that's not the point of medicine. I think these problems are getting smoothed out and the MPP will run much better in the future. I also think it will improve as more people join the department.

Dr. Jefferson agreed with Dr. Robinson that the MPP had helped the department, but he remained critical of the MPP's operations:

It's still difficult to get a handle on precisely what's going on. The process of forming the MPP did not have a salutary effect on communication problems within the department, and these problems remain.

In a way, the MPP has had no real effect on me. I do exactly what I did before and am not significantly better or worse off because of it. The available funds have allowed the department to survive, which was important, but when the MPP was formed, Dr. Wells was never as frank as he should have been about the economic problems of the department. He said "we'd make a little extra money," but we never knew that there was a significant economic problem. If we had, we might have all discussed it and come up with an agreeable solution. The emphasis was always on the medical school's guidelines.

I think Dr. Wells is a much better chief of medicine than a businessman. There are many business issues, and it was preposterous to go about them in an unbusinesslike way. I think Wells had the attitude that it isn't nice to talk about money. So because he can't talk about it, we have a major communication problem. We still need frankness about this because we're getting new people into the MPP and they have to know the details.

Dr. Lewis gave his opinion of the MPP's shortcomings:

It's a nice feature of the department to have supplemental funds. I've set up a library in my office for medical students and residents in gastroenterology. I've also used money for honoraria and visual aids, and residents have been reimbursed for expenses from various meetings.

As for the other side, I would say that reduced personal income and loss of independence are disadvantages of the MPP. And there have been mistakes. The whole concept of centralized billing was a big mistake. I've voted against it every time it's come up, but it exists. Of course, the mistake was exacerbated by the choice of a billing company.

I believe the real problem in organizing the MPP was asking people to change. People were asked to go from a liberal, laissez-faire system to a structured one, and they resisted. That's not unusual and could have been predicted.

Commenting on the MPP four years after he'd organized it, Dr. Wells noted that some questions remained unanswered:

It's a difficult situation because there still is no uniformity in the medical school. I did what I thought had to be done to keep a department of medicine functioning academically, but some departments haven't done anything. And realistically, I know academic rank doesn't always reflect someone's contribution. But what could I do?

And then there's always been the budget problem. We never really know where we stand with any of our four budgets. We have budgets for the hospital, the medical school, the grants, and the MPP; research funds for this department alone are $10 million. That's big business, and we're not trained for that.

Assignment

1. Classify the activities of Dr. Wells into the categories of strategy formulation, motivation, conflict management, authority and influence, cultural maintenance, management control, and patient management. How, if at all, does this assist you in understanding the problems faced by the MPP?

2. Was the management control structure (that is, the responsibility centers) of the MPP well designed? If not, how would you have changed it?

3. What is your assessment of the management control process of the MPP? How, if at all, would you have changed it?

4. What might Dr. Wells have done differently to achieve a smoother process of change in the department?

Notes

1. For a discussion of these activities in the context of integrated delivery systems in health care, see David W. Young and Sheila McCarthy, *Managing Integrated Delivery Systems: A Framework for Action* (Chicago: Health Administration Press, 1999). For a more general discussion, see David W. Young, "The Six Levers for Managing Organizational Culture," *Business Horizons* 43 (September–October 2000): 19–28.

2. John P. Kotter, "Leading Change: Why Transformation Efforts Fail," *Harvard Business Review*, January 2007.

3. John P. Kotter and Leonard A. Schlesinger, "Choosing Strategies for Change," *Harvard Business Review*, March–April 1979.

ANSWERS TO "TEST YOURSELF" QUESTIONS

Chapter 1

1. The four forces are demographic changes, morbidity in the nonelderly population, spending patterns for the elderly, and the complexity of the health care market.

2. The five drivers are case mix, volume, resources per case, cost per resource unit, and fixed costs.

3. The idea behind the health care food chain is that one entity's expenses represent another entity's revenue. Expense reductions for one organization (such as a health maintenance organization [HMO]) therefore result in revenue reductions for another (such as a hospital).

4. The term *value-based purchasing* expresses the idea that payers in health care need to consider benefits as well as costs when making a decision about purchasing. That is, their decision is made on the basis of "value" and not just cost.

5. Physicians can become involved in establishing clinical guidelines and monitoring their colleagues' use of them. This is important because only physicians have the clinical expertise that is required to establish these guidelines, and only physicians can effectively judge when a colleague has diverged from a guideline for an acceptable reason. Lay managers do not have the requisite clinical knowledge.

Chapter 2

1. Cost accounting is most often used for pricing decisions, profitability assessments, and comparative analyses.

2. The two factors are noncomparable costs, such as the cost of the chaplain's office in a hospital, and scale-related costs, such as the cost of governance.

3. The cost breakdown is shown in the following diagram:

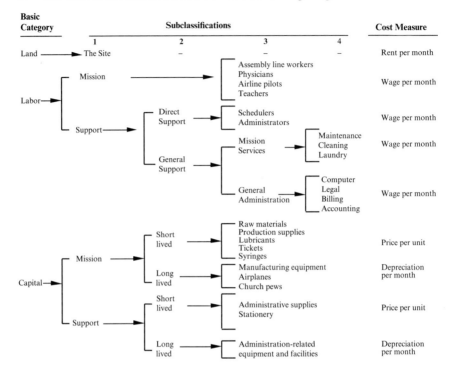

4. The six decisions are as follows:

Decision 1: Defining the cost object

Decision 2: Determining mission and support cost centers

Decision 3: Distinguishing between direct costs and indirect costs

Decision 4: Choosing allocation bases for support center costs

Decision 5: Selecting an allocation method

Decision 6: Attaching mission center costs to cost objects

5. The two that typically require the most managerial judgment are defining the cost object and the determining cost centers.

Chapter 3

1. The four types of costs are fixed costs, step-function costs, variable costs, and semivariable costs.

2. Profit = Revenue − Expenses. Revenue = Price × volume. Expenses = Fixed costs + Variable costs. Variable costs = Unit variable costs × Volume. Therefore, the basic formula is Profit = $px - (a + bx)$.

3. Unit contribution margin is the difference between price and unit variable costs, or $p - b$. The formula measures the amount that each unit sold contributes to the recovery of fixed costs.

4. It would be unstable if the products had different unit contribution margins. This situation could arise because of either different variable costs per unit or different prices. Different prices can create instability if there are different payers, each using a different reimbursement (or payment) amount. It would not be unstable if each product's unit contribution margin were roughly the same.

5. A contribution income statement is structured as follows:

Revenue
    Less: Variable costs
Equals: Margin
    Less: Fixed costs
Equals: Contribution to overhead
    Less: Overhead
Equals: Surplus (deficit)

Chapter 4

1. This is not necessarily true. If the cost is part of a program or product line and the program or product line is eliminated, the cost will also be eliminated. There may be some time that elapses due to personnel requirements, but the general point remains: a fixed cost can be differential.

2. The $15,000 is a sunk cost. It should play no role in your decision (sorry!). In contrast, the $16,000 tuition for next year is a future cost and should be considered. You need to weigh whether paying $16,000 in tuition (and presumably getting your degree) will improve your job prospects and long-term career goals. If the job being offered to you now is your dream job, well . . .

3. The traditional accounting perspective ignores depreciation as a sunk cost. The more strategic perspective uses depreciation as a surrogate for the ongoing cost of operating the program or department and thus provides a long-term (perhaps only three to five years) perspective on the department's or program's financial viability.

4. The three categories are patient sensitivity, market competition, and switching costs.

5. The other two types of alternative choice decisions are (1) keeping or dropping a product line that is unprofitable on a full-cost basis, and (2) offering a special price.

Chapter 5

1. Stage 1 was discussed in chapter 2. It is the stage in which cost centers are designated and costs are allocated from support centers into mission centers. At the end of stage 1, all costs reside in mission centers. During stage 2, mission center costs are attached to the mission center's products (goods or services). Most hospitals and other health care organizations have done a reasonably good job with stage 1 but need to put greater emphasis on stage 2.

2. In general, this is true. If a mission center works on only one product, it can use a process system in which all of its costs are divided by the number of products it works on. The average cost per product will be a meaningful number because all products are identical.

3. Direct manufacturing costs are those for such items as direct labor and direct materials, as well as other costs that can be attached to a product rather easily. Minutes of technician time for a procedure and reagents in conjunction with a laboratory test are examples. Indirect costs fall into two broad categories: (1) costs that are direct for the mission center but indirect with regard to its products (such as the cost of a supervisor or a scheduler), and (2) costs that were allocated to the mission center from support centers during stage 1. The latter two types of costs are sometimes called manufacturing overhead. (For details and other examples, go back to figure 5.1.)

4. Not all overhead fluctuates with the driver of the rate, such as with machine hours or labor hours. Some overhead costs are related to activities, such as purchasing; other overhead costs are related to material handling or to cleaning and maintenance. The solution requires creating a set of overhead cost pools, whereby the costs in each pool are more or less homogeneous, and then identifying an activity (or cost driver) for each pool that influences (or drives) the use of the costs in that pool.

5. The four general categories are facility sustaining (including such activities as building management, repair and maintenance, security, and grounds maintenance); product sustaining (activities to ensure that products are produced according to specifications, such as process engineering); batch related (activities that are performed each time a

batch of products is manufactured, such as setting up machines or inspections); and unit level (activities that are tied directly to the number of units produced, such as those related to direct labor and materials).

Chapter 6

1. The key activities are designing responsibility centers, selecting new programs, determining cost drivers, budgeting with cost drivers, and reporting on results with cost drivers. The managerial uses are improving cost control (by focusing on cost drivers), motivating key managers, measuring performance, and assigning responsibility to controlling agents

2. A responsibility center is an organizational unit led by a manager who has overall accountability for the unit's performance. There are five types of responsibility centers: revenue centers, standard expense centers, discretionary expense centers, profit centers, and investment centers.

3. A discretionary expense center's budget is fixed for the budgetary period (such as a year). A good example is an accounting department. A standard expense center does not have a fixed budget because its manager cannot control the volume of output requested from it by other responsibility centers. A good example is a hospital laundry department. Because its volume of output is unknown when the budget is prepared, the center's manager is expected to control the cost per unit rather than total costs. A standard expense center's budget is adjusted each reporting period based on the actual volume of output provided. The technique used to do this is a flexible budget (sometimes called a performance budget).

4. The fairness criterion maintains that managers should be held accountable only for those items over which they can exert a reasonable amount of control; it is sometimes characterized as "aligning responsibility with control." An example of its violation was shown in the Newport Medical Associates problem, in which the group practice was asked to be responsible for overhead allocations but could not control them.

5. The four phases are programming, budgeting, operating and measuring, and reporting. During the programming phase, senior management makes a set of decisions that have multiyear consequences. During the budgeting phase, both financial and nonfinancial

agreements about an organization's responsibility centers are reached for the upcoming year. The measuring activity of the operating and measuring phase gathers information on these financial and nonfinancial items, and senior management provides line managers with this information in an organized way during the reporting phase. Line managers are expected to take action on the basis of these reports when the organization's performance is not as planned.

Chapter 7

1. *Goal congruence* is a term borrowed from social psychology that emphasizes the importance of having the goals of each responsibility center manager aligned with the goals of the organization overall. It is important because without goal congruence, a manager may take actions that are in the best interest of his or her responsibility center but not in the best interests of the organization overall.

2. A transfer price is an internal price that is used for transactions between one organizational unit and another. An example in a department of medicine would be the amount that the department pays for a test conducted in the laboratory, such as a complete blood count. Properly designed, transfer prices can give receiving (or purchasing) responsibility centers greater control over costs, thereby enhancing fairness. They also can help ensure that a decision that is good for a given responsibility center is also good for the organization overall, thereby enhancing goal congruence.

3. An "every tub on its own bottom" (ETOB) arrangement is one in which each profit center is an independent entity and is expected to earn a surplus. A cross-subsidization arrangement is one in which the financially strong profit centers (such as cardiovascular surgery) provide subsidies to the financially weaker profit centers (such as pediatrics). An ETOB arrangement can create a "fortress-like" mentality in which there is little cooperation among profit centers even though that cooperation might be desirable. A cross-subsidization arrangement gives rise to the question of which profit centers should subsidize which others and by how much. If not well managed, this approach can lead to antagonism and distrust. Most academic medical centers have a cross-subsidization arrangement because they wish to provide a full line of services to patients and would not be able to do so if they eliminated profit centers that could not earn a surplus because of the nature of the patients they serve.

4. A typical matrix structure in an academic medical center would prob-
    ably have service lines (such as oncology and cardiology) along one
    dimension and departments (such as medicine and surgery) along the
    other. A well-run matrix structure would need a set of transfer prices
    to account for the "buying and selling" activities that take place when
    departments provide physicians (and other resources) to the service
    lines.

5. The three themes are that (1) rewards can be both extrinsic and intrin-
    sic, (2) employees need feedback, and (3) procedural justice is impor-
    tant. If the motivation process is not linked to the responsibility
    accounting system, it is possible that senior management will be
    sending mixed signals to responsibility center managers, thereby
    impeding goal congruence. If, for example, senior management wishes
    its profit centers to engage in entrepreneurial behavior, the motivation
    process must provide appropriate rewards for the risks being taken.

Chapter 8

1. The payback period technique divides the investment amount by the
    annual cash flows to determine the number of years needed to recover
    the investment. It does not consider the time value of money and hence
    does not use a hurdle rate. The net present value technique computes
    the value in today's terms of a project's cash flows and deducts the
    amount of the investment from them to see if the remainder is positive;
    if it is, the project has met or exceeded the organization's hurdle rate.
    The internal rate of return technique determines the effective rate of
    return on the project's cash flows and investment to see if it is equal
    to or greater than the hurdle rate.

2. The process begins with multiplying the interest rate of each source of
    financing by its percent of total liabilities and equity to compute its
    weighted interest rate. These weighted interest rates are then summed
    to give the weighted cost of capital. The trickiest part of this process
    is assigning an interest rate to equity.

3. The organization must make sure that its overall return on assets
    (ROA) is at least equal to its weighted cost of capital (WCC). However,
    because some assets, such as accounts receivable and inventory, do not
    earn a return, the fixed assets must earn a higher rate than the WCC.
    As a result, the organization must determine the rate its fixed assets
    must earn for the overall return on assets to equal the WCC. If the
    return on the fixed assets does not meet or exceed this hurdle rate,

the overall ROA will be below the WCC, and the organization will be atrophying.

4. Risk can be incorporated into a programming decision by (a) increasing the discount rate, (b) shortening the economic life (or using a higher discount rate after a predetermined period, such as five years), (c) giving greater weight to projected cost savings than to projected incremental financial contribution, or a combination of these options. Statistical techniques can help formalize the risk assessment, but they still require judgment and hence cannot be completely accurate.

5. There are many nonquantitative factors that might be included. Examples are (a) regulatory requirements; (b) favoritism shown toward certain managers; and (c) the impact of a project on an organization's strategic goals, such as improving patient services, enhancing the organization's image in its community, or improving physicians' attitudes toward the organization.

Chapter 9

1. Programming (discussed in chapter 8) focuses on decisions that have multiyear consequences, such as the acquisition of a new piece of equipment or the initiation of a new program. Budgeting has a one-year focus. Ideally the budget is a fine-tuning of an organization's programs for a given year, resulting in decisions about the amounts to be spent for each program during the year. The budget also specifies the organizational units that are responsible for carrying out each program.

2. The managerial context for the operating budget has an organizational context and a budgeting context. The former can be viewed in terms of the organization's environment, strategy, and culture; in most instances, it serves to constrain certain budgeting decisions. The budgeting context flows from the organizational context and has four factors: the cost structure, strategic success factors, organizational structure, and motivation process.

3. A revenue-first policy is one whereby the revenue budget is prepared before the expense budget. Preparing the revenue budget first helps provide assurance that a budgeted deficit will be eliminated (or a budgeted surplus will be increased) by reducing expenses rather than by assuming additional revenue. It requires that careful forecasts be made of revenues before expenses are estimated, and then requires that expenses be reduced to achieve the desired surplus.

4. A hospital can build its budget with six budget drivers: price, case mix, volume, resources per case, cost per resource unit, and fixed costs. Each clinical department can forecast its case mix and determine the resources that it intends to use, on average, to treat each case type (or diagnosis-related group [DRG]). Transfer prices can be used to "purchase" these resources (such as a lab test). To incorporate payer mix into the budget, the hospital needs to include estimates of the prices that will be paid by different third-parties (such as Medicare).

5. The five steps are (a) disseminating guidelines, (b) preparing revenue budgets, (c) preparing expense budgets for profit and standard expense centers, (d) preparing expense budgets for discretionary expense centers, and (e) preparing the master budget.

Chapter 10

1. The operating cycle measures the cash-related aspects of an organization's day-to-day operations: purchasing inventory, paying accounts payable, paying salaries and administrative costs, sending out bills, and collecting accounts receivable. The financing cycle measures the cash-related aspects of an organization's borrowing, fixed asset acquisitions, and debt service payments. Both cycles include billing and accounts receivable collections. The revenue cycle expands on the billing and accounts receivable collection activities to include everything from negotiating a contract with a payer to minimizing the denial of claims made in connection with that contract.

2. An organization's financial surplus includes depreciation, which is not a cash outflow, meaning that, other things being equal, the organization will have more cash than its surplus indicates. If the term of the debt is the same as the life of the asset, then the principal payment on the debt will be the same as the amount of depreciation—and therefore the surplus and the net cash inflow will be roughly the same.

3. Leverage = Assets ÷ Equity. By using leverage, an organization can have more assets on its balance sheet than its equity otherwise would permit. In increasing its leverage, which increases its financial risk, an organization must consider its business risk, which relates to the certainty of its cash flows. High business risk means that cash flows are uncertain, such that it would be unwise for an organization to have too much financial risk.

4. A surplus is a financing mechanism. It provides funds for several purposes. The two purposes discussed in the text are (a) to replace fixed
assets as they wear out (when the replacement cost is inflating) and
(b) to finance growth. A surplus also can be used to help finance the
acquisition of new assets and to provide funds for a rainy day.

5. The statement of cash flows is one of three basic financial statements.
It is organized into three areas: operating activities, investing activities,
and financing activities. It explains in a structured way how an
organization managed its cash during an operating period (usually a
year).

Chapter 11

1. A flexible budget adjusts for volume (and sometimes mix) changes
prior to measuring a manager's performance. It contrasts with a fixed
budget, which does not make such an adjustment. It is used primarily
for responsibility centers where the manager cannot control the volume
and mix of the center's outputs. It thus shows how much *should* have
been spent at the actual volume and mix.

2. Variance analysis permits a close examination of the difference between
budgeted and actual information by breaking the difference into such
factors as input efficiency or productivity and wage or unit supply
costs. It typically is used after the flexible budget has been prepared,
with computations having been made using the actual volume and mix
of outputs. It use is appropriate when a manager has responsibility for
the productivity of labor (such as technician minutes per procedure)
and the efficiency of raw materials (such as the amount of reagents
used for a lab test).

3. A good reporting process provides information on a timely basis
(which is not necessarily quickly) and has a hierarchy of information,
beginning at a highly summarized level (for senior management) and
becoming increasingly more detailed (for lower-level managers).

4. Some categories of nonfinancial information (and corresponding
examples) are quality of care (such as percentage of clinical pathways
implemented), prevention (percentage of children receiving immunizations), patient satisfaction (percentage of HMO reenrollments), and
employee satisfaction and growth (percentage of promotions).

5. A spidergram is a way to report nonfinancial (and often financial)
information in a summarized way. It allows management to see at a

glance where it is meeting (or failing to meet) its goals so that discussions can take place with the appropriate managers.

Chapter 12

1. The chapter lists thirteen characteristics. Any three would do. All are important.

2. The responsibility accounting context consists of seven activities: strategy formulation, motivation, conflict management, authority and influence, cultural maintenance, patient (or client) management, and management control. It is important because these activities must fit together and work harmoniously if the organization is to be successful.

3. The eight steps to change are (a) establish a sense of urgency, (b) form a powerful guiding coalition, (c) create a vision, (d) communicate the vision, (e) empower others to act on the vision, (f) plan and create short-term wins, (g) consolidate improvements and produce still more change, and (h) institutionalize new approaches.

4. The six methods for dealing with resistance to change are (a) education and communication, (b) participation and involvement, (c) facilitation and support, (d) negotiation and agreement, (e) manipulation and co-optation, and (f) explicit and implicit coercion.

5. It is best to start a change program by focusing on an effort that has a high impact but is of low difficulty.

SOLUTIONS TO THE PRACTICE CASES

Chapter 1 Practice Case: Central Valley Primary Care Associates

This case gives you an opportunity to think about the kinds of data needed to develop a capitation rate, which means you need to think about estimating morbidity patterns of a population, and the resulting resource requirements, on both an inpatient and an outpatient basis. As the case indicates, not only are there many considerations in developing a rate, but also physician organizations (such as group practices and independent practice associations [IPAs]) frequently do not have, and are not able to obtain easily, the information that they need to undertake an appropriate analysis. If you felt overwhelmed by the complexity of this task, welcome to the world of health care management accounting!

Question 1

There are several strategic issues. First, given Continental's 40 percent market share, Central Valley Primary Care Associates (CVPCA) cannot afford to lose this contract. To do so would have fairly drastic consequences for physician incomes, the number of physicians who affiliate with the IPA, or both.

Second, there is the nature of the contract that is being proposed. Many capitation (or subcapitation) rates are not for all health care services. This one is for primary care, specialist referrals, and inpatient hospitalization care—a fairly broad range of services. It is important to identify the contract's nature early on because it will dictate the kinds of data that Dr. Lopez needs to include in her analysis. If the rate were to cover primary care only, her analysis would be much easier. Because it includes the other two categories of services, she must rely on a broad set of data, much of which are not available to her.

Third, CVPCA consists of many small practices. With 130 physicians in 39 group practices, the average group size is 3.3 physicians. Moreover, with 57 sites, the average number of physicians at each site is 2.3. Coordinating the resource use activities of these physicians is going to be extremely difficult.

Finally, the affiliation with Valley Children's Medical Center (VCMC) is an issue. VCMC is a tertiary care children's hospital with teaching and research programs. That usually means it is high cost. We don't know the exact relationship between CVPCA and VCMC, except that CVPCA "worked closely" with VCMC's physician-hospital organization (PHO). This could be problematic for Dr. Lopez. Either she must build her budget on the assumption that CVPCA's physicians will continue to use VCMC as they have done in the past, or she must assume a different pattern of hospitalization. The former assumption will mean a higher-cost budget, and possibly the loss of the contract. The latter is quite likely to produce some difficulties not only with the physicians but also with the administration of VCMC.

These various relationships are shown schematically in exhibit B.1. Exhibit B.2 depicts the various cost drivers and their controlling agents. Exhibit B.3 shows some cost and price projections.

EXHIBIT B.1   Structure of Relationships

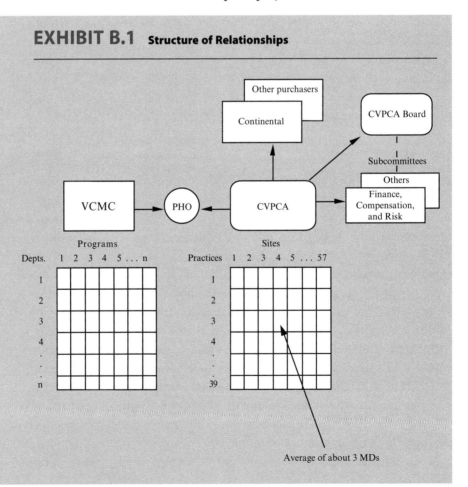

EXHIBIT B.2 Cost Drivers and Controlling Agents

Cost Driver	Controlling Agent(s)
Number of enrollees	Continental
Incidence rate	Enrollee demographics
	CVPCA's preventive activities
Resources needed per case	CVPCA's physicians, via
	Choice of outpatient versus inpatient care
	Choice of provider type (for example, nurse
	practitioners [NPs]) for outpatient care
	Use of specialists
	Lengths of stay when patients are hospitalized
	Tests and procedures used
Cost per resource unit	CVPCA, via
	Rates paid to staff (for example, NPs)
	Rates paid to specialists
	Rates paid to hospitals

EXHIBIT B.3 Cost and Price Projections

Wage and Price List	Amount
LPN wage per minute	$0.25
RN wage per minute	$0.42
Hospital low per diem charge	$1,800
Hospital high per diem charge	$2,000
Hospital low per diem cost	$1,000
Hospital high per diem cost	$1,800

Questions 2 and 3

It is important to understand that you do not have sufficient information to actually develop a budget. Rather, you need to structure the information that is available in the case so that you can identify where additional data are needed. Those data then can be obtained either by request or (more likely) by estimating. Exhibit B.4 provides a rough framework of projections, using only three outpatient activities and three inpatient diagnoses. It indicates where additional data are needed. Some of those places are the following:

- The number of enrollees. We don't know what this figure is, but presumably we could obtain it from Continental. Exhibit B.4 uses 2,000.

- The incidence of different types of outpatient activities. We don't know what the incidence rates are, and we probably could not obtain them easily. We will need to try to get a sense of them from the physicians.

- The incidence of different types of inpatient diagnoses. Again, we do not know what the incidence rates are, and we probably could not obtain them easily. We again will need to try to get a sense of them from the physicians (the hospital could tell us the number of cases of each type, but it could not tell us the incidence in the population).

- The resources needed for each outpatient activity. These can be measured in terms of the kinds of providers, the amount of time each needs to spend, and their hourly rates. We have hourly rates for everyone but physicians, so we will need to use a standard for this. Indeed, if we have some sense from Continental of what it expects to pay, and therefore have a ceiling on the capitation rate, the physicians' hourly rate actually becomes the *dependent* variable. That is, after everything else has been paid, the physicians get what is left. They can figure out how many hours they worked, and derive an hourly rate.

- The resources needed for each inpatient diagnosis, and the unit cost of each resource. Having this information will allow Dr. Lopez to compute the total cost for each resource, and thus the total cost for each inpatient hospitalization. Getting the number of units of each resource will require physician estimates. The cost per unit will need to be negotiated with the hospital. A price list, such as that shown in exhibit B.3, will need to be negotiated with the hospital for all inpatient resources.

This last negotiation can get tricky with regard to the teaching and research missions of the hospital. The physicians in the IPA will need to be ready to encourage the hospital to charge rates that are comparable to those in a community hospital, especially for relatively uncomplicated diagnoses, where a community hospital could do just as good a job as a teaching hospital. Those discussions will not be fun.

Question 4

If the budget has been set up on a spreadsheet, Dr. Lopez will need to extend the number of columns shown in exhibit B.4 to include all outpatient activities and all inpatient diagnoses (or at least most, with a buffer of some sort for the rest). Multiplying out the figures in exhibit B.4 and dividing by the number of enrollees will give a capitation rate.

EXHIBIT B.4 Projections for Capitation Rate

CENTRAL VALLEY PRIMARY CARE ASSOCIATES
Exhibit D. Projections for Capitation Rate

Children in Age Group 5-11
No. Enrollees= 2,000

Service/Diagnosis	Routine Exam (No. of Minutes)	Routine Exam (Total Cost)	CHR Nonsup OM NOS/NEC (No. of Minutes)	CHR (Total Cost)	Abn Clinical Finding NEC (No. of Minutes)	Abn (Total Cost)	Asthma Unspecified (No. of Units)	Asthma (Cost/Unit)	Asthma (Total Cost)	Pneumonia Org. Unspec. (No. of Units)	Pneumonia (Cost/Unit)	Pneumonia (Total Cost)	Convulsions (No. of Units)	Convulsions (Cost/Unit)	Convulsions (Total Cost)
Incidence (an estimate)	70.0%		58.0%		55.0%		19.0%			6.0%			5.0%		
No. of cases	1400		1160		1100		380			120			100		
Resources per case															
Professional Time (minutes)															
PCP	30	62.50													
Specialists															
RN															
LPN	30	8.97													
NP															
Hospital Stay (LOS)															
ICU							0	$1000.00	$0.00	0	$1000.00	$0.00	0	$1000.00	$0.00
Med/Surg							2.5	$900.00	$2250.00	2.9	$900.00	$2610.00	2.5	$900.00	$2250.00
Laboratory															
Special Coag									$0.00	0.00		$0.00	0.11	$129.55	$14.25
Hematology							0.20	$13.38	2.68	2.90	$13.70	39.73	1.62	14.20	23.00
Chemistry							4.18	26.13	109.22	5.75	15.43	88.72	9.90	17.81	176.32
Microbiology							0.21	27.90	5.86	1.53	37.85	57.91	0.47	35.48	16.68
Pathology							0.01	48.60	0.49	0.14	58.65	8.21	0.06	82.83	4.97
Lab processing									0.00	0.04	61.40	2.46	0.08	57.25	4.58
Blood bank									0.00	0.90	36.00	32.40	0.00		0.00
Virology							0.04	47.70	1.91	0.32	49.75	15.92	0.21	50.00	10.50
Endocrinology								42.00	0.00	0.00		0.00	0.00		0.00
Enzymology									0.00	0.00		0.00	0.00		0.00
Nephrology							0.05	25.14	1.26	0.02	120.00	2.40	0.09	100.89	9.08
CRC								30.00	0.00	0.02	37.67	0.75	0.07	58.42	4.09
													0.00		0.00
Total Lab cost per case									$121.41			$248.50			$263.47
Radiology															
Vascular							0.00		0.00	0.03	64.25	1.93	0.10	136.90	13.69
Radiology							0.90	52.54	47.29	1.85	55.20	102.12	0.78	80.54	62.82
Nuclear Medicine							0.01	210.00	2.10	0.02	306.33	6.13	0.04	273.00	10.92
Ultrasound							0.01	165.50	1.66	0.05	131.50	6.58	0.01	164.00	1.64
CT Scans							0.01	472.50	4.73	0.06	440.62	26.44	0.22	472.52	103.95
MRI							0.00			0.01	856.00	8.56	0.21	855.75	179.71
Total Radiology cost per case									$55.77			$151.75			$372.73
Pharmacy							26.50	12.78	$338.67	51.41	12.60	$647.77	30.50	8.40	$256.20
Total hospital									$2765.85			$3658.02			$3142.40

Text annotations:

"Similar estimates need to be made for other outpatient activities. Number of minutes for each provider type, multiplied by the rate per minute"

"The estimates also will need to include the various tests that will be ordered from the laboratory, and the cost per test."

"The estimates also will need to include the various procedures that will be ordered from radiology and the cost per procedure"

"The estimates also will need to include the cost of pharmaceuticals ordered for patients"

CENTRAL VALLEY PRIMARY CARE ASSOCIATES Exhibit D. Projections for Capitation Rate

Wage and Price List	Amount
LPN Wage per minute	$0.22
RN Wage per minute	$0.30
Hospital low per diem charge	$900.00
Hospital high per diem charge	$1,000.00
Hospital low per diem cost	$765.00
Hospital high per diem cost	$850.00
NP Wage per minute	$0.30
Physician Wage per minute	$2.08

One important issue to consider is catastrophic illnesses. Dr. Lopez will have to either propose that these not be included or obtain some stop-loss insurance to protect the IPA. Another critical issue is the nature of the population. If, for example, the children being covered are from certain socioeconomic groups, it is likely that their morbidity patterns will be quite different from those of children from other groups. Without this information, it is difficult to project the incidence rates, yet these rates are crucial to the budget.

Question 5

Meeting the budget will require working closely with the hospital, the specialists, and the 130 primary care providers. This will be no small challenge, given that there are 39 small practices spread over 57 sites. Resource ordering patterns for hospitalized patients will need to be carefully monitored and managed. Indeed, the decision to hospitalize and where to do so also will need to be carefully managed. Collaboration between primary care providers and specialists will become much more important than in the past in that the primary care providers are at risk for the ordering patterns of the specialists. This is more than a "gatekeeper" problem; it entails collaborating with specialists and being involved in their treatment decisions, rather than simply making the referrals.

Chapter 2 Practice Case: Mossy Bog Laboratories

This is a relatively simple exercise in calculating full costs. It requires you to assign costs to cost centers and to determine appropriate bases of allocation for support center costs.

Question 1

In the following table, amounts shown are in thousands:

Department	Initial Costs	Allocated Costs	Total to Allocate	Support Centers Maintenance	Support Centers Administration	Total
Maintenance[a]	$1,160	$0	$1,160			
Administration[b]	2,400	400	2,800	$400		
Sophisticated Tests	8,000			600	$560	$9,160
Simple Tests	4,000			160	2,240	6,400
TOTAL	$15,560			$1,160	$2,800	$15,560

[a]$1,160,000 in maintenance costs ÷ $5,800,000 in depreciation dollars (excluding depreciation dollars in the maintenance department) = $0.20 per depreciation dollar.
[b]$2,800,000 ($2,400,000 + $400,000) in administration costs ÷ 50,000 labor hours (labor hours used only in the sophisticated test and simple test departments) = $56 per labor hour.

Question 2

The next step is to use this information to set prices (or to compare existing revenues with full costs). Specifically, the organization would need to estimate the total number of tests of each type and divide total costs by that figure to get a cost per test. It would then need to mark up this cost by a percentage to obtain the profit (or surplus) it required.

Chapter 3 Practice Case A: Huntington Hospital

This is a relatively basic case on cost behavior. You need to analyze how costs have changed over a three-month period so you can construct some cost equations.

Question 1

A cost equation requires analyzing each cost for its fixed components, variable components, or both. The results are shown here, followed by the calculations for each item.

Item	Type of Cost	Behavior
Food sold	Variable	$6.00 per meal
Staff salaries and fringe benefits	Semivariable	$11,500 + $1.00 per meal
Rent and depreciation	Fixed	$4,000 per month
Utilities and other	Semivariable	$300 + $0.60 per meal

Food Sold

This is relatively easy. For each month, it is the total cost divided by the number of meals. For example, in December, it is $18,000 \div 3,000 = \$6$ per meal

Staff Salaries and Fringe Benefits

This calculation is a bit more complicated, requiring two equations and two unknowns:

1. Begin with the total cost formula:

$$TC = a + bx$$

2. Apply it to December, as follows:

$$\$14,500 = a + b(3,000); a = \$14,500 - 3,000b$$

3. Then apply it to January, as follows:

$$\$16,500 = a + b(5,000)$$

4. Substitute from the December equation, as follows:

$$\$16,500 = (\$14,500 - 3,000b) + 5,000b$$

5. Solve for b, as follows:

$$\$2,000 = 2,000b; b = \$1$$

6. Solve for *a:*

$$a = \$14,500 - (3,000 \times \$1) = \$11,500$$

Rent and Depreciation

This is a flat $4,000 per month.

Utilities and Other

This calculation requires following the same approach as that used with salaries and fringe benefits:

$$TC = a + bx, \text{ or } \$2,100 = a + b(3,000); a = \$2,100 - 3,000b$$

$$\$3,300 = a + b(5,000); \ \$3,300 = \$2,100 - 3,000b + 5,000b$$

$$\$1,200 = 2,000b; b = \$0.60$$

$$a = \$2,100 - (3,000 \times \$0.60); a = \$300$$

The cost equation is the sum of all of the individual elements, or

$$TC = (11,500 + 4,000 + 300) + (6.00 + 1.00 + 0.60)x$$

$$TC = 15,800 + 7.60x$$

Question 2

The analysis can begin with the breakeven formula:

$$px = a + bx$$

During February, x was 8,000; a was $15,800; and b was $7.60. Thus, the formula can be set up as follows:

$$p(8,000) = \$15,800 + (\$7.60 \times 8,000). \textbf{ Therefore, } p$$
$$= \$9.575, \textbf{ or (rounded)} \$9.58.$$

An alternative—and much easier—approach is simply to divide the total costs for February by the total meals served: $76,600 ÷ 8,000 = $9.58.

The $9.58 is valid only for February. In December, the figure is $12.87 ($38,600 ÷ 3,000), and in January, it is $10.76 ($53,800 ÷ 5,000). The decline from December to January to February is due to the cafeteria's fixed costs being spread over a greater number of meals each month.

Question 3

Finding the breakeven volume requires turning the equation around. We know that

$$px = a + bx,$$

$$\text{or } \$12.00x = \$15,800 + \$7.60x,$$

$$\text{or } \$4.40x = \$15,800$$

Therefore, the breakeven volume is $15,800 ÷ $4.40 = 3,591 meals.

Chapter 3 Practice Case B: Jiao Tong Hospital

Question 1

Mr. Xiong arrived at a breakeven of 53,645 visits by dividing the total of direct fixed and allocated fixed costs by the weighted average unit contribution margin [¥2,185,000 ÷ (¥73.08 − ¥32.35)]. He made several key assumptions in doing the computation, however. In large part, these assumptions take the form of givens, or constants, in his analysis, but in fact these "constants" may not be constant at all. For example:

• He assumed that fixed costs are truly fixed over the full range of operations.

• Related to this, he assumed that there are no capacity constraints, yet Dr. Cheng indicated that she cannot accommodate more patient visits unless she has more space, which would seem to imply a need to increase fixed costs.

• He assumed that there are no step-function costs, only fixed and variable costs. Both Dr. Min and Dr. Chao expressed concern that the expansion of their programs would involve some step-function costs.

• Similarly, he assumed that the unit variable costs would remain the same into the future, which would require constant efficiency and constant factor prices. All three of the physician coordinators are concerned about price increases for supplies.

• Related to this, he assumed a constant "sales mix." Any change in the mix of patients in the programs—that is, more in one, less in another, or both—will change the aggregate revenue and variable cost figures on which his chart is based. Both Dr. Min and Dr. Chao suggested changes that would have an impact on mix.

- His revenue projections assume no change in per-visit fees, yet Ms. Furong is considering an across-the-board increase.

- He has assumed that breakeven with a comfortable margin of safety is sufficient, whereas Ms. Furong sees the need for a surplus.

Considering the objections of the participants at the meeting, it is easy to see where Mr. Xiong's failure to check with physician coordinators in advance about his assumptions, or to make his assumptions explicit, has gotten him in some trouble.

Question 2

In answering this question, we must incorporate the information Mr. Xiong obtained at the meeting. Specially, the additional fixed costs (actually step-function costs) are as follows:

Pediatrics	¥62,000
Internal medicine	65,000
Total	¥127,000
Previous fixed cost level	1,385,000
New fixed cost level	¥1,512,000

Additions to unit variable costs (assumes all variable costs are supplies, which probably is not the case):

Obstetrics and gynecology	¥30.00 × 1.05 = ¥31.50
Pediatrics	¥20.00 × 1.05 = ¥21.00
Internal medicine	¥43.00 × 1.05 = ¥45.15

The across-the-board increase in fees:

Obstetrics and gynecology	¥80.00 × 1.10 = ¥88.00
Pediatrics	¥65.00 × 1.10 = ¥71.50
Internal medicine	¥75.00 × 1.10 = ¥82.50

Change in patient visits:

Obstetrics and gynecology	No change
Pediatrics	From 17,280 to 21,280
Internal Medicine	From 23,100 to 27,100

Exhibit B.5 incorporates these revisions in the same format used in exhibit 3B.1 in the case. The exhibit shows that the hospital will be considerably better off as a result of these proposed changes. In fact, the figures are almost too good to be true, and one must ask how the program managers arrived at their 4,000-visit-increase figures. They constitute a 15 to 20 percent increase for each program, which might not be achievable. Moreover, although the 62,180 visits are (barely) within the capacity constraints of the hospital, an assumption has been made that no new step-function costs (other than nurse practitioners) will be needed to support the additional 8,000 visits.

We should also remember that this analysis assumes an across-the-board increase of 5 percent in variable costs—that is, that all variable costs are supplies. Just because supplies are subject to this sort of increase does not mean that other variable cost items will be subject to some increases. A more precise analysis of unit variable costs probably is needed.

You may have treated the allocated fixed costs as unique to the individual programs, which of course they are not. Each program's share depends on the allocation basis (square meters here, but it doesn't need to stay that way). That is, the breakeven volume for any given program could be changed simply by changing the way that fixed costs are allocated, which, of course, would lead to very unstable results. The dilemma is that fixed costs cannot be treated in the aggregate, either, because a change in mix will change the weighted average unit contribution margin, and hence the breakeven figure.

Question 3

This is a pretty simple example of a breakeven analysis with multiple products and the use of a contribution income statement. Even before the changes in assumptions, internal medicine was making a contribution to the coverage of fixed costs; therefore, eliminating the department in the short run would be a mistake. Over the longer run, we need to be asking whether some other program should be initiated that could cover its fair share of allocated fixed costs.

In this regard, we need to bear in mind that using the basis of square meters is an extremely unsophisticated way of allocating these costs, which no doubt have to do with more than just space. However, the question has become somewhat moot because, with the changes in assumptions, internal medicine now is earning a small profit over its allocated costs, and the outpatient units as a whole are earning more than the ¥300,000 that Ms. Furong says she needs for the painting and minor renovations. All looks good, assuming, of course, that the new estimates are reasonable.

EXHIBIT B.5   Contribution Analysis with New Assumptions (in RMB)

JIAO TONG HOSPITAL
EXHIBIT A. Contribution Analysis with New Assumptions

	Obstetrics & Gynecology	Pediatrics	Internal Medicine	Aggregate	Breakeven	Capacity Utilization
Data from Case Exhibit 1						
Visits	13,800	17,280	23,100	54,180	53,645	86.0%
Per visit fees	80.00	65.00	75.00	$73.08		
Per visit variable costs	30.00	20.00	43.00	32.35		
Revenue	¥1,104,000	¥1,123,200	¥1,732,500	¥3,959,700		
Variable costs	414,000	345,600	993,300	1,752,900		
Contribution to fixed and allocated costs	¥690,000	¥777,600	¥739,200	¥2,206,800		
Fixed costs	350,000	470,000	565,000	1,385,000		
Contribution to allocated costs	¥340,000	¥307,600	¥174,200	¥821,800		
Allocated costs (1)	215,000	285,000	300,000	800,000		
Original surplus (deficit)	¥125,000	¥22,600	(¥125,800)	¥21,800		
New Assumptions						
Fee increase factor	1.10	1.10	1.10			
Variable cost increase factor	1.05	1.05	1.05			
Expected additional visits		4,000	4,000			
Expected additional step-function costs		¥62,000	¥65,000			
Changes with new assumptions						
Patient visits at full capacity				63,000		
Actual number of patient visits	13,800	21,280	27,100	62,180	50,151	98.7%
Fee per visit (after discounts and bad debt	88.00	71.50	82.50	79.96		
Net revenue	¥1,214,400	¥1,521,520	¥2,235,750	¥4,971,670		
Variable cost per visit	31.50	21.00	45.15	33.86		
Total variable cost	¥434,700	¥446,880	¥1,223,565	¥2,105,145		
Contribution to program fixed costs	¥779,700	¥1,074,640	¥1,012,185	¥2,866,525		
Less: Program fixed costs	350,000	532,000	630,000	1,512,000		
Contribution to allocated fixed costs	¥429,700	¥542,640	¥382,185	¥1,354,525		
Less: Allocated fixed costs (1)	215,000	285,000	300,000	800,000		
Surplus (Deficit)	¥214,700	¥257,640	¥82,185	¥554,525		
Economics of new providers						
Incremental revenue		¥286,000	¥330,000			
Incremental variable costs		84,000	180,600			
Incremental contribution		¥202,000	¥149,400			
Incremental fixed costs		62,000	65,000			
Incremental contribution		¥140,000	¥84,400			
Breakeven analysis for a new provider						
Fixed cost		62,000	65,000			
UCM		¥50.50	¥37.35			
Breakeven number of visits		1,228	1,740			

Note 1. Basis of allocation is square meters
All figures except visits in RMB Yuan

Even with these assumptions, internal medicine is just barely covering its allocated costs. If instead of 27,100 visits, it has only 24,900 visits (an increase of 1,800 over Mr. Xiong's initial assumption), it will just barely cover its fixed plus allocated costs. Anything less, and it is a full-cost loser, albeit with a contribution of over ¥300,000.

Chapter 4 Practice Case: Narcolarm

This case assists you in developing your skills in cost-volume-profit (CVP) analysis and also gives you an opportunity to examine some of the issues that arise in the context of an outsourcing decision. The outsourcing decision is interesting in that it can be turned into a CVP analysis.

Question 1

Here are the calculations to determine how may units Narcolarm must produce and sell to break even:

$$px = a + bx$$

$$\$10.00x = \$300,000 + \$8.50x$$

$$\$1.50x = \$300,000$$

$$x = 200,000 \text{ units}$$

Here is how to calculate the number of units that must be produced and sold to earn a profit of $60,000 before taxes:

$$\$1.50x = \$300,000 + \$60,000$$

$$x = 240,000 \text{ units}$$

Question 2

To find out what Dr. Black should charge per Narcolarm, we have

$$p(25,000) = \$300,000 + \$8.50(25,000)$$

$$p = \$20.50$$

Question 3

This is a tricky decision, and one that probably will require some market surveys. Note, however, that doubling the price (from $10.00 to $20.50) lowers the breakeven from 200,000 units to only 25,000 units. Dr. Black needs to determine (1) how many potential buyers there are for the

Narcolarm, and (2) how price sensitive they are. If the potential demand is low (say, 25,000 units) but buyers are unwilling to pay $20.00 for the device, she may not have much of a business.

These are matters that Dr. Black might have considered before starting the business, and certainly any smart investor would ask about them before investing in the company.

Question 4

From a purely financial perspective, the offer lowers the original breakeven volume of 200,000 units, and thus is attractive. Calculations are as follows:

$$\text{New fixed costs} = \$307,500$$

$$\text{New variable cost per unit} = \$8.00$$

$$\text{New unit contribution margin} = \$2.00$$

$$\text{New breakeven} = 153,750 \text{ units} \, (\$307,500 \div \$2.00)$$

Alternatively, because fixed costs are reduced by $7,500 and unit variable costs are reduced by $0.50, the breakeven volume for this offer is 15,000 units ($7,500 ÷ $0.50). If Dr. Black were selling more than 15,000 units, it would make sense to subcontract.

Question 5

Some of the issues Dr. Black should consider are

• Will the quality be comparable?

• What is the term of the contract, and will next year's price be $7,500 or something else?

• What is the rate of inflation, and how does it compare to the projected price increases in the contract?

• Are there ceilings on volume?

• How accurate is the projected decrease in variable costs?

Question 6

A great deal of the success of Dr. Black's venture depends on the demand for the Narcolarm. How many potential customers (individuals who get sleepy while driving) are there? How many other people might be candidates to buy the device (for friends, for example)? If 25,000 such people can be induced to pay $20 or so for the device, it looks as though she has a going concern. She needs to convince these people that $20 is not too much. Considering the stakes for the customers, she should not have too difficult a time doing that, but the big question is the actual number of people who need assistance with staying awake while driving.

Chapter 5 Practice Case A: Lincoln Dietary Department

This case allows you to make a relatively simple foray into the arena of activity-based costing (ABC). As you will see, the cost implications of a change from a single overhead rate to multiple overhead rates with multiple cost drivers can be significant.

Question 1

The predetermined overhead rate can be computed as follows:

Budgeted direct material cost:	
Regular meals ($2.25 × 300,000 meals)	$675,000
Special meals ($4.00 × 50,000 meals)	200,000
Total materials	$875,000
Total overhead	$1,533,000

The overhead rate is therefore $1.752 ($1,533,000 ÷ $875,000) per direct material dollar.

	Regular Meal	Special Meal
Cost per meal:		
Direct materials	$2.25	$4.00
Direct labor	3.20	3.70
Overhead (1.752 × Direct materials)	3.94	7.00
TOTAL COST	$9.39	$14.70
Markup (20% of total cost)	1.88	2.94
PRICE	$11.27	$17.64

Question 2

Here we begin by computing a cost per unit for each cost driver, as follows:

Activity	Cost Driver	Budgeted Cost	Budgeted Units of Activity	Cost per Unit
Purchasing	Purchase orders (POs)	$527,000	620	$850.00
Material handling	Setups	720,000	36,000	$20.00
Quality control	Batches	195,000	13,000	$15.00
Packaging	Packaging hours	91,000	14,000	$6.50

We next need to determine how many units each type of meal uses, what the associated cost is, and what the resulting overhead is, as follows:

Cost Driver	Cost per Unit	Regular Meals Number of Units	Cost	Special Meals Number of Units	Cost
POs	$850.00	120[a]	$102,000	500[b]	$425,000
Setups	$20.00	6,000[c]	120,000	30,000[d]	600,000
Batches	$15.00	3,000[c]	45,000	10,000[d]	150,000
Hours	$6.50	12,000[e]	78,000	2,000[f]	13,000
TOTAL OVERHEAD COST			$345,000		$1,188,000
OVERHEAD PER MEAL			$1.15		$23.76

[a]300,000 meals ÷ 2,500 meals per PO = 120 POs.
[b]50,000 meals ÷ 100 meals per PO = 500 POs.
[c]300,000 meals ÷ 100 meals per batch = 3,000 batches; 3,000 batches × 2 setups per batch = 6,000 setups.
[d]50,000 meals ÷ 5 meals per batch = 10,000 batches; 10,000 batches × 3 setups per batch = 30,000 setups.
[e]4 hours ÷ 100 meals × 300,000 meals = 12,000 hours.
[f]4 hours ÷ 100 meals × 50,000 meals = 2,000 hours.

We now can compute the total cost of a meal and the price, as follows:

	Regular Meal	Special Meal
Direct materials	$2.25	$4.00
Direct labor	3.20	3.70
Overhead per meal (from previous computations)	1.15	23.76
TOTAL	$6.60	$31.46
Markup (20% of total cost)	1.32	6.29
PRICE	$7.92	$37.75

Question 3

It is somewhat more complicated to use the ABC system, but if the numbers for the various overhead cost pools are accurate, the differences in cost per meal and in the resulting prices are quite dramatic. If the price of regular meals falls by about 30 percent and the price of special meals increases by about 114 percent, the resulting figures would seem to coincide more closely with the nurses' perceptions of what the meals should cost. Given that most of the work to develop the ABC system is a one-time effort, it would appear that the dietary department should adopt it.

Chapter 5 Practice Case B: Owen Hospital

This practice case follows from the discussion in the text. This case is not quite an ABC analysis because it doesn't use different cost drivers for different indirect cost pools. However, it does show that increased precision can be gained without fully implementing an ABC system.

Question 1

The computations are contained in exhibit B.6. As this exhibit indicates, whereas the average cost of an X-ray is $81.28 (as shown in exhibit 5B.2), a simple X-ray costs only $68.55, whereas a complex X-ray costs $144.93. Similar differences exist for the laboratory and inpatient care.

The reason for the differences is the same for each cost center. Exhibit 5B.4 showed that the labor and material costs differ, but the overhead also differs. Although the cost drivers may be questioned, Mr. McCarthy has determined that departmental administrative costs should be divided based on the relative proportion of units (X-rays, tests, or days). Depreciation is divided based on space occupied, as is housekeeping. Maintenance costs are divided based on the proportion of maintenance hours, and hospital A&G costs are divided based on the proportion of salary dollars.

Clearly, there can be other ways to assign these costs to a test type (or cost center within, say, radiology or pathology). Whatever approach is used, the result will almost always be a different total cost per type of test, which, when divided by the number of tests, results in a different cost per test. In effect, we have unbundled each of the three departments into two separate departments, or, in cost accounting terminology, divided a heterogeneous cost center into two more-homogeneous cost centers.

Exhibit B.7 shows the results for the two patients in question. As it indicates, patient 1 now costs $4,877.77, whereas patient 2 costs $7,930.48. This, of course, is a quite sizable difference from the results in exhibit 5B.3 of the case. With overhead aligned with cost drivers (for example, a type of X-ray), it seems safe to conclude that it is more accurate than the results in exhibit 5B.3.

Question 2

The decisions that Dr. Leddy might make with this new information differ considerably from those she would have made with the previous information. It also seems clear that the improved precision has led to an ability to better understand costs.

EXHIBIT B.6 Computing Full Cost per Unit with 3 Departments Unbundled

OWEN HOSPITAL

EXHIBIT A. Computing Full Cost Per Unit with Three Departments Unbundled

	Labor & Material Cost/Unit 1	Number of Units 2	Directly Attachable Direct Cost 3	Dept. Admin Cost 4	% of Space 5	Depreciation Cost 6	Housekeeping Cost 7	% of Maint. Hours 8	Maintenance Cost 9	% of Salary Dollars 10	A&G Cost 11	Total Cost 12	Cost per Unit 13
Radiology													
Simple x-ray	40.00	25,000	$1,000,000	$333,333	40%	$56,000	$25,720	20%	$29,540	80%	$269,057	$1,713,650	$68.55
Complex x-ray	70.00	5,000	350,000	66,667	60%	84,000	38,580	80%	118,160	20%	67,264	724,671	$144.93
Total		30,000	$1,350,000	$400,000		$140,000	$64,300		$147,700		$336,321	$2,438,321	
Laboratory													
Simple test	9.00	125,000	$1,125,000	$395,833	30%	$48,000	$20,850	40%	$69,018	60%	$232,061	$1,890,763	$15.13
Complex test	16.00	25,000	400,000	79,167	70%	112,000	48,650	60%	103,527	40%	154,708	898,051	$35.92
Total		150,000	$1,525,000	$475,000		$160,000	$69,500		$172,545		$386,769	$2,788,814	
Inpatient Care													
Ward	700.00	6,000	$4,200,000	$1,028,571	30%	$105,000	$49,680	20%	$31,650	70%	$200,111	$5,615,012	$935.84
Intensive Care Unit	1,600.00	1,000	1,600,000	171,429	70%	245,000	115,920	80%	126,600	30%	85,762	2,344,710	$2,344.71
Total		7,000	$5,800,000	$1,200,000		$350,000	$165,600		$158,250		$285,873	$7,959,723	

Notes

1 Computed based on time and motion study. See Exhibit 4.
2 Computed from departmental records. See Exhibit 4.
3 Equals column 1 * column 2.
4 Divided between unit types (e.g., tests) based on proportion of units.
5 Obtained from hospital records. See Exhibit 4,
6 From allocation in Exhibit 1, assigned based on percent of square feet occupied.
7 Same as 6.
8 Obtained from hospital records. See Exhibit 4.
9 From allocation in Exhibit 1, assigned based on percent of maintenance hours.
10 Computed from departmental records. See Exhibit 4.
11 From allocation in Exhibit 1, assigned based on percent of salary dollars.
12 Sum of columns 3, 4, 6, 7, 9, 11.
13 Column 12 divided by column 2

EXHIBIT B.7 Attaching Costs to 2 Patients (Using the ABC-Like System)

	Unit Cost	Unit	Patient 1 Number of Units	Patient 1 Total Cost	Patient 2 Number of Units	Patient 2 Total Cost
Radiology						
Simple X-ray	$68.55	X-ray	2	$137.09	0	$0.00
Complex X-ray	$144.93	X-ray	0	0.00	2	289.87
Laboratory						
Simple test	$15.13	Test	4	60.50	0	0.00
Complex test	$35.92	Test	0	0.00	4	143.69
Inpatient Care						
Ward	$935.84	Day	5	4,679.18	3	2,807.51
Intensive care unit	$2,344.71	Day	0	0.00	2	4,689.42
				$4,876.77		$7,930.48

One clear conclusion is that although both patients had the same DRG, their treatment patterns differed considerably, leading to quite different costs. Although it is possible that severity differences existed for these patients, it also is likely that the two physicians have different practice patterns, and Dr. Leddy no doubt would want to discuss the cases with the physicians in question to determine the causes of the different resource use patterns.

Question 3

If this additional information accounts for the dramatic changes in costs, the question now is whether Dr. Leddy needs to think about making the data even more precise. "Simple" and "complex" may not be sufficiently robust categories for truly understanding costs, and some additional analysis may be useful. How deeply one goes into this analytical effort depends on how much the information changes from one iteration to the next. Perhaps the categories of "simple," "moderate," and "complex" will suffice. Or perhaps there needs to be a cost for each type of test, procedure, and day that is delivered by a department. The goal, of course, is to get a reasonable balance between the macrolevel data that Dr. Leddy now has and the extremely microlevel data that would be possible if each test, procedure, and day were looked at separately. Where to draw the line is a tricky issue.

Chapter 6 Practice Case: Akron Public Health Department

This case on the use of "profit centers" in a nonprofit organization concerns a situation in which output cannot be measured by revenue. It demonstrates how establishing a profit center through the use of "shadow revenue" can create an incentive to improve performance.

Question 1

The basic fact is that the new system seems to have produced impressive results: 100 percent of the vehicles needed are now available each day, compared with less than 50 percent two years earlier, and about $3 million was saved.

One important reason, of course, was the improvement in labor-management relations brought about by the creation and active use of labor-management committees. The case does not focus on this aspect, but it must be kept in mind. From a control viewpoint, however, the basic change was that output was measured and compared with costs, so that a "profit" or "loss" could be calculated for each shop. Without such a measure, it would have been impossible to measure output in shops because of the variety of jobs done in each of them. Labeling the ratio of output to input as a "productivity factor" tied the system to productivity, even though the label was not strictly accurate.

The output measure was not completely comparable to the measure of input, or cost. It was based on the price charged for rebuilt items. Also, the outside price was undoubtedly built up from all costs plus an allowance for profit, whereas the profit center had no profit, there was no depreciation on the building, and overhead costs were not included.

As a result, the costs accumulated for jobs done inside understate the full costs of doing these jobs. Thus, if an outside shop will do a job for even less, the city would be better off outsourcing it, subject to certain provisos: (1) the quality and delivery time of the outside shop must be satisfactory; (2) the outside price should be lower than the incremental costs of doing the job inside; and (3) this policy must not create serious labor opposition (unions often seek to prohibit such a policy).

None of the defects in the system is particularly important if the measure accomplishes its aim—that is, to motivate employees. Overall, the message is that with its inherent cost advantage (not all overhead; no profit) the city shop should ordinarily be able to do the job less expensively than an outside shop. If this turns out not to be the case, something may be wrong. Competition is a powerful force.

Question 2

Job records and individual performance records were probably discontinued to focus on the new system. Employees had less paperwork to process than before, a selling point of the new system. Moreover, the detailed information evidently was not used for control, and there was no way that it could have been used in the absence of output information.

In due time, it may be desirable to reinstate record keeping, at least the record of costs for individual jobs. The focus now is on the shop as a whole. If performance is inadequate, the cause cannot be traced to individuals or to individual jobs. In a regular garage, individual job records would be kept, and they would be used for this purpose. Ordinarily, however, records of each employee's output would not be kept, although such information as idle time might be collected.

More generally, several factors seem to be at work:

- The Hawthorne effect (people perform differently when they are being watched)
- Peer pressure
- Banding together against an "outside enemy"
- The elimination of the threat associated with raised standards (note the experience with the brake shop)
- The elimination of management-labor tension

Question 3

The case focuses on the system that Mr. Edwin used *within* the Bureau of Motor Equipment (BME). This is a service organization. As the text indicates, if departments receiving services are charged for those services, there is a better record of the full cost of carrying out their programs. More important, a buyer-seller relationship is created that can have good effects. If the purchasing departments are permitted to contract outside, for example, there is additional pressure on the BME to make its costs competitive. Even if outside contracting is prohibited, the purchasing departments are likely to put pressure on the shop to keep its costs down. When they receive these services without charge against their own respective budgets, they have no incentive to worry about the costs.

The real test will come when, even if all the productivity factors exceed 1.00, the department is bumping up against the limits of its budget ceiling. At that point, "profit" as defined here is not enough; instead, some hard choices must be made for which the profit measure will not be particularly useful:

- Cut back on the number of jobs (outsourcing will not work now, assuming the contractor's cost must be covered by the budget).

- Delay work, attempting to have some (probably expensive) jobs carried forward into the next fiscal year.

- Devise some new approaches to carrying out the jobs (adopting new and improved technology, for example).

- Reduce unit prices of materials (by, for example, using reconditioned parts) or of labor (by hiring less skilled and therefore lower-wage employees).

- Improve efficiency. To the extent that efficiency—especially of an *individual worker*—becomes an issue, it may be necessary to adopt a system that focuses on more detailed units of activity than the departments contained in exhibit 6.1. This could, in the end, lead the BME back to a focus on individual workers or jobs.

Chapter 7 Practice Case: Valley Hospital

This is a fairly basic case on transfer pricing that illustrates the fact that sometimes fairness and goal congruence collide, and you have to choose between them. You should have little or no trouble making the computations, so most of your thinking can focus on the issues and how to resolve them.

Question 1

You may have made a variety of assumptions about the number of tests, variable costs of nurses, and so forth. The differential figures on a per-test basis, however, appear to be as follows:

	Ambulatory Care Division	Lab Division	Hospital Overall
Option 1: Buy from Hospital Lab Division			
Revenue	$22.00	$12.00	$22.00
Variable costs	12.00	4.00	4.00
Contribution	$10.00	$8.00	$18.00
Option 2: Buy from Biolab			
Revenue	$22.00	$0.00	$22.00
Variable cost	9.00	0.00	9.00
Contribution	$13.00	$0.00	$13.00

Question 2

The problem depicted by the figures in this table is an absence of goal congruence. Specifically, although Dr. Martin could improve the profits of her division by having complete blood counts (CBCs) conducted by Biolab, the overall profits of Valley Hospital would decline if she were to do so. That is, the hospital pays $4 out of pocket for every CBC done by the laboratory division. All other costs are fixed. Therefore, each CBC done by the laboratory division reduces the hospital's surplus by $4.

If Dr. Martin buys CBCs from Biolab, the hospital incurs an incremental cost of $9 instead of $4, and its surplus therefore is reduced by $9. That happens because for CBCs purchased from Biolab, the hospital pays a price that includes not just variable costs but also a portion of Biolab's fixed costs plus a profit margin. Clearly the hospital would prefer to have Dr. Martin purchase CBCs from the laboratory division rather than from the freestanding laboratory.

The problem is that when she purchases a CBC from the hospital's laboratory division, Dr. Martin is charged $12, not $4. As a result, for each CBC she purchases from the laboratory division, her division's surplus falls by $12, as compared to only a $9 decline if she purchases a CBC from the freestanding laboratory.

In summary, permitting Dr. Martin to purchase from outside the hospital (which fairness would allow) increases her division's surplus but reduces the hospital's overall surplus (thereby creating a *goal congruence* problem). Forcing her to buy from the laboratory division maximizes the hospital's overall surplus but reduces the surplus of her division (thereby creating a *fairness* problem). Because she is paid a bonus, requiring her to buy from the laboratory division also reduces her bonus.

Question 3

As the text discusses, this is a tricky matter. The standard answer is to require that transfer prices be at market, and market seems pretty clear in this case. It may be less clear for other tests and procedures, however, especially those that are more esoteric. Moreover, insisting that the transfer price for a CBC be at market removes control from the laboratory division, and one might argue that because it is a profit center, it should be free to charge any price it wishes.

Thus, the real question for Mr. Black is whether he wants to intervene in these sorts of decisions or leave them up to the profit center managers. Of course, leaving them up to the profit center managers may result in the hospital's surplus being less than it would otherwise be, so there is a cost to the hands-off approach. The benefit of such an approach is that over time, profit center managers will probably work out their differences, leaving Mr. Black free to spend his time on other matters. If he intervenes, he may find that a great deal of his time is occupied with resolving these sorts of disputes.

Chapter 8 Practice Case: Erie Hospital

This case requires several present value calculations to give you some practice in the technique. The case also deals with questions of sunk costs, the weighted cost of capital, and the appropriate interest rate to use for donated funds.

Question 1

For a discount rate of 5 percent, we need to extrapolate the present value factor using the midpoint between 4 percent and 6 percent. When we do so, the investment is financially feasible, as follows:

$$\text{Annual cash flows} = \$60,000$$

$$\text{Economic life} = 10 \text{ years}$$

$$\text{Net investment amount} = \$300,000$$

$$\text{Rate of return} = 20\%$$

$$\text{Net present value} = (\$60,000 \times 4.193) - \$300,000$$

$$\text{Net present value} = \$251,520 - \$300,000$$

$$\text{Net present value} = \$(48,480)$$

The investment is not financially feasible.

At a discount rate of 5 percent, the net present value can be calculated as follows:

$$\text{Annual cash flows} = \$60,000$$

$$\text{Economic life} = 10 \text{ years}$$

$$\text{Net investment amount} = \$300,000$$

$$\text{Rate of return} = 5\%$$

$$\text{Net present value} = (\$60,000 \times 7.736) - \$300,000$$

$$\text{Net present value} = \$464,160 - \$300,000$$

$$\text{Net present value} = \$164,160$$

The internal rate of return (IRR) can be calculated as follows:

Net investment ÷ Annual cash flows = Present value factor

$300,000 ÷ $60,000 = 5.000

Economic life = 10 years

Internal rate of return = 15%

The present value factor that lies at the intersection of the 10-year row and the 15 percent column of table 8A.2 is 5.019.

Question 2

The appropriate rate to use is the hurdle rate or, more specifically, the hurdle rate after the additional borrowing takes place. This raises the question of how to calculate the weighted cost of capital.

The key point here is that, as the chapter discusses, donated funds generally are not free. First, there is usually some fundraising cost associated with donations. Second, donors may expect that the earnings on their funds, but not the principal, are to be used; under these circumstances, the rate of return must be equivalent to the interest that can be earned on the funds. Finally, in an inflationary economy, unless donated funds earn a rate of return equivalent to inflation, their purchasing power will be eroded. The interest rate used therefore should be at least equal to inflation, and possibly should reflect the opportunity cost of the funds. Let's use a rate of 10 percent, a reasonable amount for a conservatively invested portfolio of funds. The result is the following weighted cost of capital:

	Percentage of Total	Average Interest Rate	Weighted Interest Rate
Debt	40.0%	12.0%	4.8%
Equity	60.0%	10.0%	6.0%
Total	100.0%		10.8%

Given the arbitrary nature of these computations, using 11 percent as the weighted cost of capital would serve the purpose. We might even use 12 percent if the organization were expecting to take on additional debt at a higher interest rate during the coming year. Alternatively, if the cost of debt were declining, we might lower the rate to 10 percent. The result would be a figure that is somewhat higher than 4.8 percent but not as high as 20 percent, and also not as high as the 15 percent IRR on Dr. Michaels's proposal.

Question 3

The mistake came about because the economic life was estimated at ten years when in fact it was only two years. If Dr. Michaels's proposed equipment had an economic life of only two years, it would have an internal rate of return of less than 1 percent, as the following calculations show:

Net investment ÷ Annual cash flows = Present value factor

$300,000 ÷ $60,000 = 5.000

Economic life = 2 years

The present value factor that lies at the intersection of the two-year row and the 1 percent column is 1.970. Therefore, the internal rate of return is less than 1 percent. If a two-year economic life had been used for the previous request, that request would not have been financially feasible either.

The fact that a mistake was made in the past does not change the conclusion that the new investment is financially feasible at 15 percent, *assuming* that the economic life and cash flows have been estimated accurately. The past decision is a sunk cost and should not be incorporated into the calculations for the decision at hand.

What is relevant here, however, is Dr. Michaels's ability to estimate economic lives. Dr. Larson should question the ten-year estimate carefully to satisfy himself that it is as accurate as possible. No matter how much he questions Dr. Michaels, though, it is impossible to predict the future with certainty, and thus a similar mistake may be made again.

Question 4

The hospital should consider a variety of nonquantitative factors in this decision: product quality, competition, researcher satisfaction, image as a hospital with the latest in technology, and others. Indeed, it is nonquantitative factors that usually tip the scales when a choice is being made between replacement technology and new technology or between research technology and technology for a support center, such as the laundry department. Nevertheless, if the hospital has the funds to invest, and if it is convinced that the estimates of cash flows and economic lives are accurate, then an investment that is financially feasible in the laundry department has just as much financial payoff as one in a clinical care department.

The process becomes complicated when the investment in, say, the laundry department has an internal rate of return that is higher than the IRR for an investment in a clinical care department. It is here that nonquantitative factors may influence the institution to make the investment in clinical care rather than in the service area.

Chapter 9 Practice Case: Los Reyes Hospital

This case allows you to see how a budget can be built using cost and revenue drivers and to experiment with different ways to set up a spreadsheet so you can test the bottom-line implications of changing various assumptions. If you have not done so already, you should try to build the budget using a spreadsheet.

Question 1

Exhibit B.8 contains a spreadsheet with the budget and shows three factors that will be useful for budget revision: number of cases, resources per case, and price/efficiency. Each is set at a level of 1.00. More factors could be used, but as the discussion of question 2 demonstrates, these three are the most important. Exhibit B.9 contains the formulas used in the computations, using columns A through E and rows 1 through 21.

Exhibit B.8 demonstrates that DRG 089 makes up about half of the contribution and DRG 014 another third. DRG 140 contributes very little. Exhibit B.8 does not calculate the contribution per case, but some simple arithmetic shows that DRG 089 contributes $3,200 ($6,000 − $2,800); the other cases have unit contributions of $3,350 (DRG 014); $3,045 (DRG 096); and $1,795 (DRG 140).

Question 2

Dr. Delgado and Mr. Cohn have two options.

Option 1: Increase Revenues

In general, as the text discusses, this option is the easiest to put into a budget but the hardest to actually pull off. It would be unwise for Dr. Delgado to increase her budgeted surplus by taking this route. If she does, however, there are three ways to go about it:

• *Raise prices.* We are told little about the market, however, so it is hard to say whether a price increase could be instituted without a decrease in volume. Frequently health maintenance organizations and other

EXHIBIT B.8   Operating Budget

	A	B	C	D	E
		Routine			
	All	Care	Radiology	Laboratory	Pharmacy
Resource factor (RF 1, 2, 3, 4)		1.00	1.00	1.00	1.00
Case factor (CF)	1.00				
Price/efficiency factor (PEF 1, 2, 3, 4)		1.00	1.00	1.00	1.00

	DRG 089	DRG 014	DRG 096	DRG 140	Total
Overall Budget					
1 Number of cases	300	200	100	50	650
2 Revenue per case	$6,000	$6,500	$5,000	$3,000	
3 TOTAL REVENUE	$1,800,000	$1,300,000	$500,000	$150,000	$3,750,000
4 Variable expenses per case	2,800	3,150	1,955	1,205	
5 TOTAL VARIABLE EXPENSES	$840,000	$630,000	$195,500	$60,250	$1,725,750
6 Contribution	$960,000	$670,000	$304,500	$89,750	$2,024,250
7 TOTAL FIXED EXPENSES					1,950,600
8 SURPLUS (DEFICIT)					$73,650
Variable Expense Detail					
Routine Care					
9 Average number of days per case	9	11	7	4	
10 Average expense per day	$250	$250	$250	$250	
11 Total average expense per case	$2,250	$2,750	$1,750	$1,000	
Radiology					
12 Average number of films per case	5	6	4	1	
13 Average expense per film	$25	$25	$25	$25	
14 Total average expense per case	$125	$150	$100	$25	
Laboratory					
15 Average number of tests per case	10	10	3	5	
16 Average expense per test	$15	$15	$15	$15	
17 Total average expense per case	$150	$150	$45	$75	
Pharmacy					
18 Average number of units per case	55	20	12	21	
19 Average expense per unit	$5	$5	$5	$5	
20 Total average expense per case	$275	$100	$60	$105	
21 TOTAL AVERAGE VARIABLE EXPENSE PER CASE	$2,800	$3,150	$1,955	$1,205	

EXHIBIT B.9 Formulas

	A	B	C	D	E
	All	**Routine Care**	**Radiology**	**Laboratory**	**Pharmacy**
Resource factor (RF 1, 2, 3, 4)	1.00	1.00	1.00	1.00	1.00
Case factor (CF)	1.00				
Price/efficiency (PEF 1, 2, 3, 4)	1.00	1.00	1.00	1.00	1.00
	DRG 089	**DRG 014**	**DRG 096**	**DRG 140**	**Total**
Overall Budget					
1 Number of cases	= 300 × CF	= 200 × CF	= 100 × CF	= 50 × CF	= B12 + C12 + D12 + E12
2 Revenue per case	$6,000	$6,500	$5,000	$3,000	
3 Total revenue	= B12 × B13	= C12 × C13	= D12 × D13	= E12 × E13	= B14 + C14 + D14 + E14
4 Variable expenses per case	= B45	= C45	= D45	= E45	
5 Total variable expenses	= B12 × B16	= C12 × C16	= D12 × D16	= E12 × E16	= B17 + C17 + D17 + E17
6 Contribution	= B14 − B17	= C14 − C17	= D14 − D17	= E14 − E17	= F14 − F17
7 Total fixed expenses					$1,950,600
8 Surplus (deficit)					= F19 − F20
Variable Expense Detail					
Routine Care					
9 Number of days per case	= 9 × RF 1	= 11 × RF 1	= 7 × RF 1	= 4 × RF 1	
10 Expense per day	= $250 × PEF 1	= $250 × PEF 1	= $250 × PEF 1	= $250 × PEF 1	
11 Total expense per case	= B26 × B27	= C26 × C27	= D26 × D27	= E26 × E27	
Radiology					
12 Number of films per case	= 5 × RF 2	= 6 × RF 2	= 4 × RF 2	= 1 × RF 2	
13 Expense per film	= $25 × PEF 2	= $25 × PEF 2	= $25 × PEF 2	= $25 × PEF 2	
14 Total expense per case	= B31 × B32	= C31 × C32	= D31 × D32	= E31 × E32	
Laboratory					
15 Number of tests per case	= 10 × RF 3	= 10 × RF 3	= 3 × RF 3	= 5 × RF 3	
16 Expense per test	= $15 × PEF 3	= $15 × PEF 3	= $15 × PEF 3	= $15 × PEF 3	
17 Total expense per case	= B36 × B37	= C36 × C37	= D36 × D37	= E36 × E37	
Pharmacy					
18 Number of units per case	= 55 × RF 4	= 20 × RF 4	= 12 × RF 4	= 21 × RF 4	
19 Expense per unit	= $5 × PEF 4	= $5 × PEF 4	= $5 × PEF 4	= $5 × PEF 4	
20 Total expense per case	= B41 × B42	= C41 × C42	= D41 × D42	= E41 × E42	
21 TOTAL VARIABLE EXPENSE PER CASE	= B28 + B33 + B38 + B43	= C28 + C33 + C38 + C43	= D28 + D33 + D38 + D43	= E28 + E33 + E38 + E43	

third-party payers dictate prices, so the hospital probably is a price taker.

- *Increase volume.* Presumably Dr. Delgado is already trying to increase volume, and her initial estimates represent her best guesses as to what is possible. They may even be optimistic. (Incidentally, to increase volume, she presumably will encourage physicians to admit their sick patients to Los Reyes Hospital rather than elsewhere.)

- *Change the mix of business so that there are more higher-contribution cases.* The analysis of this option is not quite straightforward, however. The question, assuming capacity constraints, is not which case type has the highest contribution margin but what is the total contribution that can be attained. If, for example, Dr. Delgado could admit only one more patient (and was interested in the impact on surplus), she would admit a patient with DRG 014 (with a unit contribution of $3,350). If, however, she has twelve days of capacity available, she would presumably prefer to admit three cases of DRG 140, because each case has a four-day length of stay; three cases would provide a total contribution of $5,385 (3 × $1,795), compared to only $3,350 for a single DRG 014 (which has an eleven-day length of stay).

Option 2: Reduce Costs

This is probably the more realistic option. There are two ways to go about it:

- *Reduce fixed costs.* We are told little about these costs, however, so it is hard to say whether this is feasible. In most organizations, it usually is, because costs of this sort tend to grow as the volume of activity grows but not to decline as volume falls off.

- *Reduce variable expenses per case.* There are two ways to do this:

  - Reduce the number of resource units used per case (for example, use fewer days, fewer radiology films, fewer lab tests, or fewer pharmacy units).

  - Reduce the expense per resource unit. This can be done in two ways:

    - Lowering factor prices (by, for example, lowering nursing wages, technician wages, or supply costs per unit)

    - Achieving greater efficiency (by, for example, using fewer nurses per bed day, fewer technician minutes per X-ray or lab test, or fewer supplies per X-ray or lab test)

Examining these options, we can see that it probably would be difficult to reduce factor prices. The hospital could ask nurses and technicians to work for less, but if there were other opportunities in the area, some people would be likely to leave. Replacing them with lower-wage employees could be difficult. Similarly, the hospital presumably has the best prices it can get from suppliers, although negotiation with suppliers certainly is a possibility.

This leaves the hospital with the options of reducing the number of resource units per case or achieving greater efficiency. It appears that these possibilities are where the greatest opportunities exist. However, it is not clear that Dr. Delgado can directly influence the actions needed to get greater efficiency. This is the responsibility of the service department heads. But by working with the physicians in her department, Dr. Delgado should be able to influence the number of resource units used per case. Indeed, as exhibit B.10 shows, by reducing lengths of stay to 90 percent of the original amounts budgeted, Dr. Delgado can increase the surplus to over $200,000.

Question 3

There are several problems that might arise. First, varying resource use. Dr. Delgado might wish to have greater detail on the kinds of radiology films and lab tests that are conducted or on the different wards where patients stay (some might have higher usage than others).

Second, the nature of fixed expenses. Dr. Delgado probably should see greater detail on the fixed expenses to determine whether they might be reduced. For example, some breakdown within the categories of rent, utilities, cleaning, administration, and the like might shed some light on the feasibility of reducing these expenses. If it turns out that some of these expenses are allocated to the department, she may want to suggest that the hospital establish transfer prices for them.

Third, case mix. The department deals with several hundred DRGs. Dr. Delgado may resist developing clinical protocols (or pathways) for all the DRGs, and the department may find it useful to employ the "80–20 rule." That is, it is likely that 20 percent of the DRGs seen in the department account for 80 percent of the department's costs.

Finally, Dr. Delgado may question whether some of the fixed expenses are associated with different case types. If certain fixed expenses can be associated with certain types of cases (for example, higher utility costs for a particular DRG because of the specialized equipment used), Dr. Delgado could begin to analyze whether discouraging some case types would improve her surplus.

EXHIBIT B.10   Revised Operating Budget 1: 10 Percent Reduction in Average Length of Stay

	All	Routine Care	Radiology	Laboratory	Pharmacy
Resource factor (RF 1, 2, 3, 4)		0.90	1.00	1.00	1.00
Case factor (CF)	1.00				
Price/efficiency factor (PEF 1, 2, 3, 4)		1.00	1.00	1.00	1.00

	DRG 089	DRG 014	DRG 096	DRG 140	Total
Overall Budget					
Number of cases	300	200	100	50	650
Revenue per case	$6,000	$6,500	$5,000	$3,000	
TOTAL REVENUE	$1,800,000	$1,300,000	$500,000	$150,000	$3,750,000
Variable expenses per case	2,575	2,875	1,780	1,105	
TOTAL VARIABLE EXPENSES	$772,500	$575,000	$178,000	$55,250	$1,580,750
Contribution	$1,027,500	$725,000	$322,000	$94,750	$2,169,250
TOTAL FIXED EXPENSES					1,950,600
SURPLUS (DEFICIT)					$218,650
Variable Expense Detail					
Routine Care					
Average number of days per case	8.1	9.9	6.3	3.6	
Average expense per day	$250	$250	$250	$250	
Total average expense per case	$2,025	$2,475	$1,575	$ 900	
Radiology					
Average number of films per case	5	6	4	1	
Average expense per film	$25	$25	$25	$25	
Total average expense per case	$125	$150	$100	$25	
Laboratory					
Average number of tests per case	10	10	3	5	
Average expense per test	$15	$15	$15	$15	
Total average expense per case	$150	$150	$45	$75	
Pharmacy					
Average number of units per case	55	20	12	21	
Average expense per unit	$5	$5	$5	$5	
Total average expense per case	$275	$100	$60	$105	
TOTAL AVERAGE VARIABLE EXPENSE PER CASE	$2,575	$2,875	$1,780	$1,105	

To deal with these matters, Mr. Cohn may need to make some compromises in the quality of the budget information he uses. He may not be able to prepare a budget in this way for all DRGs and hence for the department's total budget. He thus may have to live with some imprecision. This is not an easy compromise for an accountant.

Question 4

There no doubt will be considerable resistance from physicians to spending their time on financial issues. Developing protocols and linking them to financial matters can be time consuming and frustrating. Developing transfer prices for service departments can be similarly difficult.

A related matter is determining the departments for which transfer prices can be developed and those for which they cannot. It should be easy to identify a transfer price for laundry services, for example, but probably difficult to set one for administration and general services. Moreover, there is a question of the kind of responsibility center each department should be. If Mr. Cohn decides to expand the effort to the rest of the hospital, he will find that the departments fall into the four categories displayed in exhibit B.11. As this exhibit indicates, transfer pricing decisions need to be made in each category.

Chapter 10 Practice Case: Gotham Meals on Wheels

This case is an excellent spreadsheet exercise. Ideally, you prepared your analysis using spreadsheet software. One advantage of doing this is that you can see very clearly the relationships among the balance sheet, the income statement, and the statement of cash flows. The case also shows an organization that is running out of cash because its rapid growth is causing cash to be used up for working capital purposes (mainly accounts receivable and inventory).

Question 1

Exhibit B.12 has been prepared using a spreadsheet and contains income statements; balance sheets; statements of cash flows (SCFs); and reconciliations for retained surpluses, accounts receivable, and inventory. Exhibit B.13 contains the spreadsheet formulas for exhibit B.12. Note that with the exception of some beginning balances, the entire spreadsheet is driven by the case data in the first four lines. The spreadsheet exercise thus provides

EXHIBIT B.11   Responsibility Center Issues

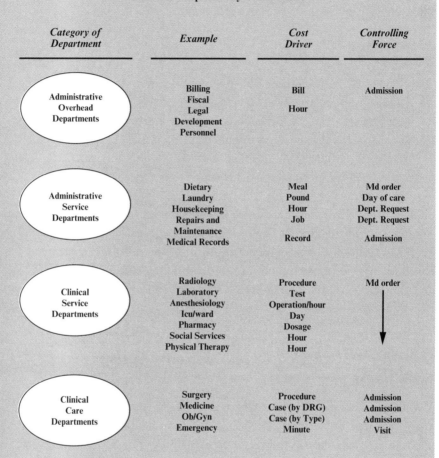

Exhibit D Responsibility Center Issues

Category of Department	Example	Cost Driver	Controlling Force
Administrative Overhead Departments	Billing Fiscal Legal Development Personnel	Bill Hour	Admission
Administrative Service Departments	Dietary Laundry Housekeeping Repairs and Maintenance Medical Records	Meal Pound Hour Job Record	Md order Day of care Dept. Request Dept. Request Admission
Clinical Service Departments	Radiology Laboratory Anesthesiology Icu/ward Pharmacy Social Services Physical Therapy	Procedure Test Operation/hour Day Dosage Hour Hour	Md order
Clinical Care Departments	Surgery Medicine Ob/Gyn Emergency	Procedure Case (by DRG) Case (by Type) Minute	Admission Admission Admission Visit

you with an opportunity to see how all three statements—income statement, balance sheet, and SCF—can be derived from the same data set.

Question 2

The problem that this organization faces is an imbalance among four factors: growth rate, profit margin, accounts receivable collection period, and inventory holding period. As the text describes, and as this case illustrates rather dramatically, it is possible for an organization to be earning a rather sizable surplus and still be running out of cash.

Mr. McCall has several options:

• Slow his growth rate.

• Widen his margin by (1) increasing the unit price, (2) lowering per-unit costs, or (3) reducing his fixed monthly expenses.

• Attempt to speed up the collection of accounts receivable by either (1) improving the office inefficiencies so the bills can be sent out sooner or (2) asking clients to pay sooner than in one month (including asking for cash on delivery).

• Attempt to get his suppliers to wait a month to get paid so that he pays for his COGS (cost of goods sold) in the same month that he incurs them instead of a month beforehand.

• Obtain more contributions.

• Obtain a loan. As the SCF in Exhibit B.12 indicates, he will need just under $11,000, which he will not be able to pay back until some time in the next year. (The interest will reduce his margin, incidentally.)

Question 3

Mr. McCall needs to act quickly. It is March, and, if the projections are correct, in April he will run out of cash. However, as the projections show, the cash deficit reaches just under $11,000 in August, and then there is a positive inflow in September. So, if he can quickly obtain a loan for $11,000 (probably a bit more just to be on the safe side), he can weather the cash flow storm. He might try to raise some more equity, but, again, unless he has an angel investor with a ready checkbook, it is too late.

In terms of the other options listed earlier, it is too late to slow growth or raise prices. He may be able to decrease costs, but it probably is too late for that also. It also is a bit late in the game to ask his customers to pay more quickly, although he probably can improve the efficiency in sending out bills. He might ask his suppliers to wait to get paid, but again, it is a little late in the game to do that. In short, unless he has an angel investor, a loan probably is his best option. He should be calling his bank in the morning!

Chapter 11 Practice Case A: Oak Street Nursing Home

This is a relatively simple case to give you practice in calculating a flexible budget and some fairly simple variances.

EXHIBIT B.12 Financial Statements

Item	October	November	December	January	February	March	April	May	June	July	August	September
Case Data												
Units sold	0	325	450	500	750	1,000	1,250	1,500	1,750	2,000	2,250	2,500
Revenue per unit	11	11	11	11	11	11	11	11	11	11	11	11
COGS per unit	7	7	7	7	7	7	7	7	7	7	7	7
Monthly expenses	300	1,400	1,400	1,600	2,000	2,000	2,000	2,000	2,000	2,000	2,000	2,000
Income Statements												
Revenue	0	3,575	4,950	5,500	8,250	11,000	13,750	16,500	19,250	22,000	24,750	27,500
COGS	0	2,275	3,150	3,500	5,250	7,000	8,750	10,500	12,250	14,000	15,750	17,500
Gross margin	0	1,300	1,800	2,000	3,000	4,000	5,000	6,000	7,000	8,000	9,000	10,000
Other expenses	300	1,400	1,400	1,600	2,000	2,000	2,000	2,000	2,000	2,000	2,000	2,000
Income (loss)	(300)	(100)	400	400	1,000	2,000	3,000	4,000	5,000	6,000	7,000	8,000
Reconcile Retained Surpluses												
Beginning balance (BB)	0	(300)	(400)	0	400	1,400	3,400	6,400	10,400	15,400	21,400	28,400
Surplus (deficit)	(300)	(100)	400	400	1,000	2,000	3,000	4,000	5,000	6,000	7,000	8,000
Ending balance (EB)	(300)	(400)	0	400	1,400	3,400	6,400	10,400	15,400	21,400	28,400	36,400
Reconcile Accounts Receivable												
BB	0	0	3,575	8,525	10,450	13,750	19,250	24,750	30,250	35,750	41,250	46,750
+	0	3,575	4,950	5,500	8,250	11,000	13,750	16,500	19,250	22,000	24,750	27,500
–	0	0	0	3,575	4,950	5,500	8,250	11,000	13,750	16,500	19,250	22,000
EB	0	3,575	8,525	10,450	13,750	19,250	24,750	30,250	35,750	41,250	46,750	52,250
Reconcile Inventory												
BB	0	2,275	3,150	3,500	5,250	7,000	8,750	10,500	12,250	14,000	15,750	17,500
+	2,275	3,150	3,500	5,250	7,000	8,750	10,500	12,250	14,000	15,750	17,500	19,250
–	0	2,275	3,150	3,500	5,250	7,000	8,750	10,500	12,250	14,000	15,750	17,500
EB	2,275	3,150	3,500	5,250	7,000	8,750	10,500	12,250	14,000	15,750	17,500	19,250

Item	October	November	December	January	February	March	April	May	June	July	August	September
Balance Sheets												
Cash	22,425	17,875	12,975	9,700	5,650	400	(3,850)	(7,100)	(9,350)	(10,600)	(10,850)	(10,100)
Accounts receivable	0	3,575	8,525	10,450	13,750	19,250	24,750	30,250	35,750	41,250	46,750	52,250
Inventory	2,275	3,150	3,500	5,250	7,000	8,750	10,500	12,250	14,000	15,750	17,500	19,250
Total assets	24,700	24,600	25,000	25,400	26,400	28,400	31,400	35,400	40,400	46,400	53,400	61,400
Contributed capital	25,000	25,000	25,000	25,000	25,000	25,000	25,000	25,000	25,000	25,000	25,000	25,000
Retained surpluses (deficits)	(300)	(400)	0	400	1,400	3,400	6,400	10,400	15,400	21,400	28,400	36,400
Total liability + Equity	24,700	24,600	25,000	25,400	26,400	28,400	31,400	35,400	40,400	46,400	53,400	61,400
SCFs—Direct												
Cash received from customers	0	0	0	3,575	4,950	5,500	8,250	11,000	13,750	16,500	19,250	22,000
Cash paid to suppliers	2,275	3,150	3,500	5,250	7,000	8,750	10,500	12,250	14,000	15,750	17,500	19,250
Other cash payments	300	1,400	1,400	1,600	2,000	2,000	2,000	2,000	2,000	2,000	2,000	2,000
Net cash from options	(2,575)	(4,550)	(4,900)	(3,275)	(4,050)	(5,250)	(4,250)	(3,250)	(2,250)	(1,250)	(250)	750
+ Beginning cash balance	25,000	22,425	17,875	12,975	9,700	5,650	400	(3,850)	(7,100)	(9,350)	(10,600)	(10,850)
Ending cash balance	22,425	17,875	12,975	9,700	5,650	400	(3,850)	(7,100)	(9,350)	(10,600)	(10,850)	(10,100)
SCFs—Indirect												
Surplus	(300)	(100)	400	400	1,000	2,000	3,000	4,000	5,000	6,000	7,000	8,000
Change in accounts receivable	0	(3,575)	(4,950)	(1,925)	(3,300)	(5,500)	(5,500)	(5,500)	(5,500)	(5,500)	(5,500)	(5,500)
Change in inventory	(2,275)	(875)	(350)	(1,750)	(1,750)	(1,750)	(1,750)	(1,750)	(1,750)	(1,750)	(1,750)	(1,750)
Net cash from options	(2,575)	(4,550)	(4,900)	(3,275)	(4,050)	(5,250)	(4,250)	(3,250)	(2,250)	(1,250)	(250)	750
+ Beginning cash balance	25,000	22,425	17,875	12,975	9,700	5,650	400	(3,850)	(7,100)	(9,350)	(10,600)	(10,850)
Ending cash balance	22,425	17,875	12,975	9,700	5,650	400	(3,850)	(7,100)	(9,350)	(10,600)	(10,850)	(10,100)

EXHIBIT B.13 Formulas (October to March Only)

Item*	B October	C November	D December	E January	F February	G March
Case Data						
8 Units sold	0	325	450	500	750	= F8 + 250
9 Revenue per unit	11	= B9	= C9	= D9	= E9	= F9
10 COGS per unit	7	= B10	= C10	= D10	= E10	= F10
11 Monthly expenses	300	1,400	1,400	1,600	2,000	= F11
Income Statements						
14 Revenue	= B8 × B9	= C8 × C9	= D8 × D9	= E8 × E9	= F8 × F9	= G8 × G9
15 COGS	= B10 × B8	= C10 × C8	= D10 × D8	= E10 × E8	= F10 × F8	= G10 × G8
16 Gross margin	= B14 − B15	= C14 − C15	= D14 − D15	= E14 − E15	= F14 − F15	= G14 − G15
17 Other expenses	= B11	= C11	= D11	= E11	= F11	= G11
18 Surplus	= B16 − B17	= C16 − C17	= D16 − D17	= E16 − E17	= F16 − F17	= G16 − G17
Reconcile Retained Surpluses						
21 BB	0	= B23	= C23	= D23	= E23	= F23
22 Surplus (deficit)	= B18	= C18	= D18	= E18	= F18	= G18
23 EB	= B21 + B22	= C21 + C22	= D21 + D22	= E21 + E22	= F21 + F22	= G21 + G22
Reconcile Accounts Receivable						
25 BB	0	= B28	= C28	= D28	= E28	= F28
26 +	= B14	= C14	= D14	= E14	= F14	= G14
27 −	0	0	= B14	= C14	= D14	= E14

Item*	B October	C November	D December	E January	F February	G March
28 EB	= B25 + B26 − B27	= C25 C26 − C27	= D25 + D26 − D27	= E25 + E26 − E27	= F25 + F26 − F27	= G25 + G26 − G27
Reconcile Inventory						
30 BB	0	= B33	= C33	= D33	= E33	= F33
31 +	= C15	= D15	= E15	= F15	= G15	= H15
32 −	0	= C15	= D15	= E15	= F15	= G15
33 EB	= B30 + B31 − B32	= C30 + C31 − C32	= D30 + D31 − D32	= E30 + E31 − E32	= F30 + F31 − F32	= G30 + G31 − G32
Balance Sheets						
36 Cash	= B43 − B37 − B38	= C43 − C37 − C38	= D43 − D37 − D38	= E51	= F51	= G51
37 Accounts receivable	= B28	= C28	= D28	= E28	= F28	= G28
38 Inventory	= B33	= C33	= D33	= E33	= F33	= G33
39 Total assets	= B36 + B37 + B38	= C36 + C37 + C38	= D36 + D37 + D38	= E36 + E37 + E38	= F36 + F37 + F38	= G36 + G37 + G38
41 Contributed capital	25,000	25,000	25,000	= D41	= E41	= F41
42 Retained surpluses (deficits)	= B23	= C23	= D23	= E23	= F23	= G23
43 Total liability + Equity	= B41 + B42	= C41 + C42	= D41 + D42	= E41 + E42	= F41 + F42	= G41 + G42
SCFs—Direct						
46 Cash received from customers	= B27	= C27	= D27	= E27	= F27	= G27
47 Cash paid to suppliers	= B31	= C31	= D31	= E31	= F31	= G31
48 Other cash payments	= B17	= C17	= D17	= E17	= F17	= G17
49 Net cash from options	= B46 − B47 − B48	= C46 − C47 − C48	= D46 − D47 − D48	= E46 − E47 − E48	= F46 − F47 − F48	= G46 − G47 − G48
50 + Beginning cash balance	25,000	= B36	= C36	= D36	= E51	= F51
51 + Ending cash balance	= B49 + B50	= C49 + C50	= D49 + D50	= E49 + E50	= F49 + F50	= G49 + G50

*This column shows row numbers from the spreadsheet in exhibit B.12.

Question 1

To reconcile the difference between budgeted and actual revenue, we begin with a calculation of unit rates:

	Actual	Budget
Revenue	$750,000	$720,000
Number of person nights	10,000	12,000
RATE PER NIGHT	$75	$60

We can now calculate the revenue price variance as follows:

$$(\$75 - \$60) \times 10,000 = \$150,000$$

We can calculate the revenue volume variance as follows:

$$(10,000 - 12,000) \times \$60 = \$(120,000)$$

To reconcile the $30,000 increase, we begin with budgeted sales revenue, and use the variances to convert it to actual sales revenue. The calculations are as follows:

Budgeted revenue	$720,000
Plus: Favorable price variance	150,000
Less: Unfavorable volume variance	(120,000)
ACTUAL REVENUE	$750,000

Alternatively, we could have calculated a flexible budget, as follows:

	Original Budget	Flexible Budget	Actual Results
Number of person nights	12,000	10,000	10,000
Fee	$60	$60	$75
Revenue	$720,000	$600,000	$750,000
Volume variance		$(120,000)	
Price variance			$150,000
Total variance			$30,000

Question 2

The flexible budget for expenses can follow the same format:

	Original Budget	Flexible Budget	Actual Results
Number of person nights	12,000	10,000	10,000
Expense per person night	$57.00	$57.00	$73.50

	Original Budget	Flexible Budget	Actual Results
Total expenses	$684,000	$570,000	$735,000
Volume variance	$114,000		
Spending variance		$(165,000)	
Total variance		$(51,000)	

To reconcile the change in income figures, we can make the following calculations:

Budgeted income	$36,000
Plus: Favorable revenue variance	30,000
Less: Unfavorable spending variance	(51,000)
ACTUAL INCOME	$15,000

Question 3

We have a good idea of the reasons underlying the revenue variance, principally a decline in the number of nights with an increase in the price per night. We need more information, however, about the reasons for the increase in expense per night from $57.00 to $73.50. Among the items of information we might like to have are

- The breakdown between fixed and variable costs
- The labor and material breakdown for the two figures
- Wage and efficiency information for labor
- Price and use information for materials

Chapter 11 Practice Case B: El Conejo Family Planning Clinic

This case lends itself to the use of a rather simple spreadsheet, which can be used to compute the variances. Once one variance has been computed accurately, the formula in that cell can be copied and pasted into the remaining cells of a similar kind.

Question 1

Exhibit 11B.3 is in the same format as exhibit 11B.1 but uses the actual volume and mix of visits.

Exhibit 11B.4 is the same as the flexible budget described in the text: that is, it holds price, resource use, and so forth at budget and changes only volume and mix. As it indicates, although the number of visits increased by 50 from the budget, the mix changed in such a way that the surplus should have been $750 lower than the original budget.

Exhibit 11B.4 also computes revenue price variances using the formulas described in the chapter. So far the analysis is sound, although the difference between the flexed surplus of $84,250 and the deficit of $218,300 clearly suggests that there is much more to be uncovered.

Question 2

Some of the other reasons for the large total variance might be the following:

- More or fewer physician minutes, nursing minutes, medical supply units, or laboratory tests per visit, on average, than at budget
- Higher or lower average wage per minute for physicians, nurses, or both, or higher or lower expenses per medical supply unit or laboratory test than budgeted
- Higher or lower fixed expenses

Question 3

The computations are shown in exhibits B.14, B.15, and B.16. The data show the following:

- Productivity and use variances (the first set of reasons given in the answer to question 2) accounted for a negative $288,250 variance (see exhibit B.14). Looking along the type-of-service dimension, we can see that over half of the total ($160,500) was for laboratory tests. Looking along the visit-type dimension, we can see that over half ($151,250) was for an IUD first visit. The highest single item was laboratory tests for an IUD first visit.
- Wage, price, and efficiency variances (the second set of reasons) actually summed to a positive variance of $2,700 (see exhibit B.15). The $2,700 masked some more significant variances, however, but none was as substantial as the productivity and use variances.
- Actual fixed expenses (the third reason given earlier) did not differ from budget.
- A summary of variances indicates that the total variance was $303,300, from a budget of a positive $85,000 to a deficit of $218,300 (see exhibit B.16). In terms of responsible groups, the area where there was the

EXHIBIT B.14 Productivity and Use Variances

	IUD 1st Visit	Oral Contraceptive 1st Visit	Special Follow-Up	Routine Follow-Up	Total
Type of Service					
Physician Care					
Budgeted minutes per visit — Actual minutes per visit	5	5	(5)	(5)	
Budgeted wage per minute	$1.00	$1.00	$1.00	$1.00	
Productivity variance per visit	$5.00	$5.00	$(5.00)	$(5.00)	
Total productivity variances	$13,750	$11,000	$(5,000)	$(3,000)	$16,750
Nursing Care					
Budgeted minutes per visit — Actual minutes per visit	(10)	(10)	5	5	
Budgeted wage per minute	$0.50	$0.50	$0.50	$0.50	
Productivity variance per visit	$(5.00)	$(5.00)	$2.50	$2.50	
Total productivity variances	$(13,750)	$(11,000)	$2,500	$1,500	$(20,750)
Medical Supplies					
Budgeted number of units per visit — Actual number of units per visit	(1)	(1)	0	0	
Budgeted expense per unit	$25.00	$25.00	$25.00	$25.00	
Use variance per visit	$(25.00)	$(25.00)	$0.00	$0.00	
Total use variances	$(68,750)	$(55,000)	$0	$0	$(123,750)
Laboratory Tests					
Budgeted tests per visit — Actual tests per visit	(2)	(1)	(3)	0	
Budgeted expense per test	$15.00	$15.00	$15.00	$15.00	
Use variance per visit	$(30.00)	$(15.00)	$(45.00)	$0.00	
Total use variances	$(82,500)	$(33,000)	$(45,000)	$0	$(160,500)
Total productivity and use per visit	$(55.00)	$(40.00)	$(47.50)	$(2.50)	
Actual number of visits	2,750	2,200	1,000	600	
Total productivity and use variances	$(151,250)	$(88,000)	$(47,500)	$(1,500)	$(288,250)

EXHIBIT B.15 Wage, Price, and Efficiency Variances

	IUD 1st Visit	Oral Contraceptive 1st Visit	Special Follow-Up	Routine Follow-Up	Total
Actual number of visits	2,750	2,200	1,000	600	
Type of Service					
Physician Care					
Budgeted wage per minute	$(0.20)	$(0.20)	$(0.20)	$(0.20)	
− Actual wage per minute					
Actual number of minutes per visit	25	5	20	10	
Wage rate variance per visit	$(5.00)	$(1.00)	$(4.00)	$(2.00)	
Total wage rate variance	$(13,750)	$(2,200)	$(4,000)	$(1,200)	$(21,150)
Nursing Care					
Budgeted wage per minute	$(0.10)	$(0.10)	$(0.10)	$(0.10)	
− Actual wage per minute					
Actual number of minutes per visit	40	30	25	5	
Wage rate variance per visit	$(4.00)	$(3.00)	$(2.50)	$(0.50)	
Total wage rate variance	$(11,000)	$(6,600)	$(2,500)	$(300)	$(20,400)
Medical Supplies					
Budgeted − Actual expense per unit	$4.00	$4.00	$4.00	$4.00	
Actual # units per visit	4	2	2	0	
Rate/efficiency variance per visit	$16.00	$8.00	$8.00	$0.00	
Total rate/efficiency variance	$44,000	$17,600	$8,000	$0	$69,600
Laboratory Tests					
Budgeted expense per test	$(1.00)	$(1.00)	$(1.00)	$(1.00)	
− Actual expense per test					
Actual number of tests per visit	5	3	5	0	
Rate and efficiency variance per visit	$(5.00)	$(3.00)	$(5.00)	$0.00	
Total rate and efficiency variance	$(13,750)	$(6,600)	$(5,000)	$0	$(25,350)
Total wage, rate, and efficiency variances	$5,500	$2,200	$(3,500)	$(1,500)	$2,700

largest problem in meeting budget was in use of the laboratory, but use of medical supplies also was quite substantial.

In terms of using this information to manage the clinic, Ms. Ramirez might start by examining why more lab tests were ordered for every visit type except a routine follow-up. She also might ask the nurses why they are spending 10 minutes more for first visits, on average, than budgeted.

EXHIBIT B.16   Summary of Variances

	IUD 1st Visit	Oral Contraceptive 1st Visit	Special Follow-Up	Routine Follow-Up	Total
Contribution margin variances	$(8,750)	$5,000	$0	$3,000	$(750)
Revenue price variances	0	(22,000)	5,000	0	(17,000)
Subtotal	$(8,750)	$(17,000)	$5,000	$3,000	$(17,750)
Productivity and Use Variances					
Physician care	$13,750	$11,000	$(5,000)	$(3,000)	$16,750
Nursing care	(13,750)	(11,000)	2,500	1,500	(20,750)
Medical supplies	(68,750)	(55,000)	0	0	(123,750)
Laboratory tests	(82,500)	(33,000)	(45,000)	0	(160,500)
Subtotal	$(151,250)	$(88,000)	$(47,500)	$(1,500)	$(288,250)
Wage, Rate, and Efficiency Variances					
Physician care	$(13,750)	$(2,200)	$(4,000)	$(1,200)	$(21,150)
Nursing care	(11,000)	(6,600)	(2,500)	(300)	(20,400)
Medical supplies	44,000	17,600	8,000	0	69,600
Laboratory tests	(13,750)	(6,600)	(5,000)	0	(25,350)
Subtotal	$5,500	$2,200	$(3,500)	$(1,500)	$2,700
Total variances	$(154,500)	$(102,800)	$(46,000)	$0	$(303,300)
Variances by Responsible Group					
Physicians	$0	$8,800	$(9,000)	$(4,200)	$(4,400)
Nurses	(24,750)	(17,600)	0	1,200	(41,150)
Medical supply department	(24,750)	(37,400)	8,000	0	(54,150)
Laboratory	(96,250)	(39,600)	(50,000)	0	(185,850)
Senior management	(8,750)	(17,000)	5,000	3,000	(17,750)
Total	$(154,500)	$(102,800)	$(46,000)	$0	$(303,300)

Is it possible, for example, that physicians are saving 5 minutes per visit by giving the nurses more work? If so, perhaps that is appropriate, but there may be quality-of-care issues that need to be examined. Moreover, there is no savings if it takes a nurse (at half the per-minute wage of a physician) twice as long to do the same task (10 minutes versus 5 minutes).

Question 4

On a regular basis, probably monthly although perhaps more frequently if the problems persist, the chief of medicine needs to see information on the variances associated with the resources being used in conjunction with each type of visit. At the moment, it would appear that some intervention is needed.

The director of nursing no doubt needs to see similar information in terms of how much nursing time is being spent per visit versus what was planned. The two managers also need to collaborate to make sure that the budgeted time spent by physicians and nurses is appropriate to the visit type, and then to compare actual time with the budget. Given the large variances with several items, there clearly is a need for a consistent flow of variance information so that they can consider what action is appropriate.

Chapter 12 Practice Case: Hillside Hospital

This case provides a good example of a change process that got out of hand and probably did not need to. To analyze the issues, we must distinguish among the cross-functional activities discussed in the text. To analyze the implementation process, we must use some of the change management concepts discussed in the text.

Question 1

Exhibit B.17 shows some of the key aspects of the seven cross-functional activities and classifies some of Dr. Wells's activities into this framework. Of particular importance in this exhibit is the fact that personnel policies (a strategy formulation activity) were developed not by Dr. Wells, but rather by the medical school, and it is important to recognize that managers frequently are responsible for management control and task control activities within the constraints of strategy formulation decisions made by others. This, in part, was Dr. Wells's problem. More generally, much of what happened was a result of factors in Dr. Wells's environment, such as the Kent Medical School guidelines; the medical school's financing problems; and a concern with the hospital's having "excessive" control, such as it did in the department of anesthesia.

Dr. Wells did make a strategic decision, however: that of initiating the Medical Practice Plan (MPP). Clearly there were other approaches that he could have taken and did not. Once he opted for the MPP, though, he constrained his management control and patient management choices.

EXHIBIT B.17   The Cross-Functional Framework

Strategy Formulation	Management Control	Patient Management
Deciding on objectives of the organization; on changes in these objectives; on resources used to attain them; and on the policies that are to govern the acquisition, use, and disposition of these resources. Personnel policies from Kent constrained strategy formulation.	Ensuring that resources are obtained and used effectively and efficiently in accomplishing organizational objectives. Poor feedback to MDs on financial results Manual versus computer billing system.	Ensuring that specific activities are carried out effectively and efficiently for each patient encounter. Improving collections. Chief-service patients allow for more collections.

Authority and Influence	Cultural Maintenance	Conflict Management
Designing the management control structure and identifying formal reporting relationships. Centralized versus decentralized billing.	Changing to a "research" culture as opposed to a "clinical care" culture. MDs who are not interested in academics leave the department.	Addressing the different perspectives that arise in a change effort.

Motivation		
Determining how people are rewarded for "good" work. Tenure and recognition become more important than clinical care income.		

Exhibit B.18 helps clarify this point by indicating the options that were open to Dr. Wells. Specifically, he was choosing between a centralized and a decentralized group practice (that is, one that involved a combination of specialties, and one that was unique to a given specialty, such as medicine). He also was choosing between an internal and an external group (that is, one inside—and working with—the hospital versus one totally separate from the hospital).

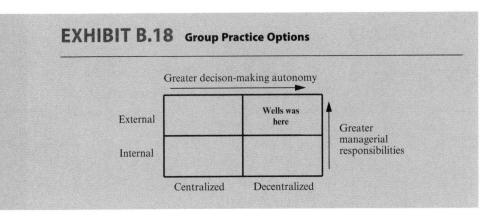

EXHIBIT B.18 Group Practice Options

By allowing us to see the categories in which Dr. Wells's activities fell, the cross-functional framework is helpful in assessing some of his implementation problems. One of his most significant problems was in the area of patient management. Because he did not spend enough time in the management control area, formulating the systems and procedures for patient management activities, he found himself immersed in the details of activities such as billing. In this regard, an important managerial activity is to move oneself out of the patient management area and into either the management control or strategy formulation areas. Dr. Wells did not do this well.

Question 2

The clue to the answer to the first part of this question is contained in the background portion of the case, which states that the medical school was "asking that patient fees support hospital clinical departments." In effect, the medical school was making each clinical department a profit center. In structuring the group practice, however, Dr. Wells turned each doctor into a revenue center, because presumably he now wanted to manage the revenue generated by each (not to maximize it, as one might normally expect in a revenue center, but to ensure that it was not too much). This is an interesting variation on the revenue center theme, in which the usual goal is revenue maximization. Keep in mind, however, that in a revenue center, the manager's performance is measured by the amount of revenue generated by his or her center. That was as true for the doctors at Hillside Hospital as for individuals in any other kind of revenue center.

The problem with this arrangement was that, as revenue centers, doctors had little interest in expenses. This meant that the responsibility for all expenses fell to Dr. Wells. This might have been okay, although it no doubt meant that he would spend a great deal of his time approving (or denying) requests for expenses, and worrying about whether the revenues generated by the doctors would be sufficient to cover the department's expenses. Because he created an incentive for doctors to earn less revenue than before (presumably by seeing fewer patients), the revenue side of his profit center would be somewhat unpredictable.

Making the doctors into profit centers would not have worked here because they were constrained on the revenue side. What might have worked, though, would have been to give each doctor a discretionary expense budget each year that he or she could use without approval. That would have freed Dr. Wells from the need to make or deny requests for many of the department's expenses.

Question 3

In terms of the management control process, there seemed to be little programming. We see scant evidence of any attempt by Dr. Wells to develop or manage the relationships among teaching, research, and clinical programs, for example, although we can assume that some of this was going on. The nature of the MPP's authority and influence process, however, had the de facto effect of channeling doctors' energies away from clinical practice and into teaching and research programs. That is, their clinical practice activities could raise their personal income, but only up to the ceiling. The only way to raise the ceiling was to get promoted, which was based on engaging in teaching and research.

We see no evidence of any budgeting activities, although, again, we might guess that some were taking place, albeit informally. However, as discussed earlier, the fact that the department was a profit center, coupled with the uncertain revenue from the doctors, created a situation in which budgeting for Dr. Wells was tricky. Indeed, budgeting for expenses had become much more critical for him than before, and it's not clear that he recognized this fact.

Both measuring and reporting activities were in quite a sorry state throughout most of the early years of the MPP. You should recognize that much of the "can of worms," as Dr. Wells described it, was in the measuring and reporting areas of the management control process.

Question 4

With regard to achieving a smoother implementation, there are several important and related issues. First, there is the question of both managerial and organizational values—that is, the department's culture. Dr. Wells's values were clearly those of academic medicine, and they were not as clinically oriented as the values of many of the doctors practicing in his department. In essence, Dr. Wells was attempting to change the culture of the department of medicine by creating a more homogeneous set of values. He was doing so through management control and motivation activities by making it increasingly difficult for doctors to earn a great deal of money while engaging only in clinical activities.

Second, given the environmental changes and the differing values, there was clearly a significant lack of goal congruence, or at least perceived goal congruence. In part, this lack of congruence came about because Dr. Wells's orientation reflected that of the Kent Medical School and its academic needs, and because Dr. Wells was dealing with a hospital administration in which the resources were quite limited. In contrast, the doctors had a stronger clinical orientation and a need to earn large salaries.

Finally, it should be pointed out that the management control process is only one aspect of attaining goal congruence (although in this situation it probably contributed more to the *lack* of goal congruence than to its resolution). In addition to the management control and cultural maintenance activities, there are various conflict management techniques that might have been used, such as the distribution of memos, letters, and reports; the use of the organizational hierarchy (although the medical school, a potential lever in doctor acceptance, apparently was unwilling to be heavy handed in this instance); and the use of committees, either permanent or ad hoc. All of this relates to both conflict management and authority and influence.

Dr. Wells's use of a permanent group (the MPP's board) was not a vehicle to resolve the lack of goal congruence, both because it was seen (probably accurately) as heavily biased in his favor and because it apparently did not concern itself with the implementation process. A more appropriate vehicle might have been a temporary group, or task force, which could have dealt with doctors' concerns and allowed issues to surface and be resolved before they reached a critical stage. Exhibit B.19 contains a summary of goal congruence issues. Exhibit B.20 lists several of the decisions that Dr. Wells made during the years when the change was under way and contrasts them with other possibilities. This is not entirely "Monday morning quarterbacking," because most of these options are pretty fundamental aspects of change management.

EXHIBIT B.19   Goal Congruence Issues

Members' Values and Needs		Dr. Wells's Values and Needs		
Need independence/ time	Need to control money (from medical school)	Anti–private practice	Teaching/ research clinical balance	Money for research/ clinical decreasing
Privacy of income				

Lack of goal congruence————> Conflict————> Need for resolution

Range of Goal Congruence Mechanisms*

Paper systems	Ad hoc hierarchy	Individual teams/ committees	Permanent integrator	Groups/ committees

What did Dr. Wells do?

- Allowed time to pass
- Held individual discussions
- Designed reward system
- Created penalties
- Avoided ad hoc meetings
- Gained control of B of T

*This is sometimes called "integrating mechanisms." See Lawrence, Paul R., and Jay W. Lorsch, *Organization and Environment* (Boston: Division of Research, Harvard Graduate School of Business Administration, 1967).

EXHIBIT B.20   Choices Made in the Implementation Process, and Possible Alternatives

Item	What Happened at Hillside	Another Possibility
Control over resources	Taken away	Give (via profit centers)
Leadership styles	Unclear and inconsistent; hidden agenda	Clear and consistent; clear agenda
Constraints imposed	Many; people had little say in the details	Few; give people a fair amount of say in details
Conflict management	No real forum for discussion of questions or management of conflict	Create an ad hoc task force or other mechanisms for answering questions and managing conflict
Pace of change	Little attention to process or the appropriate sequence of events	Pay attention to process and the appropriate sequence of events
Timing of changes in the management control system	After the MPP was formed and in place	Before the change takes place

GLOSSARY OF SELECTED TERMS AND CONCEPTS

ABSORPTION COSTING. A costing system that treats fixed manufacturing costs as product costs and hence holds these costs in inventory until the product is sold. See *activity-based costing (ABC)* and *variable cost.*

ACTIVITY-BASED COSTING (ABC). A costing system that uses multiple cost pools and overhead bases to attach manufacturing overhead to products. Considered to be more accurate than a method that uses a single rate. ABC is especially useful when there is *product diversity, cost diversity,* or *volume diversity.*

AFFORDABLE CARE ACT. A 2010 law in the United States that requires near universal coverage for health care, and provides a variety of patient protection features. For details, see http://www.hhs.gov/healthcare/rights/law/index.html

ALLOCATED OVERHEAD. The fixed and variable overhead, usually pertaining to a central office or general administration, that is distributed to individual responsibility centers, departments, and programs according to preestablished formulas. Usually a basis of allocation is chosen such that each organizational unit receives its fair share of the overhead based on its use of the basis. For example, in a hospital, the overhead cost of laundry usually is allocated on the basis of pounds processed, and housekeeping might be allocated on the basis of square feet or meters.

ALLOCATION BASES. The metrics used to distribute a support center's costs to other support centers and mission centers.

ALTERNATIVE CHOICE DECISION. A decision with one or more options. The three primary types of these decisions are (1) keeping versus discontinuing a product line or service that is unprofitable on a full-cost basis; (2) making versus buying (for example, performing an activity internally versus outsourcing it); and (3) accepting versus rejecting a special request.

BALANCED SCORECARD (BSC). A technique that measures both non-financial as well as financial performance. Non-financial measures typically are clustered into three categories: customer satisfaction, internal process improvement, and employee growth and development.

BATCH-RELATED ACTIVITIES. One of four general categories of activities that influence the use of manufacturing overhead. These are activities that are performed each time a batch of products is manufactured, such as setups for machines, material movements, and inspections.

BEHAVIORAL ASPECTS. Elements of the budgeting phase of the management control process that consider how line managers are to be involved in formulating the budget. It contrasts with the mechanical aspect.

BUDGET DRIVER. An activity or measure that can be managed and that can cause an organization's net income to increase or decrease.

BUDGET MONITORING. One aspect of the reporting phase of the management control process. It compares actual results to budgeted ones.

BUDGETING CONTEXT. A set of considerations that flows from the organizational context and consists of four features that influence and constrain how the budget is prepared.

BUSINESS RISK. Refers to the predictability or certainty of an organization's cash flows. Organizations that have a high degree of uncertainty about their cash flows have a relatively high business risk. Organizations that have a high degree of certainty about their cash flows have a relatively low business risk.

CASE MIX AND VOLUME. Refers to the different types of diagnoses that can present themselves for treatment. Examples include diabetes, liver cancer, or psoriasis. Volume refers to the number of each type of case.

CASH-RELATED CYCLES. The operating cycle and financing cycle. The former is concerned with day-to-day operations, the latter with longer-term financing. They must be managed to be certain that the organization does not run out of cash. See *financing cycle* and *operating cycle.*

CHANGE MANAGEMENT. The way an organization goes about implementing changes to its responsibility accounting system.

CHRONIC CONDITIONS. Those conditions that continue indefinitely, unlike acute conditions, which end. An example of an acute condition is viral pneumonia. Examples of chronic conditions are diabetes, Alzheimer's disease, arthritis, and asthma.

COMPLETE BLOOD COUNT (CBC). A fairly typical test for a patient in a hospital.

CONTRIBUTION. Usually the difference between revenue and variable costs but sometimes the difference between revenue and the sum of variable costs and direct fixed costs of, say, a department or a program. An example of the former is the contribution of a dialysis procedure to the dialysis unit's fixed costs. An example of the latter is the contribution of the dialysis unit to the organization's overhead costs.

CORONARY ARTERY BYPASS GRAFT (CABG). Pronounced "cabbage." A surgical procedure performed to relieve angina (chest pain or discomfort) and reduce the risk of death from coronary artery disease. Arteries or veins from elsewhere in the patient's body are grafted to the coronary arteries to improve the blood supply to the heart.

COST CENTER. Categories used to collect costs. They are divided into two categories: support centers (such as housekeeping, laundry, and plant maintenance) and mission centers (such as medicine, surgery, and pediatrics).

COST DRIVER. An activity that can be directly linked to an increase or decrease in costs. Cost drivers are frequently relatively easy to identify but sometimes difficult to measure. Thinking in terms of cost drivers allows managers to shift their focus away from the traditional departmental structure of an organization and toward the activities that cause the existence of costs and, perhaps most important, toward the managerial actions that can influence and control costs.

COST OBJECTS. The purposes for which costs are gathered. A cost object is aligned with a price. Examples include DRG100 or an ambulatory care visit.

COST PER RESOURCE UNIT. The cost of each unit of service provided to treat a case, such as the cost of a complete blood count (CBC). It needs to be distinguished from the resource unit itself. For example, one cost driver is the number of CBCs, but another is the cost of each CBC.

CROSS-FUNCTIONAL ACTIVITIES. Seven activities (or processes) that interact in an organization and must be coordinated. They comprise strategy formulation, patient (or client) management, authority and influence, conflict management, cultural maintenance, motivation, and the management control process.

CULTURE. The set of basic assumptions that underlies decision making in an organization.

DEBT STRUCTURE. The mixture of short- and long-term liabilities on an organization's balance sheet. By matching the term of the debt to the life of the asset, a company's principal payments on the debt will be equal to the asset's depreciation, and, other things equal, its cash flows will be the same as its surplus (or deficit) on an accrual basis.

DIAGNOSIS-RELATED GROUP (DRG). A DRG is a collection of several homogeneous diagnoses, and constitute a hospital's "products." A DRG is determined by "grouper" software, based on the International Classification of Diseases as well as the procedure performed, and the patient's age, sex, and discharge status, including any complications or co-morbidities. A DRG determines how much Medicare pays a hospital for each of its products. For details, see http://medicaldictionary.thefreedictionary.com/DRG.

DIFFERENTIAL COST. A cost that will change depending on a choice made by management. Differential costs are calculated for make-or-buy, keep-or-discontinue, special-price, and obsolete asset alternative choice decision making. They include the variable costs of any products involved and may include both step-function and fixed costs, depending on the circumstances. If a cost will be the same regardless of the alternative chosen (as depreciation will be, for example), it is not a differential cost.

DIRECT COST. A cost that can be attributed unambiguously to either a product or an organizational unit. If the former, it is classified as either direct material or direct labor. If the latter, it can be somewhat complicated. For example, depreciation of machines in a plant is a direct cost of the plant; however, it is generally considered an indirect cost of the products produced in the plant.

DIRECT LABOR. Labor that is unambiguously associated with a unit of finished product—for example, a worker on an assembly line or a lab technician working on a specific test. See *indirect labor*.

DIRECT MATERIAL. Material that is unambiguously associated with a unit of finished product—for example, reagents for a lab test. See *indirect material*.

DISCOUNT RATE. The interest rate used to compute the present value of a future stream of cash flows.

DISCRETIONARY EXPENSE CENTER. A responsibility center whose manager's financial performance is measured in terms of the total expenses incurred by the center regardless of how much output the center produces. See *investment center, profit center, revenue center,* and *standard expense center*.

DUAL-ASPECT CONCEPT. The accounting concept that is represented by the fundamental accounting equation: Assets = Liabilities + Equity. Assets are what an organization owns or has claim to, liabilities are funds owed to outsiders, and equity represents the combination of contributions from owners (or donors) and retained earnings.

EFFECTIVENESS. Accomplishing what the organization wants to do. The more of an organization's objectives a responsibility center accomplishes, the greater its effectiveness. See *efficiency*.

EFFICIENCY. Accomplishing something at a low cost. It can be measured by a ratio of outputs to inputs—that is, amount of output achieved per unit of input. Measures of efficiency do not consider whether the output was in support of the organization's objectives. See *effectiveness*.

FACILITY-SUSTAINING ACTIVITIES. One of four general categories of activities that tend to influence the use of manufacturing overhead. They are the highest-order activity and include work such as plant management, building repair and maintenance, security, and grounds maintenance. See *activity-based costing (ABC), batch-related activities, product-sustaining activities*, and *unit-level activities*.

FAIRNESS When a manager makes a good financial decision from the standpoint of achieving the goals of his or her responsibility center, the measurement and reporting system shows improved financial results. A lack of such fairness ordinarily means that the measurement system needs to be revised to distinguish between controllable and non-controllable items and that the manager's performance needs to be measured with regard to those items over which he or she exerts a reasonable amount of control.

FINANCIAL RISK. Synonymous with *leverage*. Other things being equal, the higher an organization's leverage, the higher its debt service obligation, and the greater the risk that it will be unable to meet this obligation, that is, the greater its financial risk. Compare to *business risk*.

FINANCING CYCLE. A set of activities that consist of borrowing to finance fixed assets, purchasing the fixed assets, generating revenue from the use of those assets, and using the collection of accounts receivable to repay both the principal and interest on the debt. See *cash-related cycles*.

FIXED COST. A cost that remains unchanged over a wide range of volume. The classic example is rent. Fixed costs ordinarily have a relevant range, that is, a certain number of units or volume of activity over which they remain fixed. Rent, for example, would increase if an organization's volume of activity increased to such an extent that it needed to move into larger and more expensive facilities. See *step-function cost* and *variable cost*.

FLEXIBLE BUDGETING. A technique that re-calculates a budget based on the actual volume and mix of output. It is used as a first step in computing variances, and isolates the impact of volume and mix on a responsibility center, allowing the manager to isolate labor and material variances. It is especially important for a standard expense center where the manager has limited or no ability to control volume and mix. See *standard expense center.*

FORMAL AUTHORITY. The influence that a manager derives from his or her position in the organizational hierarchy.

GOAL CONGRUENCE. Alignment between the goals of managers of individual responsibility centers and the goals of the organization overall. Goal congruence is an important consideration in designing a management control system, and a lack of it ordinarily results in behavior on the part of responsibility center managers that is not in the best interests of the organization as a whole. Its absence ordinarily means that some changes are needed in the nature of the organization's responsibility centers or its transfer pricing structure. See *transfer price.*

GROSS PRESENT VALUE. The value in today's terms of a future stream of cash flows. Because money has time value, cash flows received one or more years from today are not worth as much today as their dollar amount in the future. They are thus "discounted" using a discount rate.

HEALTH CARE FOOD CHAIN. The idea that each entity's expenses in the health care system represent revenue for another entity.

HOSPICE CARE. Focuses on palliative care for a terminally ill patient (one who is medically certified to have less than six months to live). For details, see http://hospicenet.org.

HURDLE RATE. The discount rate that a capital project must demonstrate to be acceptable financially. It can be determined by computing the return on fixed assets that is needed for the organization's return on assets to equal its weighted cost of capital.

INCIDENCE RATE. The frequency with which a particular event occurs. For example, if the incidence rate of a heart attack during a year is 1 percent and there are 1 million people, then 10,000 of them will have a heart attack.

INDEPENDENT PRACTICE ASSOCIATION One form of a health maintenance organization (HMO). An HMO receives its revenue from monthly premium payments made by, or on behalf of, each insured person. Its revenue therefore is essentially fixed, and it must manage its expenses so that they do not exceed its revenue.

INDIRECT COST. A cost that cannot be attributed unambiguously to either a product or an organizational unit. It must be divided among the units to which it applies.

INDIRECT LABOR. Labor that cannot be identified directly with a unit of finished product—for example, supervisors or maintenance people. The costs of indirect labor become part of manufacturing overhead. See *direct labor* and *manufacturing overhead (MOH)*.

INDIRECT MATERIAL. Material that cannot be identified directly with a unit of finished product—for example, solvents used to lubricate machines in a department. The costs of indirect material become part of manufacturing overhead. See *direct material* and *manufacturing overhead (MOH)*.

INFORMAL AUTHORITY. Influence that comes about for reasons other than a person's position in the formal organizational hierarchy.

INPUT MEASURES. Measures related to the efficiency and productivity of the resources used to produce the organization's products.

INTERMEDIATE PRODUCTS. Services that are provided to a patient during his or her stay in a hospital. The "final product" is a discharge from the hospital, but the intermediate products consist of all those services needed to provide the final product. They include lab tests, radiological procedures, meals, laundry, and others.

INTERNAL RATE OF RETURN. The discount rate that will result in a net present value of zero. See *net present value*.

INVESTMENT CENTER. A responsibility center whose manager's financial performance is measured in terms of the total revenues minus the expenses of the center, computed as a percentage of the assets used by the center—that is, the center's return on assets. *See discretionary expense center, profit center, revenue center,* and *standard expense center*.

LEVERAGE. A measure of the amount of debt relative to equity on an organization's balance sheet. Allows an organization to own more assets than would be possible if it relied only on its own equity. This, in turn, allows it to deliver more services or to produce more goods than otherwise would be possible, and therefore to earn more revenue.

LINE-ITEM FORMAT. A way of presenting a budget that classifies expenses by function, such as salaries and wages, rather than by programs. Contrasts with *program format*.

LINE MANAGER. A person responsible for the day-to-day operations of an organizational program or responsibility center. This is a person whose judgments are incorporated into the organization's plans, who must see to it that those plans are implemented, and whose performance is measured by the responsibility accounting system. Line managers are sometimes called operating managers. See *senior management* and *staff.*

MANAGEMENT CONTROL PROCESS. A sequence of activities that take place in four phases: programming, budgeting, operating and measuring, and reporting.

MANAGEMENT CONTROL STRUCTURE. An organization's network of responsibility centers.

MANUFACTURING OVERHEAD (MOH). Costs other than direct material and direct labor, such as indirect material, indirect labor, and other costs that are associated with the manufacturing effort but that cannot be associated directly with a product that is manufactured Examples include utilities, depreciation, and taxes. See *indirect labor*, *indirect material*, and *variable manufacturing overhead.*

MECHANICAL ASPECTS. The part of the budgeting phase that makes calculations and ultimately computes the resulting surplus or deficit. It contrasts with the *behavioral aspects.*

MORBIDITY. Refers to the state of disease within a population. It contrasts with *mortality*, which is the term used for the deaths in a population.

MOTIVATION PROCESS. The set of rewards and (occasionally) punishments that managers receive based on their performance.

NET PRESENT VALUE. Gross present value less the amount of the investment needed to achieve it.

NONFINANCIAL MEASURES. Information on planned outputs, usually consisting of process and results measures. Some organizations commit themselves to specific output targets for each program.

NONQUANTITATIVE FACTORS. Elements other than a financial analysis that affect senior management's decision about whether to approve a capital investment proposal.

OPERATING CYCLE. A set of activities that consist of purchasing inventory, using it in the production of goods or delivery of services, generating revenue from the sales of those goods and services, and collecting the associated accounts receivable. See *cash-related cycles.*

OPERATING MANAGER. See *line managers*.

OPPORTUNITY COST. The cost of an option not chosen. If we could earn $20,000 in contribution from selling product A and $30,000 in contribution from selling product B, and we choose to sell product A, the difference ($10,000) is the opportunity cost of selling product A.

ORGANIZATIONAL CONTEXT. A framework for budgeting that can be viewed in terms of environment, strategy, and culture. In most instances, these factors serve to constrain certain budgeting decisions.

OUTPUT MEASURES. Measures related to an organization's goals.

OUTSOURCING RISK. The chance that an outsourcing activity will have problems. It is a combination of patient (or client) sensitivity to the service's quality, the competitive nature of the market for the outsourced activity, and the cost of switching back to internal production or engaging the services of another vendor.

PAYBACK PERIOD. The number of years needed to recover an investment. It is equal to the amount of the investment divided by the incremental annual cash flows resulting from the investment.

PERIOD COST. A cost that is not assigned to a product. Period costs generally include marketing and general administration costs. They are expensed each accounting period, whether or not any products are actually sold. See *product cost*.

PRODUCT COST. A cost that is assigned to a product—for example, direct material, direct labor, and manufacturing overhead. Such costs are assets and are held in a finished goods inventory until the products are sold, at which point they become part of the cost of goods sold. See *period cost*.

PRODUCT DIVERSITY. The condition that exists when different products use overhead-related services in different proportions: for example, when one product requires considerably more inspection time than another. Product diversity is important only when the costs of the different activities are significantly different. See *activity-based costing (ABC), relative cost factor*, and *volume diversity*.

PRODUCT-SUSTAINING ACTIVITIES. One of four general categories of activities that tend to influence the use of manufacturing overhead. They are needed to ensure that products are manufactured according to specifications, and include process engineering, product specifications, engineering change notices, and product enhancements. See *batch-related activities, facility-sustaining activities*, and *unit-level activities*.

PROFIT CENTER. A responsibility center whose manager's financial performance is measured in terms of the total revenues of the center minus its total expenses. See *discretionary expense center, investment center, revenue center,* and *standard expense center.*

PROGRAM FORMAT. A way of presenting a budget that classifies expenses by program (such as community mental health), rather than by function. Contrasts with a *line-item format.*

RELATIVE COST FACTOR. A significant difference in the costs of the different activities related to the use of overhead. *See activity-based costing (ABC), product diversity,* and *volume diversity.*

RESOURCES PER CASE. The cost-related elements that are used in the treatment of a patient with a particular diagnosis. In a hospital, these resources include a day of care, a laboratory test, a radiological procedure, and a variety of non-clinical items, such as a meal or a pound of washed laundry.

RESPONSIBILITY CENTER. An organizational unit headed by a manager charged with achieving certain agreed-upon results. From a responsibility accounting perspective, the number of people in the center is relatively unimportant. The key issue is determining how senior management will measure the group's financial performance. Senior management's goal is to design responsibility centers in such a way that the responsibility center manager is responsible for those activities over which he or she exercises a reasonable amount of control. See *discretionary expense center, investment center, profit center, revenue center,* and *standard expense center.*

REVENUE CENTER. A type of responsibility center whose manager's financial performance is measured in terms of the amount of revenue earned by the center—for example, a development office in a university or a sales office in an HMO. See *discretionary expense center, investment center, profit center,* and *standard expense center.*

REVENUE CYCLE. A set of activities that typically begins with the negotiation of payment rates with a managed care plan or other insurer, registering patients, collecting some financial information, billing insurers and patients, collecting accounts receivable, and assuring the data were recorded correctly.

REVENUE DRIVER. An activity that can influence an organization's revenue. In most organizations, revenue drivers are price, volume, and mix. For example, in a company selling personal computers, operating revenue for each type of computer is the company's price for that type multiplied by the number sold of that type. Summing this revenue across all types of computers gives total revenue.

RISK. The possibility that a proposed capital investment project will not yield the return that its proponents suggest it will.

SEMIVARIABLE COSTS. Sometimes called *mixed* or *semi-fixed* costs. Costs that share features of both fixed and variable costs. A portion is fixed, but the cost line then rises. The result is a line that begins at some level above zero and then slopes upward in a linear fashion,.

SENIOR MANAGEMENT. Collectively, the individuals at the top of the organization's hierarchy. They are responsible for seeing that the organization accomplishes its objectives. They generally formulate the organization's overall strategic directions, sometimes with assistance from line management. See *line manager* and *staff*.

SOCIAL INDICATORS. Measures related to the impact an organization has on society at large

SPIDERGRAM. A reporting technique that presents results in a way that can be easily viewed in terms of their relationship to the minimum acceptable level and the desired goal.

STAFF. The individuals who collect, summarize, and present information that is useful in the responsibility accounting process. Although staff members may be numerous, they do not make significant decisions for the organization. See *line manager* and *senior management*.

STANDARD EXPENSE CENTER. A responsibility center where financial performance is measured by via a flexible budget. In each reporting period, the budgeted variable cost per unit is multiplied by the actual number of units of output, to which the budgeted fixed costs are added. The result is a budget to which the center's actual expenses are compared for the purpose of measuring financial performance. Sometimes the unit of output is adjusted by type, such as the type of test in a laboratory. See *discretionary expense center, investment center, profit center,* and *revenue center*.

STATEMENT OF CASH FLOWS. One of the three basic financial statements (the other two are the income statement and the balance sheet). It explains, in an organized way, the changes in cash that took place between two balance sheets. It classifies the changes into operating, financing and investing activities.

STEPDOWN METHOD. One of three methods for allocating support center costs to mission centers. Sometimes called the "Two Stage" method. It allocates costs to both support centers and mission centers, but all costs eventually end up in mission centers.

STEP-FUNCTION COST. A cost that is essentially fixed but for which the relevant range is relatively small. A good example of a step-function cost is supervision. When the number of employees increases to a certain level, a new supervisor must be hired. Supervision salaries thus increase or decrease in a step-like fashion rather than smoothly. See *fixed cost* and *variable cost.*

SUBCAPITATION An arrangement in which an organization that is paid under a capitated basis contracts with another organization also on a capitated basis. The first organization shares a portion of the original capitated premium with the second organization, but both are at risk for expenses that exceed the capitation payments.

SUNK COST. A cost that is associated with a past decision. It either has been committed (like the rent payments on a lease, for example) or has actually been spent (like the depreciation on a machine, for example). Sunk costs are not relevant for alternative choice decision making as they will remain the same regardless of the option that is selected.

TERTIARY CARE HOSPITAL. A hospital that deals with very sick patients. It contrasts with a community (secondary care) hospital, which deals with moderately ill patients, and a quaternary care hospital, which deals with the sickest of patients. There are no primary care hospitals. Primary care is delivered by physicians in their offices.

TRANSFER PRICE. The price at which an intra-organizational transaction takes place. For example, in a hospital, the Department of Surgery purchases lab tests from the Clinical Pathology Department. Because both are departments of the same hospital, their transaction is intra-organizational. The transfer price for such transactions can range from market price to variable cost. Transfer prices frequently are important elements of an organization's responsibility accounting system.

UNIT CONTRIBUTION MARGIN. The amount that each unit of product sold contributes to the recovery of fixed costs. Normally, it is calculated as price minus variable costs per unit.

UNIT-LEVEL ACTIVITIES. One of four general categories of activities that tend to influence the use of manufacturing overhead. They are tied directly to the number of units produced, and might include utility usage and machine hours. Unit-level activities also include direct manufacturing costs; the three other activity categories include only manufacturing overhead. See *activity-based costing (ABC), batch-related activities, facility-sustaining activities,* and *product-sustaining activities.*

VALUE-BASED PURCHASING. The idea that cost is not the only consideration in a purchasing decision; benefits also matter. An example from the computer industry is a cheap (say, $300) computer. This computer will not have much RAM, hard-drive capacity, or processing speed. So, consumers will be willing to pay more if they perceive that their benefits (e.g., processing speed) increase in greater proportion to their costs.

VARIABLE COST. A cost that increases in an almost linear fashion with volume. For example, as the number of visits in an outpatient department increases, the cost of medical supplies increases at about the same rate. See *fixed cost* and *step-function cost.*

VARIABLE MANUFACTURING OVERHEAD. Costs that are not directly associated with any given product but that vary with the activity level in the department where the product is produced. For example, a photocopying facility's toner usage would not normally be considered part of the direct material cost of a particular copying job but would increase with the volume of copying in the department. See *indirect labor, indirect material, manufacturing overhead (MOH).*

VARIANCE. A difference between an actual revenue or expense item and the budgeted one. Variances are usually due to one or more of the following: volume, mix, use, and rate.

VARIANCE ANALYSIS. A technique that computes the difference between budgeted and actual financial results in terms of different causes, such as case mix, volume, resources per case, and cost per resource unit.

VOLUME DIVERSITY. The condition that exists when products are manufactured in batches of different sizes. See *activity-based costing (ABC), product diversity,* and *relative cost factor.*

WEIGHTED COST OF CAPITAL (WCC). The weighted interest rate of all the sources used to finance an organization's assets. It uses the interest rate paid for each liability (such as a mortgage or bond) as well as the rate assigned to the organization's equity.

WEIGHTED RETURN ON ASSETS. The weighted interest rate of all of an organization's assets. It uses the interest rate earned for each asset, and weights it by the percentage of total assets that that asset comprises.

WITHHOLD. An amount removed from a physician's (normally a primary care physician's) fee that is placed in a fund for later distribution if certain goals are met. If health care costs (and other goals) do not meet a certain defined target the withheld amount is not paid out.